South University Library
Richmond Campus
2151 Old Brick Road
Glen Allen, Va 23060

D1681698

MAR 2 7 2018

Mental Health, Crime and Criminal Justice

Mental Health, Crime and Criminal Justice

Responses and Reforms

Edited by

Jane Winstone
Principal Lecturer in Criminal Justice, University of Portsmouth, UK

palgrave
macmillan

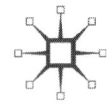

Introduction, selection and editorial matter © Jane Winstone 2016
Individual chapters © Respective authors 2016

All rights reserved. No reproduction, copy or transmission of this publication may be made without written permission.

No portion of this publication may be reproduced, copied or transmitted save with written permission or in accordance with the provisions of the Copyright, Designs and Patents Act 1988, or under the terms of any licence permitting limited copying issued by the Copyright Licensing Agency, Saffron House, 6–10 Kirby Street, London EC1N 8TS.

Any person who does any unauthorized act in relation to this publication may be liable to criminal prosecution and civil claims for damages.

The authors have asserted their rights to be identified as the authors of this work in accordance with the Copyright, Designs and Patents Act 1988.

First published 2016 by
PALGRAVE MACMILLAN

Palgrave Macmillan in the UK is an imprint of Macmillan Publishers Limited, registered in England, company number 785998, of Houndmills, Basingstoke, Hampshire RG21 6XS.

Palgrave Macmillan in the US is a division of St Martin's Press LLC, 175 Fifth Avenue, New York, NY 10010.

Palgrave Macmillan is the global academic imprint of the above companies and has companies and representatives throughout the world.

Palgrave® and Macmillan® are registered trademarks in the United States, the United Kingdom, Europe and other countries.

ISBN: 978–1–137–45386–0 hardback
ISBN: 978–1–137–45387–7 paperback

This book is printed on paper suitable for recycling and made from fully managed and sustained forest sources. Logging, pulping and manufacturing processes are expected to conform to the environmental regulations of the country of origin.

A catalogue record for this book is available from the British Library.

A catalog record for this book is available from the Library of Congress.

This book is dedicated to my mother in memory of all the years she loved and supported me. And to my family, Jon, Andrew, Lizzy, Beth, Steven and Rosa, who never cease to amaze me with how wonderful they are.

Contents

List of Figures   ix

List of Tables   x

Acknowledgements   xi

Notes on Contributors   xii

1. Crime, Exclusion and Mental Health: Current Realities and Future Responses   1
   Jane Winstone

2. A Broken Outline – Being an Observer in My Own Life: Notes from a Service User   21
   Lucy Jo Mathews

3. Troublesome Offenders, Undeserving Patients? The Precarious Rights of Mentally Disordered Offenders   28
   Rob Canton

4. Interventions and Outcomes: Accumulating Evidence   48
   James McGuire

5. Desistance in Offenders with Mental Illness   67
   Svenja Göbbels, Jo Thakker and Tony Ward

6. Medicalising 'Hatred': Exploring the Sense and Sensitivities of Classifying the Motivations for Hate Crime as Mental Disorder   91
   Jemma Tyson and Nathan Hall

7. Mental Health Needs and Neurodevelopmental Disorders amongst Young Offenders: Implications for Policy and Practice   109
   Prathiba Chitsabesan and Nathan Hughes

8. 'It Made My Mind Unwell': Trauma-Informed Approaches to the Mental Health Needs of Women in the Criminal Justice System   131
   Madeline Petrillo

9. Challenging the Cultural Determinants of Dual Diagnosis in the Criminal Justice System   147
   Aaron Pycroft and Anita Green

10 The Role of the Mental Health Clinical Nurse Specialist in the
Crown Court Setting: Towards a Best Practice Model 167
Charles de Lacy

11 The DSPD Programme: What Did It Tell Us about the Future for
Managing Dangerous Prisoners with Severe Personality Disorders? 184
Ruth Scally

12 Prosecuting the Persecuted: Forgive Them, They Know Not What
They Do 201
Taffy Gatawa

13 Successful Strategies for Working with Mentally Disordered
Offenders within a Complex Multi-Agency Environment 218
Leighe Rogers and Gillian Ormston

14 Training to Improve Collaborative Practice: A Key Component of
Strategy to Reduce Mental Ill Health in the Offender Population 242
Sarah Hean, Elizabeth Walsh and Marilyn Hammick

15 Psychological Jurisprudence: Problems with and Prospects for
Mental Health and Justice System Reform 266
Bruce A. Arrigo and Heather Y. Bersot

Index 285

List of Figures

8.1	Model	141
13.1	Mind map of early considerations	220
13.2	Breadth of identified task	221
13.3	Complex multi-agency environment and emerging governance structures	222
13.4	Current governance structures	223
13.5	Early development of scheme	227
13.6	Scoping of existing service provision	228
13.7	Key aspects of the risk management plan	230
13.8	Map of stakeholders	234
13.9	Map of stakeholders and proximal relationships	235
13.10	Data collection for evaluation	236
14.1	An activity system surrounding the requests for psychiatric reports made by the criminal justice system	250
14.2	An activity system surrounding the provision of psychiatric reports by the Mental Health Services	251
14.3	The two activity systems of mental health and court services interacting as defendants with mental issues overlap between the two	253
15.1	Diagnosing the relations of humanness in ritualised communicative intra/interaction	276

List of Tables

7.1	The prevalence of psychiatric and neurodevelopmental disorders	110
13.1	Comprehensive register of risks	231
13.2	Risks identified and action taken	232
13.3	Management stakeholder plan	235
13.4	Lessons learned log	238
14.1	Exemplars of collaborative competency frameworks and competencies to be attained by MHS and CJS professionals	256
14.2	A triple-phase model of training for enhanced collaborative practice (TCP) at the interface of the MHS and CJS	261

Acknowledgements

This book, which was a glimmer of an idea in 2012, has taken a number of years to come to fruition. Over this period I owe a huge debt of thanks to my colleagues, professional and academic, who not only contributed chapters, but also their collaboration and unwavering support. I would like to thank the peer reviewers for their helpful comments and also Julia Willan, Harriet Barker and Dominic Walker for their encouragement and skilful guidance. Last, but by no means least, thank you to my family for their steadfast confidence in my ability to bring this project to completion.

Notes on Contributors

Bruce A. Arrigo is Professor of Criminology, Law and Society and Professor of Public Policy in the Department of Criminal Justice and Criminology at the University of North Carolina, Charlotte. In the College of Liberal Arts and Sciences, he holds additional faculty appointments in the Psychology Department. In the College of Health and Human Services, he holds a faculty appointment in the Department of Public Health Sciences. Arrigo is also a faculty associate in the Center for Professional and Applied Ethics – a teaching, research and service unit of the Philosophy Department – a senior member of the University Honors College, and a faculty affiliate of Wake Forest University's Bioethics, Health and Society Program.

Heather Y. Bersot is an independent researcher and an adjunct lecturer in the Department of Criminal Justice and Criminology at the University of North Carolina, Charlotte. Her peer-reviewed articles have appeared in the *Journal of Theoretical and Philosophical Criminology*, the *Journal of Forensic Psychology Practice*, and *Contemporary Drug Problems*. She is the co-author of the book, *The Ethics of Total Confinement: A Critique of Madness, Citizenship and Social Justice*. She served as the managing editor (2008–2009) of the *Journal of Forensic Psychology Practice*, co-editor (2011) of the *Journal of Forensic Psychology Practice* Special Double Issue, and co-editor (2012–2013) of the *Routledge Handbook of International Crime and Justice Studies*. Her research interests include critical penology, psychology and the law, and ethics.

Rob Canton is Professor of Community and Criminal Justice at De Montfort University, Leicester. He worked in the probation service for many years in a variety of different practice, management and training roles before joining De Montfort. Rob has been extensively involved in recent years in work to help other countries to develop their practices in supervising offenders, mostly in Eastern Europe. He was appointed by the Council of Europe to contribute to framing the recommendation that was subsequently adopted (2010) by the Council of Europe as the *European Probation Rules*. He has a career-long interest in the challenges involved in working with mentally disordered offenders.

Prathiba Chitsabesan is a Consultant Child and Adolescent Psychiatrist (Pennine Care NHS Foundation Trust) and an honorary research fellow with the University of Manchester, Manchester Academic Health Science Centre. She has a special interest in research exploring the needs of young offenders and the subsequent implications for policy and practice. As a member of the

Offender Health Research Network she has been involved in the development of the Comprehensive Health Screening Tool (CHAT) for the Department of Health and Youth Justice Board.

Charles de Lacy is Clinical Nurse Specialist to the Central Criminal Court and head of the Mental Health Liaison Scheme for the Old Bailey. He set up the pilot Psychiatric Liaison Service for professionals, which was independently evaluated and has subsequently become fully established as the Crown Court Liaison and Diversion Service. In 2009 the service won the prestigious Lord Chancellor's Award.

Taffy Gatawa is the former Patient Safety Lead for a West London Mental Health Trust. She has many years of experience of working with individuals with mental health needs and originally trained as a mental health nurse, and has pursued academic studies in risk and security management as well as undertaking guest lectureship at the Institute of Criminal Justice Studies, University of Portsmouth. She has presented at national level on the subjects of managing violence and aggression and patient safety, including at the National Association of Psychiatric Intensive Care Unit (NAPICU) annual conference in 2011 and the Patient Safety Congress in 2010. Taffy is Head of Patient Safety and Quality in Royal Surrey County Hospital at Guildford.

Svenja Göbbels is a PhD candidate in the Centre for Forensic Behavioural Science at Melbourne, Australia. Her research interests include intimate partner violence and stalking, desistance from offending and offender cognition.

Anita Green is a Nurse Consultant in Education and Training for Sussex Partnership NHS Foundation Trust and a visiting fellow with the University of Brighton. Prior to this role she was a Dual Diagnosis Nurse Consultant working for the same Trust. She is a member of the editorial board for *Advances in Dual Diagnosis*. Her research interests include dual diagnosis and women and the application of Motivational Interviewing in mental health settings.

Nathan Hall is Principal Lecturer in Criminology and Policing at the Institute of Criminal Justice Studies, University of Portsmouth. He is a member of the Cross-Government Hate Crime Independent Advisory Group (IAG) and the Association of Chief Police Officers Hate Crime Working Group. Nathan has also acted as an independent member of the UK government hate crime delegation to the Organization for Security and Co-operation in Europe, and is a member of the Crown Prosecution Service (Wessex) Independent Strategic Scrutiny and Involvement Panel, Hampshire Constabulary's Strategic IAG, and the Metropolitan Police Service's Hate Crime Diamond Group. He has published widely in the field of hate crime.

Marilyn Hammick is a recently retired International Education and Research Consultant and visiting professor, Bournemouth and Birmingham City Universities. She was consultant to The Best Evidence Medical Education Collaboration (2003–2013), a founder member of In-2-Theory (an international interprofessional scholarship and practice network) and Chair of The UK Centre for the Advancement of Interprofessional Education. Marilyn has published widely, with peer-reviewed papers and books on evidence-informed education and interprofessional education, and is a respected editor and reviewer.

Sarah Hean is Marie Curie Senior Fellow at the University of Stavanger, Norway and an associate professor at Bournemouth University, UK. She is Chair of the In-2-Theory group promoting the application of theoretical frameworks in interprofessional and interagency working. She is an associate editor of the *Journal of Interprofessional Education* and a board member of the Centre for the Advancement of Interprofessional Education. She has extensive experience of longitudinal and cross-sectional evaluations, including those exploring the challenges of interagency working at the interface of the CJS and MHS, and the importance of training workers to cope with this complex interagency setting.

Nathan Hughes is Marie Curie Research Fellow in the Murdoch Children's Research Institute at the Royal Children's Hospital, Melbourne, and Senior Lecturer in Social Policy and Social Work at the University of Birmingham. Nathan's research explores the implications of developing understandings in biological and neurosciences for policy and practice in the criminal justice system, including how understandings of adrenarche, puberty and young adult maturation can support biosocial models of patterns of offending, and how new insights into neurodevelopmental disorders can explain trajectories of offending and inform more effective responses.

Lucy Jo Mathews has been a service user for 20 years. She completed her final years of education under home-schooled conditions achieving excellent results in her GCSEs and further education. However, her attempt to attend a full-time campus-based university course to qualify to be a primary school teacher was thwarted by her mental health needs. Her effort to address these through the mental health services is documented in her chapter. Lucy lives independently with the support of her family and friends, her GP and psychiatrist. Under supervision she has managed without daily medication for the past year, but keeps this decision under regular review. Lucy has contributed a chapter to this book in a spirit of hope that it will bring home to readers what it is like to live with the mental health needs that academics and professionals have debated.

James McGuire is Professor of Forensic Clinical Psychology at the University of Liverpool, where he was Director of the Doctorate in Clinical Psychology programme from 1995 to 2013. Before that he worked in learning disability services and for seven years in a high security hospital. He carries out psycho-legal work involving assessment of individuals for Youth and Crown Court, and for hearings of the Mental Health Review Tribunal, Parole Board and Criminal Cases Review Commission. He has conducted research in probation services, prisons and other settings on aspects of psychosocial rehabilitation with offenders, and has written or edited 14 books and numerous other publications on this and related issues. He was a member of the NICE Guideline Development Group on Antisocial Personality Disorder (2009–2010), and is a member of the NOMS Correctional Services Advisory and Accreditation Panel. He has been an invited speaker at conferences in 19 countries and has been involved in a range of consultative work or staff training with criminal justice and social welfare agencies in the United Kingdom and nine other countries.

Gillian Ormston is a project manager for Intelligent Awakenings Ltd. Gillian was previously employed by HMCTS as the Mental Health Court Pilot project manager. Since 2010, she continues to work within the Sussex Area to support further development of Liaison and Diversion Services across the county.

Madeline Petrillo is a senior lecturer at the Institute of Criminal Justice Studies, University of Portsmouth, supporting the delivery of the probation qualification programme. She previously worked as a probation officer, where she specialised in working with women offenders. She is undertaking PhD research exploring women's pathways to desistance after imprisonment.

Aaron Pycroft is Senior Lecturer in Addiction Studies at the Institute of Criminal Justice Studies, University of Portsmouth where he teaches, researches and writes on issues related to substance misuse, rehabilitation and the criminal justice system. He coordinates an international group that researches the application of complexity theory to public service settings and his two most recent books are Pycroft, A. and Bartollas, C. (eds) (2014) *Applying Complexity Theory: Whole Systems Approaches to Criminal Justice and Social Work* and Pycroft, A. (ed.) (2015) *Key Concepts in Substance Misuse*.

Leighe Rogers is a director within Surrey and Sussex Probation Trust. Leighe is Surrey and Sussex Probation Trust Director for Brighton and Hove and is the Trust lead for Restorative Justice, Health and Wellbeing and Domestic Abuse. She has represented the Trust on local and national media, entering a debate on Radio 4's 'Women's Hour' on domestic abuse. Leighe is committed to cross-sector partnership working. She joins the Office of the Sussex Police & Crime Commissioner on secondment (one day a week) and holds a similar role in the office of the Surrey Police & Crime Commissioner.

Ruth Scally is a consultant forensic psychiatrist working in a secure psychiatric hospital in Birmingham, UK. She has a particular interest in the treatment of female offenders and the management of personality disorders.

Jo Thakker is Senior Lecturer in Psychology at the University of Waikato in Hamilton, New Zealand. She holds a PhD in Psychology from Canterbury University in New Zealand in 1997 and has since worked in both clinical and university settings. Most of her clinical work has been with offenders in prisons in Australia and New Zealand. Her key research areas include cultural psychology, substance use and abuse, and sexual offenders. She also has a background in theoretical research.

Jemma Tyson is Lecturer in Criminology and Criminal Justice at the Institute of Criminal Justice Studies, University of Portsmouth. She is researching issues relating to disability hate crime for her PhD. In particular, her research examines criminal justice service provision for victims of learning disability hate crime, and builds upon the findings of her Master's thesis on a related topic. The latter research was conducted in partnership with the Cross Government Hate Crime Programme, with whom she worked as an intern for a number of years. Jemma is an IAG member for Hampshire Constabulary, sits on the Constabulary's Fairness and Equality Delivery Group (Disability) and has also represented the UK government at hate crime events overseas.

Elizabeth Walsh is Associate Professor of Offender Health at the University of Leeds. She is a registered general nurse who has worked both for and with HM Prison Service in clinical, educational and practice development roles since 1995. Much of her work is centred on the support and development of professionals caring for those in contact with the criminal justice system. Her research interests include emotional labour of prison nurses, clinical supervision, managing pain in prison and the health and social care of older prisoners. She is the elected Chair of the Nursing in Criminal Justice Services Forum at the Royal College of Nursing, a visiting professor at the University of Ottawa and a member of the editorial board of the *Journal of Forensic Nursing*.

Tony Ward is Professor of Clinical Psychology at Victoria University of Wellington, New Zealand. He has taught forensic and clinical psychology at the Universities of Canterbury, Melbourne, Deakin and Victoria. Ward is the creator of the Good Lives Model of Offender Rehabilitation and has written numerous articles, books and book chapters on this model. He has over 370 academic publications and his research interests include offender rehabilitation, forensic and correctional ethics, evolutionary criminology, and cognition in sex offenders.

Jane Winstone is a principal lecturer in community justice in the Institute of Criminal Justice Studies, University of Portsmouth. She has drawn on her professional training and experience of working as a probation officer to contribute to the probation officer qualification and currently supports the Professional Doctorate in Criminal Justice. Winstone chairs the Faculty Ethics Committee and has a keen interest in developing evidence-based and ethical practice for youth and adult offenders, with a particular focus on mental disorder. She has conducted a number of evaluations in this area, including a national evaluation of liaison and diversion provision which contributed to the Bradley Report, the Mental Health Court initiative (Brighton and Stratford MC) and the Mental Health Liaison Pilot at the Central Criminal Court.

1
Crime, Exclusion and Mental Health: Current Realities and Future Responses

Jane Winstone

When Simon Stevens took up his role as CEO of NHS England, an executive, non-departmental body established in 2012, he announced the NHS five year forward view with seven models of care (Kings Fund, 2015). In response, Laurence Moulin posted the following comment:

> Unless we redesign structure and services from the 'bottom up', starting with what will be offered for people receiving services, and ensure that the 'offer' is a single physical/mental health service, we may find at the end of the five year plan we have only succeeded in moving the deckchairs into a different pattern. (Laurence Moulin Consulting in Mental Health and Learning Disability, 2015)

This book arguably reflects both positions – positive and forward looking, identifying strategies that work, and suggesting that efforts and resources should be targeted to these. Plus, a twinge of 'moving deckchairs' pessimism. There have been many initiatives with little recognisable long-term impact. These have been well-meaning and intended to address what seems to have become an intractable problem of adequately supporting people with mental health needs, especially those who offend (Winstone and Pakes, 2007). These initiatives started with Reed (1992) and include, in the intervening decades, the Dangerous Severe Personality Disorder (DSPD) endeavour (see Scally, this volume) and various legislative policies and guidelines, including a revision of the Mental Health Act in 2007. Now, with an energising burst, the Bradley Report (2009), which was wholeheartedly welcomed, and the establishment of NHS England (2012), whose five year view was greeted with cautious enthusiasm.

In the spirit of transparency, accountability and evidence-based evaluation of publicly funded initiatives, an independent commission was set up to review the five years of progress on the 82 recommendations arising out of the Bradley Report (Durcan et al., 2014; see also Rogers and Ormston, this volume). This reports that steady progress is being made, especially in the development of increased provision of liaison and diversion teams for adults, children and young people and that early intervention is being offered in police stations and courts across the country (Durcan et al., 2014, p. 3). This is certainly encouraging given that the final recommendations of the Bradley Report were, somewhat depressingly, extraordinarily similar to the conclusions drawn by Reed nearly two decades before (Reed, 1992; see Pakes and Winstone, 2008, 2009). Reed had also concluded that a coherent framework of liaison and diversion services was required for those entering the criminal justice system with mental health needs; although in the intervening decades there was little progress to show for the, arguably sporadic, efforts of policy makers to realise this. However, there is some evidence that we live in more enlightened times, where joined-up thinking and the top-down energies and resources of Health and Justice may finally be targeting the multiple, complex needs of the same populations with equal determination and that the initiatives arising out of the Bradley Report and NHS England will have concrete, sustainable outcomes. There is certainly, both then and now, a spirit of willingness to succeed from those delivering the services. A survey of professionals working within 101 liaison and diversion schemes demonstrated their commitment and tireless efforts towards supporting this group (Winstone and Pakes, 2008; Pakes and Winstone, 2010). Some of these professionals have contributed to this volume, and many are currently participating across multi-agency settings to drive forward the new agendas in Health and Justice (see Rogers and Ormston, this volume).

Staying one day ahead of yesterday

Looking to the past helps us to understand the potential hurdles and provides learning to carry into the future. The need for change has been couched in a range of political agendas over the last two to three decades. 'Tough on crime and tough on the causes of crime' and the 'Public Protection Agenda' were the flagships of the Labour government years, whilst the coalition government forged its initiatives under the label of the 'Big Society'. The focus of these agendas can be summarised as the requirement to reduce costs (economic imperative) and to improve the ratio of costs to intended outcomes (individual, social and community impact). These broad thrusts can be identified in the current restructuring and focus of Health and Justice strategies.

The Five Year Plan set out by NHS England (Kings Fund, 2015) has attracted a good deal of attention, not least because it is a strategy to resolve the problems that have beset the service, one of which, as Simon Stevens stated, is health inequalities (Stevens, 2014). Health inequality particularly impacts on those who have mental disorders and also offend (Winstone and Pakes, 2005;

Bradley, 2009). Research that is seminal in this area, Singleton et al. (1998), demonstrated that 90% of those on remand and in custody have one or more clinically diagnosable mental health needs, with a subsequent study finding that 10% of male and 30% of female prisoners have previously experienced a psychiatric acute admission to hospital (Department of Health, 2007). In addition to the 90% of those incarcerated with a mental health need, in the period 2013/14 there were a total of 23,531 people subject to the Mental Health Act (1983, revised 2007). This is 6% (1,324) more than at the end of the previous reporting period, and 32% greater than at the end of 2008/09, the year when Community Treatment Orders were introduced (Health and Social Care Centre, 2015).

Bradley (2009) claimed that unmet, complex, multi-dimensional social and health needs have continued to allow people with mental health difficulties to end up in the criminal justice system. Partly I would argue that this is a result of over-stretched mainstream health services and social provision and partly because, having entered the criminal justice pathway, the support for mental health struggles to achieve the same standard as mainstream services; this is particularly so for in-reach prison services (Brooker, et al., 2002; Durcan, 2008; Bradley, 2009; Offender Health Research Network, 2010). These factors contribute to this group being particularly over-represented in a 'revolving door' of frequent short-term prison sentences, with no robust, centrally agreed, community, social or healthcare pathway of provision to disrupt this pattern (Revolving Doors Agency, 2007; Bradley, 2009). This affects youth and adults alike (see for example, Chitsabesan and Hughes, this volume; Göbbels, Thakker and Ward, this volume).

In recognition that the potent mix of mental disorder, multiple complex needs and offending behaviour poses a unique challenge to the criminal justice system, there has been a plethora of guidance and legislation. This includes Healthy Children, Safer Communities (2009), Government Drug Strategy (2010), Breaking the Cycle (government green paper and response, 2010/2011), No Health Without Mental Health and implementation framework (2011/2012), Ending Gang and Youth Violence (2012), Preventing Suicide in England (2012), Integrated Offender Management (2013) and PIPE (Psychology Informed Planned Environments; 2013). Not forgetting, of course, the Bradley Report (2009) and recommendations, the creation of NHS England (2012) with seven models of care, the Care Act (2014), and the Offender Rehabilitation Act (2014) which includes updated guidance for service commissioning and provider agencies to deliver the Mental Health Treatment Requirements (MHTR) locally. See also the Criminal Justice Act 2003 (CJA 2003).

Typified by the failure of the MHTR to achieve significant uptake due to funding and resourcing issues (Pakes and Winstone, 2012), none of the statutory agencies which comprise the criminal justice system have the training, resources or remit to implement and tackle alone the issues identified in this tranche of legislative activity, guidelines, reports and plans. Two broad areas particularly bedevil their efforts to address the contributory dynamic risk factors for offending in those with mental health needs (Winstone and Pakes, 2010). Firstly, the link between social exclusion, mental health needs and offending behaviour is securely established (Thornicroft, 2006; Bradley, 2009; Seymour, 2010). Social exclusion as a pre-existing contributory factor to anti-social behaviour is therefore prevalent amongst those with mental disorder who present to the criminal justice system. However, to address this, it requires community care and social provision pathways, which are at best patchy and at worst non-existent. Second, is the requirement for health care to support mental health needs once an individual has entered the criminal justice system (Blackburn, 2004); this is clearly beyond the remit of the statutory agencies. For example, with high offending rates of individuals with substance misuse and mental health needs (Pycroft and Clift, 2012), those with this dual diagnosis have been noted to be liable to fall through the net of the services. The service providers are not formally linked, are separately commissioned and therefore pose a particular challenge to multi-agency collaboration (Bradley, 2009; see Pycroft and Green, this volume).

As a result of the resourcing issues facing social and healthcare, the criminal justice system has become what some have claimed to be the 'dustbin' (Revolving Doors Agency, 2007), collecting up all those for whom other services are unable to make provision. However stretched or ill-equipped the statutory agencies, they cannot refuse an order from the court to manage/implement an offender's sentence. Neither are they in a position to routinely provide, through interagency services, the specialised provision to address the multiple, complex needs which could reduce the risk of harm to self and others.

Therefore, the policy responses, the initiatives that have been driven by the Bradley Report and the Five Year Plan to address health inequalities, face uphill work to redress and improve upon the current status quo. In the NHS, the mental health trusts in England have seen their budgets fall by more than 8% in real terms over the course of the last parliament (coalition government 2010–2015). It is calculated that this amounts to a reduction of almost £600m, whilst at the same time referrals to the service have risen by nearly 20% (Community Care, 2015). In addition, it is claimed that thousands of people have been denied the social care support that could ensure their health does not deteriorate to a crisis point, which may also leave them at risk of antisocial behaviours. All this is set against a background of a paucity of crisis housing provision, home treatment teams being insufficiently funded, and shortage of beds – meaning that people are being sent miles away from home for in-patient psychiatric treatment (Community Care, 2015). It is hard enough to have mental health needs, with all the attendant miseries incumbent upon this, without structural responses exacerbating social exclusionary factors which disrupt networks of support (see Göbbels, Thakker and Ward, this volume). This, *in extremis*, leaves many in poverty, homeless and unknown to/unregistered with GPs or other services.

Establishing the Community Rehabilitation Companies (CRC), reforming the commissioning and provider structures (Offender Rehabilitation Act 2014), innovations such as peer mentoring and supervision of those in custody for 12 months and under, transforming the work of the National Probation Service (under the auspices of the National Offender Management Service, NOMS) and a target operating model of Payment by Results (Pbr), are part of the new frameworks and strategies to manage offenders. With regard to Pbr and social care, a study by Appleby et al. (2012, vii), concludes that:

> While the introduction of Pbr may have had some positive impacts within the NHS in England, the current system as applied is not fit for our current and future health and social care needs despite efforts to develop and refine it.

Whilst not all privatisation initiatives fall within the Pbr formula, with regard to reducing recidivism some argue that even taking the broader perspective, which includes not-for-profit organisations, probation privatisation will be a disaster and likely to founder on the rocks of implementation (Garside, 2014). This is partly attributed to the Pbr formula for successful bidders for the CRCs, whereby a portion of the total payments will depend upon the degree to which they are successful in containing, possibly reducing, reoffending. It is true that the CRCs will have the responsibility for providing supervision for the first time to short-sentence prisoners (those sentenced to less than 12 months in prison) after release. It is also a fact that this group are comprised of many who will have unmet mental health and multiple social needs (Bradley, 2009). So, the CRCs will be under close scrutiny to see if they can succeed in a climate that is still focussed upon budget constraints and where health and social care inequality and social care provision pose significant challenges.

Managing risk

Given the numbers of offenders with mental health needs who are punished through the normal sentencing processes (that is, the CJA 2003), NACRO (2007a) and Bradley (2009) have argued persuasively that the legal definition of a Mentally Disordered Offender should embrace all those who enter the criminal justice system with a mental health need. Health care should begin from the moment of arrest, within a national framework of liaison and diversion (see Bradley, 2009; Durcan et al., 2014). Further, healthcare should not be confined to those who enter the criminal justice system whose mental disorder is so severe and debilitating that they are managed through the Mental Health Act once they appear in Court.

The focus of public awareness is, however, usually upon those with acute mental health needs who are assessed as posing a serious risk of harm to others. The reporting of these atypical cases through social media, newspapers, etc. has been recognised as generating a high level of public anxiety (Prins, 2005). This has had a twofold impact; firstly, it has exacerbated the stigma and stereotyping of people with mental disorder, particularly those who offend (Thornicroft, 2006; Lee, 2007). Secondly, it has resulted in a number of inquiries which have demonstrated deficiencies in the management of risk. I will briefly explore some notorious and high profile cases to consider the debates and dilemmas. If change is to mean progress, it will need to be inclusive of the identified areas of deficit as these will impact on all those with a mental disorder who offend.

In 1996 Michael Stone murdered Lin and Megan Russell. He was known to services and diagnosed as having a psychopathic personality disorder with psychotic symptoms aggravated by substance misuse. The independent inquiry reported on his treatment, care and supervision (Francis, 2006). Unusually, it also addressed the influence of the unprecedented media interest and involvement, much of which was inaccurate and misleading (Prins, 2010). The inquiry was delayed because of a lengthy appeal process, but when it was finally published it identified that mistakes were made by mental health, probation and social workers before the attack. These included the loss of medical records which jeopardized ongoing multi-agency care. There was a failure of addiction services to mount an effective care plan, in particular the denial of Stone's request for in-patient treatment. Poor ID checks with different services also allowed him to register under different names leading to poorly informed assessments of risk and need. Marjorie Wallace, the chief executive of the mental health charity Sane, said Stone and the Russells were 'failed by the psychiatric, probation and other services, none of which appeared to take responsibility for his care and treatment' (The Guardian, 2006). The Mental Health Alliance stated that 'Michael Stone...sought help, but was lost between health, criminal justice and substance misuse services....this is an all too common problem' (The Guardian, 2006).

The management of Michael Stone highlights the difficulties of multi-agency work, particularly with regard to information sharing, roles and responsibilities (see Rogers and Ormston, this volume). In addition, the original trial, appeal and later developments in this case meant that a final determination was not made until 2006. This is an example of the complex administrative and legislative framework that must be navigated by professional and lay sentencers, forensic and criminal justice professionals. The process itself also creates lengthy delays in what Nash and Williams describe as 'limiting mayhem' (Nash and Williams, 2006, p.23; see de Lacy, this volume). For example, the difficulty posed in establishing a definitive diagnosis of mental disorder and its contribution to the offence behaviours leads to a proliferation of Expert Reports to the Court (see de Lacy, this volume), each of which may take anything from six weeks plus to prepare. In addition, the legal and forensic definitions of mental disorder are widely differing and the very nature of mental disorder means that diagnoses are open to being contested between experts, leading to a diffusion of clarity in complex cases and further case management delays. You have only to look at the brief definition of mental disorder in the Mental Health Act 2007 ('MHA 2007') compared to the 947 pages of classification in DSM V (American Psychiatric Association, 2013) to see the potential for legal and diagnostic challenges to arise. Finally, the stigma and prejudice against those with mental disorders, stirred up by the reporting of this case in the media, exacerbated public fear and was a trigger factor in placing a premium upon public protection (see Canton, this volume). This was reflected in a political move to assuage these fears by strengthening public protection arrangements with a focus on the rights of the victim in the CJA 2003 (Lee, 2007). I would argue that the political rhetoric compounded by ill-informed media speculation may have proved to be somewhat self-defeating. Steury and Choinski (1995) and Thornicroft (2006), amongst many others, have identified that the stigma and prejudice associated with mental disorder, intensified by highly publicised reporting and demands for political action, only serves to escalate the social exclusionary factors for all those with a mental disorder, rendering them more vulnerable to acquiring a criminal record (see for example, Badger et al.,1999; Social Exclusion Unit, 2002; Bradley, 2009). The high numbers of those incarcerated and those subject to statutory community supervision who have a mental disorder and unmet social and care needs bears this out.

Further examples of weak multi-agency management of an offender, known to services and committing a further serious offence have been identified by the Inquiry into the murder of Naomi Bryant by Anthony Rice in 2005 (HM Inspectorate of Probation, 2006). Rice was diagnosed with a psychopathic disorder, likely contributory to his history of violent and sexual offences:

> We have found a number of deficiencies, in the form of mistakes, misjudgements and miscommunications at various stages throughout the whole process of this case that amount to what we call a cumulative failure. (HMIP, 2006, p. 2)

The findings particularly identified that, as with the management of Michael Stone almost a decade earlier, it was often not clear who was in charge of the case, leading to diffusion and discontinuities in lead responsibilities. This contributed to a major mistake in not bringing forward the files which would have informed the overly-optimistic assessment of Anthony Rice as fit for release into the community and placing him in accommodation that could not provide appropriate supervision. Many of the findings were similar to that of the Dano Sonnex report (HM Inspectorate of Probation, 2009). Sonnex, a known offender diagnosed with psychopathy, was the subject of an inquiry following the murder of two French students in London in 2008. The report also identified failed assessment processes, weak information exchange between settings and agencies, competing demands and limited resources. These were held responsible for professional failures leading to an offender, known to services, being unmonitored and unsupported. The findings of inquiries and reports from these atypical cases are strong evidence that multi-agency deficiencies in collaboration appear to be persistent over the long term and can be understood as a separate from – although perhaps dynamically interactive with – a paucity of resources.

The case of Rice, however, is distinctive because it brought to the fore the alleged causal role of the Human Rights Act 1998 (Whitty, 2007, p. 202). This reinvigorated the debate and public discourse around the rights of the offender versus the rights of the victim in the management of risk. It ultimately led to changes in the way in which those subject to Multi Agency Public Protection arrangements (MAPPA) are represented (see Nash and Williams, 2010) and raises some highly problematic ethical issues which persist to this day (see also Canton, this volume). These can be summarised as follows:

- To detain a person who is mentally capable under mental health provisions is a grievous injustice and a label for life.
- To detain a person who is not mentally capable under mental health provisions may result in a longer period of detention where that person presents only the same or similar risk factor as a person who has committed the same act but is mentally stable.
- To respond within a human rights framework to the behaviour of an individual who was mentally ill at the time of the offence but is no longer mentally ill at the time of committal/sentencing or shortly thereafter.
- To fail to detain a person who is not mentally capable under mental health provisions may present a risk to the public that is unacceptable.

Crime control models attempt to eliminate risk, possibly at the expense of balancing risk and rights (Hudson, 2001). An accurate assessment of the risk an individual poses to themselves and others is therefore key to addressing the complexities of risk management within an ethical framework in order to achieve a transparent and defensible balance (Nilsson et al., 2009). In part this will depend on the clinical diagnosis and known associated risks of the mental disorder; the difficulties of establishing a definitive forensic diagnosis have already been discussed. Contributing to the forensic assessment is a criminal justice assessment of dangerousness and risk of harm. It has long been acknowledged, however, that the accuracy of both psychiatric and criminal justice assessment can be influenced by weak assessment tools coupled with unconscious bias and stereotyping for both actuarial and clinical assessment strategies.

Nilsson et al. (2009), in a review of the predictive validity of actuarial forensic assessment tools, argued that it is not problematic to identify whether an individual from a specific subject group has a higher probability than others for violent acting out, especially re-acting out, but it is much more difficult to arrive at a reasonable conclusion about the individual risk to relapse into criminality. The Royal College of Psychiatrists holds a similar view whilst also drawing conclusions about clinical assessment:

> Actuarial approaches are based on addressing risk at a group level, but they cannot move from group to individual risk evaluations easily. Their accuracy is lowest in detecting rare events. They are able to predict at all only when the service user being assessed comes from the population for which the tool was developed... .....Clinical approaches provide individualised and contextualised assessments, but are vulnerable to individual bias and poor interrater reliability. (RCP, 2008; p. 27)

Confirmation of this can be found in the search for a definitive resolution to the assessment of cognitive disabilities and risk prediction which has contributed to a proliferation of assessment tools and what Uzieblo et al. (2012, p.43) refer to as 'diagnostic chaos'. With regard to individual bias it can also be found in the over-representation of black and minority ethnic (BME) populations in the criminal justice system (Bradley, 2009). Those from BME groups are more likely to be diagnosed with mental health problems and are more likely to be admitted to hospital (Mental Health Foundation, n.d.; Badger et. al., 1999). Figures show that black people are increasingly over-represented at each heightened level of security in the psychiatric process from informal to civil detention, and then in detention on forensic sections within the courts and criminal justice system (NACRO, 2007b, p. 1; Bradley, 2009; Department of Health, 2012). Psychotic remand prisoners are more likely to be black and older than other mentally disordered prisoners, and this is especially so for women detainees (Badger, et al., 1999; Department of Health, 2012). BME groups are over-represented in special hospitals, making up almost 20% of the population (Badger et al., 1999; see also Stevenson, 2014). It is known that the relationship between social exclusion and crime is complex (Abrams et al., 2007) and that social exclusion factors disproportionately impact on the BME population. However, it cannot be discounted that the over-assessment of BME populations when they enter the criminal justice system accounts for their disproportionate over-representation in the high secure estate, in other mental health provision and in the general incarcerated population.

This brings the debate to the case of Christopher Clunis, diagnosed as schizophrenic, who killed Jonathan Zito in 1992. It is a now familiar litany of failed multi-disciplinary responses (Stone, 2003), but the point to draw attention to here is that the media portrayed him as big, black, mad and dangerous. Neal (1998) compellingly argues that because Clunis embodied notions of black madness, conflating constructions of race, gender, mental disorder and dangerousness, that this was contributory to professional fear leading to inadequate responses and unmet complex social and care needs over a number of years leading up to the offence. Whilst I stated earlier the aspiration that we now live in more enlightened times, the current rates of entry of BME populations into the criminal justice system alongside the subsequent outcomes of screening and assessment processes, continue to suggest there is much to be done to achieve equality for this population in order to avoid the unconscious bias and stereotyping by professionals.

Whatever the difficulties of screening, assessment and multi-agency resourcing and management, the public fear aroused by high profile cases such as Clunis and Stone led to a concern that the law was not providing adequate protection to those suffering from mental disorders or to those affected by their actions. The reform of the 1983 Mental Health Act in 2007 was a response to this. It aimed to ensure that a revised Appropriate Medical Treatment Test (previously a 'Treatability Test') would allow engagement with those suffering from what had previously been considered untreatable conditions, such as personality disorders, and it redefined mental to 'any disorder or disability of the mind' to support this. The strengthening of the MHA has, however, done little to unravel the complexities of determining whether an individual should be punished under normal sentencing provisions or treated and managed through the provisions of the MHA. For an example of this I shall now turn finally to the case of Nicola Edgington.

Nicola Edgington, diagnosed as a paranoid schizophrenic after stabbing and killing her mother in 2005, was released in 2009 from a secure mental hospital where she was supposed to be indefinitely detained (it also emerged that the NHS Trust, which recommended Edgington's release in 2009, cared for 12 other patients who went on to kill, suggesting that the assessment of such patients needs to be carefully reviewed). As for Nicola Edgington, two years later, in 2011; following her repeated but unmet pleas for treatment and help, including requests to be detained under the MHA as she knew her mental health was deteriorating, she stabbed and murdered Sally Hodkin, a stranger, in the street (Independent Police Complaints Commission, 2013). She was tried and found guilty of murder at the Central Criminal Court. Putting to one side the issues around assessment and care management, it is the outcome of the trial that I want to focus on here. The CPS argued against the medical consensus by contending that Edgington was in full command of her faculties. Here the problem of the undifferentiated nature of mental disorder is highlighted, as the defence produced two senior psychiatrists as Expert Witnesses who stated that the original diagnosis of paranoid schizophrenia was robust. Nevertheless the Judge chose to give greater weight to the arguments of the prosecution and Edgington was deemed to be rational; therefore a plea of diminished responsibility was not accepted. She was given a life sentence for murder with a minimum term of 37 years. The remarks of the presiding Judge when passing sentence outraged many informed observers in that he acknowledged that Edgington may well have been experiencing some form of transient psychosis before and after the attack but that this did not absolve her from taking full responsibility for her actions.

There is little point in playing the blame game. Expert and other reports to the court are to inform sentencing, not to determine the outcome. However, a code of law for the clergy in the 8th century set out that, 'If a man fall out of his senses or wits, and it comes to pass that he kill someone, let his kinsmen pay for the victim, and preserve the slayer against aught else of that kind' (Egbert, Dialogue of Ecclesiastic Institution, n.d.). Certainly it is not too much to hope that 21st century sentencing decisions be at least as enlightened as those of an 8th century archbishop.

The lack of a shared meaning and understanding around mental disorder within and between legal and health disciplines inevitably leads to controversy and debate, particularly in the area of risk, whether to self or others, whether in terms of health outcomes or justice outcomes. The only real reform with any meaning for those with mental disorder who offend is that such scrutiny around the pathway of screening, assessment, care, management and sentencing leads to further clarity and enhanced processes and provision.

21st century thinking

We, the public, professionals and organisations, statutory, voluntary or community based, need to share a basic premise of seeing health as a whole and not just the absence of disease or infirmity – it embraces physical, social and mental well-being (World Health Organization, 1948, no. 2, p. 100). The pluralistic mix of models incorporating the interaction of biological and social factors and the silo of specialisms and expertise required to intervene and support these mean that although it is particularly complex to achieve a universal understanding and definition of what constitutes mental disorder (Ormel et al., 2013) we must strive to address this in order to achieve an effective multi-agency response.

Bradley (2009) set out the social and economic costs of failing to address provision deficits for this population and made recommendations fit for a 21st century society. In addition, within the group of those who are labelled as mentally disordered offenders, there are populations who are further disproportionately and negatively impacted in accessing already scarce and disjointed resources. This will be the challenge for the future and a challenge which this volume seeks to address, for, as Bean and Mounser (1993, p. 113) asserted, many of this group are seen as:

> Patients whose cause is not easy to espouse...not given the sympathy often granted to victims of crime, far too often the perpetrators of discord; frequently perceived as dangerous to the social order, to others or to themselves.

In the spirit of endeavour the same questions asked of old can be used to interrogate new efforts: do these people get the care they deserve? Are they managed such that their health can improve to support a reduction in the frequency and seriousness of reoffending? And, can the risk they pose to themselves and others be effectively addressed?

The contents of this book

This book examines the provision for those with a mental disorder who offend across a wide range of perspectives. The unifying feature is that of identifying best practice and provision for the future and providing a solution-focussed response to some well-known and debated issues, and also to address areas where the literature and engagement are scant. It embraces perspectives which include the need to radically re-vision perceptions of justice in the way in which mental disorder is managed, and professional contributions which identify the way in which new initiatives are learning from previous experience how to best navigate the hurdles of multi-agency implementation.

I chose to open the chapters in this book with the perceptions of a service user who translates for the reader how professional responses impact on personal life experiences. In one short narrative it captures many of the debates that academic and professional contributors explore in depth later in this volume. It is the more profound because of the balanced and reflective style of the author. It bought to my mind the belief rooted in the Muslim faith that those with a mental disorder are specially loved and particularly chosen to tell the truth. This sentiment can also be located in the humanist approach to mental ill-health with its focus upon personal growth, rather than solely on mental health needs, in order to support an individual to flourish. Enough said – Lucy tells her story better than I ever could, and it certainly lends support to those who argue that patients should be involved in the research, design and evaluation of new approaches to the management of mental disorder.

It felt particularly appropriate to follow this chapter by the contribution from Canton who debates human rights and ethical responses for offenders with a mental disorder. This is a highly current topic which is considered here in relation to philosophical and legal ambiguities; the right to be punished and not to be punished, the right to equal treatment and the rejection of unfair discrimination. It contests a holistic and deterministic approach to mentally disordered offenders as a homogenous group and argues that solution-focussed responses should start from a human rights and ethical context.

In these early sections of the volume I have also positioned the debates which address the framework from which interventions emerge. McGuire focusses on the accumulating evidence for treatment and management, and Göbbels, Thakker and Ward on desistance and mentally disordered offending. In these complementary chapters, McGuire critiques reviews and primary studies in the search for a definitive approach to take forward to the future. Addressing a range of the most problematic diagnoses, he draws on the literature to challenge the notion of untreatability and argues for a new research agenda which addresses the methodological limitations of past studies. This chapter is followed by considering in depth the use of desistance strategies. In applying the lens of desistance approaches to mental disorder, Göbbels, Thakker and Ward contribute to a sparse literature in this subject area. They draw upon studies from more well-known implementations, for example with sex offenders and the general offending population, to explore how the learning from these can be applied to mentally disordered offenders. There is a particular focus on the debates around social capital and social exclusion which disproportionately impact upon those with a mental disorder. Strengths-based approaches and the Good Lives Model are explored to consider how the different phases could be integrated with a strategy to support mentally disordered offenders. Whilst recognising that implementation would need to be appropriately adapted to individual limitations, they argue that in supporting the individual to lead a purposeful, pro-social and fulfilled life, these approaches have much to offer. Tyson and Hall address another neglected area of debate, the links between hate crime and mental disorder. In what is likely to be one of the first forays into this topic, they rose to this challenging brief by exploring whether and if the motivations for hate crime can ever be understood within a framework of mental disorder. Whilst hate crime is still a relative newcomer to criminology, mental disorder is certainly not. Exploring the two together led Tyson and Hall into debates around definitions which are not necessarily shared, the motivations for crime arising out of prejudice and whether hatred can be considered to be a symptom of mental disorder, rather than a mental disorder per se. They, as do Canton, McGuire, Göbbels, Thakker and Ward, open up new topics for debate and new ways of conceptualising mentally disordered offending in relation to future interventions.

The chapters authored by Chitsabesan and Hughes, Petrillo, and Pycroft and Green, focus upon the needs of specific mentally disordered populations. Chitsabesan and Hughes contribute to the discourse around the high rates of mental health needs and neurodisability amongst young people within the youth justice system. They explore the ways in which different types of diagnoses impact on the opportunities young people have to establish themselves in the social and educational pursuits which promote both good mental health and the protective factors which mitigate the likelihood of offending. The reader is introduced to the Comprehensive Screening and Assessment Tool (CHAT) which Chitsabesan and Hughes have been closely involved in developing. They argue that without robust and effective processes for screening and assessment, exemplified by CHAT, interventions cannot be effectively targeted. This means that young people will continue to be punished for the behaviours which their unmet mental health needs render them vulnerable to.

Petrillo explores the experiences of women in detention in relation to mental health, arguing for a trauma-informed approach and gender-responsive programme designs. She includes narratives from her research which speak to the complex needs of those with comorbidity as well as those from ethnic minorities. These draw attention to the paucity of current responses as well as to the potential of developing more fruitful pathways of interventions for the future. Pycroft and Green focus upon the theme of dual diagnosis, which is so often raised by other contributors to this volume and is central to the debates around multi-agency collaboration in management, resourcing and provision pathways. Interrogating key pieces of legislation and guidance, such as the Misuse of Drugs Act 1971, the Mental Health Acts (1983/2007), Drug Strategy (2010), Public Health Strategy (2010) and the Mental Health Strategy (2011) they explore the ways in which definitions of dual diagnosis have been conceptualised which lead to systemic problems in management. They argue for the development of a whole systems approach based on service user and co-production strategies and that this should be undertaken alongside a change in thinking in policy discourse around 'hard to reach' groups.

The chapters authored by de Lacy, Scally, and Gatawa address in depth how those with severe and enduring mental disorders posing a high risk of harm are managed once they enter the criminal justice system. De Lacy offers a unique insight into the activities of the Central Criminal Court ('Old Bailey') from the perspective of his role as Clinical Nurse Specialist. He takes us through what may, from the outside, appear to be a bewildering and winding pathway of law, case management and sentencing. In doing so, he explains how this prestigious court deals with some of the most complex cases of mental disorder and offending behaviour that are determined by the judiciary and sets out a best practice model which could be transferred to other settings. Scally focusses upon the Dangerous and Severe Personality Disorder (DSPD), a legal but non-clinical entity, arising out of proposals for Policy Development published jointly by the Home Office and the Department of Health in July 1999 (Department of Health and Home Office, 1999). The DSPD initiative, a response partly to public fears around atypical cases, was well funded and independently evaluated. Scally identifies a rich seam of learning from this now-abandoned programme and associated legal classification. Once again, this is a reminder of the difficulties posed when there is such a diffusion of shared meanings. The knowledge gleaned from the experience and evaluation of the DSPD also encourages the reader to look again at the chapter by McGuire and reflect on just how much we do already know which can be brought forward to inform impending programme development. Gatawa, a former practitioner at Broadmoor, a highly secure psychiatric hospital, provides insight into the management of further offending behaviour by in-patients. She draws attention to the dilemmas of determining whether and how to respond to such behaviours and the impact on decision-making for staff as well as for future risk assessments which inform release outcomes. It is a rare privilege to hear the voice of a professional who works so closely with those who are both mentally disordered and dangerous. The research, which gathered views from staff and patients, leads to conclusions around developing more robust guidelines and a role for the police which could better support professionals and lead to improved risk assessment information.

Throughout the chapters in this book there is a premium placed upon multi-agency practice, whether for those in the wider sentenced population or those incarcerated in prisons or secure health facilities. This is explored in depth by Rogers and Ormston and Hean, Walsh and Hammick. Rogers and Ormston are leading one of the national liaison and diversion initiatives supported by NHS England, arising out of the Bradley recommendations. Anyone who has tried to establish a liaison and diversion arrangement will know the hurdles that must be resolved around differing and competing organisational philosophies, skills, roles, training, information sharing and resources. All these, plus the diffusion of lead responsibilities, have been issues identified as leading to cumulative failures in the strategic and operational management of those with a mental disorder who offend. Rogers and Ormston, drawing upon years of professional expertise, demonstrate how they have responded to these challenges. They also go some way to answering the questions often posed of diversion which are where, when, how and to what. Hean, Walsh and Hammick contribute to these solution-focussed debates by addressing the ways in which multi-agency training can improve collaborative practice. Despite forays into multi-agency training in the past there is little to suggest that a coherent framework of content or format for such training is in place. Hean et al. respond to this by setting out in detail how it could be achieved and the ways in which this would enhance opportunities to securely embed multi-agency initiatives that take place across health and justice settings. James (1999, 2010), amongst many other authors, concludes that it is not the lack of will to start diversion and liaison schemes that is the problem, but the inability to see these through to enduring and well established pathways. Multi-agency training could play a key role in this.

The book concludes with a thought-provoking contribution from Arrigo and Bersot. Many of the authors in this volume have addressed the deterministic dialogue and public discourse around mental disorder and offending behaviours. Arrigo and Bersot take up this challenge by considering a number of concepts central to the critical philosophy of psychological jurisprudence. They argue for a transformation – metamorphosis – in the way that mentally disordered offending is conceptualised, in a closely-argued theme which centres upon human relatedness. This echoes the sentiments of Canton (this volume) that the narrow channels of social, legal and political thinking obscure the fundamental issue of respecting individual humanity – the ethical framework which should be the start-point of any and all debates around management and effectiveness.

Conclusion – harnessing the opportunity

The aim of this book is to be solution-focussed. The authors have traversed a wide range of issues and drawn upon literature, research, professional and service user experience to respond to this. However hard-pressed or tempted to pessimism when considering the trail littered with limited former outcomes, it is important not to be overwhelmed by the enormity of the task. Building upon learning and knowledge from previous experience is the way forward when constructing micro and macro legal, health and social reforms. The current reality is situated at the meeting point of the past and future. So, whilst mental health and crime may not be a new subject to criminology, research and dialogue provide constant sources of new knowledge and understanding. There is, now, a golden opportunity to ensure that this is embraced and harnessed in the renewed energies and commitment of policy-makers, practitioners and academics to resolve the hurdles. Most people with mental health needs, even those who offend, are far more likely to be a victim than to victimise, to self-harm rather than harm others. These are some of the most vulnerable, excluded and marginalised members of society; their numbers are not small and include children as well as adults. As this book makes perfectly clear, there are solutions, political, legal and social; what is needed is that these are mobilised in the development of new and future strategies.

References

Abrams, D., Christian, J., and Gordon, D. (2007). *Multidisciplinary Handbook of Social Exclusion Research.* Chichester: Wiley.

American Psychiatric Association (2013). *Diagnostic and statistical manual of mental disorders* (5th ed.) ('DSM V' or 'DSM-5'). Washington, DC: American Psychiatric Publishing.

Appleby, J., Harrison, T., Hawkins, L. and Dixon, A. (2012). *Payment by Results: how can payment systems help to deliver better care?* The Kings Fund. www.kingsfund.org.uk/sites/files/kf/field/field_publication_file/payment-by-results-the-kings-fund-nov-2012.pdf (accessed 12 February 2015).

Badger, D., Nursten, J., Williams, P., Woodward, M. (1999). *CRD Report 15 – Systematic Review of the International Literature on the Epidemiology of Mentally Disordered Offenders.* www.york.ac.uk/inst/crd/report15 .htm (accessed 12 February 2015).

Bean, P. and Mounser, P. (1993) *Discharged from Mental Hospitals.* London: Macmillan. ISBN–13: 978–033344787.

Blackburn, R. (2004). 'What Works' with mentally disordered offenders. *Psychology, Crime & La*, 10(3), 297–308.

Bradley, K. (Lord) (2009). *The Bradley Report: Lord Bradley's review of people with mental health problems or learning disabilities in the criminal justice system.* London: Department of Health.

Brooker, C., Repper, J., Beverley, C., Ferriter, M. and Brewer, N. (2002). *Mental Health Services and Prisoners: A Review.* Commissioned by Prison Healthcare Taskforce, Department of Health / Home Office. Sheffield: ScHARR, University of Sheffield.

Community Care (2015). *Mental Health Service in Crisis.* Community Care online www.communitycare.co.uk/search-results/?q=budget%20cuts%20for%20mental%20health. (accessed 17 January 2015).

Department of Health (2007). *Conference Report, Sharing Good Practice in Prison Health,* 4/5 June 2007. www.ohrn.nhs.uk/resource/policy/Yorkconferencereport.pdf

Department of Health (2012). *Post Legislative Assessment of the Mental Health Act 2007: Memorandum to the Health Committee of the House of Commons.* London: Department of Health. (accessed 14 March 2015).

Department of Health and the Home Office (1999). *Managing Dangerous People with Severe Personality Disorder. Proposals for Policy Development.* www.dh.gov.uk/prod_consum_dh/groups/dh_digitalassets/documents/digitalasset/dh_120634.pdf (accessed 12 January 2015).

Durcan, G. (2008). *From the Inside: Experiences of prison mental health care.* London: Sainsbury Centre for Mental Health.

Durcan, G., Saunders, A., Gadsby, B. and Hazard, A. (2014). *The Bradley Report five years on. An independent review of progress to date and priorities for further development.* London: Centre for Mental Health.

Egbert, Archbishop of York (n.d.). Dialogue of Ecclesiastic Institution. In D. Whitelock (ed.) (1996) *English Historical Documents Volume 1, c.500–1042.* New York: Routledge.

Francis, R., QC (2006). *Report of the independent inquiry into the care and treatment of Michael Stone.* http://hundredfamilies.org/wp/wp-content/uploads/2013/12/MICHAEL_STONE_JULY96.pdf (accessed 12 January 2015).

Garside, R. (2014). *Report from the House of Commons Justice Committee.* Centre for Crime and Justice Studies. www.crimeandjustice.org.uk/resources/coming-probation-privatisation-disaster

Health and Social Care Centre (2015). *Inpatients formally detained in hospitals under the Mental Health Act 1983, and patients subject to supervised community treatment: Annual report, England, 2013/14*. www.hscic.gov.uk/catalogue/PUB15812/inp-det-m-h-a-1983-sup-com-eng-13-14-rep.pdf (accessed 18 January 2015).

HM Inspectorate of Probation (2006). *An Independent Review of a Serious Further Offence case: Anthony Rice*. www.justiceinspectorates.gov.uk/probation/wp-content/uploads/sites/5/2014/03/anthonyricereport-rps.pdf (accessed 19 January 2015).

HM Inspectorate of Probation (2009). *Risk of Harm Inspection Report. A Stalled Journey. An inquiry into the management of offenders' Risk of Harm to others by London Probation*. www.justiceinspectorates.gov.uk/probation/wp-content/uploads/sites/5/2014/03/London_Special_Inspection_Report-rps.pdf (accessed 22 March 2015).

Hudson, B. (2001). Punishment, Rights, and Difference: Defending Justice in the Risk Society. In K. Stenson and R. Sullivan (eds). *Crime, Risk and Justice: The politics of crime control in liberal democracies*. London: Willan Publishing.

Independent Police Complaints Commission (2013). *Investigation into the police contact with Nicola Caroline Edgington prior to her fatally stabbing Sally Hodkin*. www.ipcc.gov.uk/sites/default/files/Documents/investigation_commissioner_reports/hodkin_investigation_report.pdf (accessed 23 March 2015).

James, D. V. (1999). Court diversion at ten years. Can it work? Does it work? Has it a future? *Journal of Forensic Psychiatry*, 10(3), 503–520.

James, D. V. (2010). Diversion of mentally disordered people from the criminal justice system in England and Wales: An overview. *International Journal of Law and Psychiatry*, 33, 241–248.

Kings Fund (2015). *Five Year Forward Plan for NHS*. www.kingsfund.org.uk/projects/nhs-five-year-forward-view?gclid=Cj0KEQjwmLipBRC59O_EqJ_E0asBEiQATYdNh2VXcVCvLgLojMfqNCOOWtMdWHxnToEHmUSjHXBy1bMaAms68P8HAQ

Lee, M. (2007). *Inventing Fear of Crime: criminology and the politics of anxiety*. Cullompton: Willan Publishing.

Mental Health Foundation (n.d.). *Black and Minority Ethnic Communities*. www.mental-health.org.uk/help-information/mental-health-a-z/b/bme-communities / (accessed 23 March 2015).

Moulin, L (2015) #542905 http://www.kingsfund.org.uk/publications/implementing-nhs-five-year-forward-view. (accessed 16 September 2015).

NACRO (2007a). *Effective mental healthcare for offenders: the need for a fresh approach. Mental Health and Crime Policy Briefing*. www.nacro.org.uk/data/files/nacro-2007101000-476.pdf (accessed 1 April 2015).

NACRO (2007b) *Black communities, mental health and the criminal justice system*. www.nacro.org.uk/data/files/black-communities-mh-1009.pdf (accessed 13 February 2015).

Nash, M. and Williams, A. (eds) (2006). *Handbook of Public Protection*. Cullompton: Willan Publishing.

Nash, M. and Williams, A. (eds) (2010). *Handbook of Public Protection* (2nd ed.). Cullompton: Willan Publishing.

Neal, S. (1998). Embodying Black Madness, Embodying White Femininity: Populist (Re) Presentations and Public Policy – The Case of Christopher Clunis and Jayne Zito. *Sociological Research Online*, Vol. 3, No. 4. www.socresonline.org.uk/3/4/2.html (accessed 16 February 2015).

Nilsson, N., Gustavson, C., Munthe, C., Forsman, A. and Anckarsater, H. (2009). The precarious practice of risk assessment in forensic psychiatry. *International Journal of Law and Psychiatry*, 32 (6), 400–407.

Offender Health Research Network (2010). *The pathway of prisoners with mental health problems through prison health services and the effect of the prison environment on the mental health of prisoners: A report to the National Institute of Health Research.* www.ohrn.nhs.uk (accessed 17 February 2015).

Ormel, J., Jeronimus, B. F., Kotov, M., Riese, H. et al. (2013). Neuroticisim and common mental disorders: meaning and utility of a complex relationship. *Clinical Psychology Review*, 33, 686–697.

Pakes F. and Winstone, J. (2012). The mental health treatment requirement: the promise and the practice. In: A. Pycroft and S. Clift (eds). *Risk and rehabilitation: management and treatment of substance misuse and mental health problems in the criminal justice system.* London: Policy Press. 107–118.

Pakes, F. and Winstone, J. (2010). A site visit survey of 101 mental health liaison and diversion schemes in England. *Journal of Forensic Psychiatry and Psychology*, 21 (6), 873–886.

Pakes, F. and Winstone, J. (2009). Effective practice in mental health diversion and liaison. *The Howard Journal of Criminal Justice*, 48 (2), 158–171.

Pakes, F. and Winstone, J. (2008). The fall and rise of mental health diversion. *Prison Service Journal*, 177, 43–47.

Pycroft, A. and Clift, S. (eds.) (2012). *Risk and rehabilitation: management and treatment of substance misuse and mental health problems in the criminal justice system.* Bristol: Policy Press.

Prins, H. (2005). Mental disorder and violent crime: A problematic relationship. *Probation Journal*, 52, 333.

Prins, H. (2010). *Offenders, deviants or patients? Explorations in Clinical Psychology.* London: Taylor and Francis.

Reed, J. (1992). Reed report on mentally disordered offenders. *British Medical Journal*, 305, 1448.

Royal College of Psychiatrists (2008). *Rethinking risk to others in mental health services: Final report of a scoping group.* CR150. RCP. rcpsych.ac.uk/pdf/CR150%20rethinking%20risk.pdf (accessed 21 March 2015).

Revolving Doors Agency (2007). *Prisons: Britain's 'Social Dustbins'.* www.revolving-doors.org.uk/documents/prisons-britains-social-dustbins / (accessed 22 March 2015).

Seymour, L. (2010). *Promoting and protecting offenders' mental health and wellbeing.* Centre for Mental Health. www.centreformentalhealth.org.uk/pdfs/Public_health_and_criminal_justice.pdf (accessed 1 January 2015).

Singleton, N., Meltzer, H. and Gatward, R. (1998). *Psychiatric morbidity among prisoners in England and Wales.* Office for National Statistics. London: Stationery Office.

Social Exclusion Unit (SEU) (2002). *Reducing re-offending by ex-prisoners.* London: Office of the Deputy Prime Minister. www.bristol.ac.uk/poverty/downloads/keyofficialdocuments/Reducing%20Reoffending.pdf (accessed 14 January 2015).

Steury, E. and Choinski, M. (1995). Normal crimes and mental disorder: A two-group comparison of deadly and dangerous felonies. *International Journal of Law and Psychiatry*, 18(2), 183–207.

Stevens, S. (2014). *High quality care for all, now and for future generations.* NHS England. www.england.nhs.uk/2014/04/01/simon-stevens-speech / (accessed 09 February 2015).

Stevenson, J. (2014). *Explaining levels of wellbeing in BME populations in England.* www.leadershipacademy.nhs.uk/wp-content/uploads/2014/07/Explaining-levels-of-wellbeing-in-BME-populations-in-England-FINAL-18-July-14.pdf

Stone, N. (2003). *A Companion Guide to Mentally Disordered Offenders* (2nd ed.). Crayford: Shaw. (accessed 11 March 2015).

The Guardian (2006). *Stone Report Highlights Case Errors.* www.theguardian.com/society/2006/sep/25 /1 (accessed 06 January 2015).

Thornicroft, G. (2006). *Shunned: discrimination against people with mental illness.* Oxford: Open University.

Uzieblo, K., Winter, J., Vanderfaeillie, J., Rossi, G. and Magez, W. (2012). Intelligent diagnosing of intellectual disabilities in offenders: food for thought. *Behav Sci Law*, 30(1), 28–48.

Whitty, N. (2007). Risk, Human Rights and the Management of a Serious Sex Offender. *Zeitschrift für Rechtssoziologie*, 28, Heft 2, 201–212.

World Health Organization (WHO) (1998). *Preamble to the Constitution of the World Health Organization* as adopted by the International Health Conference, New York, 19–22 June, 1946; signed on 22 July 1946 by the representatives of 61 States (Official Records of the World Health Organization, no. 2, p. 100) and entered into force on 7 April 1948. www.who.int/about/definition/en/print.html (accessed 19 February 2015).

Winstone, J. and Pakes, F. (2005). Marginalised and disenfranchised: community justice and mentally disordered offenders. In: J. Winstone and F. Pakes (eds). *Community Justice: issues for probation and criminal justice.* Cullompton: Willan Publishing. 219–236.

Winstone, J. and Pakes, F. (2007). The mentally disordered offender: disenablers for the delivery of justice. In: D. Carson., B. Milne., F. Pakes., K. Shalev and A. Shawyer (eds). *Applying psychology to criminal justice.* Chichester : Wiley. 167–182.

Winstone, J. and Pakes, F. (2008). *Report on National Criminal Justice Mental Health Team audit (England).* Commissioned by the Department of Health, Office for Criminal Justice Reform and Her Majesty's Court Service (to inform the Bradley Report, 2009).

Winstone, J. and Pakes, F. (2010). Offenders with mental health problems in the criminal justice system: the multi-agency challenge. In: A. Pycroft and D. Gough (eds). *Multi-agency working in criminal justice: control and care in contemporary correctional practice.* London: Policy Press. 169–178.

2
A Broken Outline – Being an Observer in My Own Life: Notes from a Service User

Lucy Jo Mathews

As I leant forward to blow out the candles on my cake I took an extra deep breath realising that this marked the point where I would have spent more of my life suffering from serious illness than I had not. It was my 30th birthday. I currently hold the dual diagnosis of having an Autistic Spectrum Disorder and Rapid Cycling Bipolar Disorder. I have spent much of my adult life haunted by the difficulty of defining myself as me...as a woman, as a friend, a daughter, a sister and aunt, a colleague, while battling these conditions that are so intrinsically interwoven with the very fabric of who I am. This is both on an organically physical level and also in the perceptions of myself in society and to my family and friends.

Over the course of 17 years I've seen councillors, clinical and educational psychologists, psychotherapists, psychiatrists, social workers, occupational therapists, psychiatric nurses and have experienced the NHS mental health service as both an in- and out-patient. Medical professionals have disagreed on my diagnosis to the tune of suggesting seven different psychiatric and psychological conditions and I've been prescribed anti-depressants, anti-convulsants, lithium, anti-psychotics, benzodiazepines and sleeping medications.

Medical professionals, the media, politicians, service users and the general public will probably forever disagree over the characterisation and labelling of mental health disorders. Unfortunately, despite recent campaigns to raise public awareness and change attitudes there is still wide-ranging stigma and misunderstanding surrounding mental illness. I believe this is largely because we are trying to apply a universal blanket of political and social correctness to just too wide a scope.

We are fond of using the term 'mentally ill', whereas people would think it important and entirely necessary for clarity to differentiate between diabetes or motor neuron disease, for example, and not just say 'physically ill' (see Canton, this volume). Standardising our approach and attitudes to the millions of people whose conditions land them under this universal poorly defined umbrella of mental illness serves only to reinforce and perpetuate outdated perceptions (see McGuire, this volume).

I have a severe and chronic psychiatric illness and am in receipt of the highest level of Employment and Support Allowance and various Disability Living Allowances. I am cared for by my mother and a few close friends with whose support I get to occasionally socialise and indulge in my passion for furniture making. My whole life is a balancing act though and all of it I spend feeling drained and unwell from the physiological effects of the conditions and the psychological impacts of isolation, loneliness, lost dreams and fears for my future (see Arrigo and Bersot, this volume).

Several years ago I decided that I would no longer hide the truth about either of my diagnoses in the hope of improving people's understanding. Despite this, the wide range of responses I've had to my health problems still range from the slightly ridiculous to plainly offensive to knife-twistingly painful. These have included: 'Does that mean you're crazy?', 'Oh are you like that strange woman from Eastenders?', 'Is it terminal?', 'It seems to be you're the only one who thinks that so could it be we know the truth and not you?', 'No, I don't think you've got that', 'You should really set up a business', 'You're so lucky you don't have to work' and 'You don't look sick'.

As a teenager, and following an unsuccessful course of anti-depressants, I was referred to my local Community Mental Health Team (CMHT) in 1999. I held the popular belief that some doctor or some drug somewhere would hold all the answers to a cure. As time went on, this morphed to a (seemingly) more realistic expectation of the health service offering a place of respite, recovery and support. My early experiences did not, in fact, fall too far from this. I navigated my first period of severe debilitation with a strong, consistent team of professionals including a consultant psychiatrist and consultant clinical psychologist. They managed my care over a two-year period, both as an out- and in-patient, through regular appointments and therapy.

Initially my health continued to deteriorate and my psychiatrist decided to admit me to an open in-patient ward for more intensive assessment and to keep me safe. There was no expectation of a speedy discharge and I left the hospital much stronger but more importantly having established a new medication regime based on my newly established diagnoses. My health improved and I trained as a cabinet maker ultimately entering employment and living an independent life.

I returned to my CMHT in 2005 suffering from depression. In the intervening years the mental health services within the NHS had been subject to cuts in funding and what I found was a service limping heavily under enormous strain. I appreciated that the staff were overworked and underpaid (they would tell me at every appointment) but the bottom line was that I was deteriorating rapidly with the illness pursuing me relentlessly. I was given anti-depressant medication (contra-indicated for use with Bipolar Disorder unless prescribed with an additional mood stabilising drug) and referred to the recently established 'Home Crisis Team'. There were no longer any in-patient beds available other than to those labelled as 'critically ill'.

The 'Home Crisis Team' offered one of the most disjointed, ineffectual and stressful services I have ever experienced (see Canton, this volume). This was a time when I was experiencing a state of mind that severely limited my general understanding, decision-making abilities and assertiveness. I was in urgent need of high level support, continuity of care and strong advocacy. Different people visited each day, often missing the scheduled appointment times and arriving hours later. They attempted to administer procedures such as taking blood in my kitchen but without explaining why it was necessary. After several days my mother had to request that they didn't return back to the house. My life was starting to unravel at an alarming speed and I was becoming extremely unwell, suffering from a period of mania possibly caused/accelerated by the prescription medications.

Shortly afterwards, in 2006, came my second hospitalisation. Although, prima facie, I was encouraged to make the choice of admitting myself voluntarily, I do not recall there being much of an element of encouragement or choice. I was told by the psychiatrist that if I didn't agree to a voluntary admission then she would section me under the 1983 Mental Health Act. Long gone was the day of the open unit. Having had the decision forced upon me, I was taken to a ward and held like a prisoner, stripped of my possessions with the door slammed shut and locked behind me. As a voluntary patient I was not subject to any statutory powers and legally should have been well within my rights to leave at any time, accompanied or otherwise. In reality, it was a very different situation. The ward was locked at all times and requests to leave were denied. When I challenged this situation I was told that they would not let me leave until I had seen a doctor – one doctor covering several hospitals of a major city – the wait would be over eight hours. I was desperate, alone and vulnerable, being held against my will in a place I had been promised would help me and keep me safe.

The ward was a disturbing place. The staff spent the majority of their time gathered in the nurses' station, a locked, glass-fronted room within the ward, separated from the patients. They came out only to shout at you to queue up for medications or to try and stop people inappropriately using the payphone. It was a mixed sex facility and people were free to come and go into your room as they chose. I observed countless incidents of sexual aggression and sexual attention that, had they occurred in the workplace, would have constituted harassment. One of the nurses told me she didn't really understand why I was there and she was sure that as I was a pretty girl all I needed was a boyfriend to make me feel better. They sent me home after only a few days without any sort of meaningful recovery and it came as no surprise when within a couple of months I had to be re-admitted.

The in-patient ward was supposed to offer a safe and therapeutic environment for the acutely ill. However, my experience was different. Shortly towards the end of my second stay that year a fellow in-patient offered me the use of his razor, the medical team attempted to issue me with the wrong prescription medication having gotten my notes confused (they were reading off a chart from the previous admission when my illness was in a different phase) and the psychiatrist discarded my previous history and diagnoses and told me I probably had a personality disorder. They then discharged me again. I found myself being sent back to the CMHT, having been signed up to a support group for a condition I didn't believe I had.

Most people will be familiar with images of the mental asylums of the late 18th to early 20th century – it is perhaps more disturbing that as we move through the first quarter of the 21st century mental health services still frequently remain segregated. The CMHT in my town can be found located in a building entirely separate to other healthcare facilities. It makes no attempt to disguise itself behind a name which might afford service users the privacy and confidentiality they deserve – quite the contrary in fact. The service clearly advertises itself overlooking the busy one-way system. If you wish, for whatever reason, not to be forced into disclosing the nature of your health difficulty you have to try and skulk in round the back and hope that the person across from you in the waiting room isn't someone you know who is friends on a social media site with your neighbour/old school friend/employer etc.

After months of very little progress and repeated requests for a new approach I was referred to a consultant psychiatrist who specialised in developmental disorders. This doctor met with me once and then a second time with me and my family. For the first time in years someone seemed to actually listen to and respect what I was saying (see Göbbels, Thakker and Ward, this volume) and reconfirmed my original diagnosis of ASD and Bipolar. The consultant provided written recommendations of possible avenues to explore that would offer a therapeutic treatment approach targeted to my specific conditions. I returned to my CMHT with renewed hope of finally moving forward. I was met with apathy. I said I could be flexible in where I went for treatment but I was told that the NHS's declaration that service users could choose which team they saw didn't apply and that my current CMHT was my only option. I could see the one psychologist they had (which I did to no success) and after that there was nothing more they could offer.

So once again I was back to relying heavily on the medications as the major intervention. I was passed between different team members and attended intermittent appointments with junior doctors who had little idea who I was and who felt no need to conceal that they had often had no time to read notes or familiarise themselves with my history. It's a worrying reality when internet search engines become a greater source of information about your condition and medications than your local CMHT. I identified a real need to research possible treatment options myself but unhappily my ideas were generally either met with complete disinterest or I was told there simply wasn't the money or resources available.

I continued to be severely debilitated by my health, and the medications that I was being given felt, rather ironically, like they were removing what little control I had left. I was easily distracted and everything I had ever known merged before me in an insurmountable, shapeless barrage of half-experienced thoughts and dulled senseless feeling. My concentration became increasingly fragmented to the degree that even re-reading words and sentences up to four times wasn't helping. My mind would close down and phase out the voices of the people I loved and I couldn't find the passion or inclination to pursue my hobbies.

The medications, particularly the anti-psychotics, were draining the very essence of my humanity and it may sound selfish but I needed more than to just be alive; a broken outline, forced to be an observer in my own life. I wanted to take the decision to come off my medications and only use drug intervention at times of acute crisis. It was to be one of the biggest decisions of my life and I wanted to explore and consider the implications with my medical team.

I was immediately deemed treatment resistant by the CMHT. I felt very much that the responsibility for the destruction of my life and the burden of future illness would be placed in no uncertain terms on my shoulders should I make the decision not to take regular medication for the rest of my life. My disapproving CPN said that it was 'better in the long run' and made it clear (while sitting in my home) that she felt I would be accountable for the increasing deterioration of my cognitive functioning by letting the disease destroy my brain if I didn't comply with taking daily medication.

These discussions continued with my psychiatrist and I felt increasingly isolated following these meetings. The medical team were committed to trying to establish and implement illness management plans and stress/symptom awareness strategies but without involving me in the discussion about what it was they were trying to achieve. What success looked like in terms of the intended outcomes of my treatment was being defined by the mental health professionals rather than me. I valued their input and respected their expertise but I needed someone to listen to me.

One of the things I think people underestimate is the significance of the impact of non-medical team members for providing continuity of care and an environment that best fosters a strong therapeutic alliance between service user and their healthcare team. In my early days in the late 90's/early 00's the service was largely co-ordinated by a small number of administrative staff who knew your name and had the time to engage with you and support your visits to the team. This was much needed in times of mental distress.

When I returned several years later (2006) this had all changed – harassed and stressed staff (usually a different face each appointment) greeted you rudely while carrying out other tasks. They often exhibited complete disinterest in me or my needs or were too busy discussing other service users' conditions on the phone to help. I recently bumped into the woman who for years had been the secretary of the consultant psychiatrists at the CMHT. She greeted me like an old friend, enquiring after my health. I had assumed she had retired but then, in some distress, she told me how she had been made redundant. I wonder if they felt her role was the most expendable. I would argue not. The restructuring of the service meant that I had to fight my way past reception and had been devalued and treated with hostile aggression at every turn. This meant that I was in no fit state to discuss my treatment in a productive way when I did sit down in the doctor's office. Reaching that point without a stress headache or in desperation became the exception rather than the rule.

My experience of the impact of others' attitudes to mental illness has been that tolerance, understanding and resourcing is far more readily available under the premise of one of two outcomes – you either get better or you die. There doesn't really seem to be a huge amount available for helping improve quality of life or supporting people in maintaining their status quo. Once out of crisis, the mental health services are eager to discharge you (for understandable reasons) but ease of access to re-establishing a higher level of care and support if you have a chronic illness and relapse is vital. Once discharged the process of being re-referred to the community teams is impossibly prolonged and hard work at a point in time when you are the most vulnerable and debilitated.

I believe that everyone deserves an equal standard of care and have always wished to remain committed to the NHS – there have been some fantastic and dedicated individuals who have positively affected my care over the years. I was loath to find myself feeling backed into a corner and forced to consider other options. However, after four years of frustrating, disjointed, incompetent and, at times, dangerous service provision, I found myself begging the people I loved, who had helped save my life, to promise they would let me die rather than have me end up back in an NHS psychiatric ward and I vowed to never step foot in the CMHT building ever again. It saddens me that this has turned out to be one of the most life-affirming and positive steps in my journey. I am now looked after by a private consultant psychiatrist and my fabulous and eternally patient GP.

My quest will be to continue to try and seek out both healthcare professionals and friends who will treat me with care and dignity at the times where they are required to take control of my decisions and who will see me as an equal, trust in my opinions and honour my wishes when I am healthy enough to reassume responsibility for myself. These are the people with whom I can talk about my feelings of wanting to die (when they are there) without being considered 'dangerously suicidal' or 'incredibly disrespectful to the thousands of people fighting cancer who so want to live' and people who can appreciate my acceptance of my life as it is. For thirty seconds of every minute I have to devote my time, mind and energy to balancing and fighting to stay safe and stay alive. But for the other half I can love and laugh, achieve, cry and shout just like everybody else. See me as both these people and take time to get to know and respect each equally. That's all I'd like to ask of anyone.

3
Troublesome Offenders, Undeserving Patients? The Precarious Rights of Mentally Disordered Offenders

Rob Canton

Introduction

This chapter affirms the importance of trying to establish an ethical basis for working with 'mentally disordered offenders' in the context of academic and policy debate that is often centred around ideas of effective treatment and system management. It is argued that a respect for human rights constitutes the most secure foundation not only for ethical policy and practice, but also for an approach that can contribute to solutions and to positive outcomes – both in terms of meeting the needs of mentally disordered offenders and in reducing reoffending. Rights are here understood as ethical entitlements and, although law is essential in defending and promoting these rights, it is also necessary to find a perspective from which to critique the law. The initial account suggests that human rights include both *liberties* (freedom from oppression and cruelty, for example) and *claims* (demands on government to foster circumstances in which people may thrive). The daunting question of what are the rights of mentally disordered offenders is explored by considering each of a paradoxical set of rights that have been attributed to them. It is argued that examination of these putative rights exposes some assumptions about (and ambivalent attitudes towards) mental disorder. It is likely that cultural influences and stereotypes influence reactions towards people believed to be mentally unwell and that these reactions may subvert or distort policy objectives (see Arrigo and Bersot, this volume). An understanding of the social origins of mental distress, including the effects of social disadvantage and exclusion, is set against the dominance of medical conceptions which have dominated policy debate. The chapter concludes by asserting claim rights, as well as the safeguards of liberty rights, and making connections between the entitlements of mentally disordered offenders and the 'Good Lives Model' (see Göbbels, Thakker and Ward, this volume) which is now influential in desistance research. In the context of contemporary economic difficulties and the volatile politics of crime and punishment, the fundamental importance of establishing a secure ethical foundation for policy and practice must be asserted.

The problem of how to manage offenders with mental health needs seems intractable, and has puzzled and frustrated policy makers and practitioners for a very long time. This chapter tries to distinguish and perhaps to clarify some of the complex and contested questions to which these problems give rise. How, then, are these matters to be approached and discussed? While policymakers, practitioners and researchers have often set the question 'What works?' as their priority (see McGuire, this volume), it can be argued that a better initial question is 'What's right?' Both questions are complex and irresolvably contested, but there is much to be gained from beginning criminal justice debates by foregrounding ethical considerations, especially when considering offenders with a mental disorder. It has been properly insisted that 'the mentally disordered offender [should] be treated as a person first, as an offender second, and as mentally disordered third' (Peay, 1994; p. 1123). Yet a great deal of policy discussion inverts these priorities, considering, first, the individual's needs for diagnosis and treatment; second, the contribution of the agencies of criminal justice; and, third (if indeed at all), the ethical entitlements and safeguards that derive from being a person (see Mathews, this volume).

There is a real risk that ethical considerations are obscured or lost in debates about effective treatment or about the efficient management of the notoriously complex interfaces between systems of health care and criminal justice. Discussing the institutions of punishment – but making a point that is no less well-taken when considering those who are mentally disordered – David Garland writes that '...values such as justice, tolerance, decency, humanity and civility should be part of any penal institution's self-consciousness – an intrinsic and constitutive aspect of its role – rather than a diversion from its "real" goals or an inhibition on its capacity to be "effective"' (Garland, 1990: p. 292).

History too demonstrates the imperative value of keeping sight of the ethical status of patients with mental health needs. Histories of psychiatry are replete with examples of pain and humiliation inflicted on patients, sometimes with good intention, but also arising from more complex and perhaps questionable motives (Porter, 2002; Scull, 2005). Nor should it be assumed that these cruelties and abuses have been consigned to the past. Implicating the psychiatric profession and its symbiotic relationship with 'a massively profitable psychopharmaceutical industry', Scull suggests that 'we once more live in an era where simplistic and biologically reductionist accounts of mental disorder enjoy wide currency... [and have adopted] a concept of mental illnesses as specific, identifiably different diseases, each allegedly amenable to treatment with particular drugs or "magic bullets".' (Scull, 2005: p. xii; see Mathews, this volume). It will be argued later that contemporary approaches to mentally disordered offenders tend to rest precisely on the assumptions that Scull calls into question, that policy discourse is 'over-medicalised' and that there are other ways of understanding and responding to mental distress – ways that may better respect the rights of those concerned. The history of the prison too includes any number of examples of gratuitous cruelty and degradation (Morris and Rothman, 1995; Wilson, 2014). Across the world, countless prisoners are still held in the most appalling conditions. In the USA alone – although for sure not only there – tens of thousands of inmates are held in conditions that can be argued to amount to torture, many of whom have a clinically diagnosable mental health need and/or learning need (Gawande, 2009; see also Council of Europe, 2014).

That the most fundamental rights of suspects and offenders and of people believed to be mentally disordered have been grossly violated, so often and in so many places, should be a reminder of the need to determine the ethical parameters within which debates about effectiveness may take place. Before attempting to identify these parameters, it will be important to look briefly at the ethical concepts that are to be deployed in the discussion.

Human rights

One approach to an understanding of the constraints and obligations that set the ethical boundaries of responses to mentally disordered offenders is through an inquiry into human rights. There is no suggestion that *human rights* represents the only way to think about moral issues or that all ethical considerations can be framed as rights. *What is the right thing to do* can as well be explored through reflections on welfare, duties and virtues (see Sandel, 2009, for an excellent introduction to these topics). Yet the discourse of human rights has become the best established way of asserting liberties and claims, a familiar and international 'language' in which to conduct policy debate and one that is of particular value to oppressed and vulnerable groups (Clapham, 2007).

Rights encompass both liberties and claims (Gearty, 2006). *Liberties* include an insistence on restraints on inhuman and degrading treatment, on cruel or unusual punishment, against injustice; *claims* articulate a demand for the state to meet needs for human flourishing and well-being, for example, rights to education, employment, healthcare and to an adequate standard of living. These are claims that require more than forbearance and call for positive action by the state.

Human rights are everybody's: they do not have to be earned and the sole and sufficient credentials to qualify for them are to be human. This insight is an essential reminder that, in the present context, it is not only the rights of those believed to be mentally disordered offenders that are at issue, but the rights of everyone else as well – in particular, perhaps, of actual or potential victims of their crimes. This should not, however, be discussed as a question of *balance*. As Ashworth has argued, that metaphor often leads to a utilitarian calculation that the rights of victims 'outweigh' the rights of offenders (Ashworth, 1996; see also Canton, 2009). The implication would then be that majority rights should prevail. But rights can and should function as constraints on what the state may legitimately do. As Nozick powerfully asserted: 'Individuals have rights, and there are things that no person or group may do to them (without violating their rights)' (Nozick, 1974: p. ix).

The European Convention on Human Rights distinguishes between *absolute rights* (which may never be taken or given away), *limited rights* (which may only be compromised in explicitly identified specific circumstances) and *qualified rights* (where individual rights must be considered alongside broader social and community interests) (Ministry of Justice, 2006). Notoriously, too, rights may *conflict*. To assert a right, then, even persuasively, does not by itself settle the question, but it does mean that there is a need for a principled judgement. A human right may not be ignored or merely set aside as inconvenient: if it must be infringed (because other moral considerations turn out to be more compelling), this requires an ethical justification and the infringement should take place with a sense of regret, an attempt to mitigate the consequences for the right-bearer and a stimulus to look for solutions to future similar cases which better respect the right.

In the modern era, the authority of law has been fundamental to the framing and development of human rights, as statutes and international treaties have proliferated. In the UK, the most important such statute was the Human Rights Act 1998, which incorporated the European Convention for the Protection of Human Rights and Fundamental Freedoms into national law. The government's professed intention at that time (Home Office, 1999) was that human rights should not merely be seen as a constraint on policy:

'Though it is clearly right that all public authorities should not act incompatibly with the Convention rights, the Act was intended to do more than merely avoid direct violations of human rights.…this is a constitutional measure, *legislating for basic values which can be shared by all people throughout the United Kingdom. It offers a framework for policy-making…*' (Joint Committee on Human Rights 2003 – emphasis added).

It is indeed doubtful, however, that the Act has been embraced in this way. There has certainly been progress – many cases have come to court where the Act and the Convention on which it is based have been cited. In the area of criminal justice, attempts have been made in this way to clarify, defend and promote the rights of prisoners (van Zyl Smit, 2007) and those subject to community penalties (Gelsthorpe, 2007). But this often seems to have been wrung from a grudging and reluctant administration, which has reacted with just the kind of litigious defensiveness that the government itself had originally warned against. There is little sign that the Convention has inspired penal policy. On the contrary, the Act – and indeed the very idea of human rights – now often attracts suspicion and hostility in politics and in the mass media (Gies, forthcoming).

However that may be, one of the principal advantages of framing ethical debate in the language of human rights is that their legal basis makes them *justiciable* – capable of being put to test and determined in a court of law. Political decisions can be challenged in court – domestically, through the Human Rights Act 1998, and internationally through the Convention in the European Court of Human Rights. Invoking human rights in this way has been employed to good effect in recent years. For example, the Howard League has used the processes of judicial review to clarify and promote recognition of the rights of young people in custody and the duties that are owed to them, establishing the key principle that the state is not absolved of its duties to young people because they are designated 'young offenders' (Howard League, 2008).

Yet while the legal standing of human rights affords these progressive possibilities, enabling challenge and insistence on the enforcements of rights through due process of law, the topic should not be explored solely through an analysis of statute and case law. It is important, after all, not to lose sight of a conception of human rights that can appraise, challenge and limit the powers of the state, including its legislative and judicial authority. In this paper, then, discussion about rights will not be confined to those rights that have been established by law, but will include ethical arguments about what it would be to deal with mentally disordered offenders fairly and well. (For the legal aspects of the Convention's impact on the rights of people who are mentally disordered, see especially Richardson, 2005; Prior, 2007; Hale, 2004.) Moreover, in general, a dependence on the law here will be slow to progress. Legislation takes time and courts can only have regard to cases that are brought before them.

It has been argued, then, that the discourse of human rights represents the most instructive way of exploring ethical issues in relation to mentally disordered offenders; that regard should be had to both liberties and claims; and that the foundation of rights in law is both a strength (making ethical assertions justiciable) and a limitation (because not all rights are – or perhaps even could be – articulated in statute or case law). In particular, it has been asserted that human rights are those rights that all people possess in virtue of our common humanity. The corollary of this is that to fail to take account of someone's rights may be to treat them as less than human (see Arrigo and Bersot, this volume).

Mentally disordered offenders and rights

Definitions of the term *mentally disordered offender* are discussed by others in this volume (see for example Göbbels, Thakker and Ward). Here it is enough to note that there can be no uncontroversial definition of this term, not least because any definition is 'partly dependent on the incentives for its construction' (Peay, 1994: p.1123; see Arrigo and Bersot, this volume); that there are legal, medical and lay understandings that are different, even if they sometimes overlap; that attempts to apply or to reject the application of the term to an individual is in practice strongly influenced by professional and resource interests; and that, without a sufficient definitional consensus, attempts to frame policy will founder and estimates of the numbers of people concerned should always be regarded with caution if not scepticism. It can even be argued that it is impossible to identify a 'group' of mentally disordered offenders whose members have as much in common with one another, or are sufficiently different from many offenders excluded by definition, to constitute any kind of group or category (Canton, 2002). The term mental disorder encompasses a very wide range of conditions, yet policy commonly fails to respond to this diversity.

As for ethical inquiry, the expression *mentally disordered offenders* is an unpromising start. It is a reductive term that understands people in complex and troubled circumstances in terms of their worst behaviour (as *offenders*) and assimilates people with a wide range of mental health difficulties. It 'groups' people with any number of dimensions of difference – gender, age, ethnicity, sexuality (see for example Petrillo, this volume; Chitsabesan and Hughes, this volume) – as well as widely differing offending careers. It smuggles in, at least by implication, assumptions about the connections between mental health and offending. With these cautions duly noted, discussion moves on to consider how the rights of mentally disordered offenders might be explored.

A brief historical and international review of forensic psychiatry some years ago ended by identifying a number of central themes, including:

> the right to be punished; the right not to be punished; the right to be treated; the right not to be treated; the justice of indeterminate sentences especially when associated with treatments of debatable efficacy; and the poor predictability of dangerousness. (Higgins, 1984; p. 13)

It seems to me that this paradoxical set of claims and problems offers a framework in which many of the most complex ethical concerns may be explored. Reflection on these questions illuminates some of the philosophical and legal ambivalence and confusion that are regularly acted out in practice, contributing to an explanation of why policy is so difficult to frame and so often frustrated in implementation. It may also expose certain assumptions – about the nature of mental disorder, about punishment and treatment, about the capacity of mentally disordered people to be (or to be held) responsible, about their supposed irrationality and consequent unpredictability – which are all the more influential in policy debate and in practice because they are insufficiently articulated or inspected.

The right to be punished

Among the arguments to be found in the extensive philosophical literature on the justifications of punishment is the claim that offenders have a *right to be punished*. While the origins of this claim could be traced to Kant or to Hegel, the case has been more recently developed by Bennett (2008), building on an influential paper by Strawson (1960 [1982]). Our 'reactive attitudes' to the behaviour of others, which include resentment, gratitude, forgiveness and anger, contribute to the very fabric of human society, exchange and reciprocity. Reactions to wrong-doing can only be withheld by assuming towards someone an 'objective attitude', regarding their behaviour as 'caused', rather than autonomous and done for *reasons* (which is the way in which we usually understand human conduct). While there are circumstances where this objective attitude is appropriate, it is at odds with our usual expectations of one another and 'a sustained objectivity of interpersonal attitude, and the human isolation which that would entail, does not seem to be something of which human beings would be capable' (Strawson, 1960 [1982]; p. 81). Since the capacity to be a moral agent is definitively human, to deny this capacity to someone is, in a literal sense, to dehumanise them and part of what it means to respect moral agency is to impose punishment when this is deserved.

For the present discussion, however, the issue is not whether there is a right to be punished, but rather whether, if there is such a right, there are any general grounds for supposing this right to be inapplicable to mentally disordered offenders. Instructively, when looking for examples of where the objective attitude might be appropriate, Strawson mostly refers to people who are in some way or another mentally disordered. But why does mental disorder lead to a withdrawal of our usual reactive attitudes? One likely explanation is that irrationality has often been regarded as a defining characteristic of madness (Porter, 2002). Reasons for behaviour do not apply to people with a mental disorder: it is the mental disorder that controls their conduct and their behaviour is viewed through that lens. As Nathan Filer puts it, 'If people think you're MAD, then everything you do, everything you think, will have MAD stamped across it' (Filer, 2013: p. 216). Yet as Moore insists, in more prosaic terms, '...most of the actions of a mentally ill person are a result of non-illness factors' (Moore, 1996: p. 41). Peay notes that 'Mental disorder may correlate with certain kinds of offending, but is rarely causative...' (Peay, 2012: p. 432).

In truth, mentally disordered people offend for the same broad range of reasons as everybody else – for example, through fear, greed, poverty, abuse, anger, drunkenness, arrogance and despair. The problem then becomes one of trying to understand what contribution the mental disorder made to the offence. It may, for instance, have affected motivation or perhaps been a disinhibiting factor. It should also be noted that mentally disordered offenders are at least as likely as (probably more likely than) others to use alcohol and / or illegal drugs (Watkins, et al., 2001; see Pycroft and Green, this volume). In most cases, drug use or drunkenness will not be accepted as a substantially mitigating factor, but the problem of disentangling the (legally culpable) influence of substance misuse from the mental disorder (for which they are held not to blame) is intractable. There will be cases in which these influences are more readily discernible, but there can be no general assumption that diagnosed mental ill health was 'the cause' of the offence and takes away the right to be punished.

In law, the number of cases in which mental disorder leads to acquittal are extremely few – much more commonly, it is adduced in mitigation (see De Lacy, this volume). But in that case, the Court should have regard to all the statutory purposes of sentencing (Criminal Justice Act, 2003, s. 142) and it is not at all clear why reform or rehabilitation (perhaps through treatment) should be given priority over punishment, deterrence, incapacitation or reparation. A mindset that assumes that mental disorder conclusively explains an offence will sometimes redound to the offender's advantage, but (as will be argued later) this is by no means always the case. At the same time, that mindset has profoundly disadvantaged people with mental illness and learning disabilities by setting them outside ordinary understandings of human interaction and invoking the objective attitude which Strawson (1960 [1982]) shows to be typically dehumanising. Punishment, it can be argued, is one component of respect for persons.

Finally, mention must be made of the procedural safeguards associated with punishment that may be withheld for interventions characterised as 'treatment' (see McGuire, this volume). In particular, retributive punishment insists on *proportionality* and sets principled limits determined by the seriousness of the offence. Yet if an offence is 'caused' by some impairment, then proportion can be suppressed in the name of treatment and public protection. Indeterminacy is a natural consequence, for at the time of sentence it is not at all clear when treatment may be expected to have had its effect. Such might be the basis of the right to be punished.

The right not to be punished

If there is a general right to be punished, then, the reasons for denying this right to mentally disordered offenders must be made out. The right *not* to be punished, as has been seen, might rest upon assumptions that mentally disordered offenders are somehow less culpable – an assumption made by many people, although one which can also be viewed with suspicion as the fabrication of excuses. Perhaps it is feared that the imputation of mental disorder might confuse less complicated reactions to wrongdoing and enable defendants to 'get away with' something less than their deserts (see also Webb, 1999). In this chapter, our concern is more with a moral understanding of responsibility than the legal concept (for an excellent introduction to the relevant legal debate, see Johnstone and Ward 2010, especially Chapters 4 and 5). And in these terms it is natural to think of *degrees of responsibility*, which would vary not only with the characteristics of the crime, but also with the characteristics of the offender. From a moral point of view, as well as with regard to a focus on solutions, this individualisation is an essential aspect of an appropriate response to offending by people believed to have a mental disorder.

Many excusing or mitigating conditions – duress, provocation, mistake – depend on ideas of what people of sound mind might do in the circumstances; but another set of conditions may arise from deficiencies associated with mental disorder. These might be cognitive defects or volitional deficiencies. Hallucination or delusion are paradigm examples of cognitive impairments, while compulsion, obsessions and impulsivity might all influence volition. As has been argued, however, the diversity of mental disorder makes generalisations impossible here and a 'right' of (all? most?) mentally disordered offenders not to be punished on the basis of their (limited or lack of) culpability is hard to establish.

The right not to be punished, however, might be grounded not so much on assumptions or speculations about culpability (at the time of the offence), but on the possibility that prosecution and punishment might aggravate mental ill health, as assessed at the time of sentence (see Rogers and Ormston, this volume). The right not to be treated in ways that aggravate any mental condition seems unassailable: even the most punitive-minded people reject (or should reject) any form of punishment which leads to a deterioration in someone's physical or mental health. The European Court of Human Rights has ruled that, under Article 3 of the Convention, 'the authorities are under an obligation to protect the health of persons deprived of liberty...[and] in the case of mentally ill persons, to take into consideration their vulnerability...' (*Keenan v United Kingdom* [2001] 33 EHRR 38: 111).

Yet this is a right that should be enjoyed by all defendants. The deleterious effects of punishment – especially imprisonment and, still more, solitary confinement or detention in dehumanising conditions – are well known (Shalev, 2008). It has been said that:

> Many studies assume that mental health difficulties are imported, failing to consider that the pains of imprisonment can distort the prevalence of mental health problems.... Mental health problems and confinement may then go hand in hand' (Scott and Codd, 2010: p. 24).

The regular inspections of the Committee for the Prevention of Torture (Council of Europe, 2014) often uncover evidence of psychologically damaging forms of incarceration, while in the USA even the most psychologically robust inmates are likely to be traumatised by the isolation of the regime in 'Supermax' prisons (Shalev, 2009).

There is no reason to doubt that psychiatric assessment can help courts to distinguish those who are most vulnerable in these respects (see De Lacy, this volume) but the categories of *mentally disordered offenders* and *the vulnerable* do not coincide. For example, people assessed with *personality disorder* make up a large proportion of the prison population (62% of male and 57% of female sentenced prisoners – Stewart, 2008), but it is by no means clear that this condition of itself makes them vulnerable to psychological deterioration in custody. Equally, there is no doubt that there are a number of defendants with no known psychiatric history or whose mental health has not been assessed whose psychological well-being will deteriorate in a prison.

It is possible to argue that punishment is unjustifiable and that accordingly *all* defendants have a right not to be punished (Zimmerman, 2011). Discussion here has tried to determine if there are particular considerations that apply to mentally disordered offenders. The overlooking of diversity immanent in the term *mentally disordered offenders* has complicated discussion throughout. As well as exposing assumptions that are commonly made about the capacity of people with mental disorder to reason and to act purposefully, these reflections point to possible explanations of the limited success of policy in this area. Sentencers are not persuaded that mental disorder should always constitute grounds for diversion (from the criminal justice system, from custody or other sanctions) or that imprisonment is never appropriate and generalised policies about mentally disordered offenders that guide them in that direction are likely to be limited in their effect. In the next part of this chapter, the right to be treated and the right not to be treated will be explored.

The right to be treated

The right to be treated for mental disorder seems fundamental and is affirmed prominently in the UN statement *The protection of persons with mental illness and the improvement of mental health care* (United Nations, 1991). Yet while this appears to stand as a decent aspiration of any civilised society, it is a right that, in practice, is not enjoyed by many people in mental distress in the UK. Although it has been estimated that one in four adults experience some kind of mental health difficulty in the course of a year (Mental Health Foundation, 2007), mental disorder has never been included in the time-parameters for treatment and management by the health services (for example, reduced waiting times). With the whole health system under pressure, it has been said by authoritative observers that 'The mental health service in England is in crisis and unsafe' (BBC 2013c, 2014; see also Laurance, 2003).

If there were accessible services, it might be possible for many people to gain the treatment or support that they need before their distress and bewilderment find expression in criminal offences. In that case, fewer people with mental disorders need come to the attention of criminal justice in the first place. As it is, some people unable to obtain services through community access on a voluntary basis will instead be treated compulsorily at the order of the Court and the criminal justice system is at risk of replacing primary health services as the way of accessing mental health treatment.

Primary mental health care support also seems less available to some groups. For example, there is evidence that 'there are significant and sustained differences between the white majority and minority ethnic groups in experience of mental health services and the outcome of such service interventions' (National Institute for Mental Health, 2003: p. 10). That report went on to express concerns about the adequacy of primary mental health support to people from minority ethnic groups and noted that often their access to psychiatric services is through arrest and prosecution.

Policy, especially when reasserting the value of diversion (see Rogers and Ormston, this volume), is at risk of assuming a well-resourced capacious mental health care system. But this does not exist. Nor is it clear that hard-pressed psychiatric services should give priority to defendants and offenders. Medical practitioners should presumably make judgements about resource allocation on clinical grounds, but Peay (2012) cites evidence to suggest that people sent to hospital from court tend to be (clinically) *less* needy than those referred from the community.

Treatment can mean many different things – from medication to regime management, from counselling to cognitive behavioural programmes. For that matter, as Peay notes, 'There may be a mismatch between health and criminal justice personnel in respect of the objectives of treatment' (Peay, 2012: p. 441). For health professionals the priority may be to treat the disorder believed to underlie the offending, while for criminal justice personnel the principal objective may be to avert the problem of managing difficult people safely in penal custody or in the community. Again, given the uncertain relationship between crime and mental disorder, treatment – even (clinically) successful treatment – may make little or no difference to future offending. So while from one point of view a right to treatment ought to be affirmed, it is much harder to work out what this amounts to in practice. These issues will become clearer as the right *not* to be treated is discussed.

The right not to be treated

These are ethical dilemmas in determining robust and lasting solutions to managing mental disorder. Baroness Hale (2004) makes the critical distinction between *enabling* access to treatment as of right and *enforcing* treatment, which, without due safeguard, amounts to the violation of a right. There are, to be sure, hard questions about the capacity to consent, but the (defensible) presumption should be that, as with physical ill health, people ought not to be treated against their will and their view may be overridden only after careful assessment, legal scrutiny and due process (Hale, 2004). While resistance to treatment is often construed by the psychiatric profession as an irrational refusal – the inability of an ill patient to comprehend the benefits of treatment – the outcomes (and side effects) of treatment often remain so uncertain that it is by no means clear that refusal must be 'irrational' (see Mathews, this volume). For that matter, mental health professionals themselves dispute the efficacy of certain treatments for certain conditions (for discussion see, for example, Bentall, 2003).

Discussions about treatment for mentally disordered offenders are often predicated on particular understandings of the nature of mental disorder, as well as assumptions about its relationship with offending. Drug therapies and 'talking cures' are felt to be the appropriate treatment. Yet there are other ways of understanding and responding to mental distress. Attention to the *social* influences on mental disorder – 'bad things happen and can drive you crazy' (Read and Haslam 2004) – is a reminder that social factors make a significant difference to the onset, development and treatment of a range of mental disorders and to prospects of recovery. Leff (2003) is among those who have argued convincingly that a significant improvement of the environment, especially in the quality of personal relationships, is at least as effective as medication in guarding against relapse in depression and schizophrenia. We should take more seriously the possibility that, as well as mental disorder 'causing' crime, offending and its consequences contribute to and aggravate mental distress. Offenders' lifestyles often bring them considerable anxiety and stress. The offences themselves, as well as the fears and realities of detection and punishment, can bring enormous stress as well as undermining those factors that stabilise and nurture mental health – not least (though not only) supportive relationships. Offending and its consequences – especially imprisonment – result in social exclusion, stigma, closing down of opportunities and relationships (Uggen et al., 2004). These are all factors associated with mental ill health (Canton, 2008).

It is well established that many people with a mental disorder lead lives marked by enormous social disadvantage. People with schizophrenia commonly experience stigma and discrimination in many countries, leading to their impoverishment, social exclusion and a low general quality of life (Thornicroft et al., 2009). There have been similar findings for people with major depressive disorders (Lasalvia et al., 2013). Mentally ill people are vulnerable to hate crime on the basis of their mental ill health or disability (Clement et al., 2011; see Tyson and Hall, this volume), are believed to be three times more likely to be victims of crime (BBC, 2013b) and five times more likely to be murdered than the general population (*The Independent*, 2013). Already often in poverty, they are especially vulnerable to the impact of economic recession (BBC, 2013a).

It may be argued that, whatever the origin of their mental disorder, people have a right to treatment. The point here is that if a woman living in impoverished circumstances burdened by her responsibilities and perhaps enduring domestic violence from a partner visits her doctor and reports symptoms that lead to a diagnosis of depression, a decision to prescribe anti-depressant medication is not necessarily what she most needs – nor is it politically neutral. It is well known that many women offenders have precisely this kind of profile (see, notably, Corston, 2007; see Petrillo, this volume).

A right not to be treated, then, might rest on matters of consent, but also on concerns about the efficacy of medical treatment. Whether or not a condition is 'treatable' is not always the right question and effectiveness depends on any number of variables (Allen, 1987; see McGuire, this volume; Scally, this volume). Moreover, psychiatric or psychological treatment may be inappropriate. It is at least arguable that attention to the oppressive conditions that confront so many mentally disordered offenders would be quite as beneficial for mental health as 'treatment' and that treatment is unlikely to have its effect without regard to this context. It may be convenient for politicians to translate problems of socio-economic origin into personal pathologies (both for offenders and for people with a mental disorder), but these reflections expose the radical inability of social problems to be resolved by either criminal justice or psychiatry – even working in partnership (see Rogers and Ormston, this volume; Hean, Walsh and Hammick, this volume).

To summarise: following Higgins (1984: p. 13), the chapter has so far reviewed '...the right to be punished; the right not to be punished; the right to be treated; the right not to be treated'. These notional rights have been looked at separately, but it must be recognised that they are usually interrelated. A right to be treated, for example, is often connected in debate with a right not to be punished. It has been argued that none of these rights is as straightforward as might appear and that cases can be mounted both for and against them all. It may well be that these doubts about what is fitting when a mentally disordered offender is arrested or attends court may subvert any generalised policy like *diversion*. Police and courts may well – and reasonably – be unconvinced that this is always appropriate and, most fundamentally, a policy that is intended to apply to so heterogeneous a 'group' as mentally disordered offenders is always likely to founder. Discussion moves next to the other themes reviewed by Higgins – dangerousness, 'prediction' and indeterminacy.

Indeterminacy and treatment, dangerousness and prediction

Risk and public protection have become established as the over-riding shared objectives of the agencies of criminal justice (see Arrigo and Bersot, this volume). Garland sets this in the context of a *culture of control* where public protection 'has become the dominant theme of penal policy' (Garland, 2001: p. 17; Loader and Sparks, 2002). In mental health policy, too, risk has become a determining influence on the character of the psychiatric system (Laurance, 2003). The deeply embedded cultural belief that people who are mentally ill are volatile, irrational and unpredictable fuels these fears (Porter, 2002). If prediction and knowledge are needed to manage our risks, how are risks that seem inherently unknowable and unpredictable to be managed?

The harder it is to understand why an offence has taken place, the more likely it will be that a psycho-pathological explanation will be sought. Since so many crimes of violence are in this sense unintelligible, there is a discernible trend towards understanding such crimes in psychiatric terms (Canton, 2002). Other contributors to this volume (see for example, Chitsabesan and Hughes; Gatawa; de Lacy) explore aspects of the assessment and management of risk, its potential and limitations, uncertainties about 'prediction' and the especially vexed question of the inter-related but distinct assessments of dangerousness from people variously assessed with personality disorder, psychopathy or suitability for the *Dangerous and Severe Personality Disorder* programme (Peay, 2012; see Scally, this volume). Focus here is on the implications for human rights.

Of particular concern is that the prevalence of risk-thinking in criminal justice policy has the potential to subvert valued safeguards, especially proportionality (Hudson, 2001; see Arigo and Bersot, this volume). Proportion sets limits (principled, if hard to specify) to punishment, but once the perceived imperative of public protection is allowed to supersede these safeguards, it is hard to limit intervention. While it has been an assumption of this chapter that human rights offer defences against oppression, it is to be noted here that the European Convention on Human Rights explicitly countenances detention for people with a mental disorder. Among the reasons why Mullen (1999) denounced the DSPD programme (see Scally, this volume) was precisely because this preventive / pre-emptive detention would have been unlawful unless it could be brought within the scope of Article 5 1. (e), which allows for the lawful detention of persons of 'unsound mind'.

Yet where treatment is required it may be thought impossible to say, at the time of sentence, how long it will take for it to have its effect; and where diagnosis and prognosis are uncertain, as so often with personality disorder (see, for example, Tyrer et al., 2007), it is especially difficult to know when treatment *has* had its effect. An inevitable consequence is that mentally disordered offenders will be more likely to receive indeterminate sentences, without the safeguard of (retributive) proportionality. A study in 2008 confirmed that, as well as orders under mental health legislation, offenders with mental disorders were over-represented among those sentenced to Indeterminate Sentences for Public Protection (IPP), enacted in the Criminal Justice Act 2003. This study also found that the stresses and doubts of indeterminacy add to mental distress (Sainsbury Centre, 2008).

While the psychiatric profession may be believed to possess the relevant expertise in determining risks, the claim to this authority becomes questionable once it is appreciated that criminal 'predictors' outperform diagnostic ones – that is, the risk factors of reoffending for mentally disordered offenders are much the same as for everyone else. A meta-analysis by Bonta and colleagues demonstrated that, both for general and violent forms of reoffending, 'Clinical or psychopathological variables were either unrelated to recidivism or negatively related' (Bonta et al., 1998: p. 139). In practice, it is often extremely important to distinguish psychiatric from criminogenic factors – otherwise, clinical stability or improvement could lead to overlooking the possibility that levels of risk are the same (or higher) or, on the other hand, that risks of reoffending have reduced, even though there has been no discernible clinical improvement. This is not to deny that mental disorder is sometimes associated with likelihood of recidivism, but the connection needs to be explored and understood person by person rather than resting on uncritical and over-generalised assumptions (Canton, 2005).

Reflection on risk demonstrates the ways in which a focus on public protection has the potential to infringe the rights of mentally disordered offenders. The 'psychiatrisation' of bad behaviour leads to indeterminacy and an exaggerated regard for the contribution of mental disorder to risk assessment and management. Treatment can be invoked to warrant interventions that might otherwise be unlawful (the DSPD programme), even where there is substantial doubt about the clinical efficacy of such treatment, supported by the claim that all this is taking place in the interests of the individual offenders themselves. In this way, the identification of someone as a mentally disordered offender, instead of becoming the basis for a meeting a special need, turns out to lead to special control (Peay, 2012).

Good lives and claim rights

Research in probation and rehabilitation has been refreshed in recent years by desistance scholarship (McNeill and Weaver, 2010; see Göbbels, Thakker and Ward, this volume). People desist from offending by coming to live *good lives* (Ward and Brown, 2004; Ward and Maruna, 2007), their criminogenic needs and risks transcended by ways of living in which crime increasingly has no place. These insights have encouraged a shift of attention towards the processes of personal change in which rehabilitative intervention may well have a place, but often a subordinate and supportive role to wider developments in the individual's life. Desistance has tended to emphasise the importance of social capital: people need opportunities to acquire and sustain lives that will transcend their offending behaviour. The relationships and social bonds involved depend not only upon individuals' abilities and motivation, but also on the availability of opportunities – a function of the sociopolitical order beyond the reach of criminal justice practices.

This is a perspective that is much less apparent in academic and policy debate about mentally disordered offenders and indeed is marginalised by the over-medicalised conception of mental disorder that dominates contemporary psychiatry. Yet it has been argued that there are other ways of trying to understand mental distress with rather different implications for policy. A *good lives* perspective here would attend not only to liberty rights (safeguards against oppression and injustice), but also to claim rights – including a right to fair access to the resources of civil society which are effectively unavailable to many offenders and many people with mental disorder. Adequate access to accommodation, employment and (of course) healthcare are among the rights that call for positive action (not just forbearance) from the state. Desistance research would lead us to expect that a policy that ensured due respect for these rights would enhance mental health, reduce reoffending and increase public protection.

Conclusions

Among the rights most prominently affirmed in almost all human rights conventions is the right to equal treatment and the rejection of unfair discrimination. Discrimination often arises either from an exaggeration or from a denial of difference. Mentally disordered offenders are vulnerable to both such errors and much of the argument in this chapter has opposed the exaggeration of difference: the idea that there is a discrete group of offenders with mental disorders whose rights and needs are distinct from those of others and who should accordingly be managed or treated in quite different ways. The chapter has called these assumptions into question in many ways. At the same time, there is more that should be said about the hazards and injustice of a denial of difference. All agencies will inevitably encounter offenders with mental disorders and distress and must take proper account of their circumstances if they are to do them justice.

The foundations of a respect for human rights would consider mentally disordered offenders holistically rather than reductively, be cautious of any over-generalised policy for so diverse a 'group', be critical of assumptions that there is a straightforward causal relationship between mental disorder and offending and recognise the contribution that social capital – including, but not just, 'treatment' – makes to desistance.

Looking to the future, to those initiatives that may shape the way in which offenders with mental disorder are managed and treated, it has been argued here that an approach that begins with human rights – rather than with treatment effectiveness or system management – could turn out not only to entail a better and fairer treatment for mentally disordered offenders but also to enhance the public's fundamental right to be safe.

References

Allen, H. (1987). *Justice Unbalanced: Gender, Psychiatry and Judicial Decisions.* Milton Keynes: Open University Press.

Ashworth, A. (1996). 'Crime, community and creeping consequentialism', *Criminal Law Review*, 43, 220–230.

BBC (2013a). 'Mentally ill people "hit hard by recession"' – 27 July 2013 – available online at http://www.bbc.co.uk/news/health-23463309 (accessed June 2014).

BBC (2013b). 'Crime victims with mental illness ignored, research suggests' – 7 October 2013 – available online at http://www.bbc.co.uk/news/uk-24420430 (accessed June 2014).

BBC (2013c). England's mental health services 'in crisis' – 16 October 2013 – available online at http://www.bbc.co.uk/news/health-24537304 (accessed June 2014).

BBC (2014). 'Patients sectioned "because of pressure on beds"' – 2 June 2014 – available online at http://www.bbc.co.uk/news/uk-27656241 (accessed June 2014).

Bennett, C. (2008). *The Apology Ritual: A Philosophical Theory of Punishment.* Cambridge: Cambridge University Press.

Bentall, R. (2003). *Madness Explained: Psychosis and Human Nature,* London: Allen Lane

Bonta, J, Hanson, K, Law, M (1998). The prediction of criminal and violent recidivism among mentally disordered offenders: a meta-analysis. *Psychological Bulletin*, 123 (2), 123 – 142.

Canton, R. (2002). Rights, Probation and Mentally Disturbed Offenders. In D. Ward, J. Scott and M. Lacey (eds). *Probation: Working for Justice* (2nd edition). Oxford: Oxford University Press.

Canton, R. (2005). Risk Assessment and Compliance in Probation and Mental Health Practice. In B. Littlechild and D. Fearns (eds). *Mental disorder and criminal justice: Policy, provision and practice.* Lyme Regis: Russell House.

Canton, R. (2008). Working with Mentally Disordered Offenders. In S. Green, E. Lancaster and S. Feasey (eds). *Addressing Offending Behaviour: Context, Practice, Values.* Cullompton: Willan Publishing.

Canton, R. (2009). Nonsense upon stilts? Human rights, the ethics of punishment and the values of probation. *British Journal of Community Justice*, 7 (1), 5–22.

Clapham, A. (2007). *Human Rights: A Very Short Introduction.* Oxford: Oxford University Press.

Clement, S., Brohan, E., Sayce, L., Pool, J., and Thornicroft, G. (2011). Disability hate crime and targeted violence and hostility: a mental health and discrimination perspective. *Journal of Mental Health*, 20 (3), 219–225.

Corston, J. (2007). *The Corston Report: A Review of Women with Particular Vulnerabilities in the Criminal Justice System.* London: Home Office. Available online at http://www.justice.gov.uk/publications/docs/corston-report-march-2007.pdf (accessed June 2014).

Council of Europe (2014). Committee for the Prevention of Torture. Online at http://www.cpt.coe.int/en/

Garland, D. (1990). *Punishment and Modern Society: A Study in Social Theory.* Oxford: Oxford University Press.

Garland, D. (2001). *The Culture of Control: Crime and Social Order in Contemporary Society.* Oxford: Oxford University Press.

Gawande, A. (2009). Hellhole: The United States holds tens of thousands of inmates in long-term solitary confinement. Is this torture? *The New Yorker*, 30 March 2009. Available online at http://www.newyorker.com/reporting/2009/03/30/090330fa_fact_gawande (accessed June 2014).

Filer, N. (2013). *The Shock of the Fall.* London: Harper Collins.

Gearty, C. (2006). *Can human rights survive? The Hamlyn Lectures 2005.* Cambridge: Cambridge University Press.

Gelsthorpe, L. (2007). Probation values and human rights. In L. Gelsthorpe and R. Morgan (eds). *Handbook of Probation.* Cullompton: Willan Publishing.

Gies, L. (forthcoming). *Mediating Human Rights: Culture, Media and the Human Rights Act.* London: Routledge.

Hale, B. (2004). *What can the Human Rights Act do for my mental health?* Paul Sieghart Memorial Lecture 2004. Available online at http://www.bihr.org.uk/sites/default/files/transcipt_hale.doc (accessed June 2014).

Higgins, J. (1984). The Mentally Disordered Offender in his Society. In M. Craft and A. Craft (eds). *Mentally Abnormal Offenders.* London: Ballière Tindall.

Home Office (1999). 'Jack Straw Announces Implementation Date for the Human Rights Act'. News Release 153/99 (18 May 1999).

Howard League (2008). 'Growing Up Shut Up'. Available online at http://snipurl.com/28vnoq9 (accessed June 2014).

Hudson, B. (2001). Human Rights, Public Safety and the Probation Service: Defending Justice in the Risk Society. *Howard Journal*, 40 (2), 103–113.

Johnstone, G. and Ward, T. (2010). *Law and Crime.* London: Sage.

Joint Committee on Human Rights (2003). *A Culture of Respect for Human Rights*, Sixth Report, Session 2002–2003. Available online at http://www.publications.parliament.uk/pa/jt200203/jtselect/jtrights/67/6705.htm#note24 (accessed June 2014).

Lasalvia, A. et al . (2013). Global pattern of experienced and anticipated discrimination reported by people with major depressive disorder: a cross-sectional survey. *The Lancet*, 381 (9860), 55–62.

Laurance, J. (2003). *Pure Madness: How fear drives the mental health system.* London: Routledge.

Laurance, J. (2013). Mentally ill people nearly five times more likely to be victims of murder than general population. *The Independent*, 6 March 2013. Available online at http://snipurl.com/28ybw5m (accessed June 2014).

Leff, J. (2003). *The Unbalanced Mind.* London: Phoenix.

Loader, I. and Sparks, R. (2002). Contemporary Landscapes of Crime, Order and Control: Governance, Risk and Globalisation. In M. Maguire, R. Morgan and R. Reiner (eds). *The Oxford Handbook of Criminology* (3rd edition). Oxford: Oxford University Press.

McNeill, F. and Weaver, B., (2010). *Changing Lives? Desistance Research and Offender Management.* Scottish Centre for Crime and Justice Research Report No. 3/2010.

Available online at http://www.sccjr.ac.uk/publications/changing-lives-desistance-research-and-offender-management/ (accessed June 2014).

Mental Health Foundation (2007). *The Fundamental Facts: The latest facts and figures on mental health*. Available online at http://www.mentalhealth.org.uk/publications/fundamental-facts/ (accessed December 2014).

Ministry of Justice (2006). *Making Sense of Human Rights*. Available online at http://www.justice.gov.uk/downloads/human-rights/human-rights-making-sense-human-rights.pdf (accessed June 2014).

Moore, B. (1996). *Risk Assessment: A Practitioner's Guide to Predicting Harmful Behaviour*. London: Whiting and Birch.

Morris, N. and Rothman, D. (eds) (1995). *The Oxford History of the Prison: The Practice of Punishment in Western Society*. New York: Oxford University Press.

Mullen, P. (1999). Dangerous people with severe personality disorder: British proposals for managing them are glaringly wrong – and unethical. *British Medical Journal*, 319, 1146–1147. Available online at http://www.ncbi.nlm.nih.gov/pmc/articles/PMC1116939/pdf/1146.pdf (accessed June 2014).

National Institute for Mental Health (2003). *Inside Outside: Improving Mental Health Services for Black and Minority Ethnic Communities in England*. Available online at http://snipurl.com/28zsg9p (accessed June 2014).

Nozick, R. (1974). *Anarchy, State and Utopia*. Oxford: Blackwell.

Peay, J. (1994). Mentally disordered offenders. In M. Maguire, R. Morgan and R. Reiner (eds). *The Oxford Handbook of Criminology* (1st edition). Oxford: Oxford University Press.

Peay, J. (2012). Mentally disordered offenders, mental health and crime. In M. Maguire, R. Morgan and R. Reiner (eds). *The Oxford Handbook of Criminology* (5th edition). Oxford: Oxford University Press.

Porter, R. (2002). *Madness: A Brief History*. Oxford: Oxford University Press.

Prior, P. (2007). Mentally disordered offenders and the European Court of Human Rights. *International journal of law and psychiatry*, 30 (6), 546–557.

Read, J. and Haslam, N. (2004). Public opinion: Bad things happen and can drive you crazy. In J. Read, L. Mosher and R. Bentall (eds). *Models of Madness: Psychological, Social and Biological Approaches to Schizophrenia*. London: Routledge.

Richardson, G. (2005). The European convention and mental health law in England and Wales: Moving beyond process?, *International Journal of Law and Psychiatry*, 28 (2), 127–139.

Sainsbury Centre (2008). *In the Dark: the mental health implications of imprisonment for public protection*. Available online at http://www.centreformentalhealth.org.uk/pdfs/In_the_dark.pdf (accessed June 2014).

Sandel, M. (2009). *Justice: What's the right thing to do?* London: Penguin.

Scott, D. and Codd, H. (2010). *Controversial issues in prisons*. Maidenhead: Open University Press.

Scull, A. (2005). *Madhouse: A Tragic Tale of Megalomania and Modern Medicine*. New Haven and London: Yale University Press.

Shalev, S. (2008). *A Sourcebook on Solitary Confinement*. London: Mannheim Centre for Criminology, London School of Economics. Available online at: www.solitaryconfinement.org/sourcebook (accessed June 2014).

Shalev, S. (2009). *Supermax: Controlling risk through solitary confinement*. Cullompton: Willan Publishing.

Stewart, D. (2008). *The problems and needs of newly sentenced prisoners: results from a national survey*. Available online at http://snipurl.com/28y2jx7 (accessed June 2014).

Strawson, P. (1960). 'Freedom and Resentment', as reprinted in G. Watson (ed.) (1982) *Free Will*. Oxford: Oxford University Press. Available also online at http://www.ucl.ac.uk/~uctytho/dfwstrawson1.htm (accessed May 2014).

Thornicroft, G., Brohan, E., Rose, D., Sartorius, N., Leese, M., INDIGO Study Group. (2009). Global pattern of experienced and anticipated discrimination against people with schizophrenia: a cross-sectional survey. *The Lancet*, 373 (9661), 408–415.

Tyrer, P., Coombs, N., Ibrahimi, F., Mathilakath, A., Bajaj, P., Ranger, M., ... and Din, R. (2007). Critical developments in the assessment of personality disorder. *British Journal of Psychiatry*, 190 (49), s51–s59.

Uggen, C., Manza, J. and Behrens, A. (2004). 'Less than the average citizen': stigma, role transition and the civic reintegration of convicted felons. In S. Maruna and R. Immarigeon (eds). *After Crime and Punishment: Pathways to offender reintegration*. Cullompton: Willan Publishing.

United Nations (1991). *The protection of persons with mental illness and the improvement of mental health care*. Available online at http://www.un.org/documents/ga/res/46/a46r119.htm (accessed June 2014).

van Zyl Smit, D. (2007). Prisoners' Rights. In Y. Jewkes (ed.). *Handbook on Prisons*. Cullompton: Willan Publishing.

Ward, T. and Brown, M. (2004). The good lives model and conceptual issues in offender rehabilitation. *Psychology, Crime & Law*, 10 (3), 243–257.

Ward, T. and Maruna, S. (2007). *Rehabilitation*. London: Routledge.

Watkins, T., Lewellen, A. and Barrett, M. (2001). *Dual Diagnosis: An Integrated Approach to Treatment*. London: Sage.

Webb, D. (1999). A balance of possibilities: some concluding notes on rights, risks and the mentally disordered offender. In D. Webb and R. Harris (eds). *Mentally Disordered Offenders: Managing people nobody owns*. London: Routledge.

Wilson, D. (2014). *Pain and Retribution: A Short History of British Prisons, 1066 to the Present*. London: Reaktion Books.

Zimmerman, M. (2011). *The Immorality of Punishment*. Calgary: Broadview Press.

4
Interventions and Outcomes: Accumulating Evidence

James McGuire

Introduction

Communities show understandable concern over those of their members who have mental health problems. Apart from a general compassion for the welfare of our fellow citizens, that reaction might be partly attributable to the finding of several surveys that a large fraction of the population, perhaps as many as a quarter, will themselves experience such problems at some point in their lives. This has been found in the United Kingdom (McManus et al., 2009) and also worldwide (World Health Organization, 2001). While some researchers have expressed reservations about how these kinds of data are collected, there seems little doubt that large numbers of people directly experience problems in this respect. Many more do so indirectly by supporting a troubled relative or friend.

Sometimes, however, our feelings over this are tinged with hesitation, and can rise to disquiet and alarm when attention turns to those who display more severe and enduring types of problem. Despite efforts by public health agencies to reduce it (see e.g. Mehta et al., 2009), there is still significant stigma attached to some psychiatric diagnoses, and people labelled in those ways are often feared and avoided rather than provided with meaningful support (see Canton, this volume; Arrigo and Bersot, this volume). Such difficulties are further compounded when individuals in this position have also broken the law. Working with people who have done so is not an activity that attracts a large amount of public sympathy or acclaim. Despite the formally accepted principle, codified in law, that individuals who commit offences as a consequence of mental disorder are not wholly responsible for their actions, they remain one of the most highly marginalised groups in society (Winstone and Pakes, 2005).

In the face of these challenges, many questions arise. One of them is whether the care that is given to members of this group, and the work carried out with them, achieve their intended purposes. The objective of this chapter is to address that question. In seeking to find possible answers, the chapter will survey evidence concerning the outcomes of interventions in working with people who have mental disorders and who have also committed criminal offences.

There are several sets of research findings with a direct bearing on this question. The main section of the chapter will draw together reviews of those areas, in an exercise in evidence synthesis. One issue is the very broad one of the effectiveness of psychological therapies for ameliorating mental health problems in general. A second is the overall effectiveness of interventions with offenders as a means of reducing their rates of criminal recidivism. We will briefly examine what are now quite large bodies of knowledge pertaining to these questions. Narrowing the focus, we will then look more closely at the findings of some recently published systematic reviews on the effectiveness of psychosocial interventions to reduce offending behaviour in people with mental disorders (see Petrillo, this volume). Particularly relevant within this is the gradually emerging evidence concerning the treatment of personality disorders (see Scally, this volume). An attempt will be made to integrate what has been discovered in these related but nevertheless diverse areas, and to draw out key lessons of potential practical importance.

Work with individuals who have severe mental health problems and have also broken the law places practitioners at the meeting point of two quite different paradigms of thinking: respectively those of healthcare and criminal justice (see Rogers and Ormston, this volume; Hean, Walsh and Hammick, this volume). This can produce a succession of anomalies. For example, it is difficult to avoid using the word 'treatment'. But that might not be the most appropriate term to use when discussing the material covered in this chapter. It most often refers to a medical or somatic intervention, prominently the use of psychotropic drugs. In most healthcare settings, those on the receiving end are usually willing to accept courses of action that are prescribed for them. Doing so carries implications about the relationship between the professional (who possesses expert knowledge), and the service user (who is a layperson in this context). It also introduces affiliated concepts such as 'dosage' and 'treatment adherence'. In criminal justice settings by contrast, where we work with people who have broken the law, the suitability of this model becomes debatable (see Arrigo and Bersot, this volume). Critical sociologists have castigated psychology and psychiatry for characterising individuals in this position as somehow 'sick'. But in any case, the kinds of interventions that are typically used in this setting are psychosocial rather than medical. They involve a process whereby the role of the practitioner is to encourage the service user to participate in specially designed activities. Successful engagement is believed to generate a process of skill acquisition or of reflection which might result in subsequent behaviour change. But willingness to receive help and actively pursue such change cannot be taken for granted amongst those who are at odds with society's expectations of them.

Conceptually, a better parallel for the use of the word 'treatment' might be found in the terminology of experimental design. Here it refers to the difference between one group whose members are exposed to a particular experience, or engaged in an active intervention, and another group whose members are not. The former is the experimental or treatment group, the latter the comparison or control group. The groups should as far as possible be matched in any other respects that might influence the outcome. The objective is to test the hypothesis that the experimental condition will induce a predicted change in the first group but not in the second. In criminal justice research the meanings of these words are further complicated as there are studies in which the 'treatment' group receives nothing that would be recognisable as such in the healthcare sense. Indeed, they might even be made to endure more discomfort, for example by being subjected to harsher punishment (e.g. sentenced to a physically demanding regime or 'boot camp', or to more intensive surveillance). To add further to the confused language here, in many studies the second group is often described as receiving 'treatment as usual' (TAU). Unfortunately, it is difficult to escape from this nomenclature in any discussion of intervention or evaluation research.

Psychological therapies for mental health problems

Let us turn to the first area of evidence listed above, concerning whether or not psychological therapy (of which there are numerous forms) is successful in reducing the symptoms of mental ill-health or in returning distressed individuals to a state of well-being. There have been long-running debates with regard to this. Questions addressed have ranged from the fundamental one of whether psychotherapies work at all, and whether any observed changes are simply a placebo effect, to more specific issues such as whether some types of therapy are superior to others, or have a greater impact on some problems rather than others (see Göbbels, Thakker and Ward, this volume). There have also been debates over the respective roles of therapeutic 'techniques' and relational or 'alliance' factors in influencing outcomes.

Since the innovative use of meta-analytic review methods in the 1970s by Smith et al. (1980), there has been a broad consensus that psychological therapy has significant positive and beneficial effects, and that they are far larger than those that could be explained by placebo alone. The volume of work carried out since then has been immense, and that early conclusion has been considerably strengthened. In a very broad-ranging review Lipsey and Wilson (1993) combined results from a series of 156 meta-analyses of psychologically based interventions and found strong evidence of positive effects. Focussing more exclusively on psychotherapy, in a major review Lambert (2013) regarded the question of effectiveness as largely settled, finding robust and well-established therapeutic outcomes that are both statistically significant and clinically meaningful. There is considerable evidence that psychotherapy both '...facilitates the remission of symptoms and improves everyday functioning' (Lambert, 2013, p. 205).

Thus there is substantial evidence for a positive impact of therapy on mood disorders/depression, generalised and social anxiety disorders, post-traumatic stress, and obsessive-compulsive disorder. There is strong evidence both that these effects are superior to placebo, and that gains can be maintained over time, i.e. there are lasting benefits. These findings are not confined to well-funded clinical trials with carefully selected participant samples. Studies of practical effectiveness with 'clinically representative' groups in routine conditions yield evidence of similar effects (Shadish et al., 2000; Barkham et al., 2008). Where comparisons have been made with pharmacotherapy, for example in the area of depression, outcome studies show that psychotherapies perform at least as well as and sometimes better than medication, with lower rates of relapse (Lambert, 2013). A wide-ranging overview of comparisons between pharmacotherapy and psychotherapy, encompassing 61 meta-analyses of randomised controlled trials (RCTs) found that both types of intervention produced significant effects as compared to control and placebo conditions (Huhn et al., 2014). There was a trend for larger average effects from psychotherapy, which were also better sustained over time; however 'head to head' comparisons showed a mixed pattern of results. Pharmacology studies had larger sample sizes and effects could be evaluated 'blind', although this is next to impossible in psychotherapy trials even if independent evaluators supposedly unaware of participants' group allocation are employed. Both sets of studies showed evidence of publication bias, though this seems particularly worrying with respect to medication, where pharmacology companies appear to have played an insidious role in affecting what becomes publicly available (Turner et al., 2008).

Many controversies remain, however. The most extensively tested and widely employed therapeutic method is that of cognitive-behavioural therapy (CBT) and its variants. By 2012 there had been no fewer than 269 meta-analyses on the effectiveness of this approach (Hofmann et al., 2012). Given such a background, CBT has often been seen as the most thoroughly researched and most firmly evidence-based approach (Roth and Fonagy, 2006). However, other modalities such as interpersonal therapy (Cuijpers et al., 2011), and some forms of psychodynamic therapy (Abbass et al., 2012), have also been shown to have positive outcomes for some types of problem. In consequence of this, despite the initial claims of several researchers that it is possible to identify 'empirically supported treatments' (ESTs) that are most suitable for some disorders (Chambless and Ollendick, 2001), a majority of expert opinion appears to endorse what has historically been called the 'dodo bird verdict'. This is the view that that despite theoretical and practical differences between them, most forms of therapy have roughly equivalent levels of impact. There are associated, unresolved disputes regarding the relative contribution to change of different aspects of the therapeutic process, and a developing consensus that 'common factors', such as the operation of the working alliance between therapist and service user, play a larger role than any specific type of therapy per se. For this reason a number of psychotherapy researchers have argued for the delineation of core principles underpinning effective therapies, rather than emphasising training in any specific therapeutic method (Castonguay and Beutler, 2006). Alongside this, confining their analyses to the outcomes of only the most rigorous trials, some researchers have cautioned that at least with respect to depression amongst adults, the effects of psychotherapy may be over-estimated (Cuijpers et al., 2010).

Interventions in criminal justice

We might expect that the relief of distress amongst people motivated to seek help would demonstrate better outcomes than we are likely to find in penal settings: and that, broadly speaking, is what we find. However, there are also impressive outcomes of 'offender treatment' in criminal justice services, and evidence concerning reductions of criminal recidivism following interventions in prison, probation and youth justice settings is plentiful. In the field of criminal justice this is commonly referred to as the 'what works' literature, after a debate that began over four decades ago, not unlike that surrounding the effectiveness of psychotherapy, concerning whether anything useful could be accomplished with respect to reducing criminal behaviour. Many scholars trace the origins of this debate to a much-cited journal article by Martinson (1974), which purported to review the outcomes of research evaluations in crime and justice. The author's principal conclusion, that such efforts were virtually futile, was applauded in some quarters. However, it was also widely criticised on several grounds: primarily that the author had missed or ignored key evidence, leading in due course to his withdrawal of the initial conclusions. But this and other work published in the 1970s are widely regarded as having begun a trend towards more punitive sentencing practices in both the United Kingdom and the United States, with prison populations rising steadily thereafter and reaching record levels where, at least in the UK, they have since stubbornly remained.

Despite this unfavourable beginning, a sizeable mass of research findings has accumulated since then showing the opposite of what Martinson claimed.

Many studies have shown that it is possible to reduce levels and rates of criminal recidivism. The volume of work published in this area has been such that over recent years it has been subject to a series of systematic and quantitative reviews. For the period between 1985 and early 2013, McGuire (2013) counted a total of 100 meta-analyses of different portions of this field. Several more have appeared since then. These reviews collectively show more than simply that reductions in reoffending can be secured. In aggregate they also show clear trends regarding the features of more effective versus less effective interventions. On the basis of them, Andrews and Bonta (2010) developed a model of criminal-justice-based intervention entitled the *risk-needs-responsivity* (RNR) model, which has been widely applied in the process of designing, delivering and evaluating interventions (see Göbbels, Thakker and Ward, this volume).

This body of research has yielded evidence of significant reductions in general criminal offending, in studies with both young and adult offenders, and in relation to a number of specific types of crime including violence, sexual offending against children, and substance-related crimes. It is firmly established, though official criminal justice policies often seem to be in a state of denial regarding it, that these constructive approaches to addressing criminal offending are far more effective as a means of reducing offence behaviours than the conventional punitive practices that are the core of penal practice in most jurisdictions.

Here too, however, there are controversies regarding the most effective forms of intervention, but the evidence is more compelling that CBT and allied approaches have an advantage over other methods (Lipsey et al., 2007). These methods are applied in a way that departs somewhat from a therapeutic model, introducing elements with a closer similarity to education and training. Nevertheless, some other approaches, such as therapeutic communities (see Petrillo, this volume), have also been found to have good effects for individuals with multiple problems such as a history of violence and substance misuse (Lipton et al., 2002). While it is widely accepted that good working relationships are a necessary condition of engendering change here as elsewhere, evidence suggests that this is less pivotal than in provision of therapy in mental health settings, given the greater emphasis on behavioural rather than emotional change.

Offenders with major mental illness

To summarise the ground covered so far, there is evidence of good outcomes in relation to both the treatment of mental health problems in general, and in the reduction of criminal recidivism in mainstream offender populations. The accrual of these sets of research findings represents an important advance in knowledge. In criminal justice, furthermore, the emergence of the RNR model constitutes a notable landmark in our ability to make sense of the results. But as in psychotherapy research there are numerous questions still unanswered. One is the potential applicability or transferability of the findings from this body of knowledge to working with offenders who also have serious mental health problems, a group that in different studies are called mentally disordered offenders, or offenders with mental illness, many of whom are seen in settings now grouped together as 'forensic mental health services'.

Fortunately for present purposes, there are several systematic reviews and meta-analyses of this segment of the offender treatment literature. In what follows, this material will be grouped into four partially separate, but also overlapping areas, focussing successively on major mental illnesses, personality disorders in general, antisocial personality disorder, and psychopathy. Before proceeding, to clarify the ensuing discussion, we need to note that the studies included in these reviews were conducted at a time when the version of the diagnostic framework used in most research (*Diagnostic and Statistical Manual of Mental Disorders*; DSM) was the DSM-IV, the predecessor of the DSM-5 which was published in 2013.

Martin et al. (2012) undertook a review of interventions for offenders with major mental disorders. This referred primarily to what have traditionally been called mental illnesses, and excluded studies focused on substance abuse, intellectual disability or personality disorders alone, and also excluded studies of treatment of sexual offenders. From a set of 2,035 studies initially located, after applying selection criteria Martin et al. calculated 37 outcome effects from a set of 25 studies with an aggregate sample size of 15,678. The mean effect size on criminal justice outcomes at $d = 0.19$ was positive though fairly modest. This included significant effects on arrest, time spent in jail, time to failure, and violent crime; the impact on conviction fell just short of significance, but paradoxically, treated groups had higher rates of breaching release conditions. On the other hand the fail-safe number of 797 suggested there would need to be a large amount of unpublished non-significant findings for this result to be reversed. In clinical terms, although there was no effect on an aggregate mental health measure, there was evidence of both improved functioning ($d = 0.20$) and of reduced symptom levels ($d = 0.12$) amongst treatment participants. There were large effects obtained from interventions that had both institutional and community based components. But as found in many reviews, there was considerable variability among the results.

Morgan et al. (2012) carried out a similar review of treatment of offenders with mental illness (OMI). They analysed studies that addressed either 'criminalness' (their terminology) or 'mental illness' or both. Participants in the studies they reviewed had been diagnosed with schizophrenia, bipolar disorder, or major depressive disorder. In 26 studies examined, cumulatively there were 1,649 offenders (1,369 in treatment groups and 280 in comparison samples). Mental health symptoms were the focus of intervention in 15 studies and criminal recidivism in four. For the latter studies where criminal recidivism data were reported there was a mean effect size (Cohen's d) of 0.11. This is very similar to the average effect sizes reported in the general 'offender treatment' literature. Within this figure, however, a wide range of effects emerged. Three studies reported positive effect sizes (0.25, 0.38, 0.54). But the overall mean effect was reduced by the fourth study which had a marked counterproductive result (an effect size of − 0.55).

Hockenhull et al. (2012) reported an extension to an earlier large-scale systematic review and meta-analysis of interventions for those at high risk of engaging in violent behaviour, including individuals diagnosed with major mental disorders (Leitner et al., 2006). An extensive literature search, initially screening over 102,000 references with a more focussed second-stage review of 206 items containing quantitative data, located only seven randomised controlled trials (RCTs) of psychologically based interventions. The outcomes measured in these studies were confined to short-term changes in functioning, such as improved anger control, gauged using psychometrics or observational rating scales. The odds ratio of 0.611 implies a sizeable reduction in problems, and the 95 per cent confidence interval indicates a clear-cut treatment effect. However, the small number of studies, the absence of evaluation incorporating variables such as reoffending or rehospitalisation, and the comparatively short time-scales suggest that the findings need to be interpreted cautiously.

Taken together however, whilst these three sets of results may not reveal striking effects, they are in the main positive and the trends found within them are reasonably consistent. This is drawn from a context of work with individuals who are beset by multiple problems, and for whom service provision is often limited. Given the daunting nature of these challenges, the results to date are encouraging and promising.

Personality disorders

The above studies concentrated on the problems of people experiencing major mental illnesses such as psychoses, or severe emotional disorders such as depression or anxiety states. However surveys using formal diagnostic criteria (e.g., Fazel and Seewald, 2012; Sirdifield et al., 2009) consistently show that a large proportion of persistent offenders meet criteria for a diagnosis of personality disorder (PD), and particularly the sub-type within it defined as antisocial personality disorder (ASPD) in the DSM, or dissocial personality disorder in the WHO's ICD-10 classification.

It is important to bear in mind some disputes and record some reservations concerning how these 'disorders' are conceptualised and the empirical grounds on which they are based. There are reasons for regarding their scientific status as more tenuous than is generally supposed. To be diagnosed with any kind of PD, an individual should first show a pattern of dysfunction that is pervasive across several areas of functioning, persistent over time, and inflexible in the face of different situational conditions. Then, to be diagnosed with (for example) borderline personality disorder, an individual should exhibit five out of a set of nine further specific criteria. This means that there are potentially 256 different ways in which BPD can be present. In a study of 930 patients attending a day hospital in Norway, Johansen et al. (2004) found 252 who met the diagnostic criteria for BPD, but they showed 136 different symptom permutations, with no more than six patients showing the same mix of features. Given results like these, it is difficult to say what exactly a diagnosis of BPD actually means. The 'categorical' model of PD has also been heavily criticised, and several research studies using the method of *taxometric analysis* have found that a model based on continuous variables provides a better fit for the available datasets (Edens et al., 2006). There were proposals to incorporate changes along such lines in the DSM-5 but they were not accepted, relegating this to a minor position in the diagnostic framework (Paris, 2014).

Personality disorders are often considered as potentially predisposing people to act in socially damaging ways, and in particular to be associated with criminal offending and interpersonal violence. Yu et al. (2012) reviewed studies that explored relationships between any type of personality disorder and a range of 'antisocial outcomes' including violence and criminal recidivism. They identified 14 studies, with a combined sample of 10,007 participants, and investigated associations between diagnosed personality disorder within these samples, and antisocial behaviour as the dependent variable. They also undertook comparisons between the patterns found in these samples and data from large normative population surveys, as well as amongst groups of non-mentally disordered offenders. Finally they compared rates of criminal recidivism for similar groups obtained from a separate set of 25 studies. The results, expressed as odds ratios (ORs), showed clear associations between ASPD and violent outcomes (OR = 10.4). In this respect Yu et al.'s review could be seen as restating what has been accepted as established for some time, and to that extent the findings appear almost tautological. The authors acknowledge this when they state (2012, p. 786) that '...it was not surprising that ASPD was associated with the highest risk estimates, because the criteria include antisocial acts'. But in other ways the results run counter to expectations. Amongst ASPD samples, only 10.7 per cent were violent: while that was higher than the proportion in the general population (1.2 per cent), the link between the diagnosis and violent criminal conduct was less sturdy than is often assumed. Amongst offenders with ASPD, the rate of violence was no higher than amongst offenders with other personality disorder diagnoses.

Personality disorder is viewed as a chronic and lifelong condition, and is often associated with (comorbid with) other mental health problems. Research suggests that its presence is likely to interfere with attempts to remediate concurrent mental health problems or patterns of troublesome behaviour. More fundamentally, it has often been considered as unresponsive to intervention in itself. On the basis of a growing number of results, however, there are grounds for suggesting that this view may be in need of revision.

Leichsenring and Leibing (2003) reported a meta-analysis comparing two different forms of therapy for personality disorder, namely psychodynamic and cognitive-behavioural therapy. They found 14 studies of the former and 11 of the latter. In both cases, the majority of the studies found were concerned either with one of the personality disorder 'clusters' (A, B or C) denoted within the DSM-IV, or with borderline personality disorder (BPD). Most studies were based on fairly small samples, but mean effect sizes for both kinds of therapy were positive and surprisingly large: for psychodynamic therapy, 1.46, and for CBT, 1.00. However, fewer than half of these studies employed comparison samples and random allocation, the remainder being 'naturalistic' studies with a single cohort (i.e. no comparison group) and entailing pre-post analysis only. That difference was more marked for the psychodynamic therapy evaluations (27 per cent studies randomised as compared with 62 per cent for CBT) and may partially explain the effect size difference. This weakens the conclusions that can be drawn from the review. Only one study of ASPD was located (Woody et al., 1985), concerned with individuals addicted to opiates (see Pycroft and Green, this volume), and evaluation of change was carried out at one month post-test only. This however yielded the unexpected finding that, while opiate users diagnosed with ASPD showed no treatment effect, those who were also diagnosed with depression showed responses similar to those of opiate users not diagnosed with personality disorder.

Duggan et al. (2007) also undertook a review of psychological interventions for personality disorder, but confined their analyses solely to the results of RCTs. They located 27 studies and here too the majority were either focussed on BPD or on a mixed collection of personality disorder types. Several therapeutic approaches provided evidence of clinical improvements as compared to TAU. They included dialectical behaviour therapy for BPD, cognitive-behavioural therapy for avoidant PD, and short-term psychodynamic therapy and manual-assisted CBT for mixed PD. In other studies, various experimental treatments were compared with other forms of active intervention. Amongst these there were two studies of antisocial personality disorder, in both of which different interventions were compared for participants who also had patterns of substance misuse. In one, contingency management performed significantly better than methadone maintenance for individuals with opiate dependence, whereas no differences emerged in a study of cocaine dependence. The authors noted that most evaluations were statistically underpowered, and there was considerable heterogeneity in outcome measures. These combined with other factors made the drawing of any firm conclusions difficult.

More recently Budge et al. (2013, 2014) reviewed research of the outcomes of treatment for personality disorders in general and reported a meta-analysis addressing two interconnected questions. The first was to compare the relative efficacy of designated 'evidence-based treatments' as compared to 'treatment as usual' for individuals diagnosed with these disorders. Thirty studies were found pertaining to this question. Evidence-based treatments (EBTs) were defined as psychologically based interventions with some previous demonstration of effectiveness exceeding that of placebo or control conditions. Treatment as usual (TAU) can itself consist of a variety of activities: often, they are rather poorly described and may entail little provision of service at all, whereas others may include participation in some form of therapy. Budge et al. found that the effects of EBTs consistently exceeded those of TAU and the differences were statistically significant. Perhaps surprisingly, they were largest for comparisons between EBTs and other formal psychotherapies, and lower for the comparison between EBTs and TAU services that did not appear to include formal therapy. The strongest results were for BPD which has been a particular focus of evaluation efforts.

The second question which Budge and her colleagues investigated was whether any specific type of EBT has been shown to be superior to any others in terms of treating personality disorders. They located 12 studies relevant to this. The majority showed no clear-cut difference between EBTs. However, three studies did show marked positive effects, all again involving BPD, respectively showing that dialectical behaviour therapy, mentalisation-based treatment, and schema-focused cognitive therapy, were superior to other therapeutic approaches (respectively client-centred therapy, structured clinical management, and transference-focused psychotherapy) with which they were compared. Oddly, the authors make detailed reference to two of these studies (Bateman and Fonagy, 2010; Giesen-Bloo et al., 2006) but do not discuss a third that is listed in their summary table (Turner, 2000).

Antisocial/dissocial personality diagnoses

In the DSM-IV and continuing into the DSM-5, ten types of personality disorder are delineated. The studies reviewed by Budge et al. (2013, 2014) were concerned with the broad spectrum of personality disorder types, though as we have noted a majority focussed on BPD. However, individuals seen in forensic mental health services are more likely to be diagnosed with antisocial personality disorder (ASPD), which is the classification most often associated with repeated criminal behaviour including violence.

Gibbon et al. (2010) reported a systematic review of RCTs of psychological interventions for antisocial or dissocial personality disorder. A search of 26 databases produced 48 studies of which 11 met inclusion criteria, containing a total of 14 comparisons between an intervention and a waiting list, TAU, or no-treatment control. There were several forms of intervention including contingency management, CBT, supportive/expressive psychotherapy, schema therapy, relapse prevention, social problem-solving, strengths-based case management, a driving while intoxicated (DWI) programme, and judicial supervision. As found in other reviews there was very wide variation in the outcome measures employed, making comparisons difficult. Some positive, statistically significant and practically meaningful results were found for several of these approaches, including various combinations of contingency management, maintenance therapy and CBT, plus the DWI programme. Positive outcomes were limited to the area of clinical change, levels of substance abuse, or family functioning; no positive results emerged for variables associated with antisocial behaviour. Collectively therefore, the evidence base must be regarded as rather thin. The authors' overall conclusion was that there was '...insufficient trial evidence to justify using any psychological intervention for those with a diagnosis' of ASPD (Gibbon et al., 2010, p. 28).

In a later review Wilson (2014) collated results from six studies of treatments for ASPD, although in most studies participants had other concomitant psychiatric diagnoses. There were three RCTs (one subsumed in the Gibbon et al. review) and three uncontrolled studies; two of the RCTs also yielded uncontrolled comparisons (i.e. between groups with and without ASPD). All of the odds ratios were in a direction favourable to treatment, but given wide confidence intervals only one was statistically significant. This was for a study of an institution-based therapeutic community, where the key outcome variable was rates of reincarceration at 12 months following release (McKendrick et al., 2006). Amongst the experimental sample, none of the participants was reincarcerated. Where individuals with ASPD diagnoses were compared to those without, there were no differences in outcomes between the groups; treatment was '...equally effective for individuals, regardless of ASPD status' (Wilson, 2014, p. 43).

Psychopathy

Amongst those individuals diagnosed with ASPD (or in terms of the ICD-10, dissocial personality disorder), generally a proportion are also assessed as manifesting what is regarded as a more severe pattern of disorder, namely 'psychopathic' personality (Ogloff, 2006). Concerns of practitioners may be deeper because until recently there was extreme scepticism, if not pessimism – some even called it an 'urban myth' (Wilson and Tamatea, 2013) – regarding the dim prospect of achieving any positive treatment effects with this group.

Target samples in these studies are usually assessed and classified as psychopathic according to the *Psychopathy Checklist – Revised* (PCL:R; there is also a screening version, PCL:SV) developed by Hare (see Hare and Neumann, 2008). For many years, it was widely accepted that some or all of those classified in this way were 'untreatable' or 'incurable', in the sense of being either unresponsive to, or actually resistant to, therapeutic intervention. Indeed they were sometimes described as acting in ways that undermine treatment efforts. In the bleakest account of the prospect of working with them, they have been thought to be made worse by treatment. Put another way, the effects of treatment have sometimes been believed to be iatrogenic.

Reidy et al. (2013) reported a systematic review of the relationship between psychopathy and violence. They located 17 studies published between 1992 and 2013 and found plentiful evidence of a link between psychopathic personality disorder and adverse outcomes. A high PCL:R score predicted: violence; higher rates of drop-out from therapies; faster drop-out; and lower levels of change in risk scores. Notwithstanding these results, Reidy et al. concluded that '...there is good preliminary evidence to suggest that although they are more treatment resistant likely requiring more resources and dosage, a specifically and carefully crafted intervention may be effective in reducing violence by psychopathic individuals' (2013, p. 536). The suggestion then is not that such individuals cannot be induced to change, rather that as yet, no appropriate method of doing so has been properly designed. However there is a growing consensus that such an intervention can be developed (Polaschek and Daly, 2013).

At the same time, several researchers have expressed doubts concerning aspects of the PCL:R measure. Reviews of its predictive power have often found that only the items within it that record a history of antisocial conduct (the 'antisocial facet') perform well as predictors of future violence (Leistico et al., 2009; Wallinius et al., 2012; Walters et al., 2008; Yang et al., 2010). This implies that what is being demonstrated is a link between past antisocial behaviour and the likelihood of its recurrence in the future, independently of the personality variables assessed by the check list. Thus it could well be that '... risk of criminal recidivism can be adequately assessed without recourse to the pejorative term "psychopath"' (Howard et al., 2013). This appears to weaken the argument that some kinds of personality variables render individuals incapable of change.

Several studies have generated tentative evidence that there can be treatment successes, and it is not inevitable that efforts in this direction will be doomed to fail, to be undermined, or to be counter-productive. Doren and Yates (2008) investigated the relationships between psychopathic personality and sexual offending. In a systematic review of this area they located ten studies, though they were based on work carried out at just four treatment centres (three in Canada, one in the Netherlands). They found that despite a widespread impression that psychopathic sex offenders were impossible to treat, a close examination of relevant studies showed there was a proportion of many participant samples who had responded constructively to intervention. Amongst sexual offenders who met the PCL:R criteria, a proportion had taken part in treatment and had shown some evidence of beneficial effects. Their rate of recidivism then became comparable to that of non-psychopathic individuals. While there was also a proportion of most samples for whom there was no evidence of treatment impact, it seems possible that there may be differences yet not clearly understood between those who do or do not respond to treatment. These findings contradict the expectation that the groups are uniformly unresponsive or treatment resistant. However, confidence in these conclusions needs to be tempered by the weak designs of some of the studies reviewed, the majority of which were pre-post designs with no comparison samples.

But in addition to these suggestions, there are other studies which have found evidence of both short-term and long-term changes in those classified as psychopathic. Skeem et al. (2002) reported a study of civil psychiatric patients in the United States. They analysed the progress of 871 patients from the MacArthur Violence Risk Assessment Study (Monahan et al., 2001), assessed at 10-week intervals for a period of one year. Using the PCL:SV with this group, 72 individuals were classed as psychopathic and 195 as 'potentially psychopathic'. Skeem et al. examined the relationship between the number of treatment sessions individuals attended during each 10-week phase and whether or not they acted violently during the next 10-week phase. Averaging across five successive 10-week phases, those designated as psychopaths who had attended seven or more sessions were 3.5 times less likely to commit violent offences than those who attended fewer sessions, and those designated as potentially psychopathic were 2.5 times less likely. These patterns held after a series of variables including substance abuse, ethnicity and employment status were controlled for.

In a different setting, Wong et al. (2006) evaluated the progress of people classed as psychopathic who completed an intervention entitled *Aggressive Behavioural Control* (ABC), a violence risk reduction programme implemented at the Saskatoon Regional Psychiatric Centre in Saskatchewan. Following discharge participants committed offences of lower seriousness than matched controls. There were small reductions in their general and violent recidivism rate as compared to an untreated group (effect sizes of 0.10 and 0.05 respectively). Changes in risk scores assessed using the *Violence Risk Scale* (VRS) were significantly associated with reductions in violent offending.

Subsequently Wong et al. (2012; Olver and Wong, 2013) reported evidence from evaluation of the Clearwater programme, a group-based intervention for high-risk sexual offenders lasting approximately eight months, also delivered at the Saskatoon centre. A proportion of participants had high PCL:R scores. Yet of this group, 73 per cent completed treatment, and following release they had a reoffending rate one-third lower than those who did not (60.6 versus 91.7 per cent). Here too changes in VRS scores predicted changes in rates of violent and sexual reoffending, and the length of sentence imposed on whose who did reoffend was 50 per cent lower for treated compared to control group members, implying lower gravity of offence types.

Interim findings from ongoing studies being undertaken in high secure prisons and treatment units in New Zealand (Wilson and Tamatea, 2013) and in the United Kingdom (Saradjian e al., 2013), using intensive structured programmes, have produced preliminary indications of changes in similar directions. That is, there is evidence of comparatively low drop-out, and of reductions in risk scores, though initially from only very small study samples.

Probably the most impressive findings to date have come from the Mendota Youth Treatment Center, Wisconsin, addressing the needs of young offenders with emerging 'psychopathic traits' (assessed using the *Psychopathy Checklist, Youth Version*, PCL:YV) (see Chitsabesan and Hughes, this volume). These were young people who by the age of 14 already had disturbing criminal records, and who had been found unmanageable in other units. After discharge from the Mendota programme, a four-year follow-up showed a very large and significant treatment effect (Caldwell, 2011). This had the additional advantage of a very favourable 7:1 ratio between the calculated benefits of the regime as compared to its delivery costs (Caldwell et al., 2006).

None of these findings may appear especially convincing on its own. They come from disparate sources and study designs, and none of the evaluations has the rigour of a prospective randomised controlled trial. Collectively, however, they suggest that the pessimism surrounding work with this group may be unwarranted. Results to date certainly have sufficient mass to cast doubt on the idea that the problems presented by individuals assessed in this way are somehow inherently intractable.

Conclusion

A number of conclusions can be drawn from the array of reviews and primary studies discussed above, though given the methodological limitations of the work done, some of them can be no more than provisional at present. Most fundamentally, there are grounds for optimism regarding the possibilities of effective work with people who experience mental health problems and have also broken the law. While for the most severe levels of these problems the evidence in support of this is still quite modest, there is enough of it to suggest that it is no longer tenable to apply blanket notions regarding 'untreatability'.

A new research agenda is required in which more refined analyses are undertaken to investigate the limits of this and whether there are variables not yet examined which might explain variations in treatment effects. Alongside, there is a need for better designed outcome evaluations that can permit fairer and firmer testing of treatment hypotheses.

References

Abbass, A., Town, J. and Driessen, E. (2012). Intensive short-term dynamic psychotherapy: A systematic review and meta-analysis of outcome research. *Harvard Review of Psychiatry*, 20, 97–108.

Andrews, D. A. and Bonta, J. (2010). Rehabilitating criminal justice policy and practice. *Psychology, Public Policy, and Law*, 16, 39–55.

Barkham, M., Stiles, W. B., Connell, J., Twigg, E., Leach, C., Lucock, M., Mellor-Clark, J., Bower, P., King, M., Shapiro, D. A., Hardy, G. E., Greenberg, L. and Angus, L. (2008). Effects of psychological therapies in randomized trials and practice-based studies. *British Journal of Clinical Psychology*, 47, 397–415.

Bateman, A. and Fonagy, P. (2009). Randomized controlled trial of outpatient mentalization-based treatment versus structured clinical management for borderline personality disorder. *American Journal of Psychiatry*, 166, 1355–1364.

Budge, S. L., Moore, J. T., Del Re, A. C., Wampold, B. E., Baardseth, T. P. and Nienhuis, J. B. (2013). The effectiveness of evidence-based treatments for personality disorders when comparing treatment-as-usual and bona fide treatments. *Clinical Psychology Review*, 33, 1057–1066.

Budge, S. L., Moore, J. T., Del Re, A. C., Wampold, B. E., Baardseth, T. P. and Nienhuis, J. B. (2014). Corrigendum to 'The effectiveness of evidence-based treatments for personality disorders when comparing treatment-as-usual and bona fide treatments'. *Clinical Psychology Review*, 34, 451–452.

Caldwell, M. F. (2011). Treatment-related changes in behavioral outcomes of psychopathy facets in adolescent offenders. *Law and Human Behavior*, 35, 275–287.

Caldwell, M. F., Vitacco, M. and Van Rybroek, G. J. (2006). Are violent delinquents worth treating? A cost–benefit analysis. *Journal of Research in Crime and Delinquency*, 43, 148–168.

Castonguay, L. G. and Beutler, L. E. (eds) (2006). *Principles of Therapeutic Change That Work*. New York, NY: Oxford University Press.

Chambless, D. L. and Ollendick, T. H. (2001). Empirically supported psychological interventions: Controversies and evidence. *Annual Review of Psychology*, 52, 685–716.

Cuijpers, P., Geraedts, A. S., van Oppen, P., Andersson, G., Markowitz, J. C. and van Straten, A. (2011). Interpersonal psychotherapy for depression: A meta-analysis. *American Journal of Psychiatry*, 168, 581–592.

Cuijpers, P., van Straten, A., Bohlmeijer, E., Hollon, S. D. and Andersson, G. (2010). The effects of psychotherapy for adult depression are over-estimated: a meta-analysis of study quality and effect size. *Psychological Medicine*, 40, 211–223.

Doren, D. M. and Yates, P. M. (2008). Effectiveness of sex offender treatment for psychopathic sexual offenders. *International Journal of Offender Therapy and Comparative Criminology*, 52, 234–245.

Duggan, C., Huband, N., Smailagic, N., Ferriter, M. and Adams, C. (2007). The use of psychological treatments for people with personality disorder: A systematic review of randomized controlled trials. *Personality and Mental Health*, 1, 95–125.

Edens, J. F., Marcus, D. K., Lilienfeld, S. O. and Poythress, N. G. (2006). Psychopathic, not psychopath: taxometric evidence for the dimensional structure of psychopathy. *Journal of Abnormal Psychology*, 115, 131–144.

Fazel, S. and Seewald, K. (2012). Severe mental illness in 33 588 prisoners worldwide: systematic review and meta-regression analysis. *British Journal of Psychiatry*, 200, 364–73.

Gibbon, S., Duggan, C., Stoffers, J., Huband, N., Völlm. B., Ferriter, M. and Lieb, K. (2010). Psychological interventions for antisocial personality disorder (Review). *Cochrane Library*, Issue 6. www.ncbi.nlm.nih.gov/pubmed/20556783

Giesen-Bloo, J., van Dyck, R., Spinhoven, P., van Tilburg, W., Dirksen, C., van Asselt, T., Kremers, I., Nadort, M. and Arntz, A. (2006). Outpatient psychotherapy for borderline personality disorder: Randomized trial of schema-focused therapy vs. transference-focused therapy. *Archives of General Psychiatry*, 63, 649–659.

Hare, R. D. and Neumann, C. S. (2008). Psychopathy as a clinical and empirical construct. *Annual Review of Clinical Psychology*, 4, 217–246.

Hockenhull, J. C., Whittington, R., Leitner, M., Barr, W., McGuire, J., Cherry, M. G., Flentje, R., Quinn, B., Dundar, Y. and Dickson, R. (2012). A systematic review of prevention and intervention strategies for populations at high risk of engaging in violent behaviour: update 2002–8. *Health Technology Assessment*, 16(3), 1–145.

Hofmann, S. G., Asnaani, A., Vonk, I. J. J., Sawyer, A. T. and Fang, A. (2012). The efficacy of cognitive behavioral therapy: A review of meta-analyses. *Cognitive Therapy and Research*, 36, 427–440.

Howard, R., McCarthy, L., Huband, N. and Duggan, C. (2013). Re-offending in forensic patients released from secure care: The role of antisocial/borderline personality disorder co-morbidity, substance dependence and severe childhood conduct disorder. *Criminal Behaviour and Mental Health*, 23, 191–202.

Huhn, M., Tardy, M., Spineli, L. M., Kissling, W., Förstl, H., Pitschel-Walz, G., Leucht, C., Samara, M., Dold, M., Davis, J. M. and Leucht, S. (2014). Efficacy of pharmacotherapy and psychotherapy for adult psychiatric disorders: A systematic overview of meta-analyses. *JAMA Psychiatry*. DOI: 10.1001/jamapsychiatry.2014.112

Johansen, M., Karterud, S., Pedersen, G., Gude, T. and Falkum, E. (2004). An investigation of the prototype validity of the borderline DSM-IV construct. *Acta Psychiatrica Scandinavica*, 109, 289–298.

Lambert, M. J. (2013). The efficacy and effectiveness of psychotherapy. In M. J. Lambert (ed.). *Bergin and Garfield's Handbook of Psychotherapy and Behavior Change*, 6th edition. Hoboken, NJ: John Wiley and Sons. 169–218.

Leichsenring, F. and Leibing, E. (2003). The effectiveness of psychodynamic therapy and cognitive behavior therapy in the treatment of personality disorders: A meta-analysis. *American Journal of Psychiatry*, 160, 1223–1232.

Leistico, A.-M. R., Salekin, R. T., DeCoster, J. and Rogers, R. (2008). A large-scale meta-analysis relating the Hare measures of psychopathy to antisocial conduct. *Law and Human Behavior*, 32, 28–45.

Leitner, M., Jones, S., Barr, W., Whittington, R. and McGuire, J. (2006). *Systematic Review of Prevention and Intervention Strategies for Populations at High Risk of engaging in Violent Behaviour*, Final project report to the NHS National Forensic Mental Health R&D Programme.

Lipsey, M. W., Landenberger N. A. and Wilson S. J. (2007). Effects of Cognitive-Behavioral Programs for Criminal Offenders. *Campbell Systematic Reviews*, 2007:6. DOI: 10.4073/csr.2007.6

Lipsey, M. W. and Wilson, D. B. (1993). The efficacy of psychological, educational, and behavioral treatment: confirmation from meta-analysis. *American Psychologist*, 48, 1181–1209.

Lipton, D. S., Pearson, F. S., Cleland, C. M. and Yee, D. (2002). The effects of therapeutic communities and milieu therapy on recidivism. In J. McGuire (ed.). *Offender Rehabilitation and Treatment: Effective Programmes and Policies to Reduce Re-Offending.* Chichester: John Wiley and Sons. 39–77.

Martin, M. S., Dorken, S. K., Wamboldt, A. D. and Wootten, S. E. (2012). Stopping the revolving door: A meta-analysis on the effectiveness of interventions for criminally involved individuals with major mental disorders. *Law and Human Behavior,* 36, 1–12.

Martinson, R. (1974). What works? Questions and answers about prison reform. *The Public Interest,* 10, 22–54.

McGuire, J. (2013). 'What Works' to reduce reoffending: 18 years on. In L. Craig, J. Dixon and T. A. Gannon (eds). *What Works in Offender Rehabilitation: An Evidence Based Approach to Assessment and Treatment.* Chichester: Wiley-Blackwell. 20–49.

McKendrick, K., Sullivan, C., Banks, S. and Sacks, S. (2006). Modified therapeutic community treatment for offenders with MICA disorders: Antisocial personality disorder and treatment outcomes. *Journal of Offender Rehabilitation,* 44, 133–159.

McManus, S., Metlzer, H., Brugha, T., Bebbington, P. and Jenkins, R. (2009). *Adult Psychiatric Morbidity in England, 2007: Results of a Household Survey.* London: NHS Information Centre for Health and Social Care.

Mehta, N., Kassam, A., Leese, M., Butler, G. and Thornicroft, G. (2009). Public attitudes towards people with mental illness in England and Scotland, 1994–2003. *British Journal of Psychiatry,* 194, 278–284.

Monahan, J., Steadman, H. J., Silver, E., Appelbaum, P. S., Robbins, P. C., Mulvey, E. P., Roth, L. H., Grisso, T. and Banks, S. (2001). *Rethinking Risk Assessment: The MacArthur Study of Mental Disorder and Violence.* New York: Oxford University Press.

Morgan, R. D., Flora, D. B., Kroner, D. G., Mills, J. F., Varghese, F. and Steffan, J. S. (2012). Treating offenders with mental illness: A research synthesis. *Law and Human Behavior,* 36, 37–50.

Ogloff, J. R. P. (2006). Psychopathy/antisocial personality disorder conundrum. *Australian and New Zealand Journal of Psychiatry,* 40, 519–528.

Olver, M. E. and Wong, S. C. P. (2013). A description and review of the Clearwater Sex Offender Treatment Programme. *Psychology, Crime and Law,* 19, 477–492.

Paris, J. (2014). After DSM-5: where does personality disorder go from here? *Harvard Review of Psychiatry,* 22, 216–221.

Polaschek, D. and Daly, T. E. (2013). Treatment and psychopathy in forensic settings. *Aggression and Violent Behavior,* 18, 592–603.

Reidy, D. E., Kearns, M. C. and DeGue, S. (2013). Reducing psychopathic violence: A review of the treatment literature. *Aggression and Violent Behavior,* 18, 527–538.

Roth, A. and Fonagy, P. (2006). *What Works for Whom: A Critical Review of Psychotherapy Research,* 2nd edition. New York: Guilford Press.

Saradjian, J., Murphy, N. and McVey, D. (2013). Delivering effective therapeutic interventions for men with severe personality disorder within a high secure prison. *Psychology, Crime & Law,* 19, 433–447.

Shadish, W. R., Matt, G. E., Navarro, A. M. and Phillips, G. (2000). The effects of psychological therapies under clinically representative conditions: a meta-analysis. *Psychological Bulletin,* 126, 512–529.

Sirdifield, C., Gojkovic, D., Brooker, C. and Ferriter, M. (2009). A systematic review of the epidemiology of mental health disorders in prison populations: a summary of findings. *Journal of Forensic Psychiatry and Psychology,* 20, S78–S101.

Skeem, J. L., Monahan, J. and Mulvey E. P. (2002). Psychopathy, treatment involvement, and subsequent violence among civil psychiatric patients. *Law and Human Behavior*, 26, 577–603.

Smith, M. L., Glass, G. V. and Miller, T. I. (1980). *The Benefits of Psychotherapy*. Baltimore, MD: Johns Hopkins University Press.

Turner, E. H., Mathews, A. M., Linardatos, E., Tell, R. A. and Rosenthal, R. (2008). Selective publication of antidepressant trials and its influence on apparent efficacy. *New England Journal of Medicine*, 358, 252–260.

Turner, R. M. (2000). Naturalistic evaluation of dialectical behavior therapy-oriented treatment for borderline personality disorder. *Cognitive and Behavioral Practice*, 7, 413–419.

Wallinius, M., Nilsson, T., Hofvander, B., Anckarsäter, H. and Stålenheim, G. (2012). Facets of psychopathy among mentally disordered offenders: Clinical comorbidity patterns and prediction of violent and criminal behavior. *Psychiatry Research*, 198, 279–284.

Walters, G. D., Knight, R. A., Grann, M. and Dahle, K.P. (2008). Incremental validity of the Psychopathy Checklist facet scores: predicting release outcome in six samples. *Journal of Abnormal Psychology*, 117, 396–405.

Wilson, H. A. (2014). Can antisocial personality disorder be treated? A meta-analysis examining the effectiveness of treatment in reducing recidivism for individuals diagnosed with ASPD. *International Journal of Forensic Mental Health*, 13, 36–46.

Wilson, N. J. and Tamatea, A. (2013). Challenging the 'urban myth' of psychopathy untreatability: the High-Risk Personality Programme. *Psychology, Crime & Law*, 19, 493–510.

Winstone, J. and Pakes, F. (2005). Marginalized and disenfranchised: community justice and metnally disordered offenders. In J. Winstone and F. Pakes (sds). *Community Justice: Issues for probation and criminal justice*. Cullompton, Willan. 219–236

Wong, S. C. P., Witte, T. D., Gordon, A., Gu, D. and Lewis, K. (2006). *Can a treatment program designed primarily for violent risk reduction reduce recidivism in psychopaths?* Poster presentation at the Annual Convention of the Canadian Psychological Association, Calgary, Alberta.

Wong, S., Gordon, A., Gu, D., Lewis, K. and Olver, M. E. (2012). The effectiveness of violence reduction treatment for psychopathic offenders: Empirical evidence and a treatment model. *International Journal of Forensic Mental Health*, 11, 336–349.

Woody, G. E., McLellan, T., Luborsky, L. and O'Brien, C. P. (1985). Sociopathy and psychotherapy outcome. *Archives of General Psychiatry*, 42, 1081–1086.

World Health Organization (2001). *The World Health Report 2001: Mental Health: New Understanding, New Hope*. Geneva: WHO.

Yang, M., Wong, S. C. P. and Coid, J. (2010). The efficacy of violence prediction: a meta-analytic comparison of nine risk assessment tools. *Psychological Bulletin*, 136, 740–767.

Yu, R., Geddes, J. R. and Fazel, S. (2012). Personality disorders, violence, and antisocial behavior: A systematic review and meta-regression analysis. *Journal of Personality Disorders*, 26, 775–792.

5
Desistance in Offenders with Mental Illness

Svenja Göbbels, Jo Thakker and Tony Ward

Introduction

The cessation of offending has been associated, amongst other factors, with age or maturation, intimate relationships (e.g., marriage), social support, work stability, cognitive transformation, high expectations from others (i.e., the 'Pygmalion Effect'), being able to disengage from one's criminal past ('knifing off'), and spirituality (for an overview see Laws and Ward, 2011). While there are many factors associated with desisting from crime, desistance is often defined by the *absence* rather than the presence of something. Thus, while it is most certainly *something*, desistance is quite difficult to define and to measure (e.g., Laws and Ward, 2011; Maruna, 2001; Walker et al., 2013b).

Researchers agree that desistance from offending is not a unitary event, and is more usefully construed as a gradual process with a number of false starts finally culminating in the complete cessation of offending (Laub and Sampson, 2003; Maruna, 2001). This state of desistance is to be distinguished from short periods of non-offending or non-offending due to lack of opportunity (Farrall, 2004; Laub and Sampson, 1993; Maruna, 2001; Walker et al., 2013b).

The concept of desistance originated in youth crime research (e.g., Laub et al., 1998; see also Chitsabesan and Hughes, this volume) and has been applied to adult offender populations in general (e.g., Farrall, 2004; Laub and Sampson, 1993; Maruna, 2001) as well as to specific populations, such as sexual offenders (e.g., Göbbels et al., 2012; Laws and Ward, 2011), drug-using offenders (e.g., Colman and Vander Laenen, 2012; see Pycroft and Green, this volume) and those who offend against intimate partners (e.g., Feld and Straus, 1989; Walker et al., 2013a).

A limited amount of research and theory has attempted to address desistance in mentally-disordered offenders (MDO). One notable study was conducted by Davis et al. (2004), who investigated longitudinal offending trajectories in youths involved with the mental health system. While the majority of these youths had no, few, or non-violent charges, a small subgroup started to offend early and persisted into early adulthood. Davis et al. (2004) reasoned that the factors encouraging non-mentally disordered young adults to desist from offending may be less protective in young MDOs. Alternatively, they proposed that desistance factors may simply be less available to young MDOs, or that they may only exert an impact later in life. In a similar vein, Fisher et al. (2006) argued that mental illness is associated with under- or unemployment, stigmatisation, lack of social capital, loss of housing, absence of productive, structured activity, and frequent change of life circumstances. All of those characteristic outcomes of mental illnesses deprive MDOs from desistance opportunities. Applying Laub and Sampson's (1993) and other criminologists' ideas, Fisher et al. (2006) argued that mental illness insulates people from informal social controls, which are essential to desistance. In contrast, intrusive, formal social controls are all too present in the life of MDOs.

While the application of desistance research and theory seems valuable in MDO populations (see Canton, this volume; Arrigo and Bersot, this volume; McGuire, this volume), it has to be acknowledged that MDOs are an extremely heterogeneous population. Andrews and Bonta (2010) point out that a widely accepted definition of MDOs has not been achieved as of yet (see Canton, this volume). They also mention that legal and psychological/ psychiatric definitions of mental disorder differ substantially in terms of what they define as mental illness or disorder. They state that offenders who suffer from clinical syndromes such as psychotic disorders, bipolar disorder, and depression that can result in diminished criminal responsibility may be seen as MDOs (American Psychiatric Association, 2000; see de Lacy, this volume). In addition, some personality disorders are closely associated with offending behaviour (American Psychiatric Association, 2000; Andrews and Bonta, 2010). Moreover, individuals with a vast array of disorders such as intellectual disability (e.g., Holland et al., 2002; Lindsay, 2002), Attention Deficit Hyperactivity Disorder (e.g., Young, 2007), and autism spectrum disorders (e.g., Cashin and Newman, 2009) seem to be over-represented in offending populations. In addition, substance abuse is a major risk factor for criminal offending relating to mental health (Andrews and Bonta, 2010; see Pycroft and Green, this volume). To further complicate matters, comorbidity of disorders is the rule rather than the exception (e.g., Côté and Hodgins, 1990). If an inclusive definition of MDO is used, most offenders (80–90%) meet criteria for mental disorders (for an overview of studies refer to: Andrews and Bonta, 2010).

A useful distinction between three types of MDOs has been made by Hiday (1999). She suggests that the first group of MDOs is characterised by minor offences that can be seen as survival crimes. The second group are those with a major mental illness and comorbid personality pathology, who also abuse alcohol and/or drugs. Members of this group tend to commit more serious criminal offences more often. The third group is the smallest subgroup of people who commit offences as an immediate consequence of their mental disorder. As desistance research most often investigates desistance in 'career criminals', the first two groups may be of major interest. However, as will be outlined later in this chapter, negotiating a severe offence, which was a consequence of a mental disorder, with an otherwise non-offending identity can be usefully understood within a desistance framework.

Leaving definitional issues aside, the application of desistance research and theory may be useful for the treatment and successful reintegration of MDOs. However, due to the complexity of the population, caution is warranted in taking a one-size-fits-all approach. In the present chapter, the question of whether MDOs desist will be examined. Subsequently, we will be using an existent integrative framework of desistance, the *Integrated Theory of Desistance from Sex Offending* (ITDSO; Göbbels et al., 2012), to organise the discussion of desistance in MDOs. The ITDSO was developed with other offender populations in mind. Importantly, many offenders are versatile. This means that very few specialise in one offence type (Andrews and Bonta, 2010). Thus, the ITDSO is seen as applicable to not only the sex offender population but also the MDO population. First, the four phases of the ITDSO will be described. Next, the phases will be tailored to the MDO population. Finally, conclusions will be drawn regarding the usefulness of a desistance approach to MDOs and directions for future research will be outlined.

Recidivism in mentally disordered offenders

A meta-analysis revealed that the average rate of recidivism in MDOs was 45.8 % for general recidivism and 24.5 % for violent recidivism over an average follow up time of 4.8 years (Bonta et al., 1998). Quinsey et al., (2006) summarised a number of follow-up studies in MDOs. They found that although the studies had different focuses and used a variety of samples, results were quite consistent. Violent recidivism rates ranged from 16% in schizophrenic offenders to 77% for treated psychopathic offenders. From these results they concluded that the higher the number of psychopathic offenders and the lower the number of schizophrenic offenders in a follow-up sample, the greater the base rate of violent recidivism. Thus, the question of average rates of violent and general recidivism across the heterogeneous MDO population is a complex one, as some MDOs have higher recidivism rates than prison populations, while others have remarkably lower recidivism rates.

Nevertheless, more recent studies from various countries have reported similar recidivism rates among MDOs, although not all of them had this issue as their major focus. For instance, in Australia, A. Ferguson et al., (2009) found that of 218 mentally ill offenders released from a secure forensic hospital,

57.2% committed a new offence, with 33.7% reoffending violently. In a Swedish sample, Lund et al., (2012) investigated a population-based cohort (N = 318) of mentally disordered male offenders who had undergone a pre-trial forensic-psychiatric investigation and were sentenced to undergo treatment, custodial, or non-custodial sentences. Overall, this diverse group exhibited a 17% violent recidivism rate, and a 36% overall recidivism rate. In an extension of the previous study, Lund et al., (2013) found that 47% of all subjects were reconvicted for violent crimes during the 13–20 year follow-up period. In contrast, Nilsson et al., (2011) found in a prospective study that only one in five subjects, who were court-referred for pre-trial forensic-psychiatric investigations, reoffended over a period of eight to 73 months. In Germany, Seifert and Moller-Mussavi (2005) investigated recidivism rates of 255 mentally ill offenders after a minimum time at risk of two years. Their results indicated that the general recidivism was 21.6% and 7.5% reoffended with serious violent or sexual offences. In Japan, Yoshikawa et al. (2007) investigated recidivism in a cohort of defendants with diminished or no criminal responsibility (n=489). They found that 10% were arrested or convicted of further violent offences over a median follow-up period of 10 years.

To summarise this brief review, the question of reoffending rates in MDOs is a complex one. Meta-analytic research conducted by Bonta et al. (1998) and more recent research discussed above indicates that 7.5–77% of MDOs go on to commit (violent) offences once they are released or discharged. However, depending on the population, a significant majority of MDOs either commit non-violent crimes or desist from crime altogether. Thus, it can be confidently stated that many MDOs desist from crime. To understand the desistance processes and opportunities to foster naturally occurring developments, we will apply a desistance framework to the MDO population.

The Integrated Theory of Desistance from Sex Offending (ITDSO)

According to the ITDSO (Göbbels et al., 2012) the desistance process occurs in 4 overlapping phases: (1) decisive momentum (initial desistance), (2) rehabilitation (promoting desistance), (3) re-entry (maintaining desistance) and (4) normalcy (successful maintenance of desistance over a long period of time). These phases will now be discussed.

Phase 1: decisive momentum

The first phase of the ITDSO, *decisive momentum*, starts with a life event that acts as a catalyst for change (Baumeister, 1994; Burrowes and Needs, 2009; Laub and Sampson, 2003; Sampson and Laub, 2005). This life event is hypothesised to result in a critical evaluation of the individual's identity as an offender and the degree to which his or her particular self-conception is likely to contribute to a fulfilling and meaningful life (Korsgaard, 1996, 2009; Oyserman et al., 2004; Oyserman and Markus, 1990). This evaluation may be accompanied by a crystallisation of discontent with life as an offender (Baumeister, 1994; Paternoster and Bushway, 2009). That is, all the separate problems of the individual are attributed to one single cause: being an offender. These psychological processes can be facilitated or impeded by external factors such as social supports and opportunities or their absence, respectively (Kazemian, 2007; Laub and Sampson, 2003; Laws and Ward, 2011; Maruna, 2001). The outcome of the first phase is a varying degree of readiness/openness to change (Giordano et al., 2002; Tierney and McCabe, 2002; Ward et al., 2004).

Phase 2: rehabilitation

After the first phase, the offender has ideally acquired a general readiness to change. In the second phase, *rehabilitation*, the ITDSO draws from the theoretical resources of rehabilitation theories, specifically the Good Lives Model (GLM; Ward and Maruna, 2007) and the Risk Need Responsivity Model (RNR; Andrews and Bonta, 2010; see McGuire, this volume). In addition, for MDOs recovery is central to desistance. The GLM shares many principles with the concept of secure recovery (Drennan and Alred, 2013b) such as the importance of self-directedness (i.e., agency), client-centeredness, and the emphasis on healthy, positive lifestyles (Lord, 2014). Thus, we will not only discuss the GLM and RNR models in this chapter, but also secure recovery. The major task for the desisting offender is the formulation of a more adaptive *life plan*. From an RNR perspective that means addressing one's criminogenic needs or dynamic risk factors in treatment. From a GLM perspective that means understanding how *primary goods*, which are outcomes and experiences that offenders value, can be achieved using pro-social means, and by doing so, reduce their risk of further reoffending (Laws and Ward, 2011; Ward and Gannon, 2006; Ward and Maruna, 2007; Yates et al., 2010). Primary goods can also be considered common life goals (Yates and Prescott, 2011) and include relationships, being good at work, peace of mind and experiencing pleasure. The rehabilitation phase involves offenders developing new skills to attain their life goals and managing their dynamic risk factors (Andrews and Bonta, 2010). The result is a good life plan (GLP) that is incompatible with future offending.

Phase 3: re-entry

The third phase of the ITDSO is *re-entry*. Maruna et al., (2004) define re-entry as a specific event *and* as a process at the same time. On the one hand, re-entry is the day when an ex-offender is released from prison and starts a new life back in the community. On the other hand, re-entry is a long-term process that begins well before release and continues beyond the release date. Successful re-entry encompasses lowering the risk of reoffending and, therefore, protecting communities from further crimes (Andrews and Bonta, 2010). This should result in the offender having a chance to live a fulfilling, pro-social life (Ward and Gannon, 2006; Ward and Maruna, 2007). Ideally, the offender has committed to change earlier in the desistance process and is now able to translate this choice into action. Commitment to change manifests itself in the formulation and acceptance of a realistic good life plan (GLP) and subjective change in identity (see Phase 1). The ability to maintain desistance in the community can be facilitated or hampered by external conditions. Whereas it is important that essential needs (e.g., housing) are met, the acceptance of ex-offenders as fellow citizens by the community is crucial for reinforcing more pro-social identities (Hattery and Smith, 2010; Swann and Bosson, 2010). A successful re-entry phase facilitates the ex-offender's achievement of long-term desistance.

Phase 4: normalcy/reintegration

The fourth and final phase of the ITDSO can be seen as an extension of the re-entry phase. Research suggests that desistance requires sustained determination over years or even decades (e.g., Kurlychek et al., 2012). Ex-offenders profit from trust that they experience from their social networks, which bestows hope and helps them to achieve normalcy (Burnett, 2010; Farrall and Calverley, 2006; Hattery and Smith, 2010). Thus, desistance is seen as a complex process that unfolds over time. It begins with an event that precipitates change and ends when the person makes a commitment to a new way of living.

The other side of the coin – desistance in MDOs

The brief, selective review above indicates that whereas some MDOs continue to commit (violent) offences, a significant majority either commit non-violent crimes or desist from crime altogether. Interestingly, little empirical and theoretical research focuses on *how to promote* desistance in MDOs. In the following, we will use the previously introduced ITDSO to structure ideas in regards to facilitating desistance in MDOs.

Phase 1 – decisive momentum – readiness to change

As described above, a formal and/or informal readiness to change is the first step of the desistance journey. Readiness has been defined as the presence of client or therapeutic situation characteristics, which are likely to promote engagement in therapy and thereby, are likely to enhance therapeutic outcomes (Ward et al., 2004). According to the ITDSO, this readiness arises through critical insights the offender gains due to life events such as incarceration or new social relationships. In the tradition of the desistance literature, readiness to change does not only involve the internal and external characteristics described in Ward et al.'s (2004) offender readiness model, but also reflects the agentic decision to engage in change. Low readiness for treatment can be a significant issue in MDOs (Howells and Day, 2007).

More specifically, a number of characteristics may impede treatment readiness and early desistance in MDOs. First, lack of insight into their own symptomatology and violence risk can be a significant problem in MDOs (Douglas et al., 2013; Hodge and Renwick, 2002). Second, the presence of negative symptoms common to psychotic and affective disorders can negatively impact an offender's readiness to participate in treatment (Ward et al., 2004). Third, some MDOs need to rediscover and reconstruct their sense of self as a coherent entity before the self can be perceived as an active and responsible agent able to master the environment (Davidson and Strauss, 1992; Hodge and Renwick, 2002). Fourth, individuals with substance abuse disorders suffer from a lack of perceived self-efficiency or agency that has to be restored and reinforced before change can occur (Bandura, 1999; see Pycroft and Green, this volume). All of these factors may mean that an MDO does not engage in the necessary self-reflection and self-evaluation tasks to initiate change and to begin the desistance journey. Nevertheless, even if all or some of those obstacles are present, the emergence of a more positive possible self-concept may support MDOs in attempting to change.

Similarly to the ITDSO, Ward et al. (2004) highlight that readiness to treatment is not only determined by internal (i.e., personal), but also external (i.e., contextual) factors. Unfortunately, due to most forensic facilities emphasising security concerns as opposed to treatment (see Gatawa, this volume), contextual factors often seem to hinder individual change. Moreover, personal factors such as limited intra- and interpersonal resources, limited self-awareness, and little experience with positive self-control may further reduce the capacity for transformation (Hodge and Renwick, 2002).

Hodge and Renwick (2002) examined issues surrounding the motivation of MDOs to change. They suggest that it may be unlikely that an MDO commits to change without intervention due to a lack of capacity for rational and analytical thought. In their view, practitioners must be equipped for the complex challenge of developing and supporting MDOs' motivation for change. Engagement in therapy should not be equated with motivation, as for some MDOs engagement in therapy is a 'behavioural requirement' of being in an institution without any genuine intent to change (Hodge and Renwick, 2002, p. 227; see Scally, this volume). At the same time, a lack of engagement in therapy may not necessarily mean a lack of motivation to change. For instance, there might be no tailored treatment available or the treatment method might be unsuitable, rendering the otherwise highly motivated patient to be mislabelled as treatment-resistant. Hodge and Renwick (2002) also raise the issue that while an MDO may be highly motivated to work on some problems, he or she may be unmotivated to address others. Rowe and Soppitt (2014) showed that motivation may not be a necessary precursor to engagement in desistance-focused interventions but can occur through participation in programmes. Thus, 'motivation/readiness to change' should not be treated as a global trait of an individual, but as a dynamic concept, with clients being at different stages of working on their various problems (see Petrillo, this volume). In addition, some research indicates that offender motivation to desist cannot only be construed as an individual resource, but is influenced by relational processes as well (Rowe and Soppitt, 2014).

Another problem that is not necessarily unique to the MDO population is that they may lack or not be able to capitalise on social supports. Informal social controls are thought to be central to every stage of the desistance process (for an overview see: Göbbels et al., 2012). However, many MDOs suffer from social dysfunction (Corrigan, 1991), and/or are mistrustful of others and their intentions (Cordess, 2002; Hodge and Renwick, 2002), which can not only hamper the therapeutic alliance but also impair a patient's capacity to form social bonds with non-professionals.

Nevertheless, certain recommendations can be made in regards to promoting initial desistance in MDOs. Findings by Gudjonsson et al., (2007) suggest that patient motivation may be negatively impacted by accommodating acutely ill and reasonably stable patients on the same ward, patient dynamics (e.g., bullying), staff dynamics (e.g., poor morale among staff; see Mathews, this volume), and the use of illicit drugs on the unit; these may all have an adverse effect on a patient's motivation to change. Some facilities may even create a counter-therapeutic environment that hinders initial desistance.

Community-based treatments, diversion, and mental health courts may not be readily available to the more serious MDOs (see de Lacy, this volume; Ormston and Rogers, this volume). However, even in a very restrictive environment, promoting an MDO's sense of agency can be valuable. To promote agency in non-MDOs, McMurran and Ward (2004) suggest that a therapist's style should promote autonomy and competence by giving clients a rationale for therapy, acknowledging the offender's feelings and opinions, and helping them develop new skills. Cognitive neuroscience (Synofzik et al., 2013) and narrative research (Holma and Aaltonen, 1997) alike strongly suggest that re-establishing a personal sense of agency is of crucial importance in recovering from psychosis (see Mathews, this volume). Thus, establishing an environment where MDOs can re-establish a sense of identity, agency, and being accepted, is a crucial step in the desistance journey.

Drennan and Alred (2013b) emphasise the value of a recovery-oriented approach to offender rehabilitation and link this approach to the incorporation of desistance literature into offender rehabilitation (Ward and Maruna, 2007). Drennan and Alred (2013b) distinguish between clinical recovery (absence of symptoms of mental illness), functional recovery (restoration of functional abilities to perform tasks in daily life), social recovery (social inclusion, social capital), and personal recovery (a deeply personal experience which resembles a journey). A key feature of personal recovery is establishing a positive sense of identity, which is also the major feature of the first phase of the desistance journey. However, Drennan and Alred (2013b) explain that an offender faces an additional recovery task. The offender needs to accept having offended, to realise that criminogenic personal characteristics require change, and to understand the personal and social consequences of having offended. Thus, similar to a desisting offender, MDOs in recovery must disentangle themselves from a criminal identity (Corlett and Miles, 2010). For example, research with drug-using offenders indicates that desistance is secondary to recovery, mainly because drug-using offenders see themselves as addicts rather than criminals (Colman and Vander Laenen, 2012; see Pycroft and Green, this volume). However, it can be speculated that in some offenders, desistance can be synonymous with recovery, and in others the two processes are so intertwined that they are indistinguishable. In contrast, some MDOs may need to negotiate committing a crime with an otherwise non-offending identity (Fisher et al., 2006).

Phase 2 – rehabilitation

Beyond the internal processes described above, external factors can also facilitate recovery. For example, Jacobson and Greenley (2001) explain how the implementation of human rights principles such as elimination of stigma, a positive culture of inclusion, trust, and empowerment, as well as recovery-oriented services can promote recovery in general psychiatry. More specific to recovery in forensic mental health, Drennan and Alred (2013a) defined *Secure Recovery* as acknowledging 'the challenges of recovery from mental illness and emotional difficulties that can lead to offending behavior. It recognizes that the careful management of risk is a necessary part of recovery in our service but this can happen alongside working towards the restoration of a meaningful, safe, and satisfying life.' (Preface, p. x). Thus, not only the offenders' willingness to change is of relevance, but also the approach to rehabilitation, which influences the success of interventions.

Robertson et al. (2011) reviewed different approaches to the rehabilitation of MDOs. They identified three approaches to MDO rehabilitation: therapeutic models targeting individual psychopathology, RNR, and strength-based approaches (positive psychology, GLM, etc.). Therapeutic models targeting individual psychopathologies are driven by the implicit assumption that treating MDOs is the same as treating non-offending individuals with major mental disorders (Andrews and Bonta, 2010; Robertson et al., 2011; see McGuire, this volume; Petrillo, this volume). However, this one-dimensional approach has proven ineffective in regards to risk reduction in MDOs. For example, Skeem et al. (2011) reviewed a number of programmes and found that symptom improvement achieved by mental health services was not associated with recidivism reduction, even if these mental health services were evidence-based. This means that in this research MDOs who showed symptom remission post-treatment are no less likely to recidivate than those whose symptoms remain stable or deteriorate. Andrews and Bonta (2010) reason that Skeem and colleagues' results are due to the neglect of the RNR principles in the programmes they investigated. This also resonates with Drennan and Alred (2013a), who emphasise that risk management is a central part of secure MDO recovery.

The term rehabilitation has two meanings in the criminal justice system. Rehabilitation can mean social reintegration or simply the prevention of future criminal recidivism. However, the RNR model paradigm often emphasises prevention of future offending as the criterion of intervention success, which may often neglect improving mental health outcomes for offenders (Blackburn, 2004; Ward and Maruna, 2007). Accordingly, many programmes and their evaluation focus on risk reduction. For example, Cullen and colleagues conducted a series of well-controlled studies to investigate the effectiveness of the Reasoning and Rehabilitation programme (R&R) in MDOs. The R&R makes two main assumptions: i) some offenders lack the values, attitudes, reasoning and social skills required for pro-social adjustment, and ii) that such skills can be acquired. The R&R programme aims at providing clients with a repertoire of skills and behaviours as an alternative to criminal behaviour. In a recent meta-analysis of 16 studies, Joy Tong and Farrington (2006) reported a 14% recidivism reduction in MDO samples. According to Clarke et al. (2010), R&R may be effective in reducing recidivism because it focuses on psychotic reasoning biases common in schizophrenia. They found that R&R could be implemented successfully in medium-secure hospitals, providing improved psychosocial functioning in MDOs, changes in criminal attitudes, and reduction in incidents of antisocial behaviour (Clarke et al., 2010; Cullen et al., 2011, 2012).

Duncan et al. (2006) conducted a systematic review and located 20 studies that evaluated structured group interventions with MDOs. In contrast to Cullen and colleagues' work, these studies focused on clinical outcomes. The interventions either addressed problem-solving, anger/aggression management, self-harm, or other treatment targets. Most interventions studied were based on a cognitive-behavioural approach to treatment and had moderate to high positive effect sizes. However, limitations of the studies included small sample sizes, convenience sampling, and some studies lacking a comparison group and/or randomisation.

Martin et al. (2012) conducted a meta-analysis into the effectiveness of interventions targeting MDOs. The meta-analysis included 25 studies with 37 effect sizes ($N = 15,687$). Effectiveness criteria were either improved criminal justice (fewer arrests, convictions or jail days, less violent recidivism etc.) or mental health outcomes (e.g., fewer symptoms, higher functioning), or both. They found that interventions moderately reduced involvement with the criminal justice system. In addition, they found that mental health effects were associated with criminal justice effects. That is, studies with negative mental health effects had smaller criminal justice effects than studies with positive and neutral mental health effects. They noted that very few studies included in their meta-analysis adequately described the treatment models they used (see McGuire, this volume). Thus, implications for the RNR principles are limited. In addition, moderator analyses indicated a number of significant effects. Thus, the results should be treated with caution.

To summarise, it is neither sufficient to target criminogenic needs or clinical improvement in MDOs. Recidivism reduction is important; however research suggests that it is related with improved or neutral mental health outcomes. Blackburn (2004) states that rehabilitation must go beyond skills training, especially in cases with multiple diagnoses in which personality pathology maintains symptomatology and violence risk. He also raises the issue that the RNR paradigm treats mental disorder as a specific responsivity factor on the one hand, and as a dynamic risk factor (or criminogenic need) on the other. Unfortunately, the RNR paradigm (Andrews and Bonta, 2010) has been adapted from correctional settings to forensic mental health in such a way that mental illness is often conceptualised as just another risk factor, whereas specific responsivity remains largely unaddressed. However, ideally clinicians should 'address needs specific to disorder' (Andrews and Bonta, 2010, p. 508). Not addressing specific responsivity properly may not only impact the effectiveness of the intervention, but may also contribute to retention rates. For example, Cullen et al. (2011) reported a drop-out rate of 50 %. In their analysis of factors predicting drop-out they found that high levels of impulsivity, poor behavioural control, and antisocial or psychopathic traits were higher in MDOs who dropped out of R&R, suggesting that the higher risk offenders did profit less from treatment.

Blackburn (2004) states that the aim of rehabilitation in MDOs is not only to reduce recidivism, but also to alleviate suffering as well as create a better life (see also: Drennan and Alred, 2013a). However, the RNR literature seems to equate offender rehabilitation with risk or recidivism reduction, whereas ideally rehabilitation's 'goal is to *enable* the individual to avoid further crime by increasing personal effectiveness' (original emphasis; Blackburn, 2004, p. 301).

Strength-based approaches such as the Good Lives Model – Forensic Mental Health (GLM-FMH) aim at addressing an individual's risk factors and an individual's life goals at the same time. Thus, the GLM assists offenders to live better lives. At the same time, it aims to prepare offenders for an offence-free life by providing them with the skills and resources needed to attain their life goals in socially acceptable ways. In GLM terms, the presence of a mental disorder is a major obstacle to the pro-social pursuit of an individual's life goals. In addition, mental disorders can create or further exacerbate vulnerabilities. Moreover, similar to criminal behaviour, mental disorders are associated with social stigma that can lead to social exclusion, i.e. further deprivation of social capital (Barnao et al., 2010).

Gannon et al. (2011) describe a GLM intervention addressed at mentally disordered sex offenders. This programme followed the RNR principles and incorporated the main principles and assumptions of the GLM. This is, assessing each MDO's preference for common life goals (primary goods), which are related to their personal identity and their experience of agency. In addition, offenders were supported to attain a little of each life goal whilst still being detained, providing them with experiences of agency. Finally, besides enabling patients to manage their own risk, therapists assist them in understanding their offending from a GLM perspective. Their case studies suggested that the attention to each client's life goals played a key role in promoting treatment engagement. Although generalisation and firmer conclusions would require more rigorous methodology, these results suggest that attending to a client's life goals can result in noteworthy progress in this heterogeneous, clinically complex group.

Other positive, strength-based approaches focus on the well-being of MDOs. G. Ferguson et al. (2009) argue that most interventions targeted at MDOs are typically problem-focused and address criminogenic needs and/or symptom reduction. However, working towards positive outcomes and capitalising on human growth is equally important in MDO rehabilitation as risk reduction. In their study, they evaluated a six-session well-being intervention in medium security forensic psychiatry that did not consider risk reduction as one of their aims. MDOs reported higher subjective well-being and positive future thinking. In addition, they reported lower hopelessness, depression, and negative symptoms of psychosis. Interestingly, none of the MDOs dropped out once treatment commenced, although 15% decided not to take part, before treatment started.

The second phase of the ITDSO draws significantly from the RNR as well as from the GLM. Risk assessment and the RNR principles remain a significant part of strength-based interventions. However, the GLM is not only concerned with risk reduction, but also with successfully reconstructing an offender's sense of self. This positive, strength-focused approach is consistent with central ideas in the desistance literature (Ward and Maruna, 2007). In rehabilitation, offenders and treatment providers develop a Good Life Plan, which functions as a roadmap for risk reduction and quality of life improvement. This involves identifying important life goals an offender may have, and how maladaptive pursuits of life goals have been involved in their offending. In addition, an offender is equipped with the resources and skills they need to recover from mental illness, improve their lives, and reduce their risk (as described by Gannon et al., 2011).

Strength-based approaches such as the GLM are likely to foster desistance for the following reasons: i) they promote individual agency; ii) they are compatible with recovery; iii) they reduce hopelessness; and iv) they support MDOs in acquiring social capital. As described above, GLM-based interventions take offender's preferences and interests into account. To provide MDOs with a personal sense of agency is especially important due to the restrictions they experience. Whilst non-MDOs experience restriction of their physical freedom, MDOs often face not only physical restrictions, but psychological ones as well (e.g., disintegrated sense of self). To promote human growth, a therapeutic culture is a necessity (Childs and Brinded, 2002). Dysfunctional system dynamics such as inconsistencies, unpredictability and punitiveness most likely reinforce MDOs' previous life experiences and create an anti-therapeutic environment. However, institutional life itself may threaten autonomy and self-sufficiency. Thus, the goal should not be to make patients adjust to the system, but rather to provide them with skills to live in a less structured environment (Lindqvist and Skipworth, 2000). To provide MDOs with positive personal agency experiences, a collaborative approach as advocated by the GLM is the way to go. In addition, Lindqvist and Skipworth (2000) emphasise that rehabilitation should be concerned with an MDO's life after discharge, with the ultimate goal of forming a realistic, productive and hopeful life plan.

Phase 3 – re-entry

As described by Göbbels et al. (2012), re-entry is very stressful for offenders. It can be expected that MDOs face unique challenges when re-entering mainstream society. According to the ITDSO, successfully desisting ex-offenders are hypothesised to endorse a non-offending identity, acquire important skills to live a satisfying life without harming others, and reduce their risk factors during the rehabilitation phase. All these factors contribute to an offender's ability to maintain a commitment to his or her lifestyle change. However, external factors determine desistance as well. In the following, we will outline barriers to and facilitators for desistance in MDOs once they have re-entered the community.

Barriers to desistance in mentally disordered offenders

The ITDSO outlines that a primary goods package (housing, work, health, family and friendships) is a necessary but not sufficient condition for successful reintegration. However, in MDOs these bare essentials are often not met. Mallik-Kane and Visher (2008) conducted an in-depth examination of the re-entry process in offenders with mental, physical and substance abuse conditions in a representative sample of 1,100 male and female offenders in the USA. They found that MDOs faced many challenges upon release or discharge and received only very sporadic and fragmented mental health care for acute problems. Only half of their sample reported receiving care for their symptomatology. In addition, in comparison to non-mentally ill offenders, MDOs reported poorer housing and work outcomes (see Canton, this volume). That is, they were less likely to earn a legal income and more likely to rely on disability support. The authors emphasised that many released prisoners depended on family support for employment and housing. MDOs received less functional, financial and emotional support from families, while dysfunctional family environments were more common among MDOs. MDOs in general received less family support, however female MDOs' level of support was even lower than that of their male counterparts (see Petrillo, this volume). In addition, substance abuse was a significant health challenge for MDOs and was associated with poorer housing, employment and recidivism outcomes, with women often experiencing worse outcomes than men.

Fisher et al. (2006) noted that MDOs were often exposed to social networks in which illicit drugs were all too present (see Pycroft and Green, this volume). Due to the lack of financial means to acquire the drugs, members of these social networks may engage in antisocial behaviour. In these marginalised networks, substance use and criminal behaviour may be modelled. Poverty and homelessness may also contribute to survival crimes. Thus, in such social networks, economic and pro-social capital is lacking to such a degree that desistance seems almost impossible.

Economic and social disadvantage and marginalisation stand in an interactive relationship with criminalisation and stigma. Fisher et al. (2006) describe how MDOs often get arrested for trivial charges such as trespassing or disorderly conduct. In addition, MDOs often face double or even triple stigma – mentally disordered, criminal and addicted. For example, Hartwell (2004) reviewed existing literature on individuals with dual diagnosis. A high number of MDOs suffered from a major mental disorder such as schizophrenia and comorbid substance disorders. She found that in a non-representative sample of 501 offenders, 344 were dual-diagnosed. The individuals with dual diagnosis were more likely to be serving sentences due to drug-related crimes (property offences, public order offences etc.). They were also more likely to be homeless on release, to violate probation, and to recidivate. Moreover, the double stigma of being mentally ill and a substance abuser created barriers to community-based services. Dual-diagnosed individuals are not the preferred candidates for rehabilitation or other support services, possibly because of their lower levels of compliance. In addition, having been incarcerated or a patient in forensic psychiatry may result in a triple stigma. This may be associated with continued involvement in criminal behaviours, a cyclical 'revolving door' phenomenon in which MDOs oscillate between homelessness and repeat imprisonment (Baillargeon et al., 2009; Martin et al., 2012).

It should also be acknowledged that MDOs are not only perpetrators; they are vulnerable to victimisation as well. Research suggests that MDOs who have been victimised recently are at a higher risk of committing violence (Hiday et al., 2001; Sadeh et al., 2014). Thus, especially when released in the community, MDOs face victimisation that may be a MDO-specific barrier to desistance.

How to maintain desistance in mentally disordered offenders

As this discussion indicates, there are many barriers to MDOs' desistance on community re-entry. Some of those barriers apply to most offenders while some are unique to MDOs. However, there are many factors that may facilitate desistance. Some of them apply to all kinds of offenders while others may be specific to the MDO population. In the following, two related desistance factors – pro-social capital and employment – will be discussed as examples.

a) Pro-social capital As described in the previous section, many MDOs are embedded in antisocial networks. Hence, many of them may lack pro-social capital. According to De Silva et al. (2005), it is debatable if social capital is an individual or ecological (as in groups of people) resource. This chapter focuses on the former and views social capital as an individual's resource comparable to social support and networks. Similar to other forms of capital (physical, human), social capital is productive, bringing about positive outcomes that in its absence would not occur. Social capital means a network of relationships, which facilitates pro-social action by providing resources and a sense of obligation, expectation and trust (Farrall, 2004). In a systematic review, De Silva et al. (2005) found strong evidence to suggest an inverse association between levels of social capital (e.g., feelings of trust and reciprocity) and mental disorders. Thus, higher social capital is associated with lower levels of mental illness (for similar results see: Almedom, 2005). In addition to having a protective effect against mental illness, social capital is likely inversely associated with reoffending (Farrall, 2004; Wright et al., 2001).

While pro-social family contacts should be promoted in MDOs, Bonta et al. (1998) found that poor living relationships and family dysfunction were predictors of recidivism in MDOs. Similarly, Kawachi and Berkman (2001) emphasise that strong social ties promote the maintenance of psychological well-being; however, note that social ties can also result in role strain for women who lack resources to provide support to others. Thus, before making contact with estranged family members or friends, it should be determined if benefits outweigh the risks.

In addition, formal social contacts such as counsellors may assist offenders in achieving a normalised lifestyle. For example, Rowe and Soppitt (2014) found that commitment to desistance was stronger when re-entered ex-offenders engaged with formal supports that were not part of the criminal justice system and thought staff had an authentic interest in helping them.

b) Employment While Bonta et al. (1998) found that employment and education difficulties were insignificant in the prediction of reoffending among MDOs, employment arguably exposes individuals to pro-social networks comprised of individuals who may be less likely to engage in criminal activity. Furthermore, employment provides structured activity, self-esteem enhancement and financial independence. Uggen (2000) emphasises that work can be a turning point in adult offenders' lives as it seems to promote desistance. However, many MDOs suffer from a lack of life skills and social withdrawal (Rice and Harris, 1997), which seems at odds with gainful employment. Thus, these individuals require support in their efforts to secure employment. Twamley et al. (2003) conducted a meta-analysis investigating the efficiency of vocational rehabilitation in non-offending, severely mentally ill patients. They found that supported employment programmes were more effective than other more traditional vocational rehabilitation programmes such as sheltered workshops. Supported employment aims to place individuals quickly in integrated work settings and train them on site. In addition, it aims at tailoring placement to the client's abilities and interests, and offers ongoing vocational support and integrated vocational rehabilitation in general. More specifically, those in supported employment had consistently better outcomes than traditional vocational rehabilitation in regard to both competitive employment and other employment. Although vocational rehabilitation has been identified as a valuable treatment target in MDOs (e.g., Lamb et al., 2004), few researchers have investigated its value in MDO populations yet. However, from a desistance perspective, this option appears promising.

Phase 4 – normalcy

To achieve normalcy (Farrall and Calverley, 2006), MDOs need to maintain desistance from crime over a long period of time. This also requires management of criminogenic factors of their mental illness. Thus, factors such as long-term treatment adherence are of crucial importance (Duncan and Rogers, 1998).

Obviously, achieving normalcy is a process and there is not any one point at which a person can say that it has been achieved. It takes a commitment as well as motivation to achieve a non-offending lifestyle as well as a plan on how to reach life goals in a sustainable, pro-social manner (Ward and Maruna, 2007). In terms of the various aspects of life that are important – for example, having a partner, having a job, and experiencing pleasure – these are the same whether or not a person is mentally disordered.

Conclusion

Similarly to recidivism, desistance is a multifaceted issue in a population that is as complex as MDOs. Nevertheless, the ITDSO and other desistance theories (Farrall and Calverley, 2006; Giordano et al., 2002; Laub and Sampson, 2003; Maruna, 2001; Paternoster and Bushway, 2009) can be seen as useful theoretical frameworks to apply desistance research to the MDO population. Desistance is a unifying paradigm that can accommodate many related ideas surrounding motivation, readiness, recovery, rehabilitation, positive psychology, risk management, GLM, positive re-entry and reintegration. A combination of those ideas is likely to result in a positive, future-focused and constructive approach to recidivism reduction in MDOs. In particular, desistance models focus attention on the fact that desistance is a process, which requires resources over an extended period of time. The desistance journey may start before an offender is admitted to a forensic hospital or prison and end decades after an offender has been discharged and lived offence-free in the community. Normalcy requires good mental health and a commitment to maintaining an offence-free lifestyle.

Desistance research can inform clinicians about treatment readiness and how to cultivate desistance-promoting interpersonal interactions with offenders. Clinicians should foster the development of positive future selves by taking a warm and accepting stance towards clients. This can result in clients being able to capitalise on existing social resources or establish pro-social capital (Kazemian, 2007). Desistance research also points to the importance of positive environments, as agency and external factors interact with each other (Healy, 2013). A desistance paradigm also focuses clinicians' attention on the importance of re-entry planning and aftercare.

Importantly, desistance research raises awareness of limitations of cognitive-behavioural treatments (CBT) in correctional psychology (Healy, 2013). First, the focus on personal responsibility and eradication of excuse making typical to CBT in correctional contexts may be at odds with desistance research. Maruna (2001) found that excuse making allowed successfully desisting offenders to negotiate between their criminal past and conventional identity (see also: Healy, 2013; Maruna and Mann, 2006). Thus, if poorly conducted, CBT-oriented treatments may harbour the risk of the internalisation of an offending identity as opposed to risk reduction. Alternatively, clients may show superficial compliance, which may mask true transformation. Not to forget, non-offending can happen in the absence of noticeable cognitive change (Healy, 2013).

In terms of future research there is obviously much that can be done to further understand the issues raised in this chapter. In particular, while there is much research conducted on risk factors of reoffending in MDOs, research into protective factors is sparse. It can be expected that protective factors are also desistance facilitators (Wooditch et al., 2014). Thus, Fisher et al. (2006) suggest that desistance factors are useful targets for intervention, as they most likely reduce MDOs' risk of recidivism and increase their well-being. However, simple causal models are misplaced in desistance research. For example, while social capital is robustly associated with desistance, it is unclear whether people have more social capital because they are more pro-social, or if they are more pro-social because they have more social capital. Alternatively, a third variable may explain the relationship (Barnes and Beaver, 2012; Kazemian, 2007). Clearly, more research is needed in non-MDOs and MDOs before desistance research can be applied to clinical practice. For example, while it has been recognised that employment may be a useful intervention target in MDOs (Lamb et al., 2004), in writing this chapter we had to resort to citing findings in non-offending mentally ill subjects.

Beyond, qualitative as well as quantitative studies investigating protective factors and desistance facilitators in MDO should be conducted. For example, research should find out if and how MDOs desist from crime, how they experience agency, and how they maintain desistance and eventually achieve normalcy. It is important that in this research the complexity of the MDO population is acknowledged. While it may be difficult to organise MDO groups according to diagnoses, Hiday's (1999) categorisation of three types of MDOs may be useful for further studies.

In addition, it is concerning that some MDOs who re-enter the community are at risk of victimisation, which in turn is suggested to increase their risk of offending (Hiday et al., 2001; Sadeh et al., 2014). This unique MDO risk factor and desistance hindrance should be investigated using qualitative methods to further elucidate and raise awareness of this concerning issue.

While strength-based approaches are not new to mental health as well as to correctional psychology, much needs to be done to enhance MDOs' chances to live safe, pro-social, meaningful, and personally fulfilling lives. Using a positive framework seems a good idea. However, it is also important to be realistic as to what can be achieved in a population that may face many limitations. We hope that this chapter, which may have raised more questions than it has provided answers, can contribute to ongoing enquiries in this challenging area.

References

Almedom, A. M. (2005). Social capital and mental health: an interdisciplinary review of primary evidence. *Social Science & Medicine*, 61(5), 943–964. doi: 10.1016/j.socscimed.2004.12.025

American Psychiatric Association. (2000). *Diagnostic statistical manual of mental disorders* (Revised 4th. ed.). Arlington, VA, USA: American Psychiatric Association.

Andrews, D.A., and Bonta, J. (2010). *The psychology of criminal conduct (5th ed.)*. Cincinnati, OH: Anderson.

Baillargeon, J., Binswanger, I. A., Penn, J. V., Williams, B. A., and Murray, O. J. (2009). Psychiatric disorders and repeat incarcerations: the revolving prison door. *The American Journal of Psychiatry*, 166(1), 103–109. doi: 10.1176/appi.ajp.2008.08030416

Bandura, A. (1999). A Sociocognitive Analysis of Substance Abuse: An Agentic Perspective. *Psychological Science*, 10(3), 214–217. doi: 10.1111/1467-9280.00138

Barnao, M., Robertson, P., and Ward, T. (2010). Good Lives Model Applied to a Forensic Population. *Psychiatry, Psychology and Law*, 17(2), 202–217. doi: 10.1080/13218710903421274

Barnes, J., and Beaver, K. M. (2012). Marriage and desistance from crime: A consideration of gene-environment correlation. *Journal of Marriage and Family*, 74(1), 19–33. doi: 10.1111/j.1741-3737.2011.00884.x

Baumeister, R. F. (1994). The crystallization of discontent in the process of major life change. In T. F. Heatherton and J. L. Weinberger (eds), *Can personality change?* Washington, DC American Psychological Association. 281–297.

Blackburn, R. (2004). 'What works' with mentally disordered offenders. *Psychology, Crime & Law*, 10(3), 297–308. doi: 10.1080/10683160410001662780

Bonta, J., Law, M., and Hanson, K. (1998). The prediction of criminal and violent recidivism among mentally disordered offenders: A meta-analysis. *Psychological Bulletin*, 123(2), 123–142. doi: 10.1037/0033-2909.123.2.123

Burnett, R. (2010). The will and the ways to becoming an ex-offender. *International Journal of Offender Therapy and Comparative Criminology*, 54(5), 663–666. doi: 10.1177/0306624x10383845

Burrowes, N., and Needs, A. (2009). Time to contemplate change? A framework for assessing readiness to change with offenders. *Aggression and Violent Behavior*, 14(1), 39–49. doi: 10.1016/j.avb.2008.08.003

Cashin, A., and Newman, C. (2009). Autism in the criminal justice detention system: A review of the literature. *Journal of Forensic Nursing*, 5(2), 70–75. doi: 10.1111/j.1939-3938.2009.01037.x

Childs, L., and Brinded, P. (2002). Rehabilitation of the mentally disordered offender. *Australian Psychologist*, 37(3), 229–236. doi: 10.1080/00050060210001706916

Clarke, A. Y., Cullen, A. E., Walwyn, R., and Fahy, T. (2010). A quasi-experimental pilot study of the reasoning and rehabilitation programme with mentally disordered offenders. *Journal of Forensic Psychiatry & Psychology*, 21(4), 490–500. doi: 10.1080/14789940903236391

Colman, C., and Vander Laenen, F. (2012). 'Recovery Came First': Desistance versus Recovery in the Criminal Careers of Drug-Using Offenders. *The Scientific World Journal*, 2012. doi: 10.1100/2012/657671

Cordess, C. (2002). Building and nurturing a therapeutic alliance with offenders. In M. McMurran (ed.), *Motivating offenders to change: A guide to enhancing engagement in therapy*. Hoboken, NY, USA: Wiley. 75–86.

Corlett, H., and Miles, H. (2010). An evaluation of the implementation of the recovery philosophy in a secure forensic service. *The British Journal of Forensic Practice*, 12(4), 14–25. doi: 10.5042/bjfp.2010.0611

Corrigan, P. W. (1991). Social skills training in adult psychiatric populations: A meta-analysis. *Journal of Behavior Therapy and Experimental Psychiatry*, 22(3), 203–210. doi: 10.1016/0005-7916(91)90017-Y

Côté, G., and Hodgins, S. (1990). Co-Occurring Mental Disorders Among Criminal Offenders. *Journal of the American Academy of Psychiatry and the Law Online*, 18(3), 271–281. URL: http://www.jaapl.org/content/218/273/271.abstract

Cullen, A. E., Clarke, A. E., Kuipers, E., Hodgins, S., Dean, K., and Fahy, T. (2012). A multi-site randomized controlled trial of a cognitive skills programme for male mentally disordered offenders: Social-cognitive outcomes. *Psychological Medicine*, 42(3), 557–569. doi: 10.1017/S0033291711001553

Cullen, A. E., Soria, C., Clarke, A. Y., Dean, K., and Fahy, T. (2011). Factors predicting dropout from the Reasoning and Rehabilitation program with mentally disordered offenders. *Criminal Justice and Behavior*, 38(3), 217–230. doi: 10.1177/0093854810393659

Davidson, L., and Strauss, J. S. (1992). Sense of self in recovery from severe mental illness. *British Journal of Medical Psychology*, 65(2), 131–145. doi: 10.1111/j.2044-8341.1992.tb01693.x

Davis, M., Banks, S., Fisher, W., and Grudzinskas, A. (2004). Longitudinal patterns of offending during the transition to adulthood in youth from the mental health system. *The Journal of Behavioral Health Services & Research*, 31(4), 351–366. doi: 10.1007/BF02287689

De Silva, M. J., McKenzie, K., Harpham, T., and Huttly, S. R. A. (2005). Social capital and mental illness: a systematic review. *Journal of Epidemiology and Community Health*, 59(8), 619–627. doi: 10.1136/jech.2004.029678

Douglas, K. S., Hart, S. D., Webster, C. D., and Belfrage, H. (2013). *Historical-Clinical-Risk Management, Version 3 (HCR-V3)*. Burnaby, BC, Canada: Mental Health, Law, and Policy Institute.

Drennan, G., and Alred, D. (2013a). Preface. In G. Drennan and D. Alred (eds), *Secure Recovery: Approaches to Recovery in Forensic Mental Health Settings*. New York, NY, USA: Routledge.

Drennan, G., and Alred, D. (2013b). Recovery in forensic mental health settings: From alienation to integration. In G. Drennan and D. Alred (eds), *Secure Recovery: Approaches to Recovery in Forensic Mental Health Settings*. New York, NY, USA: Routledge. 1–22.

Duncan, E. A. S., Nicol, M. M., Ager, A., and Dalgleish, L. (2006). A systematic review of structured group interventions with mentally disordered offenders. *Criminal Behaviour and Mental Health*, 16(4), 217–241. doi: 10.1002/cbm.631

Duncan, J. C., and Rogers, R. (1998). Medication compliance in patients with chronic schizophrenia: Implications for the community management of mentally disordered offenders. *Journal of Forensic Sciences*, 43(6), 1133–1137.

Farrall, S. (2004). Social capital and offender reintegration: Making probation desistance-focused. In S. Maruna and R. Immarigeon (eds), *After crime and punishment: Pathways to offender reintegration*. Devon, UK: Willan Publishing. 57–82.

Farrall, S., and Calverley, A. (2006). *Understanding desistance from crime: Theoretical directions in resettlement and rehabilitation*. New York, NY: Open University Press.

Feld, S. L., and Straus, M. A. (1989). Escalation and desistance of wife assault in marriage. *Criminology*, 27(1), 141–162. doi: 10.1111/j.1745-9125.1989.tb00866.x

Ferguson, A., Ogloff, J. R., and Thomson, L. (2009). Predicting recidivism by mentally disordered offenders using the LSI-R:SV. *Criminal Justice and Behavior*, 36(1), 5–20. doi: 10.1177/0093854808326525

Ferguson, G., Conway, C., Endersby, L., and MacLeod, A. (2009). Increasing subjective well-being in long-term forensic rehabilitation: Evaluation of well-being therapy. *Journal of Forensic Psychiatry & Psychology*, 20(6), 906–918. doi: 10.1080/14789940903174121

Fisher, W. H., Silver, E., and Wolff, N. (2006). Beyond Criminalization: Toward a Criminologically Informed Framework for Mental Health Policy and Services Research. *Administration and Policy in Mental Health and Mental Health Services Research*, 33(5), 544–557. doi: 10.1007/s10488-006-0072-0

Gannon, T. A., King, T., Miles, H., Lockerbie, L., and Willis, G. M. (2011). Good Lives sexual offender treatment for mentally disordered offenders. *The British Journal of Forensic Practice*, 13(3), 153–168. doi: 10.1108/14636641111157805

Giordano, P.C, Cernkovich, S.A, and Rudolph, J.L. (2002). Gender, crime, and desistance: Toward a Theory of Cognitive Transformation. *American Journal of Sociology*, 107(4), 990–1064. URL: http://www.jstor.org/stable/1010.1086/343191

Göbbels, S., Ward, T., and Willis, G. M. (2012). An integrative theory of desistance from sex offending. *Aggression and Violent Behavior*, 17(5), 453–462. doi: http://dx.doi.org/10.1016/j.avb.2012.06.003

Gudjonsson, G. H., Young, S., and Yates, M. (2007). Motivating mentally disordered offenders to change: Instruments for measuring patients' perception and motivation. *The Journal of Forensic Psychiatry & Psychology*, 18(1), 74–89. doi: 10.1080/14789940601063261

Hartwell, S. (2004). Triple Stigma: Persons with Mental Illness and Substance Abuse Problems in the Criminal Justice System. *Criminal Justice Policy Review*, 15(1), 84–99. doi: 10.1177/0887403403255064

Hattery, A., and Smith, E. (2010). *Prisoner Reentry and Social Capital: The long road to reintegration*. Lanham, MD: Lexington Books.

Healy, D. (2013). Changing fate? Agency and the desistance process. *Theoretical Criminology*, 17(4), 557–574. doi: 10.1177/1362480613494991

Hiday, V. A. (1999). Mental illness and the criminal justice system. In A. V. H. T. L. Scheid (ed.), *A handbook for the study of mental health: Social contexts, theories, and systems*. New York, NY, US: Cambridge University Press. 508–525.

Hiday, V. A., Swanson, J. W., Swartz, M. S., Borum, R., and Wagner, H. R. (2001). Victimization: A link between mental illness and violence? *International Journal of Law and Psychiatry*, 24(6), 559–572. doi: 10.1016/S0160-2527(01)00091-7

Hodge, J. E., and Renwick, S. J. (2002). Motivating mentally disordered offenders. In M. McMurran (ed.), *Motivating offenders to change: A guide to enhancing engagement in therapy*. Hoboken, NY, USA: Wiley. 221–234.

Holland, T., Clare, I. C. H., and Mukhopadhyay, T. (2002). Prevalence of 'criminal offending' by men and women with intellectual disability and the characteristics of 'offenders': implications for research and service development. *Journal of Intellectual Disability Research*, 46, 6–20. doi: 10.1046/j.1365-2788.2002.00001.x

Holma, J., and Aaltonen, J. (1997). The Sense of Agency and the Search for a Narrative in Acute Psychosis. *Contemporary Family Therapy*, 19(4), 463–477. doi: 10.1023/A:1026174819842

Howells, K., and Day, A. (2007). Readiness for treatment in high risk offenders with personality disorders. *Psychology, Crime & Law*, 13(1), 47–56. doi: 10.1080/10683160600869767

Jacobson, N., and Greenley, D. (2001). What Is Recovery? A Conceptual Model and Explication. *Psychiatric Services*, 52(4), 482–485. doi: 10.1176/appi.ps.52.4.482

Joy Tong, L. S., and Farrington, David P. (2006). How effective is the 'Reasoning and Rehabilitation' programme in reducing reoffending? A meta-analysis of evaluations in four countries. *Psychology, Crime & Law*, 12(1), 3–24. doi: 10.1080/10683160512331316253

Kawachi, I., and Berkman, L. F. (2001). Social ties and mental health. *Journal of Urban Health*, 78(3), 458–467. doi: 10.1093/jurban/78.3.458

Kazemian, L. (2007). Desistance from crime. *Journal of Contemporary Criminal Justice*, 23(1), 5–27. doi: 10.1177/1043986206298940

Korsgaard, C. M. (1996). *The Sources of Normativity*. New York: Cambridge University Press.

Korsgaard, C. M. (2009). *Self constitution: Agency, identity, and integrity*. New York: Oxford University Press.

Kurlychek, M. C., Bushway, S. D., and Brame, R. (2012). Long-term crime desistance and recidivism patterns – Evidence from the Essex County Convicted Felon Study. *Criminology*, 50(1), 71–103. doi: 10.1111/j.1745-9125.2011.00259.x

Lamb, H. R., Weinberger, L. E., and Gross, B. H. (2004). Mentally Ill Persons in the Criminal Justice System: Some Perspectives. *Psychiatric Quarterly*, 75(2), 107–126. doi: 10.1023/B:PSAQ.0000019753.63627.2c

Laub, J. H., Nagin, D. S, and Sampson, R. J. (1998). Trajectories of change in criminal offending: Good marriages and the desistance process. *American Sociological Review*, 63(2), 225–238. doi: 10.2307/2657324

Laub, J. H., and Sampson, R. J. (1993). *Crime in the making: Pathways and turning points through life*. Cambridge, MA: Harvard University Press.

Laub, J. H., and Sampson, R. J. (2003). *Shared beginnings, divergent lives: Delinquent boys to age 70*. Cambridge, MA: Harvard University Press.

Laws, D. R., and Ward, T. (2011). *Desistance from sex offending: Alternatives to throwing away the keys*. New York, NY: The Guilford Press.

Lindqvist, P., and Skipworth, J. (2000). Evidence-based rehabilitation in forensic psychiatry. *The British Journal of Psychiatry*, 176, 320–323. doi: 10.1192/bjp.176.4.320

Lindsay, W. R. (2002). Integration of Recent Reviews on Offenders with Intellectual Disabilities. *Journal of Applied Research in Intellectual Disabilities*, 15(2), 111–119. doi: 10.1046/j.1468-3148.2002.00112.x

Lord, A. (2014). Integrating risk, the Good Lives Model and recovery for mentally disordered sexual offenders. *Journal of Sexual Aggression*, 1–16. doi: 10.1080/13552600.2014.975164

Lund, C., Forsman, A., Anckarsater, H., and Nilsson, T. (2012). Early criminal recidivism among mentally disordered offenders. *International Journal of Offender Therapy and Comparative Criminology*, 56(5), 749–768. doi: 10.1177/0306624X11411677

Lund, C., Hofvander, B., Forsman, A., Anckarsater, H., and Nilsson, T. (2013). Violent criminal recidivism in mentally disordered offenders: A follow-up study of 13–20 years through different sanctions. *International Journal of Law and Psychiatry*, 36(3–4), 250–257. doi: 10.1016/j.ijlp.2013.04.015

Mallik-Kane, K, and Visher, C. A. (2008). *Health and Prisoner Reentry: How Physical, Mental, and Substance Abuse Conditions Shape the Process of Reintegration*. Washington DC, USA: Urban Institute Justice Policy Center.

Martin, M. S., Dorken, S. K., Wamboldt, A. D., and Wootten, S. E. (2012). Stopping the revolving door: A meta-analysis on the effectiveness of interventions for criminally involved individuals with major mental disorders. *Law and Human Behavior*, 36(1), 1–12. doi: 10.1037/h0093963

Maruna, S. (2001). *Making good: How ex-convicts reform and rebuild their lives*. Washington, D.C.: American Psychological Association.

Maruna, S., Immarigeon, R., and Lebel, T. P. (2004). Ex-offender reintegration: Theory and practice. In S. Maruna and R. Immarigeon (eds), *After Crime and Punishment: Pathways to offender reintegration*. Devon, UK: Willan Publishing. 3–26.

Maruna, S., and Mann, R. E. (2006). A fundamental attribution error? Rethinking cognitive distortions. *Legal and Criminological Psychology*, 11(2), 155–177. doi: 10.1348/135532506X114608

McMurran, M., and Ward, T. (2004). Motivating offenders to change in therapy: An organizing framework. *Legal & Criminological Psychology*, 9(2), 295–311. doi: 10.1348/1355325041719365

Nilsson, T., Wallinius, M., Gustavson, C., Anckarsater, H., and Kerekes, N. (2011). Violent recidivism: A long-time follow-up study of mentally disordered offenders. *PLoS ONE*, 6(10). doi: 10.1371/journal.pone.0025768

Oyserman, D., Bybee, D., Terry, K., and Hart-Johnson, T. (2004). Possible selves as roadmaps. *Journal of Research in Personality*, 38(2), 130–149. doi: 10.1016/s0092-6566(03)00057-6

Oyserman, D., and Markus, H. (1990). Possible Selves in Balance: Implications for Delinquency. *Journal of Social Issues*, 46(2), 141–157. doi: 10.1111/j.1540-4560.1990.tb01927.x

Paternoster, R., and Bushway, S.D. (2009). Desistance and the 'feared self': Toward an identity theory of criminal desistance. *The Journal of Criminal Law & Criminology*, 99(4), 1103–1156. URL: http://www.jstor.org/stable/20685067

Quinsey, V. L., Harris, G. T., Rice, M. E., and Cormier, C. A. (2006). Mentally Disordered Offenders. In V. L. Quinsey, G. T. Harris, M. E. Rice and C. A. Cormier (eds), *Violent offenders: Appraising and managing risk* (2nd ed.). Washington, DC, USA: American Psychological Association. 85–113.

Rice, M. E., and Harris, G. T. (1997). The treatment of mentally disordered offenders. *Psychology, Public Policy, and Law*, 3(1), 126–183. doi: 10.1037/1076-8971.3.1.126

Robertson, P., Barnao, M., and Ward, T. (2011). Rehabilitation frameworks in forensic mental health. *Aggression and Violent Behavior*, 16(6), 472–484. doi: 10.1016/j.avb.2011.03.003

Rowe, M., and Soppitt, S. (2014). 'Who you gonna call?' The role of trust and relationships in desistance from crime. *Probation Journal*. doi: 10.1177/0264550514548252

Sadeh, N., Binder, R. L., and McNiel, D. E. (2014). Recent Victimization Increases Risk for Violence in Justice-Involved Persons With Mental Illness. *Law & Human Behavior*, 38(2), 119–125. doi: 10.1037/lhb0000043

Sampson, R. J., and Laub, J. H. (2005). A life-course view of the development of crime. *The Annals of the American Academy of Political and Social Science*, 602(1), 12–45. doi: 10.1177/0002716205280075

Seifert, D., and Moller-Mussavi, S. (2005). Preliminary Recidivism Rates of the Essener Prognosis Study. Can we Speak of a Decrease in Recidivism Rates of Forensic Patients in Germany? *Fortschritte der Neurologie, Psychiatrie*, 73(1), 16–22. doi: 10.1055/s-2004-830062

Skeem, J. L., Manchak, S., and Peterson, J. K. (2011). Correctional Policy for Offenders with Mental Illness. *Law and Human Behavior*, 35(2), 110–126. doi: 10.1007/s10979-010-9223-7

Swann, W. B., and Bosson, J. K. (2010). Self and Identity. In S. T. Fiske, D. T. Gilbert and G. Lindzey (eds), *Handbook of Social Psychology*. Hoboken, NJ: John Wiley & Sons, Inc.

Synofzik, M., Vosgerau, G., and Voss, M. (2013). The experience of agency: An interplay between prediction and postdiction. *Frontiers in Psychology*, 15(4). doi: 10.3389/fpsyg.2013.00127

Tierney, D. W., and McCabe, M. P. (2002). Motivation for behavior change among sex offenders: A review of the literature. *Clinical Psychology Review*, 22(1), 113–129. doi: 10.1016/S0272-7358(01)00084-8

Twamley, E. W., Jeste, D. V., and Lehman, A. F. (2003). Vocational Rehabilitation in Schizophrenia and Other Psychotic Disorders: A Literature Review and Meta-Analysis of Randomized Controlled Trials. *Journal of Nervous and Mental Disease*, 191(8), 515–523. doi: 10.1097/01.nmd.0000082213.42509.69

Uggen, C. (2000). Work as a turning point in the life course of criminals: A duration model of age, employment, and recidivism. *American Sociological Review*, 65(4), 529–546. doi: 10.2307/2657381

Walker, K., Bowen, E., and Brown, S. (2013a). Desistance from intimate partner violence: A critical review. *Aggression and Violent Behavior*, 18(2), 271–280. doi: 10.1016/j.avb.2012.11.019

Walker, K., Bowen, E., and Brown, S. (2013b). Psychological and criminological factors associated with desistance from violence: A review of the literature. *Aggression and Violent Behavior*, 18(2), 286–299. doi: 10.1016/j.avb.2012.11.021

Ward, T., Day, A., Howells, K., and Birgden, A. (2004). The multifactor offender readiness model. *Aggression and Violent Behavior*, 9(6), 645–673. doi: 10.1016/j.avb.2003.08.001

Ward, T., and Gannon, T. A. (2006). Rehabilitation, etiology, and self-regulation: The comprehensive good lives model of treatment for sexual offenders. *Aggression and Violent Behavior*, 11(1), 77–94. doi: 10.1016/j.avb.2005.06.001

Ward, T., and Maruna, S. (2007). *Rehabilitation: Beyond the risk paradigm*. London, UK: Routledge.

Wooditch, A., Tang, L. L., and Taxman, F. S. (2014). Which criminogenic need changes are most important in promoting desistance from crime and substance use? *Criminal Justice and Behavior*, 41(3), 276–299. doi: 10.1177/0093854813503543

Wright, J. P., Cullen, F. T., and Miller, J. T. (2001). Family social capital and delinquent involvement. *Journal of Criminal Justice*, 29(1), 1–9. doi: 10.1016/S0047-2352(00)00071-4

Yates, P. M., and Prescott, D. (2011). Applying the Good Lives Model to clinical practice: Redefining primary human goods. Newsletter of the National Organisation for the Treatment of Abusers (NOTA). Retrieved from http://www.nota.co.uk/, 68

Yates, P. M., Prescott, D., and Ward, T. (2010). *Applying the Good Lives and Self-Regulation Models to Sex Offender Treatment: A Practical Guide for Clinicians*. Brandon, Vermont: Safer Society Press.

Yoshikawa, K., Taylor, P. J., Yamagami, A., Okada, T., Ando, K., Taruya, T., ... Kikuchi, A. (2007). Violent recidivism among mentally disordered offenders in Japan. *Criminal Behaviour and Mental Health*, 17(3), 137–151. doi: 10.1002/cbm.652

Young, S. (2007). Forensic Aspects of ADHD. In M. Fitzgerald, M. Bellgrove and M. Gill (eds), *Handbook of Attention Deficit Hyperactivity Disorder*. Chichester, UK: Wiley. 91–109.

6
Medicalising 'Hatred': Exploring the Sense and Sensitivities of Classifying the Motivations for Hate Crime as Mental Disorder

Jemma Tyson and Nathan Hall

Introduction

On 24 May 2014, Elliot Rodger repeatedly stabbed three men to death in his apartment, before killing two women and another man, and wounding several others, before committing suicide, during a shooting spree across ten locations in Isla Vista, close to the University of California, Santa Barbara. Rodger, it seems, had been diagnosed with Asperger's Syndrome. He had certainly been receiving psychiatric care from multiple therapists. He had published a 141-page manifesto entitled *My Twisted World* on the Internet, and posted a number of videos on YouTube, in which his hatred of others, particularly in the form of misogyny, was explicit.

Rodger is not alone. Human history is littered with incidents of extreme hate-motivated violence. One need only think of the countless examples of genocide and mass murder that have occurred around the world, or like Elliot Rodger, the similar actions of other individuals such as Timothy McVeigh, John William King, Benjamin Smith, Buford Furrow, David Copeland, Michael Adebowale, or Michael Adebolajo, to name but a few. Or, indeed, any of the seemingly nameless suicide bombers that we have now sadly become so accustomed to hearing about in the news.

In an instant, these cases encapsulate many of the complex issues associated with 'hate' and the motivations of hate crime offenders more generally: *what is 'hatred'? What connection might it have with mental ill-health? Is 'hatred' a mental disorder in its own right, or is it merely a symptom of other recognised mental illnesses? Or is it neither? Can 'hatred' ever be considered 'normal', however uncomfortable that might make us feel? And, if it is even possible to do so, what are the implications of concluding one way or the other?*

In this chapter we will explore some of the answers, such as they might be, to these frankly perplexing questions, and we shall do so with the intention of informing future directions for research and practice. Before we begin though, we must start with a confession. We are criminologists with an interest in hate crime. In our field we frequently stray into the world of psychology, but curiously, we rarely enter into the world of psychiatry specifically, or medicalisation more generally. As a result, our specific field of interest rarely engages with the study of mentally disordered offenders. Indeed, criminology largely left behind the positivist notion of the 'born criminal', the 'psychiatry movement', and more broadly the causes of crime as being located within the individual, decades ago.

Thus we accepted the invitation to write this chapter with some trepidation, feeling somewhat out of place amongst those who diagnose and treat, and who are perhaps more inclined to view behaviour as the product of individual, internal variables rather than those located in the wider social environment. As the reader, if the former is the world you predominantly occupy, we hope you will forgive our brief foray into what is for us largely uncharted territory, as we attempt to merge sociology and criminology with psychiatry and medicalisation in order to address the complex issues that underpin 'hatred', and to offer some explanation for the tragic events that all too often fill the news headlines.

Although there is not the space here to fully examine the issues in hand, the reader should be aware from the outset that hate crime is a complex phenomenon, characterised by scholarly, political and legal debates and controversies at almost every level. Within the literature, a lack of clarity surrounds aspects such as how to define and conceptualise the problem, how it has come to be formally acknowledged, or not, as a contemporary socio-legal issue, how much of it exists around the world, who should be recognised as victims and what impacts it can have on those who experience it. Also, how the problem should be responded to both via the criminal justice system and through other preventive and reformative methods, both now and in the future.

Perhaps most importantly for our purposes here, though, two particularly contentious questions serve to complicate our understanding of hate crime considerably, and in so doing make any potential association with mental ill-health more difficult to delineate: first, *what exactly does 'hate' mean within the context of hate crime*, and second, *how and why does hate become the motivation for criminal behaviour?* Given the importance of these two inter-related issues, we shall begin with a brief consideration of each, before moving on to consider the extent to which hatred can usefully be linked to mental disorder.

Thinking about 'hate' crime

i. What is 'hate' in the context of 'hate crime'?

Barbara Perry (2001) suggests that, as is the case with crime in general, it is very difficult to construct an exhaustive definition of 'hate crime' that is able to take account of all of its facets. Crime is of course socially constructed and means different things to different people, different things at different times, and what constitutes a crime in one place may not in another. As Perry suggests, crime is therefore relative and historically and culturally contingent, and this is particularly true of hate crime. This of course has important implications for understanding the boundaries of normal and abnormal behaviour – a point to which we shall return later in this chapter.

In England and Wales, the Crown Prosecution Service (CPS) and the Association of Chief Police Officers (ACPO) have agreed the following common definition of hate crime:

> Any criminal offence which is perceived by the victim or any other person, to be *motivated* by *hostility* or *prejudice* [emphasis added] based on a person's race or perceived race; religion or perceived religion; sexual orientation or perceived sexual orientation; disability or perceived disability; and any crime motivated by hostility or prejudice against a person who is transgender or perceived to be transgender (ACPO, 2014).

Whilst this details some of the characteristics of a hate offence, it acts purely as a broad operational definition and as such there are necessarily a number of separate, narrower legal definitions that also exist. Using race (see Scally, this volume) and religion as examples, arguably the most significant legal definition relates to ss28–32 of the Crime and Disorder Act 1998, which states that an offence is racially or religiously aggravated or motivated if:

(a) at the time of committing the offence, or immediately before or after doing so, the offender *demonstrates* towards the victim of the offence *hostility* [emphases added] based on the victim's membership (or presumed membership) of a racial (or religious) group or;
(b) the offence is *motivated* (wholly or partly) by *hostility* [emphases added] towards members of a racial (or religious) group based on their membership of that group.

For our purposes in this chapter, a central problem relates to the word 'hate' and what, exactly, is meant by it. Despite the frequency with which the term is used, for the purpose of furthering our understanding of hate crime, the word hate is distinctly unhelpful. As Sullivan (1999) points out in a dated but nonetheless still relevant observation, for all our zeal to attack hate we still have a remarkably vague idea of what hate actually is, and despite the powerful and emotional images that it invokes, it is still far less nuanced an idea than prejudice, bias, bigotry, hostility, anger or just a mere aversion to others. The question is, then, when we talk about 'hate', do we mean all of these things or just the extremes of them? In contemporary explanations of hate crime, it is often the former (see Hall, 2013). If we consider the two definitions presented above then we can see that neither of them speak of 'hate' as a causal factor. Rather, the definitions refer to prejudice, hostility or bias, or -isms. Clearly, then, hate crime thus defined is not really about hate, but about criminal behaviour motivated by prejudice, of which hate is just one small and extreme part.

To illustrate this position, in the absence of a precise legal definition of 'hostility' the Crown Prosecution Service (2012) advises prosecutors that consideration should be given to ordinary dictionary definitions, which include ill-will, ill-feeling, spite, contempt, prejudice, unfriendliness, antagonism, resentment and dislike – all emotions far removed from what we might call 'pure' hatred. As Sullivan (1999) rightly suggests, if 'hate' is to stand for all of these varieties of human experience, and everything in between, then the war against it will likely be so vast as to be quixotic.

In seeking to explain hate and hate crime, American legal scholars Jacobs and Potter (1998) have created what has since become a seminal model for understanding modern conceptualisations of the phenomena. They correctly explain that for a crime to become a hate crime, two core elements are required. First, there needs to be a perpetrator who 'hates' their victim and, second, there needs to be a causal link between the offender's 'hate' and the commission of the offence. As such, at the most basic level, hate crimes are offences motivated by prejudice; pre-existing criminal incidents or offences in which the offender's prejudice against the victim or the victim's group plays some part in their victimisation. But of course it is not that simple, and this basic definition masks a number of crucial issues that cannot easily be ignored.

Consequently, in attempting to adequately conceptualise 'hate crime', we must consider a number of key questions; what prejudices when transformed into action are we going to criminalise (a crucial question if we are to suggest that these 'hates' are somehow innate)? How will we know if these actions truly constitute a hate crime? What crimes are we going to include in our definition? Which groups will be acceptable to us as victims? How strong must an offender's 'hatred' be? How strong must the relationship between the 'hatred' and the offence be? Must that link be wholly or just partially causal? Who will decide? How will we decide? How can we guard against hatred without impinging upon people's basic democratic freedoms? And, of course, why is it important to consider these questions? The answer to this last question is crucial. As Jacobs and Potter (1998, p. 27) suggest, how much hate crime there is and what the appropriate response should be depends upon how hate crime is conceptualised and defined.

As a result of the need to address these questions, Jacobs and Potter (1998) suggest that hate crime, as a contemporary social construct, is a potentially expansive concept that covers a great many offenders and situations. This, they argue, can be usefully conceptualised into four categories reflecting variations in the degree of the offender's prejudice (high or low, or in other words, prejudiced or not very prejudiced), and the strength of the causal relationship (strong or weak) between the criminal behaviour and the officially designated prejudice.

As far as understanding hate and hate crime is concerned, offenders that are highly prejudiced, and whose prejudice is a strong (or indeed the sole) cause of the offending behaviour, are relatively unproblematic. Indeed, these offenders are the ones that we probably associate most when we think of the word 'hate' in its most extreme form. As such this conceptualisation represents clear-cut hate crimes where there is little doubt that the offender *hates* his or her victim in the truest sense of the word (such as, for example, those identified at the start of this chapter). Within the criminological literature, these are often referred to as 'mission' offenders, based upon a typology created by McDevitt et al., (2002), where such individuals are totally committed to their hate and view the objects of this hate as an evil that must be removed from the world. It is this obsessive attachment, or 'paranoid partnership', that Gaylin (2003: 5) suggests is definitive of true hatred. Jacobs and Potter (1998) argue, therefore, that if hate crimes included only cases like these, the concept would not be ambiguous, difficult to understand, or controversial, and nor would there be many hate crimes occurring because cases like these, generally, are rare – a point reiterated by McDevitt et al.'s typology.

However, the contemporary social construction of hate crime as a political and legal artifact does not draw the line at these 'clear cut' cases, and it is when we consider the other three conceptualisations that things become more complicated. The second (high prejudice but low causation), for example, refers to highly prejudiced offenders, such as those referred to above, but whose offending is not strongly or solely motivated by 'hate' but by some other motive, for example economics, or hunger. In the strictest sense such offences would not, and indeed should not, be considered hate crimes because they are not motivated by prejudice, but by something else, despite the fact that the offender may hold prejudices against the victim.

The third and fourth conceptualisations present different challenges for understanding hate and hate crime. Low prejudice but high causation refers to offenders who are not particularly prejudiced, or whose prejudices may be largely subconscious, but which nevertheless have a strong causal link to the offence. In other words, here the strength of the motivation is often overlooked at the expense of a perceived causal relationship. That is, a crime is committed by a member of *one group* against a member of *different group* and a hate crime is *assumed* to have occurred. For Jacobs and Potter, it is these inter-group incidents that erroneously dominate official hate crime statistics.

Finally, low prejudice and low causation represents many incidents or offences that are described by Jacobs and Potter (1998, p. 26) as being 'situational' in that they arise from ad hoc disputes or short tempers, but are neither products of strong prejudicial attitudes nor are they strongly causally related to the incident in question. In essence, there is something of a 'normality' to the 'hate' conceptualised here – a position also noted elsewhere within the hate crime literature (see for example Sibbitt, 1997 and Iganski, 2008). Whilst conceiving hate as 'normal' might seem a little odd, Sullivan (1999, p. 3) illustrates two examples that may well resonate:

> Of course by hate we mean something graver and darker than this lazy kind of prejudice. But the closer you look at this distinction, the fuzzier it gets. Much of the time we harbour little or no malice toward people of other backgrounds or ethnicities or ways of life. But then a car cuts you off at an intersection and you find yourself noticing immediately that the driver is a woman, or black, or old, or fat, or white, or male. Or you are walking down a city street at night and hear footsteps quickening behind you. You look around and see that it is a white woman and not a black man, and you are instantly relieved. These impulses are so spontaneous they are almost involuntary. But where did they come from?

This, of course, is a key question. Moreover, Jacobs and Potter's model illustrates that under some definitions and interpretations, such as the broad definitions used in England and Wales, the 'hates' and the associated incidents found in each of the four cells of their model have the potential to be labelled as hate crimes (or at least hate incidents), and under others they do not. The number of hate crimes in society is therefore entirely determined by how hate crime is defined, conceptualised and interpreted, as is our interpretation of what 'hate' is, or might be. The problem is that the definitions currently in use in many jurisdictions around the world ensure that the majority of officially labelled hate crimes are not motivated by hate at all, but by prejudice, which is often an entirely different thing.

In short, Jacobs and Potter's model serves to illustrate that hate crimes, and the 'hates' that underpin them, are in effect a social construction, and, as Sullivan (1999) puts it, the transformation of a 'psychological mystery' into a 'facile political artefact', often far removed from the 'true hatred' to which McDevitt et al. and Gaylin both refer, has served to considerably complicate our understanding of hatred. Reflecting on this point, Sullivan (1999, p. 54) notes that:

> Hate used to be easier to understand. When Sartre described anti-Semitism in his 1964 essay 'Anti-Semite and Jew', he meant a very specific array of

firmly held prejudices, with a history, an ideology and even a pseudo-science to back them up. He meant a systematic attempt to demonise and eradicate an entire race...And when we talk about hate, we often mean this kind of phenomenon. But this brand of hatred is mercifully rare...These professional maniacs are to hate crime what serial killers are to murder. They should certainly not be ignored but they represent...'niche haters': cold-blooded, somewhat deranged, often poorly socialised psychopaths...But their menace is a limited one, and their hatred is hardly typical of anything widespread.

As such, any discussion about whether the motivations behind hate crime offending should, or even can, be classified as mental disorder is therefore necessarily complicated by the reality that, *in contemporary conceptualisations at least, hate crime is rarely motivated by hate*. It would seem, then, that if we are to usefully explore the utility of considering the motivations for hate crime as a form of mental disorder, then we arguably need to skew our attention towards the narrow motivations and behaviours that are likely to be found in Cell One of Jacobs and Potter's model. Here we are likely to find the types of haters of whom Sullivan and others speak, where the focus is less on hate and hate crime as socially constructed political artefacts, but rather more specifically on hatred as an extreme psychological phenomenon.

ii. Hate as the motivation for criminal behaviour

It is worth noting at this juncture that hate crime is still relatively new to the criminological lexicon. Its origins are traceable to the late 1970s and early 1980s, and its emergence as a contemporary social problem has been largely driven by concerns relating to the disproportionate victimisation of certain groups based on various inherent personal characteristics (see Hall, 2013, for a wider discussion). Consequently, Perry (2009) has suggested that research on, and theorising about, *perpetrators* and their *motivations* has been scant partially because hate crime is 'new' to the criminological horizon, partially because it has predominantly concentrated on issues of victimisation. But also because of a lack of agreement about how exactly we should define 'hate crime', and of course, the implications that necessarily follow for the production of reliable data upon which to base research and to construct conceptual frameworks. Indeed, writing in 1999, Bowling suggested that research into perpetrators was so scarce that they represented a 'devilish effigy' within the criminological literature. Although progress in this area has since been made, Bowling's statement remains uncomfortably close to the truth.

Perhaps unsurprisingly given the often secular nature of the social sciences, explanations of hate and hate crime offending have been proffered in a rather disparate and often isolated manner, leaving us with a somewhat disjointed framework of analysis. To paraphrase Stern's (2005) view of the analytical frameworks proffered by different scholarly disciplines:

- if we think of hate as a mental disorder, then analysis and treatment is considered the cure;
- if hate is a product of the individual or the individual in a group context, then psychology or social psychology may hold the answers;
- if it is a product of economics, then economic recovery is the solution;
- if political events are the cause, then we need to effect social change;
- if it is considered to be criminal, then we need criminology and an effective criminal justice system;
- if a lack of education is the underpinning factor, then we should educate;
- if it is a product of the social world, the answer is in sociology;
- if it is caused by culture, then anthropology may assist;
- if politics is a causal factor, then let us turn to political science, and so on.

From this brief overview though, it should at least be clear that notwithstanding both Bowling's and Perry's concerns, potential explanations for hate and hate offending are many and varied, and come from a range of disciplines. But they are also inconclusive. Moreover, Gaylin (2003, p. 14) argues that socio-economic and political explanations are insufficient because they assume a rational basis for hatred and suggest a direct link between the hater's needs and the selection of their victims, and in so doing deny the pathological core of hatred. Clearly, there is not the space here to consider the contributions of each of these available analytical frameworks to our understanding of hate and hate crime (see Hall, 2013, 2014, for a more detailed discussion). So, for the purposes of this chapter, and in line with Gaylin's observations, we shall concentrate on those made by psychology and, of course, psychiatry, in an attempt to establish the extent to which hatred might be usefully considered to be a mental disorder.

Hatred and the individual

i. Psychology

The various definitions of hate crime in existence around the world illustrate, as we have noted, that this form of offending is not always about *hate*, but rather it is predominantly about *prejudice*, of which hate is just a small part. It follows then that if we want to understand hate crime then we should explore the nature of prejudice. Fortunately, as Stangor (2000) points out, there are few if any topics that have engaged the interests of social psychologists as much as those of *prejudice, stereotypes* and *discrimination* where, as Paluck and Green (2009) note, the 'remarkable volume' of literature on prejudice ranks amongst the most impressive in all of social science. This, Stangor suggests, is a consequence of the immense practical importance that such studies hold for understanding the effects of these issues on both individuals and societies, particularly given the increasing diversity of the world we live in. And as Perry (2009) suggests, these concepts mark the starting point for theorising about the perpetrators of hate crime. Indeed, she notes that the literature has been dominated by psychological and social-psychological accounts that necessarily emphasise individual-level analyses (Perry, 2009, p. 56), including significant contributions from Allport on the nature of prejudice (1954); Adorno et al. on authoritarianism (1950); Tajfel and Turner on social identity (1979); Sherif and Sherif on realistic conflict (1953); Bandura on social learning (1977), and Stephan and Stephan (1996) on integrated threat, to name but a few (see Hall, 2013, 2014, for a broader discussion of psychological theorising in relation to hate crime).

However, for all our theorising about these concepts, the existing literature tells us remarkably little about *how* prejudice transforms into actions that would constitute hate crimes. Indeed, there is little consensus for theories that seek to explain this phenomenon. It is also clear that there are many kinds of prejudice that vary greatly and have different psychological dynamics underpinning them, and this can have important implications for responding to hate crimes. Furthermore, because prejudices are independent psychological responses they can be expressed, as Allport illustrates, in a bewildering number of ways, ranging from a mild dislike or general aversion to others to extreme acts of violence. But (and this is crucial for our understanding of hate-motivated offending), the position as Green et al. (2001, p. 27) suggest is one that still holds true today;

> It might take the better part of a lifetime to read the prodigious research literature on prejudice...yet scarcely any of this research examines directly and systematically the question of why prejudice erupts into violence.

Stern (2005) reiterates this point. Whilst *psychology* informs us that most people are capable of hatred and gives us some insights into the relationship between identity and hate, its rather narrow focus on the individual as an explanation is necessarily limited and needs, if it is to provide more comprehensive answers, to be integrated into a larger framework. The broader approach taken by *social psychology*, which considers the individual in social situations where certain attributes may come to the fore, offers arguably greater insight into intergroup conflict and, as Stern points out, this 'treasure trove' of research also suggests some possibilities for responding to the problem. Nevertheless, whilst collectively psychology has some important contributions to make to our understanding of hate, it does not provide the complete explanation of hate-motivated offending that we might hope for.

Moreover, the psychological literature is clear that the holding of prejudices, both positive and negative, is an inevitable part of human nature. But, as Gaylin (2003) argues, to suggest that *hatred* is normal to the human condition is too simplistic an argument to sustain. After all, he suggests, even given the opportunity and freedom to hate or express hatred without obstruction or sanction, most of us would still not choose to do so. So whilst prejudice might be normal, hatred it would seem is not – a point arguably lost in the contemporary social construction of hate crime, and indeed in the understanding of how 'hate' and 'mental disorder' intersect.

A significant contributor to this lack of distinction between prejudice and hatred within the literature, it seems, has been psychology's preoccupation with prejudice and its normality to the human condition as an aspect of personality, rather than a specific focus on hatred as an 'abnormal' psychological disorder. Indeed, even Allport's (1954) seminal text *The Nature of Prejudice*, which ran to 519 pages and is considered to be the departure point for most, if not all, subsequent research into prejudice, dedicated just three pages directly to hatred (pp. 363–365, although as Gaylin points out, Allport was a psychologist studying normal personality, not a psychiatrist involved with mental illness). Gaylin, however, emphasises the importance of distinguishing between prejudice and bigotry and hatred, describing the former as a waystation on the road to the latter, and argues that there is indeed an important role for psychiatry in the understanding of pathological hatred:

> To understand hatred...we must get into the head of the hater. We now have a psychological framework for doing this. We must apply modern psychological understanding of perception, motivation, and behaviour to discover what hatred is. Only when we have identified the nature of the beast can we properly address the environmental conditions that support it...Hatred is a severe psychological disorder. The pathological haters...externalis[e] their internal frustrations and conflicts on a hapless scapegoat population. They are 'deluded', and their self-serving and distorted perceptions allow them to justify their acts of hatred against the enemy they have created. We must start our investigation, therefore, with an examination of the hater's mind rather than his milieu...To date there has been little call for such information, and little volunteered from the psychological community (Gaylin, 2003, pp. 14–15).

ii. Psychiatry

Bell and Dunbar (2012) echo Gaylin's final point above, noting that, unlike sociology that has a long-held interest in intergroup relations and prejudice, particularly in the form of racism, the field of mental health has rarely concerned itself with such issues. Echoing the fields of criminology and hate studies, they suggest that the emphasis of mental health studies has been on the *effects* of racism on those that are on the receiving end, with limited attention given to the mental health status of the holder of virulent racist or xenophobic beliefs, with (so far as we can ascertain) even less attention being paid to other forms of hatred (homophobia, religious bias, transphobia, and so on).

This can perhaps in part be explained, as Gaylin (2003) suggests (again echoing the outcomes of the contemporary social construction of hate crime more generally), by confusion resulting from the modern expansion of the definition of mental disorder far beyond its original conception, where the associated terminology has come to be used differently depending upon both the environment and the user. In seeking some clarity, Gaylin (2003, pp. 28–29) suggests that hatred, as opposed to prejudice and bigotry, should be viewed not as an *alternative*, but rather as a *prerequisite* to investigating the social conditions that encourage its emergence, and as such is best understood through the exploration of its three major components:

1. For Gaylin, hatred is an intense emotion, and therefore to understand it, one should have a sophisticated understanding of human emotions.
2. Beyond simply being an emotion, for Gaylin hatred is also a psychological condition; a disorder of perception; a form of quasi-delusional thinking, and as such one must also understand the nature of a delusion as a symptom of severe mental disease. He also argues that one must similarly examine the meaning of the paranoid shift that is central to the thinking of a hating individual and a culture of hatred, which will ultimately lead, he suggests, to a concern with symptom formation.
3. Finally, Gaylin argues that hatred requires an attachment to an object, the choice of which may be rational or irrational. Obsessive hatred, he suggests, is by definition irrational, and the choice of victim is more often dictated by the unconscious needs and the personal history of the hater than by the nature or actions of the hated.

There is not the space here to fully explore Gaylin's position, but he emphasises that in order to understand the mind of the hater, one must be aware that both hatred and paranoia are symptoms, and that the symptom should be viewed as a misguided repair, and therefore one should try to locate the underlying conflict that the hatred attempts to accommodate (Gaylin, 2003, p. 108). Similarly to the way in which phobics find ways to displace their anxiety, he suggests, so the hater, deluded by a severely damaged and debased sense of self, finds a person or group on whom they can displace their rage and anger at being a *victim* at the hands of *some manipulative and vindictive enemy* who is deemed to be responsible for the *desperate straits* in which the hater perceives themselves to be.

Crucially though, Gaylin acknowledges that in Western societies in particular, there will always be sources of anxiety and insecurity that will lead many to experience paranoia, but for the hater, this feeling is likely to be more permanent than transient. Thus, he suggests that the paranoid personality shares all of the elements observed in the paranoid psychotic – *negativism, suspicion, chronic anger, self-referentiality, narcissism,* and *paranoid shift* (or *projectionism*) – whilst retaining a modicum of reality

The mention of *reality* necessarily brings us to the key issue of differentiating between *normal* and *abnormal* behaviour, and between *abnormal* behaviour and *illness* – a distinction that necessarily has the potential to cloud our understanding of human behaviour considerably and, in the case of the latter, open up the possibility of mitigating circumstances and diminished responsibility within criminal proceedings. In much the same way that definitions of crime, and more specifically definitions of hate crime, vary from place to place, so the extent to which an individual is considered mentally disordered will also vary depending on cultural norms. So, for example, whilst to us in the West the motivations of a suicide bomber in the Middle East might seem incomprehensible, they may be considered within the boundaries of normalcy in the culture from which they emerged. As Gaylin (2003) rightly notes, this situation is compounded as a consequence of the porous boundary between normal and sick behaviour, and defining the latter is dependent upon defining the former which, given the diversity of human life and the range of cultural norms, is no easy task.

Bell and Dunbar (2012, p. 696) acknowledge that any attempt to examine the psychological aetiology and consequences of *racism* does indeed need to consider the larger social context, and as with the study of any pathological state needs to be measured against norms, tolerance, and sanctions found within that larger social context. However, they argue that clinical experience demonstrates that racism in particular may indeed be a manifestation of a delusional process, a consequence of contact-derived anxiety, or a feature of an individual's personality, and that racism usually results from a multitude of biopsychosocial factors that interact in complex ways. They suggest, however, that a central problem is that racism (along with other forms of hatred) has consistently been omitted from each edition (including the most recent, published in 2013) of the American Psychiatric Association's *Diagnostic and Statistical Manual of Mental Disorders*. The consequence, they lament, is that there has been little awareness of racism as being a symptom of psychiatric disorders or thoughts, feelings, or behaviour that should be observed and explored in regard to personality disorders.

Nevertheless, Bell and Dunbar (2012) suggest that it is feasible to include racism, and indeed other forms of 'hate', as 'pathological bias', proposing the following specific clinical problems of pathological bias as warranting attention: *outgroup avoidance*; *trauma-induced*; *antisocial*; *narcissist/labile*; and *paranoid*. Crucially, they clarify the position that:

> Of critical importance in assessing pathological bias is the linkage between beliefs concerning a specific outgroup and the mental health of the individual holding the beliefs. In other words, simply being biased is not presumed to be a mental disorder or a co-occurring clinical problem. Rather, when the bias is a significant moderator upon the mental health and social functioning of the individual, then serious attention to the consequences of the condition is warranted (Bell and Dunbar, 2012, p. 699).

Moreover, they suggest that there are three signifiers of pathological bias: intrusive ideation and rumination concerning outgroup persons; aversive affects associated with outgroup ideation and contact experience; and relationship-damaging behaviours employed in benign contact situations (Bell and Dunbar, 2012, p. 699). Although there is not the space here to fully explore the case proffered by Bell and Dunbar in relation to the five subtypes of pathological bias that they identify, it is worth briefly noting their position in relation to each:

1. *Avoidant*: For Bell and Dunbar, the avoidant subtype is characterised by the conscious effort to minimise contact with, and awareness of, an outgroup in order to alleviate the distress associated with these activities. These are thought to co-occur, they suggest, with avoidant and obsessive-compulsive personality disorder diagnoses, together with social phobia and generalised anxiety disorder.
2. *Trauma-induced*: Bell and Dunbar explain that the clinical features of this subtype are similar to those of *Post-Traumatic Stress Disorder*, such as avoidance of outgroup contact, intrusive thoughts relating to victimisation experiences by that outgroup, and hypersensitivity. They also suggest that this subtype may co-occur with borderline, and antisocial, personality disorder, specifically in members of racist gangs.
3. *Paranoid*: For Bell and Dunbar, this subtype reflects a more serious form of pathological bias, where, they suggest, the cognitions of the individual are 'constricted, enduring and chronically attentive to the malevolent intentions of denigrated outgroups'. Probable co-occurring diagnostic disorders, they argue, include paranoid disorder, personality disorders (notably paranoid, schizoid, and schizotypal), and obsessive-compulsive disorder.
4. *Narcissist/labile:* This subtype, Bell and Dunbar (2012, p. 700) suggest, is most consistent with the clinical criteria of narcissistic personality disorder, and may be a co-occurring problem of bipolar disorder, especially hypomania, as well as neurocognitive dysfunction. This subtype, they note, is 'marked

by the articulated ingroup entitlement, affect dysregulation, and overt hostility in their conceptualisation and interactions with outgroups'.

5. *Antisocial*: The final subtype identified by Bell and Dunbar is characteristic of individuals who engage in aggression and provocation in contact situations, and who have a conscious, articulated hostile worldview concerning members of outgroups. Developmentally, they suggest, these individuals may have prior experiences of childhood trauma and/or adult intergroup victimisation experiences as found with the trauma-based subtype.

Thus, Bell and Dunbar state that for all five types, in their experience, the problems of pathological bias adversely impact upon the individual's level of functioning. In addition, they argue (2012, p. 701) that:

> There is evidence to support the idea that personality characteristics may reveal either a vulnerability to, or a protective buffer against, pathological bias, contingent upon stable and enduring dimensions of personality. Knowing which personality characteristics are conducive to either problems or protective factors is integral in accurate indication, prognosis, and prevention. Unfortunately the question of extreme or pathological forms of bias as a stable personality characteristic has been infrequently examined.

So, despite the thought-provoking arguments visited above, it seems our quest to *comprehensively* link hatred to mental disorder is rather thwarted by a lack of research in this area. Nevertheless, the necessarily limited evidence presented here leaves us with plenty of food for thought concerning the questions we posed at the very start of this chapter, which we shall revisit here.

Discussion and concluding comments

As we sit down to write this final section (Sunday 14 September 2014), our televisions are awash with the breaking news of the beheading of David Haines, the British aid worker held hostage by Islamic State militants. The news feeds are full of commentary and opinion replete with terms such as *brutal, barbaric, despicable, evil, inhumane, monstrous, grotesque, sick, cancerous, psychopathic*, and of course, *hateful*. Whilst there is considerable debate within the literature concerning the extent to which hate crime, terrorism, and extremism overlap (again, a product of the social construction of the problem), the motivations for this behaviour, the latest in a series of beheadings of Western hostages, largely transcend these academic debates, and as such are central to many of the discussion points within this chapter. Moreover, as we write this, these same news commentaries are also discussing the possible avenues open to the British government to exact *retribution*. Whilst the response from the West remains to be seen, the discussions in the news relating to the options available serve as a powerful reminder of the wider impact and very real local and global implications that hatred, and the need to combat it, can have.

If you recall, in this chapter we set out to explore questions relating to the meaning of 'hatred'; the connection it might have with mental ill-health; whether 'hatred' can or should be considered a mental disorder in its own right or merely regarded as a symptom of other recognised mental pathologies; whether 'hatred' can ever be considered as 'normal' behaviour; and what the implications of applying such labels might be. In line with much of the literature in this area, conclusive answers are thin on the ground.

To our minds, it is undoubtedly the case that as 'hatred' has become framed as a specific socio-legal problem, its meaning has shifted considerably from the somewhat narrower conceptualisations to be found within more medically oriented circles, as illustrated in Jacobs and Potter's model, described earlier. In particular, questions surrounding both the strength of an individual's prejudice and the strength of the causal relationship between that prejudice and the resulting behaviour, often differentiated in law in the form of offences *motivated* or *aggravated* by broader interpretations of 'hate'. Thus, before any meaningful discussion concerning whether or not the motivations for hate crimes can reasonably be classified as a mental disorder can take place, it is first crucial to ensure that we are in fact talking about the same thing. As we have seen, this is not currently an assumption that can be readily made.

The question of hatred's link with mental ill-health, including whether or not it is a mental disorder in its own right, or is instead a symptom of other mental disorders, is simultaneously both easier *and* more difficult to ascertain. Let us explain what we mean by this. Formally, hatred (or extreme forms of pathological bias) in any incarnation is *not* a mental disorder, and nor is it a symptom of other existing mental disorders. It does not, and has never, appeared in the American Psychiatric Association's *Diagnostic and Statistical Manual of Mental Disorders* – a rejection dating back to the 1960s and consistently rooted in concerns surrounding the medicalisation of what is held to be a widespread social problem for culture, and not medicine, to solve (Rooks, 2012). But as we have seen in this chapter, notwithstanding the APA's stance, this remains a contentious area of debate within psychiatry, and thus the matter of whether or not hate *should* be considered as a mental disorder, or otherwise as a symptom, in *some* individuals, is rather more tricky to ascertain and remains far from settled.

Moreover, scholarship's preoccupation with the broader notion of prejudice as an aspect of personality, as opposed to hatred as a psychological disorder, as highlighted by the four cells of Jacobs and Potter's model and illustrated by Sullivan's contention, mentioned earlier, gives oxygen to the argument that the motivations for the vast majority of hate crimes thus defined may be considered more normal than abnormal. For example, we would contend that it requires a considerable stretch of the imagination to believe that each of the 278,000 or so hate incidents that occur each year in England and Wales are committed by individuals with a mental disorder (Home Office, Ministry of Justice and Office for National Statistics, 2013, p. 12). This principle similarly applies even in extreme examples. For example, the idea that each of the half a million or so individuals who took part in the Holocaust, or indeed in any other genocide, possessed a mental disorder requires an even greater imaginationary leap. As Waller (2002) and others (for example, Goldhagen, 1996; Browning, 2001) point out, in such circumstances it is the acts that are perpetrated, rather than the individuals who perpetrate them, that are extraordinary.

In explaining how this can occur, Waller points in part to a *culture of cruelty* that enables individuals to initiate, uphold and manage their 'evil'. Ordinary people, he suggests, are influenced by a complex web of social forces that enable them to commit extreme acts. This reference to culture and cultural norms, which has been a feature of many of the discussion points in this chapter, returns us to the pivotal issue of how we distinguish between normal, abnormal, disordered and sick behaviour. As we have seen, this too is culturally contingent, and needs to be measured against relevant social norms. So for all the revulsion at the murder of David Haines and others, which we share, it is of course likely that these actions and the motivations behind them, that many will perceive to be *abnormal,* are considered *anything but* in the cultural milieu in which the Islamic State militants are operating. In this sense then, identifying abnormal behaviour is dependent on defining normal behaviour. In a wildly diverse world this is no easy task either, and in effect this means that labeling something as a mental disorder is never absolute.

Finally, we come to the implications of the different positions presented in this chapter. Once again, there are pros and cons to be considered here, but for our purposes they can usefully be clustered into two central issues. On the one hand, as Leon (2005) explains, there are a number of potential benefits, but also a number of challenges, associated with psychiatry's involvement in this area. Using racism as a lens, he argues that:

> ...we might view racism as a public health problem as well as a moral and ethical problem. Putting racism in the public health arena provides us with additional options for dealing with the problem. By including racism in the *DSM* we might classify it as a delusional disorder or a personality disorder among some individuals. But what do we do about the culture or the subculture that harbors the virus of racism and prejudice? Research does not help us with this issue now but may do so in the future. It would involve psychiatry's taking a hard look at pathology in the society as a whole. Are racism and other forms of so-called cultural beliefs that harm others psychopathology? Is psychiatry prepared to confront this question? Maybe it is time that we did.

On the other hand, however, one of the most prominent and persistent arguments against the medicalisation of hatred was starkly presented by the President of the American Psychiatric Association in September 2000:

> Brutal, violent hate crimes are usually committed by mean, not sick, individuals and groups. We must not provide the convenient excuse of mental illness for those who are not genuinely ill. In the instances in which an individual has a psychiatric illness, our criminal justice system makes a clear distinction between those whose illness prevents them from knowing right from wrong in contrast to those whose illness has little bearing on their criminal behavior. Should individuals with antisocial personality disorders and no other psychiatric illnesses be excused for their crimes because they are 'mentally ill'? Of course not. (Borenstein, 2000)

And so, as is the case with much of the literature around hate and hate crime, it seems we are left with as many questions as there are answers. There is clearly an ongoing debate between those who believe that hatred can and should, in some cases, be medicalised, and thus should be a greater concern for psychiatry, and those who do not. Notwithstanding the complex issues involved in doing so, the former argue that alternative insights and treatments for this social problem are indeed achievable. For the latter, there is something of a futility associated with this process, and a danger that criminal behaviour may become excusable, and offenders absolved from criminal responsibility. So, is it useful and sensible to classify the motivations for hate crime as mental disorder? *Sometimes. Maybe.*

References

ACPO (2014). True Vision. http://www.report-it.org.uk/what_is_hate_crime.
Adorno, T. W., Frenkel-Brunswick, E., Levinson, D. J. and Sanford, N. (1950). *The Authoritarian Personality*. New York: Harper.
Allport, G. (1954; 1979). *The Nature of Prejudice*. New York: Addison-Wesley Publishing Company.
Bandura, A. (1977). *Social Learning Theory*. New York: General Learning Press.
Bell, C. C. and Dunbar, E. (2012). Racism and Pathological Bias as a Co-occurring Problem in Diagnosis and Assessment. In T. A. Widiger (ed). *The Oxford Handbook of Personality Disorders*. New York: Oxford University Press.
Borenstein, D. (2000). From the President – Prejudice – Racism. *Psychiatric News*. 15 September . Retrieved 8 September 2014 from http://psychnews.org/pnews/00-09-15/pres9b.html.
Bowling, B. (1999). *Violent Racism: Victimization, Policing and Social Context*. New York: Oxford University Press.
Browning, C. R. (2001). *Ordinary Men: Reserve Police Battalion 101 and the Final Solution in Poland*. London: Penguin.

Crown Prosecution Service (2012). *Hate Crimes and Crimes against Older People*. London: CPS.

Gaylin, W. (2003). *Hatred: the psychological descent into violence*. New York: Public Affairs.

Goldhagen, D. J. (1996). *Hitler's Willing Executioners: Ordinary Germans and the Holocaust*. London: Little, Brown and Company.

Green, D. P., McFalls, L. H., and Smith, J. K. (2003). Hate Crime: An Emergent Research Agenda. In B. Perry (ed.). *Hate and Bias Crime: A reader*. New York: Routledge. 27–48.

Hall, N. (2013). *Hate Crime* (2nd edition). Oxon: Routledge.

Hall, N. (2014). Understanding Hate Crimes: perspectives from the wider social sciences. In N. Hall, A. Corb, P. Giannasi and J. G. D. Grieve (eds). *The Routledge International Handbook on Hate Crime*. Oxon: Routledge.

Home Office, Ministry of Justice and Office for National Statistics. (2013). *An Overview of Hate Crime in England and Wales*. Retrieved from: https://www.gov.uk/government/publications/an-overview-of-hate-crime-in-england-and-wales

Iganski, P. (2008). *Hate Crime and the City*. Bristol: Policy Press.

Jacobs, J., and Potter, K. (1998). *Hate Crimes: Criminal Law and Identity Politics*. Oxford: Oxford University Press.

Leon, R. L. (2005). Racism and Mental Illness. *Psychiatric Services*, 56, 6, doi: 10.1176/appi.ps.56.6.753.

McDevitt, J., Levin, J., and Bennett, S. (2002). Hate Crime Offenders: An Expanded Typology. *Journal of Social Issues*, 58 (2), 303–317.

Paluck, E. L. and Green, D (2009). Prejudice reduction: what works? A review and assessment of research and practice. *Annual Review of Psychology*, 60: 339–367. doi: 10.1146/annurev.psych.60.110707.163607.

Perry, B. (2001). *In the Name of Hate: Understanding Hate Crimes*. New York: Routledge.

Perry, B. (2009). The Sociology of Hate: Theoretical Approaches. In B. Perry (ed.) *Hate Crimes* (vol. 1). Westport: Praeger.

Rooks, N. M. (2012). Is Racism an Illness? *Time*. 4 May 4. Retrieved 8 September 2014 from http://ideas.time.com/2012/05/04/is-racism-an-illness/.

Sherif, M. and Sherif, C. W. (1953). *Groups in Harmony and Tension: An Integration of Studies on Inter-group Relations*. New York: Harper.

Sibbitt, R. (1997). *The Perpetrators of Racial Harassment and Racial Violence*. Home Office Research Study No. 176. London: Home Office.

Stangor, C. (ed.) (2000). *Stereotypes and Prejudice*. Philadelphia: Psychology Press.

Stephan, W. G. and Stephan, C. (1996). Predicting prejudice. *International Journal of Intercultural Relations*, 20, 1–12.

Stern, K. (2005). *Hate Matters: The Need for an Interdisciplinary Field of Hate Studies*. New York: American Jewish Committee.

Sullivan, A. (1999). What's so bad about hate? The illogic and illiberalism behind hate crime laws. *New York Times Magazine*, 26 September.

Tajfel, H. and Turner, J. C. (1979). An Integrative Theory of Intergroup Conflict. In W. G. Austin and S. Worchel (eds). *The Social Psychology of Intergroup Relations*. Monterey, CA: Brooks/Cole. 33–47.

Waller, J. (2002). *Becoming Evil: How Ordinary People Commit Genocide and Mass Killing*. Oxford: Oxford University Press.

7
Mental Health Needs and Neurodevelopmental Disorders amongst Young Offenders: Implications for Policy and Practice

Prathiba Chitsabesan and Nathan Hughes

Background

There is growing evidence that young people within the youth justice system have high levels of needs in a number of different areas, including health, education, and social and emotional well-being (Chitsabesan et al., 2006; Lader et al., 2000). In particular, studies consistently suggest high levels of mental health needs (see, for example, Teplin et al., 2002) and neurodevelopmental disorders amongst young offenders (as summarised by Hughes et al., 2012). Despite evidence of high prevalence, many of these needs are unmet due to lack of appropriate screening and identification and poor continuity of care (Harrington and Bailey, 2005). This is particularly apparent amongst young people in custody. A review by the Office of the Children's Commissioner for England (2011) raised concerns about the lack of provision in place for supporting and promoting the emotional well-being and mental health of children and young people in the youth justice system. In this chapter we explore the prevalence of a wide range of mental health needs and neurodevelopmental disorders amongst young offenders, offering comparison to rates in the general population. We then consider the implications for approaches to screening, assessment and intervention to support the identification and effective management of these needs.

The prevalence of mental health needs and neurodisability amongst young offenders

Table 7.1 summarises a range of studies that identify rates of specific mental health needs and neurodevelopmental disorders amongst young people within

Table 7.1 The prevalence of psychiatric and neurodevelopmental disorders

Type of disorder	Reported prevalence rates amongst young people in the general population	Reported prevalence rates amongst young offenders
Psychotic disorder	0.4%[1]	1–3.3%[2]
Depressive disorder	0.2–3%[3]	8–29%[4]
Anxiety disorder	3.3%[5]	9–21%[6]
Post-traumatic stress disorder	0.4%[7]	11–25%[8]
Substance misuse disorder	7%[9]	37–55%[10]
Learning disabilities	2–4%[11]	23–32%[12]
Dyslexia	10%[13]	21–43%[14]
Communication disorders	5–7%[15]	60–65%[16]
Attention deficit hyperactive disorder	3–9%[17]	11.7–18.5%[18]
Autistic spectrum disorder	0.6–1.2%[19]	15%[20]
Traumatic brain injury	24–31.6%[21]	65%[22]

the youth justice system and the general population. Identifying and comparing such rates is problematic for a number of reasons. For example, rates of specific disorders are diverse due to differences in methodology between studies, including differences in sampling techniques and assessment tools, as well as variations in sample sizes. Differences in legal processes and models of service delivery within secure institutions may also contribute to differences in population samples and consequently influence the generalisability of study findings. Nonetheless the studies discussed below consistently indicate a higher prevalence of a broad range of disorders amongst young offenders.

Psychiatric disorders and mental health

Research on the prevalence of serious psychiatric disorders amongst the general population suggests rates of between 7% and 12% (Roberts et al., 1998). In comparison, studies exploring similar disorders in young offenders suggest higher rates. For example, Golzari et al. (2006) report the prevalence of psychiatric disorders amongst young males in custody in the United States (US) to be between 60% and 70%, and between 60 and 80% for young females in custody. The North West Juvenile Project (NWJP) screened a large random sample of offenders detained at Cook County Juvenile Temporary Detention Centre in the US using the Diagnosis Interview Schedule for Children, Version 2.3 (DISC-2.3). The study found that 61% of males and 70% of females met the criteria for a psychiatric disorder, and that affective disorders and substance misuse problems were common (Abram et al., 2003; Teplin et al., 2002). The following sections explore the prevalence of a wide range of specific psychiatric disorders, as identified by studies conducted within the UK and internationally, each of which demonstrate further the higher rate of mental health needs amongst youth offending populations. These studies can contribute to a greater understanding of the needs of young people within the criminal justice system and thereby the development of appropriate services and strategies to support them.

Psychotic disorders

Psychotic disorders are defined by symptoms of delusion (false beliefs about self or others that effects normal social functioning) or hallucination (sensing things that are not there, whether by seeing, hearing, smelling or feeling). The National Institute for Health and Clinical Excellence (NICE) report an estimated prevalence rate of 0.4% for psychotic disorders in children aged between 5 and 18 years (NICE, 2011a). This is in comparison to an observed prevalence rate of 10% for young males serving a custodial sentence in England and Wales (Lader et al., 2000). This figure is, however, notably higher than the incidence rates reported elsewhere. The few studies exploring the prevalence of psychotic disorders in young offenders suggest rates of 1–2% (Gosden et al., 2003; Teplin et al., 2002). This is comparable to the meta-regression by Fazel et al. (2008) which found that 3.3% of males and 2.7% of females in youth custody were diagnosed with a psychotic illness.

Reasons for differences in prevalence rates between studies may be secondary to the screening tools used, criteria for diagnosis and the professional background of the administrator. For example, Teplin et al. (2002) found that in the NWJP prevalence rates of psychosis dropped from 25% to 1% if additional criteria were included, such as persistent symptoms for at least a week, no substance use during this time, and if assessed by a psychiatrist or clinical psychologist. Nonetheless, even the lower of these figures suggests an approximately tenfold increased risk of psychotic disorder amongst young people in custody when compared to the general youth population.

Anxiety disorders

Anxiety disorders are characterised by cognitive rumination and autonomic over-activity and can be associated with an identifiable stimulus, although this is not always the case. Anxiety disorders include a range of different disorders, from generalised anxiety disorder to panic attacks and phobias. Green et al. (2005) report that around 3.3% of young people have an anxiety disorder, including 2.2% of those aged between 5 and 10, and 4.4% of those aged between 11 and 16.

Once again these figures seem to be significantly higher amongst offending populations. In their UK-based study of young males in secure care, Kroll et al.

(2002) diagnosed anxiety disorder in 17% of cases. Results from international studies from the US and Holland report rates of diagnosis typically ranging from 9% to 21% (Domalanta et al.,2003; McCabe et al., 2002; Teplin et al., 2002; Vreugdenhil et al., 2004; Wasserman et al., 2010).

The NWJP study (Teplin et al., 2002) also explored rates of trauma and post-traumatic stress disorder (PTSD). The vast majority of offenders had experienced at least one trauma in their lifetime (93%), while 11% were found to meet the criteria for PTSD. A prevalence rate of 9% was found in a UK study of young offenders (Chitsabesan et al., 2006), although, a much greater rate of 25% was found in a study of male young offenders in custody in Russia, with higher PTSD scores associated with higher scores of violence exposure (Ruchkin et al., 2002). This compares to a rate of 0.4% amongst young people aged 11–15 years in the general population (Meltzer et al., 2000).

Substance misuse disorders

Substance misuse disorders are defined by sustained maladaptive behaviours related to or caused by substance misuse (see Pycroft and Green, this volume). In the US, a survey of school-aged children 11–15 years old found that 7% of young people within the general population had used drugs within the last month, with cannabis use being the most common (National Treatment Agency, 2011). In contrast, prevalence rates of substance misuse disorder in young offenders in custody from international studies have ranged from 41% to 55% (Gosden et al., 2003; Teplin et al., 2002; Vreugdenhil et al., 2004) with slightly lower rates (37%) reported for adjudicated non-custodial offenders (McCabe et al., 2002). Within the UK, Kroll et al. (2002) found that 69% of young offenders in a secure unit had substance misuse problems on admission. Similarly high rates of substance misuse were reported in the Office of National Statistics survey of young offenders in custody across England and Wales (Lader et al., 2000).

Analysis of the literature has been complicated by differences in terminology, assessment process and the period of use identified within the study (see Canton, this volume; Pycroft and Green, this volume). Positive associations have also been shown between substance misuse and other disorders, including depression (Pliszka et al., 2000) and Attention Deficit Hyperactivity Disorder (ADHD) (Gudjonsson et al., 2012). Longitudinal studies also show an association with persistent offending (Chitsabesan et al., 2012), and both depressive symptoms and drug use into adulthood (Weisner et al., 2005).

Depression

Depression is a state of prolonged low mood associated with other symptoms, such as loss of enjoyment, reduced motivation, and disturbed sleep and appetite.

Green et al. (2005) suggest that about 0.9% of young people aged 5–15 suffer from depression with increasing prevalence associated with increasing age.

Studies evaluating major depression in male offenders in the US suggest prevalence rates of between 8% and 10% (Domalanta et al., 2003; Wasserman et al., 2010). Similarly, a study of 370 male young offenders in custody in Russia found that 10% of young people had major depression (Ruchkin et al., 2002). Within the UK, higher prevalence rates have been reported. Kroll et al. (2002) followed a group of 97 male young offenders admitted to a secure unit and found that 22% met the criteria for major depression. This was similar to a rate of 18% found in a large national study of young offenders in custody and in the community across England and Wales (Chitsabesan et al., 2006).

Fazel et al. (2008) conducted a meta-analysis of 25 surveys of psychiatric morbidity amongst children and young people in custody, including studies from the UK as well as other international contexts. Their findings suggest that around 11% of boys and 29% of girls had a major depressive disorder (Fazel et al., 2008). The high prevalence of depression in young offenders may be partially explained by the presence of shared risk factors with the development of antisocial behaviour, including social and familial disadvantage and trauma (Farrington, 2002; Loeber and Farrington, 2000).

Self-harm and suicidal behaviour

An association between antisocial behaviour and self-harm or suicidal behaviour has also been demonstrated in research studies. A study of young offenders within the UK found that 1 in 10 offenders reported some episode of self-harm within the last month (Chitsabesan et al., 2006). Self-harm is more prevalent among offenders as certain risk factors for self-harm are more common among this group, including many of those associated with the causes and expression of the psychiatric disorders described above. Predictors of an increased risk include previous attempts, prolonged low mood, attention deficit hyperactivity disorder (ADHD; see below for further discussion), impulsivity, and substance misuse (Putnins, 2005; Sanislow et al., 2003). Studies suggest that while rates of suicidal ideation in young offenders may not be dissimilar from the general adolescent population, lifetime risk of suicide attempts was high at 14% with 2% of young people having made a suicide attempt within the last month (Wasserman et al., 2010). Ruchkin et al. (2003) found that ADHD, but not depression, independently predicted suicidal behaviour, although findings from studies are inconsistent. Rates of suicide are similarly much higher in the offender population compared with non-antisocial peers, possibly as a consequence of greater impulsive behaviour and substance misuse which are more common in this group of young people (Putnins, 2005).

Neurodisability and neurodevelopmental disorders

Childhood neurodisability occurs when there is a compromise of the central or peripheral nervous system due to factors such as genetic vulnerability, birth trauma or brain injury in childhood. It is often the result of a complex mix of influences, including biological factors, such as genetics, and environmental factors, such as trauma, nutritional and emotional deprivation. Such compromises can lead to a wide range of specific neurodevelopmental disorders, with common symptoms including cognitive delay, communication difficulties, and problems with emotional and behavioural control and social functioning. The following sections evidence an association between a diverse range of neurodisabilities and the subsequent development of antisocial behaviour. Antisocial behaviour is a broad construct that may or may not include offending behaviour, but often precedes it. Within England and Wales, youth justice services are increasingly aware of the importance of identifying young people who may be at risk of developing offending behaviour through the role of youth offending prevention teams and development of early help and prevention teams within local authorities.

Learning disability

Many young people who offend will have educational needs secondary to learning, emotional and behavioural difficulties. However, so as to allow young people to access appropriate support, it is important to differentiate this broader group from a smaller subgroup of young people who have a learning disability. A learning disability is defined as an IQ score of less than 70, together with significant difficulties with adaptive or social functioning (i.e. problems with everyday tasks), and onset prior to adulthood (British Psychological Society, 2001). Subsequently, an IQ score of less than 70 is not synonymous with learning disability on its own, although the measurement of adaptive behaviour may be more difficult to assess in criminal justice settings.

Amongst the general population in the UK, McKay and Neal (2009) report that approximately 2% would be anticipated to reach the diagnostic criteria for a learning disability. Generalised learning disability is significantly more common in young people in custody, with research studies suggesting a prevalence of 23–32% (Hughes et al., 2012). High prevalence rates (27% and 32%) are also reported in two recent UK-based studies of young offenders in the secure estate using the Wechsler Intelligence Scale for Children (3rd edition, WISC-III) (Kroll et al., 2002 and Rayner et al., 2005 respectively). Chitsabesan et al. (2007) assessed the learning needs of 301 young offenders in custody and the community using the Wechsler Abbreviated Scale of Intelligence (WASI). The study found that 20% of young people within the youth justice system have a learning disability, with a further 41% assessed as having borderline low average intellectual functioning. The majority of young offenders with a learning disability identified in their study had an IQ in the 'mild range' (between 50 and 69) and may therefore be less likely to have had their learning needs identified in mainstream schools, where those needs are often overshadowed by their challenging behaviour (Herrington, 2009).

Specific learning difficulties

While diagnosis of a learning disability often implies global developmental delay, a learning difficulty is a specific area of difficulty in the context of an individual's overall intelligence, and therefore relative to their IQ. A young person with a specific learning difficulty may be of average or above-average intelligence, yet performance in one or more aspect of their educational achievements may not match this level of intelligence. Within the current UK international classification system for psychiatric disorders (ICD-10; World Health Organization, 1992) specific learning difficulties are classified as relating to reading (dyslexia), written expression (dyspraxia) and mathematics (dyscalculia). More recently the latest edition of the Diagnostic and Statistical Manual of Mental Disorders (DSM-V; American Psychiatric Association, 2013) has moved to a single overall diagnosis, incorporating deficits that impact on academic achievement, rather than limiting learning disorders to diagnoses particular to reading, mathematics and written expression. It is hoped that this new classification will contribute increased diagnostic accuracy and more effective targeting of support.

There are currently few studies exploring prevalence rates of different specific learning difficulties in young offenders. Nonetheless, specific reading difficulties, such as dyslexia, appear significantly more common in young people who offend, with one study suggesting a prevalence of about 43% (Snowling et al., 2000) compared to around 10% of the general population (British Dyslexia Association: www.bdadyslexia.org.uk/about-us.html). A study of male and female offenders serving community orders in Australia found that 21% of young people assessed had significant reading difficulties and 64% had arithmetic problems using the Wechsler Intellectual Achievement Test (Kenny et al., 2006).

In addition, within the UK, one study found that almost half of young offenders had a reading or reading comprehension age below 10 years (Chitsabesan et al., 2007). Whilst this is not necessarily indicative of a neurodevelopmental disorder, this is significant, as the age of criminal responsibility within England and Wales is 10 years, which suggests that many young people within the youth justice system may struggle to follow the legal process and make informed decisions.

Communication disorders

Communication disorders relate to problems with speech, language and communication that significantly impact upon an individual's academic achievement or day-to-day functioning. Tomblin et al. (2000) suggest that between 5% and 7% of children have a developmental disorder of language. This compares to a study by Bryan (2004) which indicated that 60% of a sample of male offenders screened in one young offender institution had specific speech or language difficulties. Similar high rates were found in a study of 72 young offenders accessing a community Intensive Supervision and Surveillance Programme (ISSP) within a youth offending service (Gregory and Bryan, 2011). The results suggested that 65% of those screened had profiles indicating that they had communication difficulties, including expressive language difficulties (28%), receptive language difficulties (45%) and articulation difficulties, such as a stammer (8%).

Particular deficits in verbal skills may also be highlighted through a discrepancy in verbal and performance IQ scores (Moffitt, 1993). Similar differences have been shown to be associated with greater hostile attribution bias (perception deficits of a neutral stimulus as hostile and threatening) or social problems solving tasks in one study of male young offenders (Wong and Cornell, 1999). A meta-analysis exploring performance and verbal IQ scores in antisocial populations across the age span found that this discrepancy was smallest in early childhood and greatest in adolescence (Isen, 2010). Subsequently, verbal deficits may also accumulate over time in childhood, secondary to school failure and exclusion.

Attention deficit hyperactivity disorder

ADHD is characterised by early onset symptoms of inattention, hyperactivity and impulsivity across multiple settings. Whilst these symptoms can be commonplace in children's behaviour, ADHD is characterised by their consistence and persistence (NICE, 2008). Prevalence rates of ADHD in young offenders have varied across studies dependent on the methodology of the study; however, identified rates of ADHD are significantly greater in young offenders in comparison with the general population. Rates of 3–7% are commonly identified in the general population of young people, with the prevalence in boys approximately four times that amongst girls (NICE, 2008). In contrast, a meta-analysis reviewing 25 international studies found a rate of 11.7% for males (Fazel et al., 2008). This is comparable to a prevalence rate of 11% found in both the NWJP (Teplin et al., 2002) and a study of male offenders in secure care within the UK (Kroll et al., 2002).

Longitudinal studies suggest that childhood ADHD predicts later antisocial behaviour (Moffitt, 1993). However, recent research suggests that this association is indirect and mediated through the development of conduct disorder (persistent and pervasive pattern of behavioural difficulties), illicit drug use and peer delinquency (Gudjonsson et al., 2012). Young people with conduct disorder and ADHD have been shown to have greater severity and persistence of antisocial behaviour (Eme, 2009).

Autism

Autism is a neurodevelopmental disorder characterised by a triad of impairment in social communication. These include qualitative differences and impairments in reciprocal social interaction and social communication, combined with restricted interests and repetitive behaviours (NICE, 2011b). These difficulties are manifest early, are lifelong and are associated with delay and deviation in the development of language and social relationships. Like many young people with neurodevelopmental disorders, those with autism can struggle with emotional regulation, displaying marked anxiety, excitement or distress to situations. Certain features of autism may predispose young people to offend, including social naïvety, misinterpretation of social cues and poor empathy.

Baird et al. (2006) report a prevalence rate of about 1% for all autistic spectrum disorders (ASD) in young people, but there is some concern that young people who experience autism may be over-represented among offending populations. The National Autistic Society (2008) suggests that young people with Asperger's syndrome are seven times more likely to come into contact with the criminal justice system than their peers. In one study of 130 young offenders from two institutions in Sweden, 15% of young people were assessed as having an autistic spectrum disorder using structured interviews based on DSM-IV criteria (Anckarsater et al., 2007). However, there are few prevalence studies of young people with autistic spectrum disorders within the youth justice system, and many studies demonstrating an increased prevalence rate have been conducted on a forensic psychiatry sample of offenders suggesting further research is required (Hughes et al., 2012).

Traumatic brain injury

A traumatic brain injury (TBI) is any injury to the brain caused by an impact, and the severity is typically measured by the depth of loss of consciousness (LOC). Whilst there is variation in the definitions, a minor injury is often classified as an injury resulting in a LOC of 5 to 10 minutes or less; mild injuries are those with a LOC of between 10 and 20 minutes; moderate are those with LOC of 20 minutes to 1 hour; and severe injuries are those with LOC for anything above an hour. A recent birth cohort study conducted in New Zealand found that 31.6% of males and 24.2% of females had suffered a head injury by age 25 (McKinley et al., 2008).

A traumatic brain injury can be associated with wide ranging cognitive and behavioural problems. The majority of TBIs appear to be mild and have no lasting effects, although long-term effects on academic performance, behaviour, emotional control and social interactions were reported by over a third of the parents of offenders in one study (Hux et al., 1998). This is reflected in a range of studies which have demonstrated an association between traumatic brain injury and antisocial behavior including an earlier onset of offending history (Timonen et al., 2002) and more violent offending (Williams et al., 2010). Greater severity of TBI was also found to be associated with greater impairment of cognition, earlier onset of criminal behaviour and increased rates of mental illness and substance use (Perron and Howard, 2008).

Identified prevalence rates of TBI among young offenders are variable, however, ranging from 4.5% to 72% (Hughes et al., 2012). A recent study of UK incarcerated young offenders between the ages of 16 and 18 found that of 186 participants, 65.1% report a TBI that left them feeling 'dazed and confused', 46% suffered a TBI with LOC, and 16.6% reported TBI with a LOC of over 10 minutes (Williams et al., 2010). Within this sample, 32% self-reported suffering more than one TBI. These rates are corroborated by Davies et al. (2012) who found that 72.1% of incarcerated young offenders in one UK institution self-reported suffering at least one TBI of any severity, with 41% reporting experiencing a LOC and 45.9% reporting suffering more than one injury.

Comorbidity

Comorbidity is defined as the presence of more than one disorder and is commonplace among young people as many risk factors such as trauma and social disadvantage are shared between disorders. Studies suggest rates from a third to a half of all offenders have comorbid disorders (Vreungendhil et al., 2004; Wasserman et al., 2010). In the NWJP, 57% of females and 46% of males met the criteria for two or more psychiatric disorders (Abram et al., 2003). In this study co-occurrence with substance misuse was common, especially for those with ADHD and conduct disorder. Rates of comorbidity are especially high among young people with early onset behavioural problems (Ruchkin et al., 2003) and offenders misusing substances (Domalanta et al., 2003).

High comorbidity may contribute to increased complexity in both the assessment process as well as successful treatment of these young people. Comorbidity with other needs such as physical health and education is also common and of clinical relevance, as young offenders have needs in multiple domains, not just mental health (Chitsabesan et al., 2006; Golzari et al., 2006; Lader et al., 2000).

Gender and ethnicity

Whilst the evidence of a higher prevalence of various mental health needs and neurodevelopmental disorders seems clear, there appears to be limited and at times contradictory evidence regarding rates amongst different subgroups within the population, including in consideration of gender (see for example Petrillo, this volume) and ethnicity (see for example Canton, this volume). Whilst studies of mental health needs have to date predominantly focused on male offenders, gender differences have been reported. For example, in the NWJP, girls were 14 times as likely as boys to meet the criteria for at least one mental disorder across a broad range of diagnoses excluding substance misuse and psychotic disorders (Teplin et al., 2002). Elevated rates of mental health needs for female offenders have also been found in studies within the US and UK, particularly for depressive and anxiety disorders (Chitsabesan et al., 2006; McCabe et al., 2002; Vincent et al., 2008). A meta-analysis of 25 studies of adolescent offenders found that major depression was four to five times more common in female offenders and twice as common in males in comparison with the general population (Fazel et al., 2008). Additionally, rates of PTSD and self-harm have also been found to be significantly more prevalent in females (Chitsabesan et al., 2006). Female offenders have been shown to experience more abuse, neglect and family history of mental illness than male offenders (McCabe et al., 2002). Other explanatory mechanisms may include greater genetic vulnerability as well as increased exposure to trauma and chaotic family lifestyles.

With regard to neurodisability, there is some evidence from international studies that boys with antisocial behaviour performed significantly poorer in reading and spelling (Svensson et al., 2001) and had lower verbal and full-scale IQ scores than female offenders (Moffitt et al., 2001: Chitsabesan et al., 2007). Rates of language problems were also lower amongst female offenders in custody within the US at between 14% and 22% (Sanger et al., 1997), in comparison with 60% of male offenders (Bryan, 2004). However a systematic review of prevalence rates of ADHD noted significantly higher rates in female adolescent offenders (19%) in comparison to males (12%), although both were higher than the general adolescent population (Fazel et al., 2008). It should be noted that there was significant heterogeneity among studies included, influenced by the sample size, population and instruments used.

There are concerns that there is an over-representation of some ethnic minority groups within the criminal justice system and that these groups of young people have poorer access to services (NACRO, 2001; Shelton, 2005). However, studies exploring differences in prevalence of mental disorders among young offenders by ethnicity have been sparse and difficult to interpret. Those studies that are available are US-based and offer variable conclusions. For example, the

NWJP found that prevalence rates of mental disorder were significantly lower in black or Hispanic offenders (Abram et al., 2003). However, a national study within the US using the Massachusetts Youth Screening Instrument (MAYSI-2) found that differences in prevalence rates varied across sites and were generally small (Vincent et al., 2008).

Implications for policy and practice

The range of research studies discussed in the previous section consistently illustrate high rates of mental health needs and neurodisability amongst young people within the youth justice system. This provides greater understanding of the role of developmental pathways in relation to the onset and continuation of offending behaviour, and suggests a number of implications for the youth justice system, from screening to effective early intervention and multi-agency collaboration.

Understanding developmental pathways

The development of antisocial behaviour involves a complex interaction of intrinsic and psychosocial factors, mirroring the complex aetiology and expression of mental health needs and neurodevelopmental difficulties. Intrinsic risk factors can be comprised of cognitive processing bias (hostile attribution bias; see Tyson and Hall, this volume), temperament and poor emotional regulation (Farrington, 2002; Moffitt, 1993). The neurocognitive profiles of young offenders include deficits in language skills, attention and impulse control as well as low IQ scores (Loeber and Farrington, 2000; Moffitt, 1993). Deficits in executive function can affect the young person's ability to regulate their behaviours, plan and generate alternative strategies. However, antisocial behaviour also shows strong associations with psychosocial adversity. Parental mental illness, family breakdown, parenting style and association with other antisocial peers influence outcomes. The association between academic problems and antisocial behaviour has also been well established. Detachment from school increases the risk of offending through reduced supervision, loss of any positive socialisation effects of school and by creating delinquent groups of young people (Stevenson, 2006). In considering a solution-focussed response, it should be integrated with the research that consistently demonstrates that the high rate of psychopathology in young offenders may be secondary to shared risk factors, as the lives of these young people are often characterised by attachment difficulties, trauma, familial psychopathology and disadvantage (Loeber and Farrington, 2000; McCabe et al., 2002). Increased genetic vulnerability, birth trauma and injury may also contribute to elevated risk.

Distinctive pathways are apparent for those with early or late onset of offending behaviour, with some gender differences suggested. Girls have historically been found to have a later onset to their antisocial behaviour compared with boys. This has led to the suggestion by Moffitt and colleagues (2001) that adolescent onset of antisocial behaviour occurs in the context of deviant peer relationships and affects girls as well as boys, while early onset, life-course persistent antisocial behaviour is neurodevelopmental in origin and predominantly affects boys.

This complex and varied interaction of intrinsic and psychosocial factors mean that an understanding of the developmental trajectories of young people requires consideration of a complex array of experiences impacting upon them, including the social and environmental, as well as the biological. This suggests a need to consider and apply a range of professional understandings, avoiding the dominance of one particular approach or culture. Currently the DSM (see APA, 2013 for the most recent edition) acts as the dominant framework for defining, diagnosing and determining entitlement and access to support for those with psychiatric or neurodevelopmental difficulties. The approach of the DSM has, however, been criticised with regard to the appropriateness, accuracy and distinctiveness of definition of specific 'disorders' as a means of representing the experiences of an individual (Krueger et al., 2005), and as historically and socially constructed, based on the dominance of specific scientific disciplines and discourses (Mallett, 2006; see Arrigo and Bersot, this volume). The use of the DSM is seen to ensure the dominance of a 'medical model' of understanding and categorising impairment, which emphasises individual deficit to be addressed through medical intervention, over a 'social model' that instead emphasises social and environmental causes and implications, and systemic and institutional processes that impact upon individual experiences of impairment, disability and discrimination (Baldry et al., 2008). Nonetheless, recognising the complex but strong associations between causes and symptoms of mental health needs and neurodevelopmental difficulties and pathways into offending is vital in supporting effective assessment and intervention, as discussed in the next two sections.

Screening

Timely screening and assessment are essential to the successful identification and management of mental health needs and neurodisability, and to the recognition of the possible relationship between offending behaviour and underlying needs in young offenders. However, problems obtaining informant history and engaging young people with mental health services due to fear of stigma can contribute to difficulties in the assessment process.

Screening is a brief process that helps to identify current needs and should be applied universally to all offenders in the youth justice system at the point of entry. It helps to differentiate young people who are at higher risk and requiring more detailed assessment from those whose needs are minor. Identifying offenders with neurodisability such as learning disabilities or communication disorders is therefore essential, not only to tailor interventions appropriately, but also because such impairments may affect the young person's capacity to engage in the legal process, including the court process, and consequently to effectively defend themselves (Snow and Powell, 2005).

Screening should inform legal decision making, diverting young people where appropriate to evidence-based interventions and away from the youth justice system, towards more specialist support (see Rogers and Ormston, this volume). Any universal screening tool for young offenders should be feasible for use by youth justice staff and also have defined processes to differentiate those at risk that require further specialist assessment. This should be supported by regular supervision and access to consultation with specialist health professionals to enable staff to practise within a robust clinical governance framework. Seeking additional information from key informants in the young person's life is also essential to developing a better understanding of the young person's strengths and needs, as many young people may minimise symptoms for fear of stigma.

In recognition of these difficulties, a health assessment tool has been developed and validated for use with young offenders within the secure estate across England and Wales. The Comprehensive Health Assessment Tool (CHAT) consists of five parts: an initial reception screen, followed by a physical health, mental health, substance misuse and neurodisability screen for all offenders (Chitsabesan et al., 2014; Offender Health Research Network, 2013). The launch of the *Healthcare Standards for Children and Young People in Secure Settings* (Royal College of Paediatrics and Child Health, 2013) has also provided an opportunity to standardise good practice guidelines and support the use of the CHAT.

Whilst identification within the secure estate provides a basis for intervention, for many people who offend there are opportunities for earlier recognition of mental health needs and neurodisability prior to contact with the youth justice system. Many of these young people with challenging behaviour may be identified earlier within educational and social work settings, though their underlying mental health and neurodevelopmental needs may not be recognised, suggesting that more robust screening within these environments is paramount.

However, varied professional cultures and frameworks ensure varied terminology, assessments and diagnoses through which to understand and address the needs of a young person. This is apparent in the potentially differential diagnosis of, and response to, the needs of young people exhibiting early problem behaviour. For example, those with impairment relating to language and communication difficulties in early childhood commonly struggle to make the transition from 'learning to read', to 'reading to learn'. 'For boys in particular, this is often a time (around 8 years of age) when externalising behaviour difficulties becomes apparent in the classroom' (Snow and Powell, 2012, p. 2). As such, without sufficient understanding, there is the potential that underlying communication issues reflecting neurodevelopmental difficulties may be expressed and interpreted as behavioural difficulties, warranting a very different professional response or intervention.

This highlights a significant set of training needs across a range of services in order to ensure appropriate assessment and response (King and Dwyer, 2009; see Hean, Walsh and Hammick, this volume). Staff in education services, family intervention projects, social services and primary health care settings require support to recognise and understand issues relating to mental health and neurodisability. This should include those working with vulnerable or 'troubled families' and 'at-risk' young people, as well as general practitioners, health visitors and midwives providing prenatal and antenatal support. Community youth justice services are also vital to early identification and intervention at the point of initial onset of offending.

Intervening effectively

Screening in educational and social work settings is vital given the growing evidence of the benefits of early intervention for young people with mental health needs and neurodisability, to prevent the development of secondary impairment such as detachment from education and substance misuse. For example, identification of neurodevelopmental difficulties at primary school age can allow young people to be appropriately supported on transition to secondary school, thereby reducing the risk of disengagement and exclusion.

The identification of an underlying neurodisability allows for services that are responsive to specific needs and learning styles in order to successfully engage with the young person, such as through a focus on behavioural rather than cognitive behavioural strategies for young people with significant learning or language difficulties. This is essential in order to develop individual care plans and to allow resources to be used more cost-effectively, rather than attempting to engage young people in generic interventions which may not take into account their specific profile of needs. In addition, the complex interaction of various risk factors and the likely co-occurrence of resultant needs and negative outcomes, as discussed above, imply a frequent need for integrated multi-professional support (see Rogers and Ormston, this volume; Hean, Walsh and Hammick, this volume), rather than approaches dominated by one agency or approach. This multi-agency approach was a key recommendation of the Bradley Report (King and Dwyer, 2009), which, in recognition of the high number of offenders with mental health needs or learning disabilities, emphasised the importance of mental health and social care services being involved in every stage of the criminal justice process. More recently, youth justice policy has focussed on the important role of education in reducing reoffending with the proposed introduction of secure colleges where education and rehabilitation are to become the focus of secure detention (Ministry of Justice, 2014).

While there is good evidence for the effectiveness of early interventions such as parenting programmes (NICE, 2009; Scott, 2008), for a subgroup of young people with more complex needs antisocial behaviour can be persistent despite these interventions (Chitsabesan et al., 2012; Loeber and Farrington, 2000). Young people with identified mental health and neurodevelopmental difficulties require access to a range of tiered and evidence-based interventions. Awareness-raising across a range of practitioners and professionals will support referral to relevant specialist services for further assessment and intervention regarding mental health needs and specific neurodevelopmental disorders. National guidelines on the treatment of many of these disorders exist through the National Institute for Health and Clinical Excellence (NICE, www.nice.org.uk), although they may require adjustment for this group of young people. There is increasing evidence for the effectiveness of multi-modal approaches, including multi-systemic therapy and multi-dimensional family therapy. Multi-systemic therapy (MST) is a multi-modal intervention where interventions are targeted at not only the young person, but also their family, school and peers. Evaluation studies of MST have been promising (Hengeller et al., 2009). In particular, it has also been shown to be effective for young people with substance misuse disorders (Ogden et al., 2007). However, criticisms of MST include the requirement for a high level of therapeutic expertise, as well as the cost of implementation. Therefore, while MST is unsuitable as a universal intervention for all offenders, it may be cost-effective for those at risk of more serious or long-term antisocial behaviour, such as those with complex neurodevelopmental support needs.

A more cost-effective alternative with a focus on young people with substance misuse problems (see Pycroft and Green, this volume) is multi-dimensional family therapy (MDFT). MDFT is a family-based outpatient treatment for adolescents with drug abuse problems and behavioural difficulties. It attempts to address the needs of the young person through therapy sessions with the family and wider social systems using a systemic model (Liddle et al., 2008; Phan et al., 2011). However, despite increasing evidence supporting the effectiveness of specific treatment programmes, there are concerns that few high-risk offenders have access to these treatments.

There is evidence that suggests many persistent offenders have an early onset to their behavioural difficulties in childhood and a greater prevalence of neurodisability and health needs. It is therefore essential to apply interventions at an early stage and to identify those young people and families who would benefit from a more intensive multi-agency approach. Greater integration between the youth justice services and key partner agencies, including schools, mental health services and social care would enable the recognition and prevention of risk factors, such as school exclusion, and provide support to families and young people in a more timely manner. This should be supported by a national multi-agency public health strategy with clear recommendations for the role of key agencies and commissioners at a local level (see Rogers and Ormston, this volume).

Recent developments in policy and practice

Politicians and professionals have begun to acknowledge the importance of meeting the needs of offenders, as long-term costs to society become increasingly apparent (Scott et al., 2001). The Bradley Report (King and Dwyer, 2009) highlighted a number of problems within the criminal justice system in England and Wales, from difficulties identifying offenders with mental health needs and learning difficulties to problems accessing appropriate treatment. Similar difficulties have been found in the provision for young offenders in custody (Office of the Children's Commissioner, 2011). Such reviews have precipitated change within the youth justice system, including the development of health standards and universal health screening through the introduction of the Comprehensive Health Assessment Tool. The development of healthcare quality standards for all young offenders within the secure estate is a joint intercollegiate initiative led by the Royal College of Paediatrics and Child Health (2013). It demonstrates the increasing importance of providing a standardised and evidence-based approach to screening and intervention for a variety of health needs whilst young people remain within the secure estate. Assessing and managing unmet health needs can inform individual care plans, help to address offending behaviour and provide a valuable opportunity to re-engage young people with health and educational services to address unmet needs. Initiatives within the community include the development of Liaison and Diversion teams (see Rogers and Ormston, this volume) within police and court interfaces to screen and divert young people away from the criminal justice system where possible. Within the current financial climate and with competing priorities for commissioners and agencies at a local level, the needs of young offenders are at risk of being overshadowed. Information from screening tools used to assess health needs could be utilised by commissioners locally to target resources more effectively. Opportunities also exist through multi-agency partnerships, as well as in engaging local clinical commissioning groups and health and well-being boards locally to emphasise the cost-effectiveness of early and effective intervention. Early coordinated care is essential in meeting the complex needs of this group of young people, highlighting the important role of a multi-agency public health strategy with cross-departmental government support and assigned resources.

Conclusion

This chapter has evidenced the high prevalence of mental health needs and neurodisability in young people who offend and outlined the implications for policy and practice, including recent developments. It is clear that young people would benefit from a standardised screening framework across the youth justice system and access to multi-modal evidence-based interventions adapted to their needs. This will require training and awareness-raising across a range of services and professionals so as to broaden understandings, challenge particular practice cultures and support joint working. Responding to the clear and identifiable needs associated with mental health and neurodisability can ensure more effective and cost-efficient interventions to prevent the onset of antisocial behaviour and break a common cycle of persistent and serious offending, as well as offering the means to support rather than simply punish young people for the risks and vulnerabilities associated with their mental health needs.

References

Abram, K.M., Teplin, L.A., McClelland, G.M. and Duclan, M. (2003). Co-morbid psychiatric disorders in youth in juvenile detention. *Archives of General Psychiatry*, 60, 1097–1108.

American Psychiatric Association (2013). *Diagnostic and statistical manual of mental disorders* (5th ed., text rev.). Washington, DC: APA.

Anckarsater, H., Nilsson, T., Saury, J., Rastam, M. and Gillberg, C. (2008). Autism spectrum disorders in institutionalized subjects. *Nordic Journal of Psychiatry*, 62(2), 160–167.

Baird, G., Simonoff, E., Pickles, A., Chandler, S., Loucas, T., Meldrum, D. and Charman, T. (2006). Prevalence of disorders of the autism spectrum in a population cohort of children in South Thames: the Special Needs and Autism Project (SNAP). *Lancet*, 368, 210–215.

Baldry, E., Dowse, L., Snoyman, P., Clarence, M. and Webster, I. (2008). A Critical Perspective on Mental Health Disorders and Cognitive Disability in the Criminal Justice System. In C. Cunneen and M. Salter (eds). *Proceedings of the 2nd Australian and New Zealand Critical Criminology Conference*, Sydney, June 19 –21. 30–45.

British Psychological Society (2001). *Learning Disability: Definitions and Contexts*. Leicester: The British Psychological Society.

Bryan, K. (2004). Prevalence of speech and language difficulties in young offenders. *International Journal of Language and Communication Disorders*, 39, 391–400.

Chitsabesan, P., Bailey, S., Williams, R., Kroll, L., Kenning, C. and Talbot, L. (2007). Learning disabilities and educational needs of juvenile offenders. *Journal of Children's Services*, 2 (4), 4–14.

Chitsabesan, P., Kroll, L., Bailey, S., Kenning, C., Sneider, S., MacDonald,W. and Theodosiou, L. (2006). National study of mental health provision for young offenders. Part 1: Mental health needs of young offenders in custody and in the community. *British Journal of Psychiatry*, 188, 534–540.

Chitsabesan, P., Lennox, C., Theodosiou, L., Law, L., Bailey, S. and Shaw, J. (2014). The development of the comprehensive health assessment tool for young offenders within the secure estate. *Journal of Forensic Psychiatry and Psychology*, 25 (1), 1–25.

Chitsabesan, P., Rothwell, J., Kenning, C., Law, H., Carter, L., Bailey, S. and Clark, A. (2012). Six years on: a prospective cohort study of male juvenile offenders in secure care. *European Child and Adolescent Psychiatry*, 21 (6), 339–347.

Davies, R.C., Williams, W.H., Hinder, D., Burgess, C.N. and Mounce, L.T (2012) Self-reported traumatic brain injury and postconcussion symptoms in incarcerated youth. *Journal of Head Trauma Rehabilitation*, 27 (3), 21–27.

Domalanta, D.D., Risser, W.L., Roberts, R.E. and Risser, J.M. (2003). Prevalence of depression and other psychiatric disorders among incarcerated youths. *Journal of the American Academy of Child and Adolescent Psychiatry*, 42, 477–484.

Eme, R. (2009). Attention deficit hyperactivity disorder and the family court. *Family Court Review*, 47 (4), 650–664.

Farrington, D. P. (2002). Developmental criminology and risk-focused prevention. In M. Maguire, R. Morgan and R. Reiner (eds). *The Oxford Handbook of Criminology*. Oxford: Oxford University Press. 657–701.

Fazel, S., Doll, H. and Langstrom, N. (2008). Mental disorders among adolescents in juvenile detention and correctional facilities: A systematic review and metaregression analysis of 25 surveys. *Journal of the American Academy of Child and Adolescent Psychiatry*, 47, 1010–1019.

Golzari, M., Hunt, S.J. and Anushiravani, A. (2006). The health status of youth in juvenile detention facilities. *Journal of Adolescent Health*, 38, 776–782.

Gosden, N., Kramp, P., Gabrielsen, G. and Sestoft, D. (2003). Prevalence of mental disorders among 15–17 year old male adolescent remand prisoners in Denmark. *Acta Psychiatrica Scandinavica*, 107, 102–110.

Gregory, J. and Bryan, K. (2011). Speech and language therapy intervention with a group of persistent and prolific young offenders in a non-custodial setting with previously undiagnosed speech, language and communication difficulties. *International Journal of Language and Communication Disorders*, 46, 202–215.

Green, H., McGinnity, A., Meltzer, H., Ford, T. and Goodman, R. (2005). *Mental health of children and young people in Great Britain 2004*. London: Office for National Statistics.

Gudjonsson, G., Sigurdsson, J.F., Sigfusdottir, I.D. and Young, S. (2012). A national epidemiological study of offending and its relationship with ADHD symptoms and associated risk factors. *Journal of Attention Disorders*, 18, 3–13.

Harrington, R. and Bailey, S. (2005). *Mental health needs and effectiveness of provision for young people in the youth justice system*. London: Youth Justice Board.

Hengeller, S.W., Scoenwald, S.K., Borduin, C.M., Rowland, M.D. and Cunningham, P.B. (2009). *Multi-systemic therapy for antisocial behaviour in children and adolescents* (2nd edition). New York: Guilford Press.

Herrington, V. (2009). Assessing the prevalence of intellectual disability among young male prisoners. *Journal of Intellectual Disability Research*, 53 (5), 397–410.

Hughes, N., Williams, P., Chitsabesan, P., Davies, R. and Mounce, L. (2012). *Nobody made the connection; the prevalence of neurodisability in young people who offend*. London: Office of the Children's Commissioner.

Hux, K., Bond, V., Skinner, S., Belau, D. and Sanger, D. (1998). Parental report of occurrences and consequences of traumatic brain injury among delinquent and non-delinquent youth. *Brain Injury*, 12 (8), 667–681.

Isen, J. (2010). A meta-analytic assessment of Wecshler's P>V sign in antisocial populations. *Clinical Psychology Review*, 30, 428–435.

Kenny, D., Nelson, P., Butler, T., Lenning, C., Allerton, M. and Chapman, U. (2006). *NSW Young people on community orders health survey 2003–2006: key findings report.* Sydney: The University of Sydney.

King, G. and Dwyer, P. (2009). *The Bradley report: Lord Bradley's review of people with mental health problems or learning disabilities in the criminal justice system.* London: Offender Health Programme, Department of Health.

Kroll, L., Rothwell, J., Bradley, D., Shah, P., Bailey, S. and Harrington, R. (2002). Mental health needs of boys in secure care for serious or persistent offending: a prospective longitudinal study. *Lancet,* 359, 1975–1979.

Krueger, R.F., Watson, D., and Barlow, D.H. (2005). Introduction to the Special Section: Toward a Dimensionally Based Taxonomy of Psychopathology. *Journal of Abnormal Psychology,* 114, 491–493.

Lader, D., Singleton, N. and Meltzer, H. (2000). *Psychiatric morbidity in young offenders in England and Wales.* London: Office for National Statistics.

Liddle, H.A., Dakota, G.A., Turner, R.M., Henderson, C.E. and Greenbaum, P.E. (2008). Treating adolescent drug abuse: a randomised trial comparing multi-dimensional family therapy and cognitive behavioural therapy. *Addiction,* 103, 1660–1670.

Loeber, R. and Farrington, D.P. (2000). Young people who commit crime: epidemiology, developmental origins, risk factors, early interventions, and policy implications. *Development and Psychopathology,* 12, 737–762.

McCabe, K.M., Lansing, A.E., Garland, A. and Hough, R. (2002). Gender differences in psychopathology, functional impairment, familial risk factors among adjudicated delinquents. *Journal of the American Academy of Child and Adolescent Psychiatry,* 41, 860–867.

McKay, J. and Neal, J. (2009). Diagnosis and disengagement: exploring the disjuncture between SEN policy and practice. *Journal of Research in Special Educational Needs,* 9 (3), 164–172.

McKinlay, A., Grace, R., Horwood, L., Ridder, E., MacFarlane, M. and Fergusson, D. (2008). Prevalence of traumatic brain injury among children, adolescents, and young adults: prospective evidenced from a birth cohort. *Brain Injury,* 22 (2), 175–181.

Mallett, C. A. (2006). Behaviorally-based disorders: The social construction of youths' most prevalent psychiatric diagnoses. *History of Psychiatry,* 17 (4), 435–457.

Meltzer, H., Gatward, R., Goodman, R. and Ford, T. (2000). *The Mental Health of Children and Adolescents in Great Britain.* London: The Stationery Office.

Ministry of Justice (2014). *Transforming Youth Custody.* London: MoJ.

Moffitt, T. (1993). Adolescent limited and life course persistent antisocial behaviour: a developmental taxonomy. *Psychological Review,* 1000, 674–701.

Moffitt, T., Caspi, A., Rutter, M. and Silva, P. (2001). *Sex Differences in Antisocial Behaviour: Conduct Disorder and Delinquency and Violence in the Dunedin Longitudinal Study.* Cambridge: Cambridge University Press.

NACRO (2001). *Youth Offending Teams, Race, and Justice: After the Watershed (Part One),* Youth Crime Briefing. London: NACRO.

National Autistic Society, The (2008). *Autism: a guide for criminal justice professionals.* London: NAS.

National Institute for Health and Clinical Excellence (2008). *Attention deficit hyperactivity disorder: Diagnosis and management of ADHD in children, young people and adults.* London: NICE.

National Institute for Health and Clinical Excellence (2009). *Antisocial personality disorder: treatment, management and prevention.* London: NICE.

National Institute for Health and Clinical Excellence (2011a). *Psychosis and schizophrenia in children and young people: final scope*. London: NICE.

National Institute for Health and Clinical Excellence (2011b). *Autism: recognition, referral and diagnosis in children and young people on the autism spectrum*. London: NICE.

National Treatment Agency for Substance Misuse (2011). Substance misuse among young people. London: NHS.

Offender Health Research Network (2013). *The Comprehensive Health Assessment Tool (CHAT): Young people in the secure estate – Version 3*. Manchester: University of Manchester.

Office of the Children's Commissioner (2011). *I think I must have been born bad: emotional well-being and mental health of children and young people in the youth justice system*. London: OCC.

Ogden, T., Hagen, K.A. and Andersen, O. (2007). Sustainability of the effectiveness of a programme of multisystemic treatment (MST) across participant groups in the second year of operation. *Journal of Children's Services*, 2, 4–14.

Perron, B. and Howard, M. (2008). Prevalence and correlates of traumatic brain injury among delinquent youths. *Criminal Behaviour and Mental Health*, 18 (4), 243–255.

Phan, O., Henderson, C., Angelidis, T., Weil, P., Van Toorn, M., Rigton, R., Soria, C. and Rigter, H. (2011). European youth centre sites serve different populations of adults with cannabis use disorder. Baseline and referral data from the INCANT trial. *BMC Psychiatry*, 11, 110.

Pliszka, S., Sherman, J., Barrow, M. and Irick, S. (2000). Affective disorder in juvenile offenders: a preliminary study. *Am J Psychiatry*, 157, 130–132.

Putnins, A.L. (2005). Correlates and predictors of self-reported suicide attempts among incarcerated youths. *Int Journal of Offenders Ther Comp Criminol*, 49 (2), 143–157.

Rayner, J., Kelly, T.P. and Graham, F. (2005). Mental health, personality and cognitive problems in persistent adolescent offenders require long-term solutions: a pilot study. *Journal of Forensic Psychiatry and Psychology*, 16, 248–262.

Roberts, R.E., Atkinson, C.C. and Rosenblatt, A. (1998). Prevalence of psychopathology among children and adolescents. *American Journal of Psychiatry*, 155, 715–725.

Royal College of Paediatrics and Child Health (2013). *Healthcare Standards for Children and Young People in Secure Settings*. London: RCPCH.

Ruchkin, V., Schwab-Stone, M., Koposov, R.A., Vermeiren, R. and Steiner, H. (2002). Violence exposure, post-traumatic stress and personality in juvenile delinquents. *Journal of the American Academy of Child and Adolescent Psychiatry*, 41, 322–329.

Ruchkin, V., Schwab-Stone, M., Koposov, R.A., Vermeiren, R. and King, R. (2003). Suicidal ideations and attempts in juvenile delinquents. *Journal of Child Psychology Psychiatry*, 44, 1058–1066.

Sanger, D.D., Hux, K. and Belau, D. (1997). Oral language skills of female juvenile delinquents. *American Journal of Speech-Language Pathology*, 6, 70–76.

Sanislow, C., Grilo, C., Fehon, C., Axelrod, S.R. and McGlashan, T.H. (2003). Correlates of suicide risk in juvenile detainees and adolesecent inpatients. *J Am Acad Child Adolesc Psychiatry*, 42, 234–240.

Scott, S. (2008). An update on interventions for conduct disorder. *Advances in Psychiatric Treatment*, 14, 61–70.

Scott, S., Knapp, M., Henderson, J. and Maughan, B. (2001). Financial cost of social exclusion; follow up study of anti-social children into adulthood. *British Medical Journal*, 323, 1–5.

Shelton, D. (2005). Patterns of treatment and service costs for young offenders with mental disorders. *Journal of Child and Adolescent Psychiatric Nursing*, 18, 103–112.

Snow, P. C. and Powell, M. B. (2005). What's the story? An exploration of narrative language abilities in male juvenile offenders. *Psychology, Crime and Law*, 11 (3), 239–253.

Snowling, M. J., Adams, J. W., Bowyer-Crane, C. and Tobin, V. (2000). Levels of literacy among juvenile offenders: the incidence of specific reading difficulties. *Criminal Behaviour and Mental Health*, 10 (4), 229–241.

Stevenson, M. (2006). *Young People and Offending: Education, Youth justice and Social Care Inclusion*. London: Williams.

Svensson, I., Lundberg, I. and Jacobson, C. (2001). The prevalence of reading and spelling difficulties among inmates of institutions for compulsory care of juvenile delinquents. *Dyslexia*, 7, 62–76.

Teplin, L.A., Abram, K.M., McClelland, G.M., Dulcan, M. and Mericle, A. (2002). Psychiatric disorders in youth in detention. *Archives of General Psychiatry*, 59, 1133–1143.

Timonen, M., Miettunen, J., Hakko, H., Zitting, P., Veijola, J., Von Wendt, L. and Rasanen, P. (2002). The association of preceding traumatic brain injury with mental disorders, alcoholism and criminality: the Northern Finland 1966 Birth Cohort Study. *Psychiatry Research*, 113 (3), 217–226.

Tomblin, J. B., Zhang, X., Buckwater, P., and Catts, H. (2000). The association of reading disability, behavioural disorders and language impairment among second-grade children. *Journal of Child Psychology and Psychiatry*, 41 (4), 473– 482.

Vincent, G.M., Grisso, T., Terry, A. and Banks, S. (2008). Sex and race differences in mental health symptoms in juvenile justice: The MAYSI-2 National Meta-analysis. *Journal of the American Academy of Child and Adolescent Psychiatry*, 47, 282–290.

Vreugdenhil, C., Doreleijers, T., Vermeiren, R., Wouters, L. and Van der Brink, W. (2004). Psychiatric disorders in a representative sample of incarcerated boys in the Netherlands. *Journal of the American Academy of Child and Adolescent Psychiatry*, 43, 97–104.

Wasserman, G., McReynolds, L., Schwalbe, C., Keatings, J. and Jones, S. (2010). Psychiatric disorder, comorbidity and suicidal behaviour in Juvenile Justice Youth. *Criminal Justice Behaviour*, 37 (12), 1361–1376.

Weisner, M., Kim, H. and Capaldi, D. (2005). Development trajectories of offending; validation and prediction to young adult alcohol use, drug use and depressive symptoms. *Developmental Psychopathology*, 17, 251–270.

World Health Organisation (1992) *The ICD-10 Classification of mental and behavioural disorders: clinical description and diagnostic guidelines*. World Health Organisation, Geneva.

Williams, H.W., Giray, C., Mewse, A.J., Tonks, J. and Burgess, C.N.W. (2010). Self-reported traumatic brain injury in male young offenders: A risk factor for re-offending, poor mental health and violence? *Neuropsychological Rehabilitation*, 20 (6), 801–812.

Wong, W. and Cornell, G. (1999). PIQ>VIQ discrepancy as a correlate of social information processing and aggression in delinquent adolescent males. *Journal of Psychoeducational Assessment*, 17, 104–112.

8
'It Made My Mind Unwell': Trauma-Informed Approaches to the Mental Health Needs of Women in the Criminal Justice System

Madeline Petrillo

Introduction

Studies have shown that the mental health needs of women who come into conflict with the law are more acute, widespread and diverse than those of men in the criminal justice system (CJS). Interventions and programming in prisons and community corrections are largely designed 'by men for men'. This has triggered debate about their ability to respond to and address the specific needs of women. The principles of gender-responsive approaches to treatment take the perspective that trauma frequently plays a part in the onset and persistence of mental health and substance use disorders amongst women who have engaged in offending behaviour. This chapter will consider how trauma-informed approaches can offer a gender-responsive framework for working with women in the criminal justice system with mental health needs. The discussion in this chapter is supported by extracts from interviews with women in HMP Holloway undertaken between May 2013 and August 2014 as part of an ongoing research project into women's pathways into and out of crime.

The gender bias in gender-neutral service provision

Proponents of gender-responsive treatment and interventions argue that at the root of many women's mental health and substance use problems are traumatic experiences that are gendered in nature (see for example Van Wormer, 2010; Bloom and Covington, 2008; Corston, 2007; Covington and Bloom, 2006). Alice's story illustrates this point:

> I used to hate myself. I used to self-harm my face. That's why I've got scars on my face. I used to self-harm quite a lot, but only my face. I used to take a lot of

drugs because of it. And I've got children and they're not allowed to live with me because I've got paranoid schizophrenia now from being raped. I used to think about it quite a lot and then it started to make my mind a bit unwell and my judgement a bit different, clouded and stuff, so my children can't live with me, so I feel very resentful now for being raped. (Alice, aged 27.)

Alice was imprisoned for six months for an offence of burglary. She has been hospitalised for mental health problems nine times over the past nine years. Her mother is diagnosed with paranoid schizophrenia which Alice believes was caused by her father 'doing lots of evil stuff' to her. Alice was first raped when she was 13 years old and started cutting her face soon afterwards because she 'did not want to be pretty anymore'. She was raped for the second time when she was 18. Alice experienced a violent relationship, losing her unborn child as a result of being punched in the stomach when five months pregnant. She was raped for a third time around six months before our conversation. This triggered an attempted suicide which resulted in Alice being hospitalised for four months, relapse into substance misuse and her involvement in the burglary. For Alice, the inter-relatedness of her experiences of abuse and loss, her mental health issues, her substance misuse and her offending is unambiguous. Yet in committing an offence, Alice's victimisation and related needs become subsumed by the State's compulsion to punish her criminality over all else (see Arrigo and Bersott this volume). As Maidment (2008) explains, 'criminal transgressions constitute the "master status" which needs to be studied, explained and corrected' (p. 36). Equality in provision in most correctional services continues to be understood as parity of provision, which would render gender-neutral treatment programmes desirable. However, it has been argued that as a minority of the offender population, women are disadvantaged by treatment programmes designed around the needs of men (Borrill et al., 2003; Corston, 2007; Van Wormer, 2010). As Alice's story indicates, what is desirable for women is that treatment approaches are gender-*informed* rather than gender-neutral and are able to respond to the gendered nature of their experiences.

Gender, mental health and substance misuse: related issues requiring a holistic response

Alice has multiple mental health related and complex needs and she is not unusual among women in the CJS. Women prisoners report poorer mental health than male prisoners in relation to psychosis, anxiety, depression, suicide attempts and self-harm (Light et al., 2013). Studies consistently estimate that around 75% of female prisoners have mental health problems (James and Glaze, 2006; Plugge et al., 2006). Maden et al. (1994) found a higher prevalence of neurosis, personality disorder, learning disability and substance misuse in women but higher levels of psychosis in men. However a recent UK Ministry of Justice study on gender differences in substance misuse and mental health amongst prisoners found a higher prevalence of *all* mental health disorders in women (Light et al., 2013). In this study, 14% of women and 7% of men serving prison sentences were found to have a psychotic disorder; 25% of women and 15% of men in prison reported symptoms indicative of psychosis; 30% of women have had a previous psychiatric admission before entering prison; 49% of women and 23% of male prisoners were assessed as suffering from anxiety and depression; 46% of women prisoners reported having attempted suicide at some point in their lives (Light et al., 2013). Women accounted for 28% of all self-harm incidents in 2012 despite representing under 5% of the total prison population (Ministry of Justice, 2014). Studies have shown women are more likely to have experienced gender-related adversity in the form of childhood abuse, poverty, domestic abuse, sexual assault and single parenthood (Ministry of Justice, 2011, 2014; Covington and Bloom, 2006; Carlen, 1988).

Although there is no unitary concept of a 'female offender', Alice is representative of women who end up populating prison and probation services. She is from a minority ethnic background, has been convicted of a drug-related offence (see Pycroft and Green this volume), experienced ruptured family relationships in childhood, is a survivor of repeated physical and sexual abuse, has multiple mental health needs, is the primary carer of young children and has limited educational or work experience (Chesney-Lind and Pasko, 2013; Corston, 2007; Covington and Bloom, 2006). Over half of women prisoners report having experienced emotional, physical or sexual abuse as a child, compared with 27% of men, and a third report experiencing domestic abuse: 52% state that they had used heroin, crack, or cocaine powder in the four weeks prior to custody (Ministry of Justice, 2011). A close correlation of repeated trauma, mental health issues, personality disorders, self-harm and other maladaptive coping behaviours such as substance misuse is repeated in the stories women tell about their pathways into offending (Belknap, 2007).

Bette's explanation for her assault of her ex-partner illustrates the challenges of untangling how mental health, personality disorder, responses to trauma and substance use disorders impact on offending behaviour. Bette was diagnosed with bipolar disorder at the age of 18 and has experienced psychotic episodes and problems with alcoholism and self-harming behaviour throughout her adult life. The offence resulted in an additional diagnosis of emotionally unstable personality disorder. Bette's account reinforces how the interaction of mental health problems, trauma and maladaptive coping mechanisms contributed to her violent behaviour:

> I was with the children's dad for 12 years. I've got bipolar disorder, things in the relationship weren't going very well, I found out he was having an affair.

We separated, things got nasty, my bipolar took a turn for the worse which meant me being sectioned. It wasn't a very nice experience... When we split, that's when the psychotic episodes come into it and emotionally unstable personality disorder... but it's because I was hiding things, I was hiding things about him and the degrading stuff he did to me as a woman... If I did sleep in the bed, I'd wake up, he was having sex with me. That's rape, and I would say to him, 'What are you doing? That's rape.' 'Don't be silly, you're my wife.' *(Bette, aged 37.)*

As illustrated by Alice and Bette, for women in the CJS, mental health problems are often part of a complex pastiche of environmental, social and emotional challenges that weave the fabric of their lives. Despite the interrelatedness of issues of gender, mental health and substance misuse problems, these tend to be treated as distinct sites for treatment or intervention in the correctional settings (Covington and Bloom, 2006). Gender-responsive approaches to programming for women with mental health needs in the criminal justice system take the perspective that trauma frequently plays a part in the onset and persistence of all these conditions (Bloom and Covington, 2008). This, together with the frequency with which these disorders co-occur, supports them being viewed as manifestations of attempts to cope with trauma as opposed to separate problems requiring distinct treatment (Bloom and Covington, 2008; Van Wormer, 2010).

Trauma-informed approaches

What is trauma?

The American Psychological Association (APA) define trauma as an emotional response to a sudden, unexpected, terrifying event ('Trauma', APA, 2014). The sense of trauma is amplified when the person feels unable to exert any agency or control over what they are experiencing. It is of particular relevance to women in the criminal justice system that rape and violent assault are named as examples of events that can cause trauma ('The effects of trauma do not have to last a lifetime' APA, 2004). Studies generally report the proportion of women in the criminal justice system who have experienced domestic and/or sexual abuse to be between 50% and 80% (Norman and Barron, 2011) though it has been found to be as high as 98% (Green et al., 2005). Trauma is believed to be fundamental to the onset and development of women's mental health problems particularly depression, post-traumatic stress disorder (PTSD) and anxiety disorders (Bloom and Covington, 2008). It has been argued that childhood victimisation is the primary causal factor that steers girls into offending lifestyles (Belknap, 2007). Women frequently come into the criminal justice system as a result of the criminalisation of their striving to survive experiences of abuse and poverty (Chesney-Lind and Pasko, 2013; Daly, 1992). Misha's experiences illustrate this familiar pathway. She was taken into the care of the local authority as a result of her mother's substance misuse and mental health problems. She spent time out of the local authority home to escape abuse. At an early age, alcohol and then drugs provided a means of coping with the trauma of bereavement, repeated abuse and the severe instability of her life. The relationship between sexual exploitation, addiction and physical abuse followed Misha into adulthood as she endured repeated domestic abuse and was coerced into sex work and offending to support her and her partner's addictions (Cusick et al., 2003).

> I went into care when I was 7. And I've been abused...in care. And social services didn't believe it was through being in care. They thought it was my family. And that emotionally traumatised me. As well as being abused your thinking 'it's my dad or my uncles'. So, really emotionally traumatised me. And I've got a lot of mental health in my family as well. So I suffer from bipolar and paranoid schizophrenia so that never helped. I started hearing voices when I was younger. And then my sister passed away when I was 12. So, I was drinking...cos by the time I was 11 I was in 34 different children's foster placements. And that's a lot yeah from 7 till then. My sister got leukaemia and I started drinking more and more. When she passed away, when I was 12, I got drunk and was gang raped in a park. So when that happened, I then turned to my mum. When I turned to my mum, my mum started selling me [...] That's a lot of abuse do you know what I mean. [...] And then I just got in an abusive relationship. I was put on the game. Cos he was feeding me drugs. And then when he got me proper hooked on heroin, he sent me out to work. *(Misha, aged 23.)*

There is clear evidence that traumatic experiences are linked to increased risks of mental health difficulties and substance misuse (DeHart et al., 2014). DeHart and colleagues (2014) found women in the criminal justice system have high prevalence rates of repeated trauma and poly-victimisation, as exemplified by Misha, Bette and Alice. Turner et al. (2006 in DeHart et al., 2014) found they are also likely to have endured 'nonvictimization adversity' such as bereavements, the imprisonment of primary caregivers, persistent family conflict and living with parents with substance misuse and mental health problems. Incarcerated women's lifetime experiences of interpersonal violence predicted greater severity of symptoms of depression, PTSD, general distress and substance misuse (Lynch et al., 2012). Symptoms and behavioural manifestations of trauma include hypervigilance, violent outbursts, suicidal ideation, self-harm, disassociation, flashbacks, mood disorders and eating disorders (Blume 1990; Hermann, 1992; in De Cou, 2002). Evidence is mixed as to whether women are more likely to experiences such symptoms (Widom, 2000). That said, incarcerated women are more likely than men to report extensive histories of abuse (Williams et al., 2012).

Why a trauma-informed approach is a gender-responsive approach

Gender differences are a critical consideration when designing programmes for women. Across jurisdictions women commit fewer offences, less serious offences, and present a lower risk of harm than men (Ministry of Justice, 2014; Corston, 2007). Women have distinct criminogenic needs (dynamic risk factors) and whilst there is debate about the *nature* of the link between victimisation and offending behaviour in women, it is incontrovertible that a relationship exists (Blanchette and Brown, 2006). As has been illustrated, trauma is often at the root of mental health and substance misuse problems for women in the criminal justice system (Alleyne, 2006) and in turn, mental health and substance misuse problems are often at the root of offending behaviour (see Pycroft and Green this volume). Bloom and Covington (2008) make the point that although PTSD is a common diagnosis associated with abuse, the most common mental health problem for women who are trauma survivors is depression. Light et al. (2013, p. 22) found an association between depression and reconviction for women who have been in prison. Women suffering depression were significantly more likely to be reconvicted in the year after release than those without such symptoms (66% compared to 31% respectively). This is not to say that victimisation causes offending, but that responses to cope with victimisation can be criminogenic (Blanchette and Brown, 2006). This suggests that trauma-informed approaches to treatment and intervention may help reduce recidivism amongst women with mental health and substance misuse needs. Bloom and Covington (2008) reiterate this point in citing Jordan and colleagues' findings that despite having been in mental health treatment, some women continued to engage in criminal behaviour (Jordan et al., 2002). They hypothesise that women's mental health disorders are often trauma-related and previous treatment has focused on the psychological after-effects of the victimisation: the substance misuse, the self-harm, the diagnosed mental disorder, but not the trauma itself.

The principles of gender-responsive interventions

Prisons are not primarily therapeutic environments. The necessities of security and control will always create a challenging environment for delivering care to those with mental health and substance misuse problems. However, as statistics quoted earlier show, the female estate is increasingly populated by women with mental health and substance use disorders. In 2006, Human Rights Watch found there to be three times as many men and women with mental health problems in prisons as in mental hospitals (Human Rights Watch, 2006). The prison environment can re-invoke past trauma by recreating feelings of disempowerment and loss, stigmatisation, betrayal and traumatic sexualisation (Short and Barber, 2004; Heney and Kristiansen, 1998). Although services that acknowledge women's victimisation experiences are becoming more widespread, such services tend to be unstructured, fragmented and unable to respond holistically to women's gender-related needs. In the UK, for example, this means that where provision exists, a woman can find herself attending a group with a non-statutory provider to help her manage self-harming behaviour, a cognitive behavioural group run by prison staff to address offending behaviour, a 12-step group with Narcotics Anonymous or Alcoholics Anonymous to address substance misuse or alcoholism, appointments with the Mental Health In-Reach Teams provided by the Department of Health for medication to manage diagnosed mental illness, and appointments with a voluntary bereavement counsellor to explore issues related to loss. Whilst a multi-agency approach to women's mental health problems is desirable, these need to function holistically.Consideration needs to be given as to whether a person with multiple complex problems can sufficiently cope with the demands of the provisions to take advantage of the services offered unless they are structured in a pathway of support.

The Women Offender Case Management Model (WOCMM) (National Institute of Corrections, 2006) in the US and the Offender Personality Disorder Strategy for Women (OPDSW) (Ministry of Justice and Department of Health, 2011) in the UK are examples of attempts by the correctional services (together with health services in the case of the UK) to provide structured, therapeutic, holistic, gender-responsive pathways through the CJS for women with mental health and substance use disorders.

The WOCMM is a community-based programme for women assessed as high risk and high need. Whilst not specifically designed for women with mental health problems, over 50% of the women involved in one pilot evaluation of the programme had a diagnosed mental health disorder, over 60% had a substance misuse problem and 74% disclosed past abuse (Millson et al., 2010). The WOCMM is based on the work of Barbara Bloom, Stephanie Covington and colleagues on the principles and theoretical underpinnings of gender-responsive interventions (Bloom et al., 2003; Bloom et al., 2004; Covington and Bloom, 2006; Covington, 2008).

The OPDSW aims to provide a clear pathway of psychologically informed, gender-specific interventions for women with personality disorders. It is targeted at women who have a committed a sexual or violent offence and/or offences where the victim is a child, and are assessed as presenting a high risk of committing another serious offence, are likely to have a severe form of personality disorder, *and* there is a clinically justifiable link between these factors.

The OPDSW treatment strategy utilises women-centred provision provided by both the National Health Service and the Prison Service, including the only female democratic therapeutic community (DTC) at HMP Send (see boxed text) and the CARE accredited programme. CARE aims to enable women with a history of violence and complex needs to better understand and reduce the risk they pose to themselves and others and to live a more satisfying and pro-social life. It comprises thirty group work sessions with ten individual narrative therapy sessions and up to two years mentoring and advocacy support (Ministry of Justice, 2011). The OPDSW will also develop 'Psychologically Informed Planned Environments' (PIPEs), which provide support following or prior to treatment in custody. The women's strategy aims to develop all six of the women's probation run hostels and the whole of one female prison (HMP Drake Hall) into PIPEs. Both models incorporate key principles which mean they can be deemed 'gender-responsive' approaches.

Box 8.1 A day as part of a women's democratic therapeutic community

Compassion is not a word I've heard a lot in prisons but it came up again and again when staff in the DTC at HMP Send spoke about their work with the women in the community. The DTC, the only one of its kind in the UK, is home to women who have committed serious crimes and have a diagnosis of personality disorder. The women attend a variety of therapy groups each morning and then engage with the general prison regime in the afternoons.

The day started with the community meeting chaired by a community member. Each of the women shared how they were feeling, most making reference to events over the weekend. Community members and staff took equal roles in asking questions to enable the speaker to reflect on their emotional responses. They offered observations that supported the more reserved women or challenged people's openness. Their observations were at once insightful, challenging and gentle. The group's questions and observations had the effect of holding a metaphorical mirror up to the speaker and encouraging her to scrutinise her reflection. The group felt safe and non-judgemental. But it was challenging. The women could not easily evade the mirror. The women were held to account for their behaviour and challenged to really think about the emotions the behaviour was expressing. The women responded in different ways. With some, the sudden recognition and understanding of an aspect of their behaviour was palpable. Others remained more resistant. But in each case it was evident that a seed had been planted that would continue to be nurtured, preened, uprooted, re-planted until it grew into something that could be recognised and used.

The DTC is based on a relational model; the community is encouraged to be together as much as possible. This is in acknowledgement that the women's problem behaviours have often been related to ruptured attachments and problems in managing relationships. So in the community, the relationship becomes the vehicle for change. Skills training (e.g., DBT/CBT) is needed because to access trauma it is better if the person has some skills with which to cope, but the skills are not what brings about change.

> The next meeting that day was the case management meeting. This involved the staff sharing thoughts and information on two community members in detail. It is a multi-disciplinary meeting attended by healthcare nurses, Probation and the DTC psychological and prison staff. The case formulation was presented. This is an important element of the meeting as all staff need to have a good understanding of the women in the community. The formulation was written as a letter to the woman and is shared with her outside of the meeting. It did not retreat from using clinical professional terms and concepts, but explained them in ways that can be easily understood. This made the 'assessment' personal and individual. The case formulation acknowledges risk and the seriousness of the crimes, but it also highlights the women's strengths. It seeks carefully for offence-paralleling behaviour and how trauma has impacted on the woman's behaviour. There was careful consideration of how to use interactions that occurred organically as learning. The discussion was open and honest and did not minimise or ignore issues with the women's behaviour but was always respectful of them and compassionate.
>
> The women's behaviours are assessed from a place of compassion. They are interpreted as resulting from trauma and ruptured attachments rather than as a symptom of personality disorder. The label somehow places blame with the individual when their behaviours are so often rooted in what has happened to them. Despite this, the women are not left in the victim role. It felt empowering. There are high expectations of the women, they are held to account and expected to take responsibility for their therapy. So the therapy sees their behaviour in terms of their trauma experiences but takes a forward-looking approach from this, seeking how to understand and stop the damaging behaviours that have resulted from the trauma.
>
> After a day at the DTC I was left thinking about how similar the women in the community are to women in the general prison population, like Alice, Bette and Misha. They had committed more serious crimes, but the stories of neglect, abuse, distress, addiction, mental health problems are stories that you hear often in women's prisons. In this environment, the women were given a chance to change their stories; to be someone who is helpful, insightful, supportive, creative, who can work with and relate to others positively, is compassionate, someone who can change. Surely all women in prison deserve that chance.

Theoretical underpinnings of trauma-informed, gender-responsive interventions

Covington and Bloom have identified four key theoretical perspectives that should inform gender-responsive treatment. These are: pathways theory, relational theory, trauma theory and addictions theory (Covington, 2000; Covington and Bloom, 2006; Bloom and Covington, 2008).

Pathways theory: Pathways theory suggests the onset of criminality in women is triggered by experiences that are gendered. It identifies experiences of abuse, mental illness related to early life experiences, substance misuse and addiction, economic and social marginalisation, and relationships as key issues producing and sustaining female criminality (Daly, 1992; Brennan et al., 2012).

Relational theory: Relational theory proposes that women's psychological maturity is not based on disconnection and individuation but on building a sense of relatedness with others. As Covington (2007) explains, 'women develop a sense of self-worth when their actions arise out of and lead back to connections with others' (p.139). The relationships experienced by women in the CJS are characterised by rupture and exploitation, therefore a primary goal for gender-responsive interventions is to promote and model healthy connections to family, friends and community (Calhoun et al., 2005). Instead of the 'self' being the key site for change, the focus is on relationship development.

Trauma theory: Trauma is both an event and a response to an event that causes overwhelming fear, powerlessness and horror. High rates of severe childhood maltreatment and repeated physical and sexual abuse in adolescence and adulthood are a feature of the life stories of most women in the CJS but in particular those with mental health and substance misuse problems. Trauma-informed services are those that are provided for problems other than trauma but require knowledge concerning the impact of trauma (Covington, 2000, 2008; Bloom and Covington, 2006).

Addiction Theory: The holistic health model of addiction understands addiction as a disease with emotional, psychological, spiritual, environmental and socio-political dimensions (see Pycroft and Green this volume). It is consistent with research that indicates drug addiction is a brain disease that disrupts the mechanisms responsible for generating, modulating, and controlling cognitive, emotional and social behaviour and that is it a progressive disease with increasingly severe biological, psychological and social problems over time. This is the theoretical understanding of addiction recommended for the development of gender-responsive services (Covington, 2008; Covington and Bloom, 2006).

They also suggest six principles that should form the basis of trauma-informed, gender-responsive treatment. The leading principle is an acknowledgement that gender makes a difference and that treatment for women needs to be responsive to this difference. Principle two is the creation of an environment based on safety, respect and dignity. Principle three is that interventions should be relational and promote healthy connections to children, family, significant others and the community. Principle four states that interventions should provide women with the opportunities to improve their socio-economic circumstances through education and training in recognition that most women in the CJS are economically disadvantaged. Principle five is the establishment of a system of community supervision and re-entry with comprehensive, collaborative services to support women in navigating through disparate and fragmented services. As Bloom and Covington explain, 'There is a need for wraparound services – that is, a holistic and culturally sensitive plan for each woman that draws on a coordinated range of services within her community' (Bloom and Covington, 2006, p.14).

Therapeutic approaches

- Person-centred: develops strong therapeutic relationships.
- Narrative therapy: helps the storyteller analyse events for alternative meanings, co-creates a story that contains solutions as well as problems.
- Family & group therapy.
- Expressive therapies: art, psychodrama.
- Centralises attachments: provides a secure base consisting of safe physical boundaries, transparent rules and procedures, and good relationships.
- Teaches mindfulness and relaxation techniques.
- CBT/DBT: to enhance life and social skills.
- Establishes a system of community and post-release supervision services.

Theoretical underpinnings

- Pathways theories.
- Relational theories.
- Addictions theories.
- Trauma theories.

Principles

- Holistic: includes advice, treatment, assessment & referral across a range of areas including family/social, personal and life skills.
- Takes a unified treatment approach that addresses both mental health & substance use disorders as primary.
- Based on women's competencies & strengths and promotes self-reliance.
- Conveys enthusiasm for and confidence in the women's abilities.
- Women-only groups.
- Based on individualised treatment planning.
- Provides the opportunity to improve socio-economic conditions.
- Culturally competent: sensitive to the messages and values that are shaped by culture and the impact of these on the lives of women
- Uses gender-responsive screening and assessment tools.

Environment

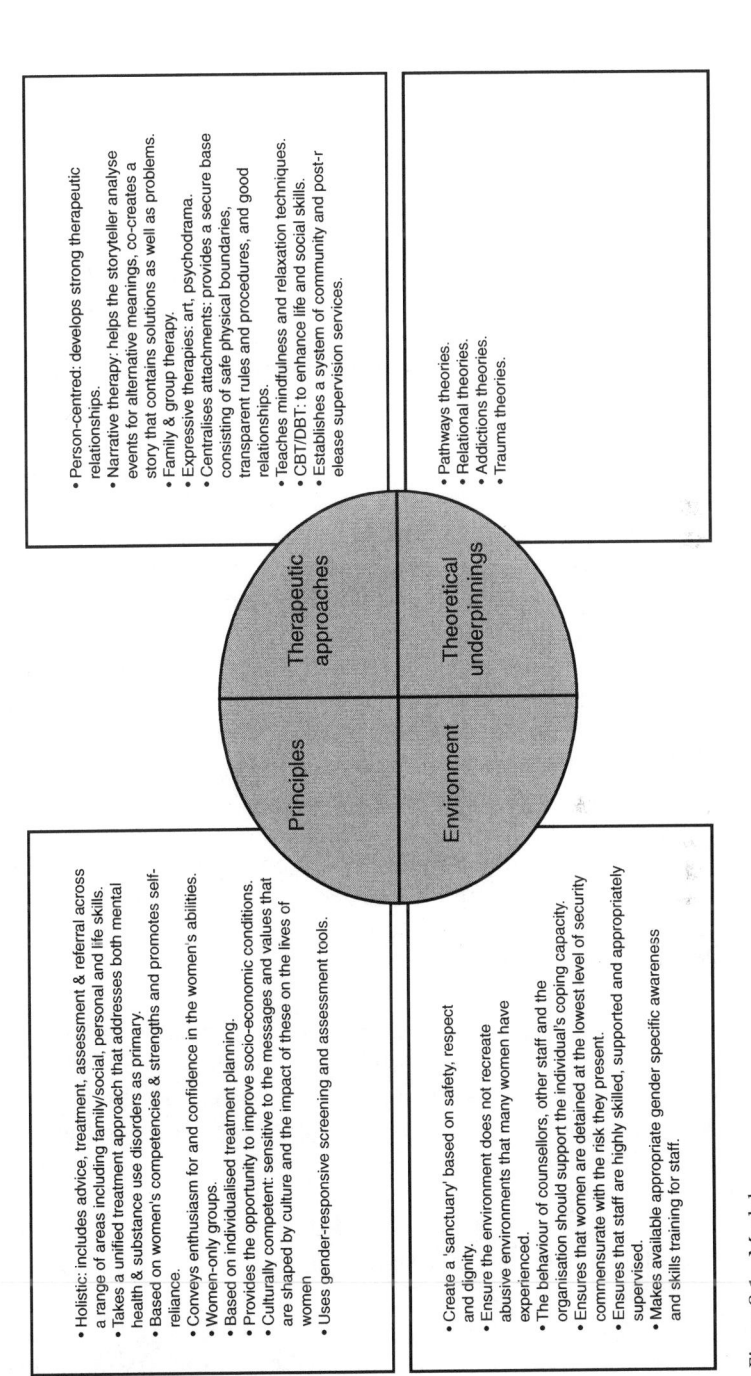

- Create a 'sanctuary' based on safety, respect and dignity.
- Ensure the environment does not recreate abusive environments that many women have experienced.
- The behaviour of counsellors, other staff and the organisation should support the individual's coping capacity.
- Ensures that women are detained at the lowest level of security commensurate with the risk they present.
- Ensures that staff are highly skilled, supported and appropriately supervised.
- Makes available appropriate gender specific awareness and skills training for staff.

Figure 8.1 Model

Conclusions: evaluations of gender-responsive approaches

Gender-responsive treatment has been developed in response to the body of research documenting the higher prevalence of trauma exposure and co-occurring substance use and mental health disorders among women in the CJS. Prior research has highlighted the importance of addressing the role of trauma in women's mental health, substance use and criminality but few studies have examined whether trauma-informed, gender-responsive treatment produces different outcomes in relation to these.

Morash et al., (1998) undertook surveys asking women in prison in the USA to name women's programmes in their jurisdictions that were effective, innovative, or promising. Elements the women deemed conducive to success included many that were gender specific: staff who provided strong female role models, the opportunity to form supportive peer networks, and attention to women's particular experiences as victims of abuse, as parents of children, and in negative relationships with men. Survey respondents also cited the need for more programmes providing drug treatment and mental health services.

Saxena et al., (2014) carried out a randomised control trial between 2006 and 2008 of two treatment groups at the Valley State Prison for Women in California, comparing outcomes of a standard therapeutic community (TC) programme with a gender-responsive programme. These programmes were *Helping Women Recover: A programme for treating substance abuse* and *Beyond Trauma: A healing journey for women* developed by Stephanie Covington. The results of the trial indicate positive effects on psychological and substance misuse outcomes for women who have experienced trauma. The study measured the impact of gender-responsive treatment on depression and number of substances used. Those who had experienced prior sexual or physical abuse and received gender-responsive treatment had reduced odds of depression and reduced rates of substances used. It concluded:

> GRT (gender-responsive treatment) has shown potential for mitigating negative outcomes (depression and substance use) associated with histories of abuse for incarcerated women. Women who had experienced prior traumatic events improved their psychological status and decreased the number of substances they used in the trauma-informed, gender-responsive substance abuse treatment group. Even when controlling for the presence of clinical level trauma distress (i.e., PTSD), GRT successfully moderated the associations between abuse and depression and abuse and substance use. (Saxena et al., 2014, p. 427.)

These findings support previous evaluations that found women who completed these programmes reported less substance misuse, less depression and fewer trauma symptoms including anxiety, sleep disturbance and disassociation after completion of the programmes (Covington et al., 2008).

Women in the CJS have higher rates of abusive experiences, mental health needs and substance misuse problems than women in society in general and men in the CJS. A link between suffering depression and reoffending in women has been established. There is debate about whether victimisation is a criminogenic need for women (see Blanchette and Brown, 2006 for a summary of the research); however the number of women with mental health needs who have experienced trauma in the CJS indicates trauma needs to be incorporated into any holistic treatment intervention for women. Ideally, more use would be made of gender-informed community provision. The network of women's centres in the UK provides holistic, multi-modal, woman-centred services that can respond to the diverse needs of women who enter the CJS. Women's problem-solving courts are another innovative scheme that could divert women with mental health problems from prison (Ward, 2014). However, at present, the CJS remains one of the primary treatment providers of mental health and substance misuse programmes to women. If addressing trauma through gender-responsive interventions can alleviate some of the psychological effects of abusive experiences among the group that suffer the effects of them the most, it has a duty to further research and develop such interventions throughout women's community and custodial correctional settings.

References

Alleyne, V. (2006). Locked up means locked out: Women, addiction and incarceration. *Women and Therapy*, 29(3), 181–194. Retrieved from : http://dx.doi.org/10.1300/J015v29n03_10.

American Psychological Association (2004). *The effects of trauma do not have to last a lifetime*. Retrieved from: http://www.apa.org/research/action/ptsd.aspx

Belknap, J. (2007). *The invisible woman: Gender, Crime and Justice* (3rd ed.). Belmont, CA: Wadsworth, Cengage Learning.

Blanchette, K. and Brown, S.L. (2006). *The assessment and treatment of women offenders: An integrative perspective*. Chichester: John Wiley & Sons Ltd.

Bloom, B. and Covington, S. (2008). Addressing the mental health needs of women offenders. In R. Gido and L. Dalley (eds). *Women's mental health issues across the criminal justice system*. Retrieved from: http://www.stephaniecovington.com/assets/files/FinalAddressingtheMentalHealthNeeds.pdf.

Bloom, B., Owen, B., and Covington, S. (2003). *Gender responsive strategies: Research, practice and guiding principles for women offenders*. National Institute of Corrections: US Department of Justice. Retrieved from: https://s3.amazonaws.com/static.nicic.gov/Library/018017.pdf

Bloom, B., Owen, B., and Covington, S. (2004) Women offenders and the gendered effects of public policy. *Review of policy research* 21(1): 31–48.

Borrill, J. Maden, A. Martin, A. Weaver, T. Stimson, G. Farrell, M. and Barnes, T. (2003). *Differential substance misuse treatment needs of women, ethnic minorities and young offenders in prison: prevalence of substance misuse and treatment needs*. Home Office Online Report 33/03. London: Home Office Research, Development and Statistics Directorate.

Brennan, T. Breitenbach, M. Dieterich, W. Salisbury, E.J. and Van Vooris, P. (2012). Women's pathways to serious and habitual crime: A person-centred analysis incorporating gender responsive factors. *Criminal Justice and Behaviour*, 39 (11), 1481–1508. Retrieved from: http://dx.doi.org/10.1177/0093854812436777.

Calhoun, G.B. Bartolomucci, C.L. and McLean, B.A. (2005). Building connections: Relational group work with female adolescent offenders. *Women and Therapy*, 28 (2), 17–29. Retrieved from: http://dx.doi.org/10.1300/J015v28n02_02.

Carlen, P. (1988). *Women, Crime and Poverty*. Milton Keynes: Open University Press.

Chesney-Lind, M. and Pasko, L. (2013). *The female offender: Girls, Women and Crime* (3rd ed.). London: Sage.

Corston, J. (2007). *The Corston Report: A review of women with particular vulnerabilities in the criminal justice system*. London: Home Office.

Covington, S. (2000). Helping women recover: A comprehensive integrated treatment model. *Alcohol Treatment Quarterly*, 18 (3), 99–111. Retrieved from: http://www.stephaniecovington.com/assets/files/9.pdf.

Covington, S. (2007) The relational theory of women's psychological development: Implications for the criminal justice system. In Ruth Zaplin (Ed.) *Female Offenders: Critical perspectives and effective interventions* (pp. 135–164). Sudbury, M.A. Jones and Bartlett Publishers. Retrieved from: http://www.stephaniecovington.com/assets/files/FinalTheRelationalTheorychapter2007.pdf

Covington, S. (2008). Women and addiction: A trauma-informed approach. *Journal of Psychoactive Drugs*, 40 (5), 377–385. Retrieved from: http://dx.doi.org/10.1080/02791072.2008.1040665.

Covington, S. and Bloom, B. (2006). Gender responsive treatment and services in correctional settings. *Women and Therapy*, 29 (3/4), 9–33. Retrieved from: http://dx.doi.org/10.1300/J015v29n03_02.

Covington, S. Burke, C. Keaton, S. and Norcott, C. (2008). Evaluation of a trauma-informed and gender-responsive intervention for women in drug treatment. *Journal of Psychoactive Drugs*, 40, 387–398. Retrieved from: http://dx.doi.org/10.1080/02791072.2008.10400666.

Cusick, L. Martin, A. and May, T. (2003). *Vulnerability and involvement in drug use and sex work*. Home Office Research Findings 207. London: Home Office.

Daly, K. (1992) Women's pathways to felony court: Feminist theories of lawbreaking and problems of representation. *Review of Law and Women's Studies* 2: 11–52

De Cou, K. (2002) A gender-wise prison? Opportunities for and limits to reform. In Pat Carlen (Ed.) *Women and punishment: The struggle for justice* (pp: 97–109). Devon. Willan Publishing.

DeHart, D. Lynch, S. Belknap, J. Dass-Brailsford, P. and Green, B. (2014). Life history models of female offending: The roles of serious mental illness and trauma in women's pathways to jail. *Psychology of Women Quarterly*, 38, 138–151. Retrieved from: http://dx.doi.org/10.1177/0361684313494357.

Green, B., Miranda, J., Daroowalla, A., and Siddique, J. (2005) Trauma exposure, mental health functioning and program needs of women in jail. *Crime and Delinquency* 51(1): 133–151

Heney, J. and Kristiansen, M. (1998). An analysis of the impact of prison on women survivors of childhood sexual abuse. *Women and Therapy*, 20 (4), 29–44. Retrieved from: http://dx.doi.org/10.1300.J015v20n04_03.

Human Rights Watch (2006) *U.S.: The number of mentally ill in prisons quadrupled.* Retrieved from: https://www.hrw.org/news/2006/09/05/us-number-mentally-ill-prisons-quadrupled

James, D.J. and Glaze, L.E. (2006). *Mental Health Problems of Prison and Jail Inmates.* Bureau of Justice Statistics. Retrieved from: http://www.ojp.usdoj.gov/bjs/abstract/mhppji.htm.

Jordan, B.K., Federman, E.B., Burns, B.J., Schlenger, W.E., Fairbank, J.A.. and Caddell, J.M. (2002) Lifetime use of mental health and substance abuse treatment services by incarcerated women felons. *Psychiatric Services* 53:317–325

Light, M. Grant, E. and Hopkins, K. (2013). *Gender differences in the substance misuse and mental health amongst prisoners: Results from the Surveying Prisoner Crime Reduction (SPCR) longitudinal cohort study of prisoners.* Ministry of Justice Analytical Series. Retrieved from: https://www.gov.uk/government/uploads/system/uploads/attachment_data/file/220060/gender-substance-misuse-mental-health-prisoners.pdf.

Lynch, S.M., Fritch, A., and Heath, N (2012) Looking beneath the surface: The nature of incarcerated women's experiences of interpersonal violence, treatment needs and mental health. *Feminist Criminology* 7(4): 381–400

Maden, A. Swinton, M. and Gunn, J. (1994). A criminological and psychiatric survey of women serving a prison sentence. *British Journal of Criminology*, 34 (2), 172–191. Retrieved from: http://bjc.oxfordjournals.org/content/34/2/172.full.pdf+html.

Maidment, M.R. (2006). 'We're not all that criminal': Getting beyond the pathologizing and individualizing of women's crime. *Women and Therapy*, 29 (3/4), 35–56. Retrieved from: http://dx.doi.org?10.1300/J015v29n03_03.

Millson, B., Robinson, D., & Van Dieten, M. (2010): *Women Offender Case Management Model: An outcome evaluation.* Washington, DC: U.S. Department of Justice, National Institute of Corrections. Retrieved from: http://www.cjinvolvedwomen.org/sites/all/documents/Women%20Offender%20Case%20Management%20Model.pdf.

Ministry of Justice (2011). *The Correctional Services Accreditation Panel Report 2009–2010.* Retrieved from: https://www.gov.uk/government/uploads/system/uploads/attachment_data/file/217266/correctional-services-accreditation-panel-report-09-10-annex-a-c.pdf.

Ministry of Justice (2014). *Statistics on women in the criminal justice system 2013: A Ministry of Justice publication under Section 95 of the Criminal Justice Act 1991.* Retrieved from: https://www.gov.uk/government/statistics/women-and-the-criminal-justice-system-2013.

Ministry of Justice and Department of Health (2011). *Offender personality disorder strategy for women.* Retrieved from: http://www.womensbreakout.org.uk/wp-content/uploads/downloads/2012/07/Offender-Personality-Disorder-Strategy-Summary.pdf.

National Institute of Corrections (2006) *Women Offender Case Management Model.* Retrieved from: http://static.nicic.gov/Library/021814.pdf.

Morash, M. Bynam, T. and Koons, B.A. (1998). Women offenders: Programming needs and promising approaches. Retrieved from: https://www.ncjrs.gov/pdffiles/171668.pdf.

Norman, N. and Barron, J. (2011) *Supporting women offenders who have experienced domestic and sexual violence.* Produced by the Women's Aid Federation of England for the National Offender Management Service. Retrieved from: www.womensaid.org.uk/core/core_picker/download.asp?id=3409

Plugge, E. Douglas, N. and Fitzpatrick, R. (2006). *The health of women in prison study findings.* Oxford: University of Oxford.

Saxena, P. Messina, N.P. and Grella, C.E. (2014). Who benefits from gender-responsive treatment? Accounting for abuse history on longitudinal outcomes for women in prison. *Criminal Justice and Behavior*, 41 (4), 417–432. Retrieved from: http://dx.doi.org/10.1177/0093854813514405.

Short, J. and Barber, M. (2004). Troubled inside. Vulnerability in prison. In N. Jeffcote and T. Watson (eds). *Working therapeutically with women in secure mental health settings*. London: Jessica Kingsley Publishers.

Trauma (2014) Retrieved from American Psychological Association website: http://www.apa.org/topics/trauma/index.aspx

Van Wormer, K. (2010). *Working with female offenders: A gender-sensitive approach*. Hoboken, NJ: John Wiley & Sons, Inc.

Ward, J. (2014) *Are problem solving courts the way forward for justice?* Howard League What Is Justice working papers 2/2014. Retrieved from: https://d19ylpo4aovc7m.cloudfront.net/fileadmin/howard_league/user/pdf/Research/What_is_Justice/HLWP_2_2014.pdf.

Widom, C.S. (2000) Child victimization: Early adversity, later psychopathology. *National Institute of Justice Journal*. Retrieved from: https://www.ncjrs.gov/pdffiles1/jr000242b.pdf

Williams, K. Papadopoulou, V. and Booth, N. (2012). *Prisoners' childhood and family backgrounds: Results from the Surveying Prisoner Crime Reduction (SPCR) longitudinal cohort study of prisoners*. (Ministry of Justice Research Series 4/12). Retrieved from UK Ministry of Justice website: http://www.gov.uk/government/publications/prisoners-childhood-and-family-backgrounds.

9
Challenging the Cultural Determinants of Dual Diagnosis in the Criminal Justice System

Aaron Pycroft and Anita Green

Introduction – what is in a name?

In itself the term 'dual diagnosis', which is used by practitioners in mental health, substance misuse services and the criminal justice system (CJS) to define a person who uses 'illegal' drugs (this can include the misuse of prescribed or over the counter medication) and/or alcohol and has a mental health problem, denotes something relatively straightforward. However in reality the use of this medically influenced term is misleading (Green, 2015), and in practice it is used more as a term of convenience to define what is a complex and heterogeneous group of service users who are often perceived as challenging to work with. In relation to the CJS, for example, dual diagnosis does not capture the complex reality of the person's criminal status or take into consideration the increased health concerns that are inevitable when someone misuses alcohol and/or illegal drugs. For example, we know in relation to physical health that diabetes, coronary heart disease, and hepatitis B or C increases. This has been highlighted recently by the Kings Fund and Centre for Mental Health (Naylor et al., 2012). Though not focussing specifically on dual diagnosis, the authors state the strong link between long-term physical health conditions and co-occurring mental health problems results in poorer health outcomes, so reducing the quality of life. There are also other social and psychological challenges that include: domestic and sexual violence (as a survivor or perpetrator), homelessness and unstable housing, financial difficulties, childhood abuse (physical, emotional or sexual), a decreasing family network, and learning needs. This group of people experience disproportionate levels of social exclusion, isolation and marginalisation, which can contribute to premature death due to illness or increased risk of suicide (see also Göbbels, Thakker and Ward, this volume; Scally, this volume). There are an estimated 60,000 people with complex needs and exclusions at any one time in England (*Making Every Adult Matter,* Clinks et al., 2009, p. 8) with an estimated prevalence of between 30% and 70% in health and social care services (Crome et al., 2009).

In 2002 the UK Government's Social Exclusion Unit (SEU, 2002) found that dual diagnosis significantly increases the problems faced by prisoners in accessing services, with drugs workers, for instance, being reluctant to take on prisoners with neurosis, while mental health staff would not work with a prisoner while he or she was addicted to drugs. The SEU pointed out that this was not unique to the prison system as it was also mirrored in the community where people with dual diagnosis typically fell between services. These concerns were also highlighted by the Bradley Report (Department of Health, 2009) which argued that dual diagnosis should be regarded as the norm, rather than the exception, and provided evidence that 74.5% of users of drug services and 85.5% of users of alcohol services experienced mental health problems, while 44% of mental health service users reported drug use and/or were assessed to have used alcohol at hazardous or harmful levels in the past year. The report found that a lack of both service provision and coordinated care was also the norm.

Leahy and Hawker, as far back as 1998 (p. 275), highlighted some of the problems associated with the diagnosing and labelling of dual diagnosis:

> Our concern as mental health workers should not be to debate whether certain people suffer a certain syndrome known as 'dual diagnosis' but rather how we can ensure that individuals with these intensive and complex problems are able to access a service which understands and responds appropriately to their multiple needs.

Guest and Holland (2011, p. 163) argue that people with dual diagnosis receive unpredictable care and treatment because the 'intricate and often complex relationship' between the person's different problems does not always make sense to those working in mental health services; for example the person with a dual diagnosis may require different responses from health, social and criminal justice services dependent upon such factors as their motivation, physical health status, links with the CJS and whether or not they are drug or alcohol dependent and mentally unwell. They may have one main need complicated by others or a number of lower-level problems which in combination are a cause for concern (Page, 2011, p. 174). Despite ongoing academic and policy work the debates surrounding who facilitates and coordinates the care and treatment required by the person presenting in any of these ways continues. Who needs to address what issue/s is still not always transparent and coherent, which we argue is symptomatic of a shortfall in policy and statutory guidance at both a local and national level.

Despite the plethora of research evidence, the ongoing expression of frustration by practitioners and service users and the setting up of commissions of inquiry, very little seems to have actually changed and the question of why that is needs to be addressed.

This chapter will offer an analysis of the ways in which the concept of dual diagnosis has developed through analysing the key legislation in the form of the Mental Health Act 1983 (as amended in 2007) and the Misuse of Drugs Act 1971. It is our contention that this legislation provides a set of conditions that are deterministic in nature and which bring about the systemic problems with dual diagnosis which are all too familiar to service users, clinicians and commissioners of services. Dual diagnosis is a socially constructed and complex problem brought about by the reductionism inherent in contemporaneous approaches to psychiatric classification, mental health and substance misuse legislation, and the ways in which services are then created to meet particular needs. In conceptualising the nature of the problem we are taking the view that problems in complex systems require higher-order solutions rather than a perpetuation of reductionist solutions (see Pycroft, 2014). This chapter will therefore argue for the development of whole-systems approaches based on service user and co-production strategies. We contend that the policy discourse of 'hard to reach' groups and complex needs requires a change in thinking to allow for an understanding of the structural determinants of health inequality. These structural determinants are political and social and are underpinned by moral and cultural systems that create disadvantage for some and advantages for others (see McPherson and McGibbon, 2014; Arrigo and Bersot, this volume). This structural inequity (see also Göbbels, Thakker and Ward, this volume) provides for an inability to access social and health care, leading to a spiralling down as aspects of mental and physical health deteriorate further, for those with a dual diagnosis. A failure to understand and coordinate the support, guidance and interventions a person with complex needs requires can lead to higher costs not only to themselves, their families, but also the local community and government resources. Whilst the language of whole systems is prevalent in contemporaneous policy discourse, including service user perspectives, there is still a treatment policy and delivery void that creates and perpetuates significant disadvantage for people who experience dual diagnosis.

Dual diagnosis strategies, policies and guidance

As might be expected, dual diagnosis has been seen as a problem of psychiatry as this profession has been the lead in diagnosing and dealing with mental health problems and substance misuse (see also Scally, this volume). A formal classificatory recognition of dual diagnosis in the form of drug-induced mental health disorders first appeared in the 3rd edition of the *Diagnostic and Statistical Manual of Mental Disorders* (DSM-III) in 1980 (American Psychiatric Association, 1980). Dual diagnosis was first mentioned in UK policy in 1999 in the *National Service Framework for Mental Health: Modern Standards and Service Models*. However, there was little emphasis on dual diagnosis, let alone specific guidance for service development or helpful interventions.

In the UK it was not until 2002 that dual diagnosis was given some focus in relation to dedicated national policy (Department of Health, 2002). The dual diagnosis good practice guide was informed by the work of Drake et al. (1993) in the USA, with the plan that local areas develop their own dual diagnosis strategies across agencies and partners who were already providing care and treatment for dual diagnosis service users. Historically, in the UK and in most countries, mental health and substance misuse policy development had not been linked because of the services being developed separately, due in part to the differing legislation. Previously, substance misuse policy focussed on control and prohibition, and more recently a health-related agenda, for example management of the harmful effects of substance misuse. Mental health has generally focussed on community care, which has evolved from closing the large mental health institutions to providing community services aimed at reducing admissions (Morgan and Dar, 2011, p. 9; see below).

The Department of Health has produced a number of 'dual diagnosis' policy guides since 2002. As Hughes (quoted in Cooper, 2011, p. 121) argues 'Clinical guidelines are only as good as the people implementing them.' It has not always been clear who should be the lead agency or professional grouping in relation to implementation, leading to a shortfall in policy implementation at local and national level. However, a small number of mental health trusts have chosen to employ dual diagnosis Nurse Consultants whose role has focussed on ensuring dual diagnosis is addressed through strategy and policy development, training practitioners, role modelling clinical expertise and research (www.dualdiagnosis.co.uk). The later guidance for mental health inpatient and day hospital settings did go further in providing some guidance on managing specific clinical concerns and challenges. There were:

- *Dual diagnosis in mental health inpatient and day hospital settings.* (Department of Health, 2006b).
- *A guide for the management of dual diagnosis in prisons.* (Department of Health and Ministry of Justice, 2009).

It is our contention that because these were 'guidance', i.e. encouraging the adoption of principles rather than creating a requirement to do so, they lacked strength and the ability to influence commissioners and mental health and substance misuse services at a local level, because there were no specific recommendations about treatment and care interventions. This lack of clear policy was a missed opportunity to gain the political and financial resources necessary to drive implementation. However what is clear is that any requirements for compliance with a nationally driven dual diagnosis strategy would run into significant difficulty due to the problems brought about by existing legislation, and would require changes to that legislation. The key legislation is discussed below, but with respect to change it is important to remember that the Mental Health Act 1983 was amended in 2007 and failed to significantly address dual diagnosis, and that there is currently no political appetite to reform the Misuse of Drugs Act 1971.

The sociopolitical determinants of dual diagnosis and health inequality in the criminal justice system

It is important to note that it was following the process of de-institutionalisation in the 1980s (a process that occurred across western democracies) that the concept of dual diagnosis first emerged. Whilst this approach was based upon the noble aspirations of care in the community, the reality was one of people with mental health problems finding themselves in poor quality accommodation, unemployed and vulnerable to the availability of alcohol and illicit drugs (Mueser et al., 1998; see Göbbels, Thakker and Ward, this volume) and also coming into contact with the criminal justice system.

When people who are experiencing dual diagnosis are subject to the requirements of a criminal justice system, whose ostensible aims to rehabilitate are conflated with punishment, deterrence and risk aversion (see Pycroft and Clift, 2012), then there are added levels of complexity and determinism which challenge us (or more precisely *should* challenge us) to address the ethical basis for dealing with mental ill health and substance misuse within that system (see also Canton, this volume). In particular, the principle of less eligibility is a powerful sociopolitical and ideological process that discriminates most profoundly against already vulnerable people. The sociocultural dynamics which shape institutions and service delivery are discussed by Arrigo and Bersot (this volume) through the critical philosophy of psychological jurisprudence and its analysis of alienation and dehumanisation. The evidence clearly demonstrates that dual diagnosis as currently conceptualised and practised leads through structural service exclusion to social exclusion and there is as a matter of urgency a need to humanise the system. First we will look at the nature of those key determinants, and then make suggestions for evidence-based approaches based upon principles of human agency that seek novel solutions to these deterministic factors.

Legislation

The two major pieces of UK legislation that in practice create a systemic concept of dual diagnosis are the Misuse of Drugs Act 1971 and the Mental Health Act 1983 (as amended 2007).

The Misuse of Drugs Act 1971 adopts the principles of punishment and deterrence predicated upon an 'evidence-based' approach to the relative harm of particular drugs, e.g. the more harmful the drug the more severe the sentence. The role of scientific evidence in political decision making is heavily contested and beyond the scope of this chapter to address in full, but for an interesting discussion in relation to drug policy see Stevens (2011). The legislation also allows for the setting up of treatment centres and in many ways reflects a continuation of the so called 'British System' of drug control, which seeks a balance between care and control in drug policy (see Strang and Gossop, 2005a, 2005b). However, what is clear from the approach taken, despite the creation of resources for the treatment of drug users, is that drug use is seen as a consequence of rational choice and that punishment and the threat of punishment would deter people from engaging in this illegal activity. The Act calls for greater multi-agency cooperation to address drug issues but there are no specific links made with mental health issues. An added level of complexity is brought about by the fact that the Act does not cover alcohol, despite its indisputable harms to individuals and society. The consequence of this is that successive governments have focussed on the harms brought about by illicit drugs with well-funded drug strategies, whilst alcohol policy has very much been an afterthought. For example the New Labour Government produced its first drug strategy in 1998 (Home Office, 1998) with its Alcohol Strategy, which was not well funded, taking until 2004 (Home Office, 2004). This has meant, for example, that despite a need to address multiple and complex needs within clinical populations, such as substance misuse and mental health, that funding has either been ring-fenced for addressing illicit drugs only or simply non-existent.

A good example is in the provision of the CARAT service (Counselling, Assessment, Referral, Advice and Through care) as a universal drug treatment service in every prison establishment across England and Wales. This is funded to work with illicit drug use only, despite the realities of complex needs including a strong correlation between drug use and alcohol use (see the Drug Treatment Outcome Research Study (DTORS.org) for details of drug use including alcohol for those entering drug treatment). Pycroft and Cook (2010), in a needs assessment for one prison, found that the impact of this was that alcohol interventions were being provided by the education department in an effort to at least try and address this important but under-resourced issue.

The Mental Health Act (1983/2007) specifically adopts exclusion criteria for drugs and alcohol. The amendments to the Act take the position that drug and alcohol problems and dependence should not be regarded as mental disorders but rather as social and behavioural problems characterised by varying degrees of habit and dependence. This approach is completely at odds with psychiatric classification and is further compounded by the Mental Health Act Code of Practice (Department of Health, 2008, section 3.10) which states:

> Alcohol or drug dependence may be accompanied by, or associated with, a mental disorder which does fall within the Act's definition. If the relevant criteria are met, it is therefore possible to detain people who are suffering from mental disorder, even though they are dependent on alcohol or drugs. This is true even if the mental disorder in question results from the person's drug or alcohol dependence.

The realities brought about by the legislation lead Noyce (2012, p. 46) to conclude that:

> What we have in practice is a recipe of diagnostic and legal contradictions, fluid in nature and open to interpretation, resulting in a form of assessment that is neither unified nor codified in any meaningful way. This lack of coherence and systemization, coupled with decisions about resources determined at best by the agendas of individual practitioners and agencies, is made worse by discrepancies in clinical and diagnostic assessment.

In addition there is other legislation that impacts directly on the commissioning and delivery of services. With respect to mental health, the NHS and Community Act 1990 has established the Care Programme Approach (CPA) to ensure the appropriate assessment and coordinated care of people with mental health problems. With the establishment of the partnership between the Prison Service and the NHS this now needed to be implemented in prisons. The Sainsbury Centre for Mental Health (2008) reported the difficulties of implementing CPA in prison settings with a quarter of in-reach clients not on CPA, with the added complication of getting community services to engage with prisoners on release, particularly when resources were limited. At the heart of the NHS and Community Act 1990 is the principle of service user involvement and the Sainsbury report also highlighted the near impossibility of involving family members or carers in CPA in prison. This is also compounded by the fact that any concept of service user involvement has been anathema to criminal justice generally (see Pycroft, 2006) and prison particularly.

In the UK the Department of Health (2002, p. 4) had promoted the view that those with a dual diagnosis should receive their care and treatment from secondary mental health services; an approach which generally has come to underpin local dual diagnosis policies and strategies. It was seen as a helpful approach to reduce the incidence of service users being missed by one service or another. However, the implementation of 'mainstreaming' by Mental Health Trusts has been an upstream battle; perhaps because such a reductionist approach does not fit or work for a large and heterogeneous group of service users (Green, 2015).

Providing 'mainstreaming' integrated care and treatment remains a strategic challenge for Mental Health Trusts, particularly in a climate of competitive tendering when substance misuse services can be provided by partners outside the National Health Service (NHS). These partners may provide services underpinned by alternative philosophies and have different priorities due to the way the service is funded. This highlights the potential for a lack of joined-up thinking when you consider the recommendation made by the Centre for Mental Health, DrugScope and the UK Drug Policy Commission (2012, p. 3) stating that 'joint commissioning of mental health and drug or alcohol services needs to become the norm. Integrated care for those with a dual diagnosis appears far beyond the horizon when commissioners are choosing to commission services in isolation of each other. Even though Public Health England (PHE) identify substance misuse and mental health as key priorities the lack of national and local joined up systems may prevent an effective response to the delivery of integrated care and treatment'.

To further compound and potentially exacerbate the plight of the dual diagnosis service user accessing mental health services is the debate of how they 'fit' into the Payment by Results approach (PbR). PbRs is a systematised commissioning approach for the payment of mental health care and treatment outcomes. It uses clustering of symptoms for specific diagnostic care and treatment (there are 20 care clusters). Care cluster 16 is allocated to those with a dual diagnosis who have enduring, moderate to severe mental health symptoms with unstable, chaotic lifestyles and co-existing substance misuse. It could be argued that this may ensure those with serious and enduring symptoms will have their complex needs met. However, it could be questioned if service users with many problems fall below the PbR threshold there will be a repeat of the serious gaps in service provision that has long been a criticism of meeting the needs of those with a dual diagnosis.

The principle of less eligibility

The principle of less eligibility is directly linked with the use of deterrence as one of the aims of punishment within criminal justice. It is a powerful ideological concept that stems from the work of the utilitarian philosopher Jeremy Bentham, was foundational to the English Poor Laws, and argues that:

> If the condition of persons maintained without property by the labour of others were rendered more eligible than that of persons maintained by their own labour then...individuals destitute of property would be continually

withdrawing themselves from the class of persons maintained by the labour of others. (Bentham, cited in Sieh, 1989)

When considering health care in criminal justice (and especially in prison) it is important to consider the contemporaneous nature and re-emergence of less eligibility in an age of austerity and financial cuts with a dominant discourse of the deserving and undeserving of help. It is argued by Sieh (1989) that the concept is both vague and flexible and allows for the exercise of discretion in criminal justice. This is important because within the prison estate the fundamental and overriding concern of prison staff is security with everything else being subordinate to this consideration, for which there are some very powerful examples. Such as that of female prisoners giving birth with prison officers being present in the hospital room and being handcuffed immediately before and after the birth itself (http://www.theguardian.com/lifeandstyle/2010/feb/21/pregnant-women-in-prison) (see also Petrillo, this volume).

The principle as applied to the Work House now applies to prison (and to community sentences where it is more often referred to as 'less superiority'), whereby the prisoners or those on community sentences should not receive a standard of lifestyle or services superior to a non-criminal. This principle is evident in the 2010–2015 UK Coalition Government's approach to, for example, capping welfare benefits to a level that does not exceed the average wage of 'hard-working' people. This was emphasised by the Chancellor of the Exchequer when he said that, 'The welfare state needs to reflect the British sense of fair play...Unless they have disabilities to cope with, no family should get more from living on benefits that the average family gets from going out to work' (cited by http://www.cpag.org.uk/content/cap-it-all%E2%80%A6). With respect to criminal justice the Secretary of State for Justice has argued that prisoners must work harder to earn privileges such as having TVs in their cells or earning wages, or even having books. He said, 'I want the arrival in prison for the first time to be an experience that is not one they'd want to repeat. That means an environment where they arrive [where] standards are pretty basic and then they start to gain extras by contributing...and if they won't do it, then they can't expect to start gaining those privileges' (cited by http://www.bbc.co.uk/news/uk-22341867).

This is the context in which we need to understand healthcare in prison, which only became part of mainstream NHS service provision in 2003. This welcome change was intended to ensure that prisoners received equality of and access to care equivalent to that available in the community, and that local primary care providers were commissioning services within prison. But as Sieh (1989, pp. 169–170) notes:

Any reform which ignores the concept of less eligibility is doomed from the start. Divergent sentiments on the treatment of inmates become manifest and slow progress when a change occurs in the handling of an inmate. Bureaucrats view innovation as troublesome and see any reform...as troublesome because of the difficulties associated with implementation.

In their research, Cornford et al. (2008) found that prisoners reported difficulties accessing services and deficiencies in medical care in prison, expressed fears about dying in prison, and were less reassured during consultations than people in the community. Likewise health staff in prison reported problems of truthfulness in consultations and working in an organisation where healthcare is not the main priority, with often a high turnover of patients, rapid assessment of new patients, deficiencies in care provision outside, and professional isolation. With respect to substance misuse (including alcohol), mental health and dual diagnosis, the impact of this is stark, as prisoners are more likely than the general population to have substance misuse and mental health problems; women prisoners have higher rates of self-harm and overdose than male prisoners (see also Petrillo, this volume); injecting drug users are eight times more likely to die in the two weeks following release than at any other time in their lives; 50% of prison suicides occur in the first 28 days of custody; and drug-dependent prisoners have double the risk of suicide in the first week of custody compared to the general prison population (Department of Health, 2006a).

Recognising and addressing the problem?

In 2009 Lord Bradley published his review of people with mental health problems or learning disabilities in the criminal justice system (Department of Health, 2009) and highlighted the ways in which offenders are now generally seen as a socially excluded group, and where possible diversion from the criminal justice system for people with mental ill health should be specifically considered (see Hean, Walsh and Hammick, this volume). The report argued that custody in particular may well exacerbate mental health problems and increase the risk of self-harm and suicide. This report has been seen as an important milestone in addressing mental health problems in the criminal justice system, and states that:

> Throughout the course of this review it has become apparent that the issue of dual diagnosis...is a vital component of addressing the issue of mental health and criminal justice. In fact...stakeholders (have) sent out a clear message that no approach to diverting offenders with mental health problems from prison and/or the criminal justice system would be effective unless it addressed drug and alcohol misuse. (Department of Health, 2009, p. 21)

Bradley observed that despite the recognised high prevalence of dual diagnosis among offenders with mental health problems, services were not well organised to meet this need; rather, services were organised in such a way as to positively disadvantage those needing to access services for both mental health and substance misuse/alcohol problems. Individuals needing both services were having to access one service at a time, or even miss out on treatment altogether, and due to a lack of coordination and collaboration prisoners often fell between the two sets of support, receiving no treatment at all. This latter state of affairs was mirrored in the community, where people with dual diagnosis typically fell between services. Bradley argued that mental health and substance misuse services in prisons needed to provide appropriate, flexible care to those dually diagnosed, rather than using dual diagnosis as a reason for exclusion from services.

The Bradley Report also referenced specialist courts, such as drug courts, in several recommendations, and was concerned for how people with dual diagnosis are served in those courts. The Bradley Commission in its five-year follow-up report (Durcan et al., 2014) found that there does not appear to have been the expansion in these courts that the Bradley Report anticipated and there is no published work on new dual diagnosis arrangements. However the Bradley Commission was heartened by developments in the New Liaison and Diversion Arrangements and Operating Model for mental health (see Rogers and Ormston, this volume), which attempts to merge and integrate with substance misuse services and considers dual diagnosis as part of its brief. The Commission stated that it 'is therefore satisfied that people with concurrent mental health and substance misuse problems will have their needs identified in both police custody and courts if these new arrangements are fully implemented and available to all these settings' (Durcan et al., 2014, p. 30).

However, despite the promise the Liaison and Operating Model (NHS England, 2014) itself makes 33 references to mental health, 21 to substance misuse, and absolutely none to dual diagnosis, or comorbidity, or concurrent mental health and substance misuse problems. This reflects the fact that in practice since 2002 there has been little governmental focus on dual diagnosis. The Drug Strategy of 2010 (Home Office, 2010) stated it was providing guidance on a different way of approaching drug and alcohol use, and whilst it gives dual diagnosis a mention it in no way highlights the significance of the problem and how this may be solved. Following the Drug Strategy, the Public Health Strategy (Department of Health, 2010) and the Mental Health Strategy (Department of Health, 2011) were published. The Mental Health Strategy provides no guidance at all, giving dual diagnosis only a mention in relation to homelessness; and finally the Public Health Strategy does not give the subject of dual diagnosis any mention at all!

Empowering service users in addressing dual diagnosis

It would appear that, despite a groundswell of opinion confirming the complexities that dual diagnosis presents, it has become an intractable problem both within and without the criminal justice system. At one level it would seem that an obvious solution would be to address the deterministic nature of the legislation through allowing the Mental Health Act (1983/2007) to adopt the psychiatric definitions of addiction as contained in DSM-V and ICD-10. This solution is certainly worthy of consideration but has some potential risks of increased coercion and medicalisation, especially in a period of time when service users are securing more control over the kinds of services that they receive and the outcomes from those services (see Barnes and Bowl, 2001; McKinley and Yiannoullou, 2012; Pycroft et al., 2013). As Polak (2000) argues, medicalisation increases the risk of becoming a form of repression itself by removing choice from service users and has the potential of net widening to incorporate significant numbers of drug/alcohol users in the mental health system, who may be recreational drug/alcohol users, or experiencing problems rather than addiction.

What appears to be missing from the national guidance is a specific service user-based approach that offers flexibility and sustainability to help a person's changing mental health, drug and /or alcohol use needs; an approach that considers where the person is in relation to their motivation to change their behaviour, personal and social circumstances (Green 2015; see also Göbbels, Thakker and Ward, this volume). The spirit of engagement and inclusion must be the basis of any care and treatment; it must not be based on exclusion due to a specific diagnosis or contact with the CJS.

The National Institute for Health and Clinical Excellence (NICE, 2011) guidance for psychosis and co-existing substance misuse problems states that service users should have the opportunity to make informed decisions about their care and treatment in partnership with their health care professionals (see Mathews, this volume). Pycroft (2006) argues this is also true for those who come into contact with the CJS; that approaches should be based on a therapeutic relationship using person-centred principles and approaches such as motivational interviewing in conjunction with a knowledge and understanding of the social context of the person and their offending behaviour. The importance of developing a positive alliance that provides flexibility for the individual is fundamental; though this may be viewed as challenging, particularly in the CJS where the practitioner is viewed as holding some power in the relationship due to the CJS legal parameters.

Co-production

Despite (or perhaps because of) the increased marketisation of public services, there has been increased interest in the co-production of services across the public sector (see Bovaird, 2007), including the criminal justice system (see Weaver, 2011). When commissioned by the mental health charity Mind to review the literature on co-production in mental health, the six foundation stones of co-production were outlined by the New Economics Foundation (NEF) (2013, p. 3) as:

1. Taking an assets-based approach: transforming the perception of people, so that they are seen not as passive recipients of services and burdens on the system, but as equal partners in designing and delivering services (see also Mathews, this volume).
2. Building on people's existing capabilities: altering the delivery model of public services from a deficit approach to one that provides opportunities to recognise and grow people's capabilities and actively support them to put these to use at an individual and community level (see Göbbels, Thakker and Ward, this volume).
3. Reciprocity and mutuality: offering people a range of incentives to work in reciprocal relationships with professionals and with each other, where there are mutual responsibilities and expectations (see Göbbels, Thakker and Ward, this volume).
4. Peer support networks: engaging peer and personal networks alongside professionals as the best way of transferring knowledge.
5. Blurring distinctions: removing the distinction between professionals and recipients, and between producers and consumers of services, by reconfiguring the way services are developed and delivered (see also Arrigo and Bersot, this volume).
6. Facilitating rather than delivering: enabling public service agencies to become catalysts and facilitators rather than being the main providers themselves.

NEF (2013, p. 9) identified that the key themes emerging from the literature are: improved social networks and social inclusion; addressing stigma; improved skills and employability; prevention; and well-being-related outcomes, including improved mental and physical well-being. In one way or another, depending on their focus, all the chapters in this volume address these persistent features of the multiple, complex needs of service users.

There are examples of co-production within the criminal justice system; for example the charity User Voice (http://www.uservoice.org/) argues that only offenders can stop reoffending, and works closely with different agencies to provide co-produced services. Service user engagement and co-production exist on a continuum and present significant challenges where issues of coercion and punishment exist, as with aspects of mental health and criminal justice legislation. However we would argue that increasing self-organisation for service users across all policy sectors including criminal justice is essential to positive outcomes (see Pycroft and Bartollas, 2014) and we offer some specific examples of areas of development with respect to dual diagnosis.

The dual diagnosis service user's voice needs to be heard to ensure a much greater say in research, policy and practice in mental health and substance misuse services. Historically, the medical model approach with its 'objectivity' has denied the validity of first-person knowledge and experience to guide strategic vision, research, policy and practice (Webb 2010, p. 34). Public and Patient Involvement (PPI) is vital to ensure the service user's voice is heard equally and their views included in the decision making from the inception of a research proposal to the planning of a new service. Advocates of PPI suggest that involvement in design before ethical approval leads to better quality ethical research that is more relevant to the target populations and thus more likely to be used.

Case Study: hearing the voices of dually diagnosed women through research

(Taken from Green and Chandler, 2012.)

The following case study is an example of how service users can be included in the development of a research proposal; including the research design, research questions and methodology. The case study does not discuss the research topic in detail, just the consultation process to highlight the significance of PPI influence through total integration in the research process from the beginning. The women involved identified themselves as having a dual diagnosis (see also Petrillo, this volume). The case study also captures the learning journey for the researchers through the consultation process and the ethical dilemmas encountered (see also Canton, this volume).

PPI consultation

We consulted with five women with dual diagnosis who were members of an established mixed gender support group. We met with the facilitator of the group, himself a person with lived experience of using substance misuse services, and discussed the project with him prior to consultation. We discussed whether we should seek the views of dually diagnosed men and women around gender-sensitive assessment but decided that the priority need was to focus exclusively on women (see also Petrillo, this volume). A small grant was awarded by the local research design service to pay for the PPI consultant's time and expenses. The consultation was jointly facilitated by a clinical and service user researcher. A second meeting was held to check the analysis and interpretation with the women and make any final adjustments.

The first part of the consultation introduced the broad aims of the research and then took an unstructured approach to facilitating the views of the women about their experiences and the research topic. The second part focussed on what the women thought was most important to research, and on developing PPI tasks and roles to be included in the research proposal. It also became clear at this point that we needed to develop peer researcher roles to be able to find out more from women who may not come forward for interview or disclose to professional researchers.

Ethical considerations

PPI consultation in the design and scoping phase takes place before ethics committee approval and consultants are therefore not protected by the same stringent ethical protocol that protects the rights and dignity of research participants and peer researchers who have direct contact with research participants. However, we considered there was a duty of care to conduct the consultation ethically, given the mental health vulnerability of the women and the sensitive nature of the topic. The consultants were asked for informed consent and made aware that they did not have to answer any questions they did not choose to and could withdraw from the consultation without giving a reason. Permission was sought to record and transcribe the focus group and the women were made aware that their views would inform the development of the research proposal and would be published in anonymised form in this and a journal article.

The biggest ethical dilemma faced by us was how to analyse the focus group as a consultation based on lived experience rather than qualitative research of the lived experience expressed. On the one hand, we thought it was important to respect the time and emotional investment given by the women in sharing their lived experience to shape the research proposal by optimising use of the information given through approaches to analysis informed by qualitative research. On the other, we felt that over-analysis of the lived experience views brought to discussion could blur the distinction between research participant and consultant. We navigated this dilemma by adopting a phenomenologically informed approach to analysis of the information to enable the categories and themes brought by the women to emerge without superimposition of our preferred meanings and perspectives. The researchers believe this compromise enabled them to draw a line between respectful curiosity in consultation, in which some categories of analysis were imposed to retain provenance as a consultation, and the more open-ended curiosity with which lived experience can be explored in ethically safeguarded research. By combining both approaches, the researchers hoped to have optimised the information given by the lived experience perspectives of the women and preserved their rights and dignity within a consultative framework. The key themes that arose were reflected in such statements as: 'I am more than the sum of my different diagnoses' (see also Mathews, this volume); 'talk to me about "dual diagnosis" and what it means to me'; 'ask me what I need'; 'what do I have to do to be heard'; 'it is harder to disclose if you have children'; 'we still care about and love our children'; 'the experience of having our children taken away from us'; 'stigma'; 'finding the right service for treatment and care'; 'learning from women in our pasts – having to cope because we are the nurturers'; and 'joined-up working with knowledgeable staff'.

The second part of the consultation asked the women to make study recommendations on the basis of the lived experience expressed in part one, and to consider PPI roles in the proposed research. As researchers we wanted to capture the 'lived experience' of the dual diagnosis woman and ensure they had a safe space to tell their stories and confirm with them the significance of the first person voice (Webb, 2010, p. 35). We approached women because there appeared to be a gap in the research literature about women with dual diagnosis, and in order to start considering what research needed to be done we believed that consulting with them and acknowledging their wealth of knowledge and experience was the first stage in finding the missing data that could be used to inform policy and practice.

Developing practice through research, training and education

Enabling and empowering practitioners to work with dually diagnosed service users is vital; however, ensuring professional training meets these needs is fundamental. The addition of attitudinal work and the exploration of prejudice and stereotyping will help to ensure the dual diagnosis service user's social, psychological, physical and economic needs are considered. The voice of the service user must be heard and viewed by those providing the training as integral partners in developing the professional curriculum. Their voices and 'lived experience' can play an important part in exploring stereotypes and prejudice (see Webb, 2010).

Robust, service user-informed training can help aspects of practice that include; being more dual-diagnosis aware, sensitivity and confidence to improve clarity in what needs to be prioritised in assessment, care planning, treatment and care. Mental health practitioners need to know how to do a full drug and alcohol assessment (or access to one when required). Likewise, substance misuse practitioners need the same for mental health assessments, to identify the risks associated with the substance use behaviour or help service users make decisions about what they see as a priority in relation to the problems and concerns they have. The service user's concerns and needs may also be different from what the practitioner perceives as important; for example, abstinence (the practitioner's view) or an attempt at controlled drinking (the service user's view) (Green, 2015). Additional training to include Motivational Interviewing would help practitioners understand what is meant by a meaningful therapeutic alliance, the manifestations of ambivalence and providing choices.

The implementation of effective interventions for people with a dual diagnosis requires good multi-agency collaboration, clear care and service pathways, and opportunities for shared learning and networking (Guest and Holland, 2011). Shared learning and education across professional groups may help address some of these challenges (see Rogers and Ormston, this volume; Hean, Walsh and Hammick, this volume). This, combined with good, consistent and sustainable clinical supervision as a model for learning in practice, will help to ensure practitioners develop a knowledge base that informs their practice and encourages them to be more service user centred in their interactions with dual diagnosis service users.

Conclusion

In conclusion there would appear to be a great deal still to be pessimistic about with respect to developments in addressing dual diagnosis, as we seem to be tied into a Gordian knot which we seem unable to untie. The cultural and political deterministic factors that bring about this situation are complex and any changes in legislation would be monumental in their impact politically, socially and with respect to service provision (see Arrigo and Bersot, this volume). However in relation to the policy process the All Party Parliamentary Group (APPG) on complex needs and dual diagnosis was established in 2007. APPGs are informal cross-party groups that have no official status within parliament and tend to be facilitated by Members of the Commons and Lords. The complex needs and dual diagnosis APPG was formed in response to concerns raised by those in parliament regarding the needs of those with complex health problems. It is hoped that the group will help keep dual diagnosis on the political agenda and contribute to informing future policy and guidance. Likewise there are glimmers of hope in the way that service users, organisations and practitioners are starting to self-organise in a variety of ways to seek to address these issues, and the umbrella of co-production would seem to offer some promising ways forward.

References

American Psychiatric Association (1980). *Diagnostic and statistical manual of mental disorders* (3rd edition) (DSM-III). Washington DC: American Psychiatric Association.
Barnes, M. and Bowl, R. (2001). *Taking over the asylum: Empowerment and mental health.* Basingstoke: Palgrave.
Bovaird, T. (2007). 'Beyond Engagement and Participation: User and Community Coproduction of Public Services' in *Public Administration Review*, 846–860.

Centre for Mental Health, DrugScope and the UK Drug Policy Commission (2012). *Dual Diagnosis: A challenge for the reformed: A discussion paper.* NHS for Public Health England.

Clinks, DrugScope, Homeless Link and Mind (2009). *In from the margins. Making every adult matter.* London: Gulbenkian Foundation.

Cornford, C., Mason, J. et al. (2008). A survey of primary and specialised health care provision to prisons in England and Wales. *Primary Health Care Research & Development,* 2008 (9), 126–135.

Crome, I., Chambers, P., Frisher, M., Bloor, R. and Roberts, D. (2009). *The relationship between dual diagnosis, substance misuse and dealing with mental health issues.* SCIE Research Briefing 30. Available at: www.scie.org.uk/publications/briefings/briefing30/index.asp

Department of Health (1999). *National Service Framework for Mental Health: Modern Standards & Service Model.* London. HMSO.

Department of Health (2002). Mental health policy implementation guide: Dual diagnosis good practice guide. London: Stationery Office.

Department of Health (2006a). *Clinical Management of Drug Dependence in the Adult Prison Setting.* London: Department of Health.

Department of Health (2006b) *Dual diagnosis in mental health inpatient and day hospital settings.* London: Stationery Office.

Department of Health (2008). *Mental Health Code of Practice.* London: Stationery Office.

Department of Health (2009). *The Bradley Report.* London: Department of Health.

Department of Health (2010). *Healthy lives, healthy people: our strategy for public health in England.* London: Stationery Office.

Department of Health (2011). *No health without mental health: a cross-government mental health outcomes strategy for people of all ages.* London: Stationery Office.

Department of Health and Ministry of Justice (2009). *A guide for the management of dual diagnosis in prisons.* London: Stationery Office.

Drake R., Bartels S., Teague, G., Noordsy, D. and Clarke, R. (1993). Treatment of substance abuse in severely mentally ill patients. *The Journal of Nervous and Mental Disease,* 18 (10), 606–611.

Durcan, G., Saunders, A., Gadsby, B. and Hazard, A. (2014). *The Bradley Report five years on.* London: Centre for Mental Health.

Green, A. J. (2015). Dual Diagnosis and the Context of Exclusion. In: A. Pycroft (ed.). *Key Concepts in Substance Misuse.* London: Sage. 83–91.

Green, A.J. and Chandler, R. (2012). *Hearing the voices of dual diagnosis women through the consultation process.* Unpublished paper.

Guest, C. and Holland, M. (2011). Co-existing mental health and substance use and alcohol difficulties – why do we persist with the term 'dual diagnosis' within mental health services? *Advances in Dual Diagnosis,* 4 (4), 162–169.

Home Office (1998). *Tackling Drugs to Build a Better Britain.* London: Home Office.

Home Office (2004). *Alcohol Harm Reduction Strategy for England and Wales.* London: Home Office.

Home Office (2010). *Drug Strategy 2010, reducing demand, restricting supply, building recovery: supporting people to live a drug free life.* London: Stationery Office.

Hughes, L. (2011). Guidelines for working with mental health-substance use. In: D B Cooper (ed.). *Developing services in mental health – substance use.* Oxford: Radcliffe Publishing.

Leahy, N. and Hawker, R. (1998). Re-inventing the wheel. *Mental Health Care*, April, 1(8), 275–289.

McKinley, S. and Yiannoullou, S. (2012). Changing minds: Unleashing the potential of mental health service users – a critical perspective on current models of service user involvement and their impact on wellbeing and 'recovery'. In: M. Barnes and P. Cotterell (eds). *Critical Perspectives on User Involvement*. Bristol: Policy Press. 115–128.

McPherson, C. and McGibbon, E. (2014). Intersecting contexts of oppression within complex public systems. In: A. Pycroft and C. Bartollas (eds). *Applying Complexity Theory: Whole Systems Approaches to Criminal Justice and Social Work*. Bristol: Policy Press. 159–180.

Mueser, K.T., Drake, R.E. and Wallach, M.A. (1998). Dual diagnosis: A review of etiological theories. *Addictive Behaviours*, 23 (6), 717–734.

Morgan, K. and Dar, K. (2011). Historical policy context of mental health-substance use. In: D B Cooper (ed.). *Developing services in mental health – substance use*. Oxford: Radcliffe Publishing.

National Institute for Health and Clinical Excellence (NICE) (2011). *Psychosis with co-existing substance misuse*. Clinical guidance 120. London: NICE.

Naylor, C., Parsonage, M., McDaid, D., Knapp, M., Fossey, M. and Galea, A. (2012). *Long-term conditions and mental health: The cost of co-morbidities*. London: The King's Fund and Centre for Mental Health.

New Economics Foundation (2013). *Co-Production in mental health: A literature review*. London: New Economics Foundation.

NHS England (2014). *Liaison and Operating Model 2013/14*. NHS England Liaison and Diversion Programme.

Noyce, G. (2012). The Mental Health Act: dual diagnosis, public protection and legal dilemmas in practice. In: A. Pycroft and S. Clift (eds). *Risk and rehabilitation: management and treatment of substance misuse and mental health problems in the criminal justice system*. Bristol: Policy Press. 43–64.

Page, A. (2011). Turning the tide: a vision paper for multiple needs and exclusions. *Advances in Dual Diagnosis*, 4 (4), 173–179.

Polak, F. (2000). Thinking About Drug Law Reform: Some Political Dynamics of Medicalization. *Fordham Urban Law Journal*, 28(1), 350–361.

Pycroft, A. (2006). Too little, too late? *Criminal Justice Matters*, 64 (1), 36–37.

Pycroft, A. (2014). 'Probation Practice and Creativity in England and Wales: A Complex Systems Analysis' in Pycroft, A and Bartollas, C (eds) (2014). *Applying Complexity Theory: Whole Systems Approaches to Criminal Justice and Social Work*. Bristol. Policy Press. 199–220

Pycroft, A. and Bartollas, C. (eds) (2014). *Applying Complexity Theory: Whole Systems Approaches to Criminal Justice and Social Work*. Bristol: Policy Press

Pycroft, A. and Clift, S. (eds) (2012). *Risk and rehabilitation: management and treatment of substance misuse and mental health problems in the criminal justice system*. Bristol: Policy Press.

Pycroft, A. and Cook, I. (2010). *HMP Kingston Integrated Drug Treatment Service: Needs Analysis. Final Report*. Unpublished report for Portsmouth City Council.

Pycroft, A., Wallis, A., Bigg, J. and Webster, G. (2013). Participation, engagement and change: a study of the experiences of service users of the Unified Adolescent Team. *The British Journal of Social Work*. ISSN 0045–3102 10.1093/bjsw/bct089

Sainsbury Centre for Mental Health (2008). *Briefing 39: Mental Health and the Criminal Justice System*. London. Sainsbury Centre for Mental Health.

Sieh, E. (1989). Less Eligibility: The Upper Limits of Penal Policy. *Criminal Justice Policy Review*, 3, 159–183.

Stevens, A. (2011). *Drugs, Crime and Public Health: The Political Economy of Drug Policy.* Abingdon. Routledge.

Strang, J. and Gossop, M. (eds) (2005a). *Heroin Addiction and the British System: Volume One, Origins and Evolution.* Abingdon: Routledge.

Strang, J. and Gossop, M. (eds) (2005b). *Heroin Addiction and the British System: Volume Two.* Abingdon: Routledge.

Social Exclusion Unit (2002). *Reducing Re-offending by Ex-prisoners.* London: Stationery Office.

Weaver, B. (2011). Co-Producing Community Justice: The Transformative Potential of Personalisation for Penal Sanctions. *British Journal of Social Work*, 41, 1038–1057.

Webb, D. (2010). Consumer perspectives. In: P. Phillips, O. McKeown and T. Sandford (eds). *Dual diagnosis: Practice in context.* Chichester: Wiley-Blackwell.

10
The Role of the Mental Health Clinical Nurse Specialist in the Crown Court Setting: Towards a Best Practice Model

Charles de Lacy

Introduction

Over the last two decades, since the Reed Report (Reed, 1992), there have been countless well-intentioned initiatives to support a formal, professionalised liaison role for those appearing in court with mental health needs, and also for an effective service to support diversion from the Criminal Justice System. Despite this, the Bradley Report (Bradley, 2009), and many other scholarly publications over the years, noted that such initiatives appeared doomed; starting out brightly and fizzling out quietly. This was mostly contingent upon some combination of weak strategic and operational support and funding over the long term, resulting in difficulty in ensuring appropriate staffing and/or being haunted by difficulties around multi-agency collaboration. In response to the Bradley Report and the resulting 82 recommendations that were accepted in full, there has been a concerted effort to identify a nationally co-ordinated response to the problem of supporting offenders with mental health needs through the criminal justice process (see Durcan et al., 2014; Rogers and Ormston, this volume). The need for an effective liaison role in the Courts is central to this current effort.

This chapter is based upon my experience over seven years working in the Central Criminal Court in the lead role of Mental Health Nurse Specialist and of being part of an evaluation of best practice (Winstone and Pakes, 2010). In looking to develop a model of best practice for the Mental Health Clinical Nurse Specialist in the Crown Court – a model that has the potential to be sustainable and transferable to other settings and can liaise effectively across the legal and medical contexts – it is first necessary to outline where the Crown Court sits in the trial process.

The Crown Court

There are 77 Crown Court Centres across England and Wales (Ministry of Justice, 2013a). They include: First Tier Centres dealing with all classes of offence in criminal cases as well as High Court Civil Work; Second Tier Centres visited by High Court Judges for all classes of criminal work; and Third Tier Centres not normally visited by High Court Judges and handling class 2 and class 3 criminal works. (Class 1 work consists of murder, attempted murder and treason. Class 2 work offences include rape, and Class 3 kidnapping, burglary, grievous bodily harm, and robbery etc.) (Ministry of Justice, 2011).

Cases originate in the Magistrates' Courts and consist of: 'indictable only' offences which can only be dealt with in the Crown Court; 'either way' cases which can be dealt with either in the Magistrates' Court or the Crown Court; and Summary Offences which the Magistrates deal with. (The allocation of cases to the Crown Court is covered by Schedule 3 to the Criminal Justice Act 2003, i.e. offences triable on indictment exclusively, offences that must be or can be sent for trial in the Crown Court without allocation for trial because they relate to offences already sent, and offences triable either way that are allocated for trial in the Crown Court.)

In 2013, of the 83,000 cases that were allocated to the Crown Court for trial, in 68,000 defendants were found guilty. There were an additional 18,000 cases on summary conviction that were allocated to the Crown Court for sentence (Ministry of Justice, 2013e). The total number of people and companies dealt with by the Criminal Justice System in 2013 totals 1.76 million. Only around 6% of all those proceeded against are actually allocated for trial at the Crown Court (Ministry of Justice, 2013e). This is consistent in demonstrating that psychiatric morbidity among prisoners is high, with 90% of those on remand and in custody having one or more clinically diagnosable mental health needs (Sainsbury Centre, 2009). It is difficult to know the rates of mental disorder among those who go for trial at the Crown Court. However, given that around 35% of those sent for trial at the Crown Court in 2013 were remanded into custody (Ministry of Justice, 2013d), set alongside the rates of mental disorder being higher among remand prisoners than those who are sentenced (see for example, Singleton et al., 1998; Bradley, 2009), then it can be concluded that significant numbers of defendants in the Crown Court may have disorders. These include drug and alcohol dependency and dual diagnosis, psychosis, neuroses and personality disorders.

The average time between offence and completion of the Court process for all criminal cases is 157 days (Ministry of Justice, 2013b). There can be substantial waiting times for cases sent for trial to the Crown Court. In 2012 this was up to 24 weeks for the substantive court hearing of those cases where a not guilty plea was entered (Ministry of Justice, 2013b). Delays may be greatly increased where there are substantial mental health issues. These delays may be caused by a variety of factors. Unwell defendants in prison are likely to be referred for an assessment with a view to considering a transfer under section 48 of the Mental Health Act 1983, amended 2007 (hereafter 'MHA'). Defence teams will need to instruct special experts and this will require quotes for the work to be served on the Legal Aid Agency and funding agreed. Special experts for the defence may well advise awaiting the outcome of any hospital based assessment before preparing any final opinion (psychiatric reports to the court are discussed in further detail below).

The Central Criminal Court Mental Health Liaison Scheme

The Central Criminal Court (often called the 'Old Bailey') is one of 11 Crown Courts in London. However its jurisdiction extends to all of England and Wales (Central Criminal Court Act 1856). Class 1 work in Crown Courts consists of attempted murder and murder.

The Central Criminal Court Mental Health Liaison Scheme (hereafter the MHLS) began life in May 2008. The Court had approached Central and North West London NHS Foundation Trust and Oxleas NHS Foundation Trust to discuss establishing a scheme. Its working arrangement with the two Trusts is based on a memorandum of understanding that has continued to shape its operations. This is a crucial point as it is the Court that has defined what it needs from this service and the MHLS works primarily to that agenda. The MHLS consists of a consultant forensic psychiatrist for half a day per week, and a full time Clinical Nurse Specialist based at the Court five days per week. This was an exceptional level of cover as at that time mental health specialists in either the Magistrates or Crown Court were only provided on a patchy basis (Pakes and Winstone, 2009, 2010).

When the Court approached the two Trusts, it was concerned that homicide cases attracted psychiatric reports and psychiatric issues were a cause of delay to the progress of cases. It was estimated that in excess of 30% of homicide cases would require assessments and reports and these were typically undertaken by defence teams. This figure is borne out by the National Confidential Inquiry into Suicide and Homicide (Health Quality Improvement Partnership, 2013; hereafter 'NCISH') which calculates that 32% of homicides between 2001 and 2011 attracted psychiatric reports (NCISH, p.39). In my experience this figure is likely to be conservative as defence teams do not have to disclose psychiatric reports to the court or even disclose that any assessment has been undertaken.

The Central Criminal Court's agenda for the MHLS is assistance with case management. Unlike diversion work in police stations and magistrates' courts (see Rogers and Ormston, this volume), assessment and reports are not the essential elements of the work undertaken by either the Consultant or the Clinical Nurse Specialist. Rather the primary purpose of the MHLS is to assist in the progression of cases through the Court processes to a legal conclusion. In homicide cases this conclusion can range from the defendant being found not guilty and discharged, or being convicted of murder and sentenced to life imprisonment.

The Court faces two fundamental difficulties when a defendant has health issues. Firstly, it will often not know the nature of those health difficulties and therefore be unable to evaluate how those issues may impact on the trial process. Secondly, once it has established the nature of any health issues, it may need to adjust the trial processes to ensure that the defendant receives a fair trial through the Court's powers to employ special measures. Special measures may include the use of an intermediary (see below) if the defendant has, for example, learning difficulties or marked mental disorder (for further information see Criminal Practice Rules and Practice Directions, 2013, Sec3D–3G, covering vulnerable witnesses and defendants; Ministry of Justice, 2013c.)

The responsibility of the Court is to ensure that the defendant receives a fair trial; the role of the MHLS and the Clinical Nurse Specialist in particular is to broker relevant medical information that impacts on the trial process and ensure that any arising issues of a practical nature are addressed. Given the agenda of assisting the Court in its case management the MHLS has to act as a link between the Judiciary, Clerks, List/Case Progression Office, Defence and Prosecution, Police Murder Investigation Teams, Probation Service etc. In addition there must be liaison with the Health Systems to obtain relevant information, for example Liaison and Diversion Services for Police Stations and Magistrates Courts, Prison Hospital Wings, Prison In-Reach Teams, High Secure and Regional Secure Units, Community Forensic Services, General Adult Services and, where there are physical issues, liaison with the GP or relevant hospital-based specialisms. Those who have brokered multi-agency collaboration will know that this is not without its hurdles (see also Rogers and Ormston, this volume).

Some legal realities

Any psychiatric system embedded in a Court needs to have a broad understanding of the Court's processes if it is to act in a facilitative way. Any defendant appearing before a Crown Court is legally innocent and is de facto regarded as fit to plead until the issue is raised; normally this will be by the defence. The burden of proof in terms of any charges on the indictment lies with the Crown and the defendant is not required to prove their innocence. The interests of the defendant are protected by the legal team he or she instructs. The dispute between the parties (prosecution and defence) as to the guilt or innocence of the defendant is determined before a jury of twelve people who are the deciders of fact. The role of the Judge is to direct on the law.

Most people charged with murder will be remanded into custody. There are limits to the length of time a defendant can be held in custody on an indictable offence and it is initially 182 days (see Prosecution of Offences Act 1985 amended and CPS Prosecution of Offences [Custody Time Limits] Regulations 1987 amended; Crown Prosecution Service, 2015). Whilst Custody Time Limits (CTL) can be renewed the aim will be for the case to be trial ready within that period. If the Crown applies for the CTLs to be extended it must show that it has acted with due diligence. If there is a failure of due diligence then the defendant may object to the extension of the CTL and apply for bail.

The default position is for the Crown to serve its case on the defence team within 50 days (see Crime and Disorder Act 1999, Service of Prosecution Evidence Regulations 2000 [Criminal Law England and Wales, 2005, No. 902]). In murder cases the defendant, if found guilty, gets an automatic life sentence and there are no psychiatric disposals open to the Court. However in cases of insanity and diminished responsibility there may be medical recommendations for disposal under Part III of the MHA.

Psychiatric issues and the trial process

There is not space in this chapter to cover all the pathways that can open up in the trial process but I have explored fitness to plead as this exemplifies the way in which the expert knowledge and understanding of the Clinical Nurse Specialist can be utilised.

Fitness to plead

Psychiatric issues in homicide cases that occur in the pre-trial process may impinge on two distinct issues: firstly whether the defendant is unfit either physically or mentally for a trial process, and secondly whether the defendant has a defence to a charge of murder by way of diminished responsibility, or in rare cases a defence of legal insanity. It is important not to confuse these distinct issues. The first scenario, that due to physical ill health or more typically mental disorder the defendant may not be fit for a trial process, needs to be identified early so that the defence can appoint an independent expert to explore the defendant's fitness.

The criteria relating to fitness was laid down in the case of Pritchard 1836 and are referred to commonly as the Pritchard Criteria (updated in the case of R v M (John) 2003). Essentially a defendant must be able to comprehend the charges, be able to plead guilty or not guilty, exercise their right to challenge a juror, instruct their defence team, follow the course of the proceedings and be able to give evidence in their own defence. Where the role of the Clinical Nurse Specialist fits with this process I will now discuss.

The Clinical Nurse Specialist may become aware of significant concerns around the defendant's fitness through a number of routes which may include custody and diversion services operating at the Police Station, the Magistrates Court or the Police summary of the alleged offence, which is served on the Court. (The Police summary served on the Court is called an MG5, see ACPO, 2011.) This indicates that the defendant was mentally unwell at the time of the arrest and also if there is a known history of mental disorder, for example, paranoid schizophrenia. Information may be received from the prison mental health services or there may be a referral from the Metropolitan Police Murder Investigation Team. Finally, of course, it may be the defence team who report that they have found their client to be unwell and they are unable to take instructions.

The Clinical Nurse Specialist assists in a number of ways in this scenario. The attention of the Judge will be drawn to the matter before the bail hearing so that the Judge can raise this in open court as something that will require addressing as the case unfolds. The Clinical Nurse Specialist will also liaise with the defence, assisting in two key ways. Firstly, by providing details of potential special experts who can assist in preparing a report on the matter of unfitness to plead. Special experts in psychiatry need to be section 12 approved (Sec 12 (2) (2A) MHA), and in serious crime Consultants in Forensic Psychiatry who are well experienced in Court work may be required. Often defence teams will have their own experts they regularly work with but they appreciate alternative suggestions if for any reason their usual expert is unavailable. Suggested experts should also include forensic psychologists who may be required to carry out assessments in relation to suspected Learning Disability and personality structure. In addition the defence may want to look at discrete areas, for example neurological issues, and therefore require assistance in locating an appropriate neurologist or neuro-psychiatrist. It is legitimate for the Clinical Nurse Specialist to discuss the options if requested so to do by the defence, but final decisions must be taken by the defence.

Where there is a defendant with a known history of mental disorder the defence would also be assisted by the Clinical Nurse Specialist as to who they approach for any medical records – whether from the community or prison. These records may become a fundamental ingredient in a trial process where there is a history of psychosis and where the Crown and defence are disputing the defendant's mental state at the time of the offence.

Unfit to plead
The Clinical Nurse Specialist should advise all parties that where fitness to plead is an issue before the Court, and the defendant has been transferred to

hospital, that an initial period of three months for assessment and treatment would not be unreasonable. The Court, with the agreement of the parties, may order a Report from the Responsible Clinician at the end of the agreed period which will enable the Court to decide the next steps to be taken. The alternative would be for the defence to obtain the Report. It can never be assumed that the parties to the case are familiar with the intricacies of the law when it comes to providing Expert Reports and the role of the Clinical Nurse Specialist is to be available to provide support, as well as to liaise with Responsible Clinicians to ensure the case progresses in as timely a way as possible. All Expert Reports are governed by the requirements set out in the Criminal Procedure Rules Part 33, and the Clinical Nurse Specialist must be familiar with these so that advice can be provided to the parties seeking to commission such a Report. The scope of the Expert Report will vary from case to case. In some situations the Court may simply ask for the Responsible Clinician to comment on fitness to plead. In other scenarios the Court may order a global report that not only addresses matters of fitness but also whether the defendant has any psychiatric defences to the charges. In murder this may include diminished responsibility or insanity.

At this point the Clinical Nurse Specialist can assist the Clerk whose responsibility it is to draw up the Court Order on a pro-forma, by ensuring that the Clerk knows who to send the order to and the address details. Without attending to the minutiae of such details the process can be significantly delayed (see Winstone and Pakes, 2007). The Clerk may also appreciate assistance with the wording so that the Responsible Clinician is clear what the question or questions are that the Court wants answering. In complex cases the Clerk will confirm with the Judge that all is in order. The Clinical Nurse Specialist may also ensure that the relevant witness statements (Court papers) reach the Responsible Clinician so that the background information necessary to write the Report is available in a timely fashion. The Clinical Nurse Specialist will liaise with the office of the Responsible Clinician to ensure that the Report reaches the Judge within the agreed time frame. It is the Judge and not the Clinical Nurse Specialist who will determine to whom the Report should be released. This may be defence-only initially or defence and prosecution depending on the view of the Judge. The key principle in the process is that the Clinical Nurse Specialist operates within the parameters set by the Court so that the Court process is not compromised by any unilateral action by the Clinical Nurse Specialist which may be well-intended but legally unwise.

If at the end of the period of treatment and assessment the defendant remains unfit for a trial process the Court will need to consider its next steps. The Court will look closely at the recommendations of the Responsible Clinician but may also invite the defence and the prosecution to prepare their own Reports before finally determining the next step. If there is a consensus between defence,

Crown and the Responsible Clinician that the defendant is indeed unfit, and that there is a prospect of the defendant becoming fit, then the Court is likely to agree an adjournment. It is in everybody's interests, including the defendant's, that he or she should be able to participate in a full trial process.

However, if the time comes and the defendant remains unfit then the Court will move to a formal determination of the issue. This determination is made by a Judge sitting alone without a jury (Domestic Violence Crimes and Victims Act, 2004, S22) and it is based primarily on the written and / or oral medical evidence. The Judge requires two medical reports, one of which must have been prepared by a psychiatrist who is section 12 (MHA) approved (see Criminal Procedures Insanity Act 1964 S4(6) and 8(2), as amended by the Criminal Procedures Insanity and Unfitness to Plead Act 1991). The Judge may well take oral evidence especially where the issue of fitness is contested between the parties. The Court process is largely inquisitorial in its approach with counsel for the defence and prosecution leading their respective experts as they give their evidence and cross questioning one another's experts. The Judge is likely also to have his or her own questions.

The Clinical Nurse Specialist can assist the Court by checking whether the Reports before the Court from defence and prosecution are in agreement. Where the Reports differ and one side argues fit and the other side states unfit then the Judge may wish to use the Clinical Nurse Specialist to obtain an independent psychiatric report before determining the issue. Such an order for an additional Report will be made in open Court following discussion with the defence and prosecution. The Clinical Nurse Specialist will, in this scenario, advise the Judge of the options in terms of an appropriate special Expert. For example, if the defendant was elderly and the issue was one of dementia and fitness for trial then it would be a case of seeking an appropriately qualified psychiatrist to offer an opinion, who ideally would also have some forensic experience. Consideration will also need to be given by the Court business manager to the costs of this, as it will be met out of central funds. If there was a trial date for examining the issue the Clinical Nurse Specialist will assist to also ensure that the independent Expert who is undertaking the work is available to attend the hearing.

The Court may invite the Experts to meet at Court and identify the areas of agreement and any areas of disagreement between them in order to facilitate an efficient hearing (see Criminal Procedure Rules part 33; Ministry of Justice, 2013g). The Clinical Nurse Specialist facilitates this process by making arrangements for the Experts to meet in confidence and by providing the resources for producing any brief summary of the Experts' positions. It is a matter for the Judge to determine the issue on the basis of the evidence. The Judge is not bound for instance to follow the majority view. Where the Court has, for example, three Reports before it, two indicating the view that the defendant was unfit, and a minority view arguing that the defendant was fit, the Judge is free to go with the minority view if he or she finds that evidence more cogent. The Court is there to test the evidence against the legal criteria (see R v Walls (2011) EWCA Crim 443). At the end of the process the Judge will give his or her ruling and set out the reasoning behind any decision reached.

If the defendant is found to be fit to plead then there is nothing to prevent the issue being raised again at a later date during the trial if there is fresh evidence that the defendant is mentally unwell to the point of being legally unfit. If the defendant is found to be unfit by the Judge then the Court will proceed to what is known as the trial of the facts to determine whether the defendant did the act or made the omission charged against him or her. This is conducted under Sec 4A, Criminal Procedures and Insanity Act 1964 and is a determination by a jury. For example, if the Crown alleges that the defendant stabbed the victim, the jury is invited to determine whether *that defendant* stabbed *that victim*. The purpose of the trial is to prevent defendants being consigned to hospital under the Mental Health Act when they may have not been responsible for the act at all!

A trial of the facts is, in some ways, not a criminal trial per se and carries no criminal sanction if the defendant is found to have committed the act. At the end it must be decided whether to make a Hospital Order, if warranted by the relevant medical recommendations under the Mental Health Act, or a Supervision Order (see the Criminal Procedures Insanity and Act 1964, Schedule 1A) which can be with or without medical treatment where a Local Authority agrees to supervision, or an absolute discharge. Arranging Supervision Orders under local authorities is a time-consuming process. If the supervision route is the preferred option to an absolute discharge the Clinical Nurse Specialist should assist the Court in explaining the complexity of the process and therefore why an adjournment of up to two months may be necessary. If the Court wishes to act in a shorter time frame then the Clinical Nurse Specialist must do all possible to achieve the result by whatever date the Court sets. Occasionally significant problems and delays may arise and the Clinical Nurse Specialist will liaise with the trial Judge and suggest ways that the Court might intervene, for example, writing to the Health Commissioners if a doctor cannot be identified to consider the option of medical supervision.

Sec 4A hearings provide a compassionate way for the Court to deal with seriously ill defendants. In one such case a severely ill defendant suffering from an active psychosis that was responding poorly to treatment and who faced allegations of a non-violent nature was found unfit by the Court, found to have committed the act by the jury and then duly given an absolute discharge. During this process the MHLS expedited a second fitness to plead report undertaken by the Consultant for the MHLS who also gave oral evidence at the hearing addressing unfitness to plead. Through liaison with the Responsible

Clinician it was established engagement with treatment was good and a supervision order unwarranted. This brought to a satisfactory conclusion a case that was causing distress to a seriously ill defendant and enabled the prosecuting authorities to draw a line under the matter.

Where defendants are unfit for trial and charged with serious offences such as murder or attempted murder and found to have done the act the likely outcome will be hospital orders with restrictions (Sec 37/41 MHA).

There is now an agreed protocol between the Mental Health Casework Section, the National Offender Management Service, the Crown Prosecution Service and Her Majesty's Court and Tribunal Service, on the management of cases where defendants have been found unfit and to have committed the act. These can be disposed of by way of S37/41 (MHA) (see Criminal Procedures Insanity Act 1964, ss5 or 5A). Essentially the Mental Health Casework Section will keep under regular review the fitness of the defendant and the Secretary of State will refer the matter to the Crown Prosecution Service for their consideration of reinstituting proceedings when deemed fit by the Responsible Clinician. The role of the Clinical Nurse Specialist is to ensure that he/she is fully apprised of the views of the Responsible Clinician. Where the Responsible Clinician takes the view that the defendant is not detainable in hospital, but should be returned to custody, then a listing with defendant to attend would result in their return to the prison system – assuming the Judge remands into custody as opposed to bailing. The Clinical Nurse Specialist can usefully draw to the attention of the Court that the defendant remains detained under the original hospital order until their appearance at Court or their return to prison. If the Responsible Clinician is planning to keep the defendant in hospital because they remain unwell then a fresh section 48 warrant would need to be applied for after the appearance of the defendant and the Court has remanded into custody. With prior planning this may be done administratively by the hospital, providing the Mental Health Casework Section with fresh section 48 reports so that following the patient's appearance at Court and their remand into custody by the Court, they may, with the issuing of the section 48 transfer warrant to the Court, be returned to the hospital from which they came. This reduces the risk of having a patient in need of urgent, ongoing treatment in hospital being unnecessarily returned to prison with all the attendant risks to themselves or others. It also reduces the costs of an empty hospital bed.

If the Clinical Nurse Specialist is aware that the Responsible Clinician does not regard the defendant as any longer detainable in hospital but should be returned to custody then the Clinical Nurse Specialist can liaise between the Responsible Clinician and the mental health services in the receiving prison to ensure the necessary medical information reaches the prison to assist in offering ongoing treatment and care to what will now be an informal patient.

Although the defendant has been found fit by the Responsible Clinician the issues of fitness may remain live issues for the Court. For example the hearing date may be in excess of a year after the Responsible Clinician found the defendant fit to plead and the pressure of a remounted prosecution may lead to a deterioration of the defendant's mental health. An option is for the Clinical Nurse Specialist to liaise with defence and prosecution and see if there is any mileage in obtaining an addendum from the Responsible Clinician to the original report to see if there is any change. If both parties agree that an update would be helpful, ideally that should be before the Court at the first opportunity. The Court may be willing in some instances to order the report administratively, the request being made to the Judge in chambers, with the accompanying evidence of the CPS and defence support for such a process. Alternatively the updated report from the Responsible Clinician on the fitness issue may be requested at the first mention hearing with the defendant not attending. The Clinical Nurse Specialist can liaise with the Responsible Clinician on behalf of the Court in the production of the Report. If there is time slippage in the production of the report then the Clinical Nurse Specialist should liaise with the List Office who will contact the Court and all parties to see if there is any objection to rescheduling the next listing date.

As you can see, the process is complex and can be lengthy. It requires an in-depth understanding of the law and a good relationship with key personnel across multi-agency settings to bring about an outcome which minimises delays. The Clinical Nurse Specialist should act as a single point of contact for all parties in order to maintain the momentum of proceedings, to ensure all parties are kept equally well informed and that correct procedures are utilised to maximise efficiency in the interests of the Court, the patient and – it must not be forgotten – the victim, who may feel lost in what may seem laborious and possibly mystifying proceedings from the perspective of a lay person.

It is time now to turn to two further key aspects in the Court process which are supported by the Clinical Nurse Specialist. Firstly, I will discuss intermediaries and after that look at the issues posed by transfers from prison to hospital.

Intermediaries

The Court also regards vulnerable defendants as being entitled to Special Measures to enable them to participate in their trial and give their evidence (see Criminal Procedural Rules 3.8(4)(a)&(b), 2013, Vulnerable Defendants and Criminal Practice Directions 2013, sections 3D–3G; Ministry of Justice, 2013f, h). This can include the use of intermediaries on behalf of defendants. Registered intermediaries trained by the Ministry of Justice have been made available to vulnerable complainants and witnesses and some will also undertake defence work.

Typically intermediaries are speech and language therapists; however, they may also be drawn from mental health professionals such as psychologists. They assist witnesses to give their evidence (Ministry of Justice, 2012). When assisting defendants in criminal trials intermediaries enable them to understand the trial process, to engage with counsel, and to give their evidence.

The need for an intermediary is normally raised in the report by the defence instructed Expert, typically a psychologist or a psychiatrist. The defence solicitors must identify an intermediary and commission a further Report. Assuming that an intermediary is recommended for the trial, or part of the trial, it will be for the defence team to serve the Report on the Court for a final determination of the issue by the Judge. Assuming the Judge agrees that the defendant should have an intermediary there will be a Court hearing with the intermediary in attendance and the ground rules for their intervention in the trial will be agreed.

The Clinical Nurse Specialist will have developed resources to support the recruitment of an intermediary, including a list of registered intermediaries who undertake defence work. When they act for the defence they do not appear as a registered intermediary per se but the fact that they are registered offers a standard because they have been through formal training with the Ministry of Justice (MOJ); see the Advocate's Gateway (2015) that offers extensive and very helpful information on intermediaries.

Transfers to hospital from prison

Transfers to hospital from prison are known to be problematic – in terms of transport, communication, transferring records, identifying a suitable bed, etc. (see for example, McKenzie and Sales, 2008). The Clinical Nurse Specialist assists by keeping the defence and all parties (the Court, the Crown and the defence) abreast of any developments around transfer to hospital from prison following remand. The serving prison for the Central Criminal Court is HMP Belmarsh and there is liaison between the mental health services at the prison and the MHLS at the Court. The Clinical Nurse Specialist alerts all parties where it is known that sec 48 MHA referrals have been made to the relevant Regional Secure Unit and notifies the parties of developments as matters unfold. It will confirm to all parties when transfer is accomplished and the name of the Responsible Clinician and the contact details. The prison is assisted with the necessary case summary and previous convictions which must be served on the Mental Health Casework Section, National Offender Management Service, before any section 48 transfer order will be agreed by the Secretary of State. If the defendant has been categorised as a potential 'Category A' prisoner, the Mental Health Casework Section, who have to approve transfers, may well request that the defendant be assessed by a high security hospital. They may also request a high security assessment where they take the view that the alleged offence details warrant management in high security, irrespective of whether any Regional Secure Unit concerned regards the risk as manageable in medium security (see also Scally, this volume; Gatawa, this volume). It is hardly surprising given the complexity of this process that significant problems can occur in the implementation of section 48 and that the Clinical Nurse Specialist has a pivotal role in relation to liaison.

The relevant high secure hospital will undertake their own assessment and determine whether the defendant is appropriate for admission. On occasions high secure may refer the case back to medium secure services if they assess that the risk can be adequately managed. However the final decision remains with the office of the Mental Health Casework Section who can, in some cases, direct that the defendant be moved to high secure care under section 48 MHA. On occasions a prison may refuse to issue a movement order for the defendant to be transferred to a medium secure hospital if the prisoner is regarded as a significant risk. This may occur although the Mental Health Casework Section has agreed the transfer and issued the necessary warrant to the mental health services in the prison. All of this can cause delays and it is important that the Court and all parties are kept apprised by the Clinical Nurse Specialist of these developments as delays will impact on trial management. The Court has no powers to enforce a transfer under section 48 as it is a matter for the Secretary of State. The Court is therefore in a somewhat passive position whilst this scenario unfolds but the Clinical Nurse Specialist can assist by knowing what is going on and liaising with all parties.

Finally the Mental Health Casework Section may refuse to agree the transfer to hospital on the evidence of the medical reports before them. I have known cases where defendants have been refused transfer because the reports are deemed not to meet the threshold for *urgent transfer* (sec 48 1(a) & (b) MHA). This creates significant problems for the trial process. The reason for this is that any admission to hospital potentially becomes an evidence gathering exercise that may assist the defendant in mounting a psychiatric defence to the charges. This would be a situation where the Clinical Nurse Specialist may assist the defence in the pre-trial process by highlighting the options within the MHA. The Court's powers under the MHA are limited where the charge of homicide applies because section 36 MHA (an order for the admission and treatment in hospital for up to 12 weeks) does not apply where the sentence is fixed by law.

In the above example, the Clinical Nurse Specialist may suggest consideration is given to a sec 35 MHA order. The problem here is that sec 35 does not permit the compulsory treatment of the defendant and if the admitting hospital felt it needed powers to treat compulsorily it would need to consider an assessment under section 3. (The Court of Appeal R v North West London

Mental Health NHS Trust ex p Stewart (1997) upheld that part 2 (S2) and part 3 (S35) of the Mental Health Act can coexist independently of each other.)

Post sentence

Following conviction and sentence, where there have been psychiatric reports before the Court it will be desirable for those reports to follow the person to hospital or to the mental health team at the prison. These reports cannot be sent unilaterally on the basis of health information sharing but rather the permission of the Court is required. This is just one example of where hurdles can be encountered with regard to whether and what information can be shared. This blights many liaison efforts (Winstone and Pakes, 2007; Pakes and Winstone, 2009; Bradley, 2009) and is where the Clinical Nurse Specialist can explain to the diverse parties involved across the legal, health and wider criminal justice sector how to share and access information legally. For example, where prison sentences have been passed, an approach may be made to the MHLS for Court papers. Perhaps during sentence the prisoner becomes unwell and is transferred on a section 47 MHA and the hospital wants the depositions and any mental health reports from the original trial. The Clinical Nurse Specialist should, in such circumstances, explain to the hospital that this will require the Court's express permission. There will need to be a request to the Court for the files to be obtained from storage, and a copy of the e-mail request or letter from the hospital will be given to the relevant Judge, who will then decide how matters should proceed.

Conclusion

The value of the Clinical Nurse Specialist in the Crown Court is as a facilitator of both Court and health processes, as the defendant who is mentally unwell will straddle both systems. Effective intervention requires a reasonable understanding of both systems – which is learnt on the job (through experiential learning and continuous professional development). The evaluation of the liaison role of the Clinical Nurse Specialist at the Central Criminal Court (which won a national award) identified features of excellence that a best practice model could adopt (Winstone and Pakes, 2010). These factors are sufficiently generic and could be adopted across a range of settings and contexts where multiple agencies intersect in the sentencing process and where there is a need to collaborate in order to achieve a fair outcome in a timely fashion. Given the current initiatives to support liaison and diversion in the Courts (see introduction; see also Rogers and Ormston, this volume) it seems to be the right time to attempt to crystallise the essence of these factors as set out below.

Firstly, the fundamental lesson from the Clinical Nurse Specialist's experience at the Central Criminal Court is that inter-agency liaison and problem solving focussed on attaining a fair trial process works for all stakeholders (Court administration, Judges, Crown and defence, Probation, Police, Court cells etc.). This is because the brokering of knowledge into the system empowers all parties to more effectively play their respective parts. The use of e-mail and telephone, coupled with attendances at Court hearings, and informal discussion with parties, contribute to an unfolding conversation where decisions can be reached which move cases forward to Court-determined conclusions. The Court processes naturally protect the respective interests of the parties and the role of the Clinical Nurse Specialist is not designed to alter the balance of power within the trial processes. The processes are by nature adversarial and the parties properly protective of their distinctive duties.

Secondly, the Clinical Nurse Specialist provides a means by which Court decisions can be effectively enacted. Good examples of this would be the ordering and delivery of reports in a timely fashion or the obtaining of medical records required for a trial process. Another example would be the arranging of the provision of equipment and nursing cover to manage the physical needs of defendants during a trial. The Clinical Nurse Specialist can achieve this more effectively than those working outside the health system for obvious reasons. Anyone who works in health knows from their own experience liaising within and across Trusts and different health systems can be a fraught process – how much more so for those who do not work in the system?

Thirdly, it is important that health agencies can communicate with the Court. The Clinical Nurse Specialist is a neutral point of contact for prison mental health teams and secure hospitals if they have issues they wish to raise. Following court hearings they can be updated with the unfolding court process and given details of forthcoming trial dates and pre-trial hearings etc. Where there are changes to original hearing dates they can be notified. Where hospitals have video link systems compatible with the Court system these can be used for pre-trial hearings, which reduces costs substantially.

Finally, the Clinical Nurse Specialist should have a thorough understanding of the law and Criminal Procedures Rules. In places, in this chapter, I have gone into detail about how these apply to, for example, the commissioning of Expert Reports, fitness and unfitness to plead, hospital transfers, intermediaries, Court Time Limits and extensions. Managing the expectations of all the parties to the proceedings by being able to provide accurate information regarding the law and Criminal Procedures Rules will help to ensure that a potentially lengthy process is not further complicated by lack of clarity as to who needs to do what and when and who needs to be kept informed.

In all this, we should never lose sight of the fact that effective Court liaison actively ensures that justice is done by the victim, the perpetrator and in the public interest.

References

ACPO (2011). *Prosecution Team Manual of Guidance.* National Policing Improvement Agency. http://library.college.police.uk/docs/appref/MoG-final-2011-july.pdf

Advocates Gateway (2015). *Intermediaries.* www.theadvocatesgateway.org/intermediaries

Bradley, K. (Lord) (2009). *The Bradley Report: Lord Bradley's review of people with mental health problems or learning disabilities in the criminal justice system.* London: Department of Health. www.centreformentalhealth.org.uk/pdfs/Bradley_report_2009.pdf

Crown Prosecution Service (2015). *Prosecution of Offences (custody time limits).* CPS. www.cps.gov.uk/legal/a_to_c/custody_time_limits/

Criminal Law England and Wales (2005) No. 902. *The Crime and Disorder Act 1998 (Service of Prosecution Evidence) Regulations 2005.* www.legislation.gov.uk/uksi/2005/902/pdfs/uksi_20050902_en.pdf

Durcan, G., Saunders, A., Gadsby, B. and Hazard, A. (2014). *The Bradley Report five years on. An independent review of progress to date and priorities for further development.* London: Centre for Mental Health. www.centreformentalhealth.org.uk/pdfs/Bradley_report_five_years_on.pdf

Health Quality Improvement Partnership (2013). *National Confidential Inquiry into Suicides and Homicides (NCISH).* www.hqip.org.uk/national-confidential-inquiry-into-suicide-and-homicide/

McKenzie, N. and Sales, B. (2008). New procedures to cut delays in transfer of mentally ill prisoners to hospital. *The Psychiatrist,* Jan 2008, 32 (1), 20–22.

Mental Health Act (1983, amended 2007). www.mentalhealthlaw.co.uk/Mental_Health_Act_1983

Ministry of Justice (2011). *Judicial and Court Statistics 2011.* www.gov.uk/government/statistics/judicial-and-court-statistics-annual

Ministry of Justice (2012). *The Registered Intermediary Procedural Guidance Manual.* Ministry of Justice www.cps.gov.uk/publications/docs/RI_ProceduralGuidanceManual_2012.pdf

Ministry of Justice (2013a). *Court Statistics Quarterly, January to March 2013.* MOJ. www.gov.uk/government/statistics/court-statistics-quarterly-jan-mar-2013

Ministry of Justice (2013b). *Court Statistics Quarterly, April to June 2013.* www.gov.uk/government/statistics/court-statistics-quarterly-april-to-june-2013

Ministry of Justice (2013c). *Criminal Practice Rules and Practice Directions (2013).* www.justice.gov.uk/courts/procedure-rules/criminal/rulesmenu

Ministry of Justice (2013d). *Criminal Justice Statistics Quarterly.* www.gov.uk/government/collections/criminal-justice-statistics-quarterly

Ministry of Justice (2013e). *Statistics.* www.gov.uk/search?q=court+statistics+2013

Ministry of Justice (2013f). *Criminal Practice Directions (consolidated) 2013.* www.justice.gov.uk/courts/procedure-rules/criminal/practice-direction/pd_consolidated

Ministry of Justice (2013g). *Criminal Procedures Rules 2013, Expert Evidence.* http://www.justice.gov.uk/courts/procedure-rules/criminal/docs/2012/crim-proc-rules-2013-part-33.pdf

Ministry of Justice (2013h). *Criminal Procedures Rules 2013, Vulnerable Defendants.* www.judiciary.gov.uk/wp-content/uploads/JCO/Documents/judicial-college/ETBB_Children_Vulnerable_adults+_finalised_.pdf

Pakes, F. and Winstone, J. (2009). Effective practice in mental health diversion and liaison. *The Howard Journal of Criminal Justice,* 48 (2): 158–171.

Pakes, F. and Winstone, J. (2010). A site visit survey of 101 mental health liaison and diversion schemes in England. *Journal of Forensic Psychiatry and Psychology*, 21 (6): 873–886.

Reed, J. (1992). Review of health and social services for mentally disordered offenders and others requiring similar services. (Reed Report.) London: Department of Health and Home Office.

R v M (John) [2003] EWCA Crim 3452 Court of Appeal. www.e-lawresources.co.uk/R-v-M-%28John%29.php

R v Walls (Robert) [2011] EWCA Crim 443 Court of Appeal. www.bailii.org/ew/cases/EWCA/Crim/2011/443.html

R v North West London Mental Health NHS Trust, ex parte Stewart [1997] 4 All ER 871. www.lawandjustice.org.uk/LJcases.htm

Sainsbury Centre (2009) *Briefing 39: Mental health care and the criminal justice system*. Sainsbury Centre for Mental Health. www.centreformentalhealth.org.uk/pdfs/briefing39_mental_health_care_in_criminal_justice_sys.pdf

Singleton, N., Meltzer, H. and Gatward, R. (1998). *Psychiatric morbidity among prisoners in England and Wales*. London: Office for National Statistics.

Winstone, J. and Pakes, F. (2007). The Mentally Disordered Offender: disenablers for the delivery of justice. In: D. Carson, B. Milne, F. Pakes, K. Shalev and A. Shawyer (eds). *Applying Psychology to Criminal Justice*. London: Wiley. 167–182.

Winstone, J. and Pakes, F. (2010). Evaluation of a pilot project to develop mental health services in the Central Criminal Court. Commissioned by: Her Majesty's Court Service, Central and North West London NHS Foundation Trust, Oxleas NHS Foundation Trust.

11
The DSPD Programme: What Did It Tell Us about the Future for Managing Dangerous Prisoners with Severe Personality Disorders?

Ruth Scally

Introduction

Personality disorders have been described since the 19th century, as psychiatrists attempted to explain how apparently sane individuals could commit incomprehensible crimes (Prins, 1995, pp. 121–122). The terminology and definitions have evolved but the currently accepted clinical definition of a personality disorder is a 'deeply ingrained and enduring behaviour pattern, manifesting as inflexible responses to a broad range of personal and social situations' (World Health Organization, 2007). Both leading diagnostic manuals, the *Diagnostic and Statistical Manual of Mental Disorders* (DSM) published by the American Psychiatric Association, and the *International Classification of Diseases* published by the World Health Organization, describe constellations of traits required for the diagnosis of different personality disorders, and both include an antisocial type disorder characterised by disregard for social norms, callous unconcern for others and for the consequence of their actions, a low tolerance of frustration and a low threshold for aggression (World Health Organization, 2007).

In July 1999 the British government published the proposal paper 'Managing Dangerous People with Severe Personality Disorder' (Department of Health, 1999) which presented the government's response to the perceived challenges posed by certain high risk offenders. It should be noted that, prior to this paper, there was no clinical entity of 'dangerous and severe personality disorder' and this was seen as a political invention (Gunn, 2000, p. 73). A definition was established that was derived from the offender's score on the Psychopathy Checklist (Revised) (PCL-R) (Hare, 2003) – a clinical tool used to diagnose psychopathy – and a DSM-IV (which was the version available at that time) diagnosis of personality disorder (Kirkpatrick et al., 2010, p. 265). It was also explicit that there should be a functional link between the personality disorder and the offending behaviour and that the individual should be assessed as being likely to commit a serious offence within the next five years (Tyrer et al., 2010, p. 95).

Over the following decade a number of different initiatives were trialled under the auspices of the Dangerous and Severe Personality Disorder (DSPD) Programme, but the focus of the investment was in the establishment of two prison and two hospital high secure units (Sizmur and Noutch, 2005, p. 35). Medium secure hospital and community projects were also piloted and the Primrose Project was established at HMP Low Newton to provide support for women who met the DSPD criteria (Sizmur and Noutch, 2005, pp. 36–37).

In this chapter the background and genesis of the DSPD programme will be reviewed to elucidate why this particular approach was undertaken. It will then be analysed from the perspective of different professional disciplines to assess to what extent the programme succeeded in its aims, and what can be learnt from it in the future.

Background to the development of the DSPD programme

To understand how the DSPD programme came into being, one needs to look back at the antecedents over the preceding decade and the wider political and cultural context. Changes within psychiatry and the legal system's approach to dangerous offenders, the attitude of the general public to such individuals and significant news events have all been identified as contributory factors.

The case of Michael Stone, a man who in 1996 attacked a young family killing the mother and her six-year-old daughter, has been identified by some as the impetus for the government to reconsider their strategy for managing dangerous offenders (Beck, 2010, p. 278). Stone had been diagnosed as psychopathic several years previously but had been discharged from hospital as being untreatable (Beck, 2010, p. 279). At that time, treatability was a condition for detention under the Mental Health Act 1983 in England and Wales. When this emerged, public attention was focussed on the apparent inability of the health service to contain such individuals (Beck, 2010, p. 279). It provided pressure from the media and the public for the government to be seen to act to address the 'monster' (Chiswick, 2001, p. 283) of the frightening prospect of such personality disordered offenders in the community (Prins, 2001, p. 89). A more accurate interpretation, then, is that the Stone case was the catalyst for the new strategy, not the beginning but the culmination of a period of shifting attitudes to dangerous offenders (Duggan, 2011, p. 431) and frustration at the refusal of mental health services to manage them (Tyrer et al., 2010, p. 95).

In parallel to the development of the DSPD programme was a consultation process regarding amendments to the mental health legislation. One of the most significant amendments suggested was to remove the treatability criterion that had contributed to Stone's discharge from hospital (Morgan, 2004, p. 105). Like DSPD, this consultation was underwritten jointly by the Home Secretary and the Health Secretary, illustrating that although the onus was on the health service, a criminal justice agenda was an equal driver (Morgan, 2004, p. 105). Indeed, it was openly stated that public safety and concerns about risk should take precedence over the medical argument that detention should be for therapeutic purposes only (Morgan, 2004, p105–106; see Canton, this volume). This change in the law was an integral part of the DSPD proposals, as it would allow the detention of those deemed to have a DSPD even if there was no potential for them to be treated (Appelbaum, 2005, p. 874).

The legislative changes were hotly contested by a range of stakeholders, including the Royal College of Psychiatrists and mental health charities (Pilgrim, 2007, p. 79). The government was accused of selecting the recommendations that best fitted their public protection agenda while dismissing others that placed more emphasis on care (Pilgrim, 2007, p. 82). The opposition to the new legislation was successful in reducing a proposed new Act to amendments to the existing Act. However, the adaptations that were carried forward were those that were congruent with the government's social control agenda (Pilgrim, 2007, p. 94). Perhaps, though, the arguments against this were fatuous in that mental health legislation has always to some extent been a means of social control, targeting those perceived at greatest risk to themselves or others (Pilgrim, 2007, pp. 80–82, 91; Chan, 2002, p. 403); posing a risk to oneself or others have always been criteria for detention (see Canton, this volume).

The development of the DSPD proposals emerged from a background of increasing awareness and pressure to address the perceived issue of psychopaths in the community. There were legitimate concerns regarding the management of those with personality disorders and the lack of provision within the health service (Coid, 2003, p. s3). The public pressure for the government to be seen to act with a public safety agenda was clearly a big impetus for both the DSPD programme and the changes in the Mental Health Act.

The DSPD programme: managing dangerous people with severe personality disorder

'Proposals for Policy Development' was published jointly by the Home Office and the Department of Health in July 1999 (Department of Health, 1999). The first paragraph of the introduction refers explicitly to the 'challenge to public safety presented by the minority of people with severe personality disorder' and states that the objective of the proposals was to establish a coordinated package of arrangements to offer better protection to the public (Department of Health, 1999, p. 2). The government estimated that there would be approximately 2,000 individuals who would have a DSPD, the majority of whom would already be in either prison or a secure hospital (Department of Health, 1999, pp. 3, 9). However, the definition of the disorder was vague in the initial consultation, merely summarised as 'people who have an identifiable personality disorder to a severe degree, who pose a high risk to other people because of their serious antisocial behaviour resulting from their disorder' (Department of Health, 1999, p. 9). There was no indication of what features would merit the designation of a severe personality disorder.

Two options were put forward for consultation. The first relied upon existing frameworks within the health and criminal justice systems. The second was more revolutionary, which would include new legislation to allow the detention of dangerous individuals in facilities that would be managed separately to the current prison and healthcare provision. Most controversially, it was proposed that this would include changes that would allow for the detention of those deemed to have a DSPD whether or not they had been convicted of an offence (Department of Health, 1999, p. 4; see Canton, this volume). When the outcome of the consultation process was published, it was revealed that the majority had supported the second more innovative solution although opposition on civil liberty grounds was acknowledged (Department of Health, n.d., p. 1). Despite this the government chose to pursue the less radical amendments to the existing systems, citing the need to pilot and evaluate assessment processes and treatment programmes (Department of Health, n.d., p. 3). In 2001 they made a manifesto commitment to providing 300 high secure places for dangerous personality disordered offenders (Sizmur and Noutch, 2005, p. 34).

The initial pilot of the DSPD programme included three prison sites – HMP Frankland and HMP Whitemoor for men and HMP Low Newton offering places for 12 women – two high secure hospitals, Rampton and Broadmoor, offering places for 140 men between them, and a range of medium secure and community initiatives in five areas of the country (Forrester et al., 2008, p. 556). Places became available from October 2002 with a gradual increase in beds ultimately offering care for 240 people by 2010 (Tyrer et al., 2010, p.95). The criteria for admission were:

- the individual is more likely than not to commit an offence within five years that might be expected to lead to serious physical or psychological harm from which the victim would find it difficult or impossible to recover;
- they have a significant disorder of personality; and
- the risk presented appears to be functionally linked to the significant personality disorder (Tyrer et al., 2010, p. 95).

The definition of a 'significant' disorder of personality was clarified as:

- two or more DSM-IV personality disorders;
- very high score on the PCL-R, defined as greater than 30; or
- a score on the PCL-R between 25 and 29 and at least one other DSM-IV personality disorder diagnosis other than antisocial (Bell et al., 2003, p. 16).

The risk of future reoffending was assessed with a combination of actuarial tools and structured clinical judgement in order to minimise the risk of false positive assessments, or over-estimating those who would reoffend (Bell et al., 2003, p. 16). The treatments and interventions offered by the different units were diverse (Farr and Draycott, 2007, pp. 64–65; Moore and Freestone, 2006, p. 193) but was broadly based on the 'What Works' cognitive behavioural approach that had formed the basis for offender programmes in prison (Hogue et al., 2007, pp. 58–59; see McGuire, this volume). This identified the three principles of matching the intensity of the intervention with the risk posed, focussing on the needs and deficits of the offender and being responsive, matching treatment modalities with the offender's characteristics (Langton, 2007, p. 100). The primary targets for treatment were factors that had been identified by previous research to have a causal relationship to the individual's offending and dynamic, or changeable, risk factors (Bell et al., 2003, p. 18).

It should be noted that although the aspirations for the programme were clearly articulated, the processes for achieving them were less explicit. In the original proposal the government accepted the dearth of research in the area and outlined a research agenda as part of the programme (Department of Health and the Home Office, 1999, p. 40).

Implementation of the DSPD programme

Staff supervision and training were key components of the pilot programmes, recognising that the DSPD population would make heavy demands on the staff working with them (Davies and Tennant, 2003, p. 91). Perhaps a strength of the pilots was the involvement of prison staff in the therapeutic programmes, empowering them to manage personality disordered offenders more constructively (Bennett, 2002, p.12) but this clearly required a significant amount of support and education for those involved (Fox et al., 2006, p. 29).

Universal difficulties in recruiting staff, across hospital and prison sites, were noted, but once employed two thirds of staff reported that they were satisfied with their work (Ramsay, 2011, p. 5; Fortune et al., 2010, p. 193). Prison sites tended to have lower staffing levels than their hospital counterparts, which is of particular interest when juxtaposed with the finding that prison staff were noted to be more positive about the programme than hospital staff (Ramsay,

2011, p. 5). When the findings of the DSPD research emerged, it was recommended that prison sites were better placed to provide the right context for the treatment of dangerous offenders (Ramsay, 2011, p. 8). Thus, the DPSD programme can be seen as an example of staff of one discipline, prison officers, working with mental health professionals to develop innovative services to manage high risk offenders (see also Rogers and Ormston, this volume; Hean, Walsh and Hammick, this volume).

A research programme formed a core part of the design of the DSPD programme. Unfortunately the research that emerged from the DSPD programme did not vindicate the rationale for the initiative. The studies confirmed that the men (none of the studies referred to female offenders) were a heterogeneous and complex population (Kirkpatrick et al., 2010, p. 270). The treatments offered were more limited than suggested by the proposals with only ambiguous benefits in the short term (Ramsay, 2011, pp. 6–7). The financial analyses were particularly powerful, suggesting that despite the investment there was in fact a deterioration in the prisoners' functioning and that there was no support for the cost-effectiveness of the programme (Tyrer et al., 2010, p. 98). It is likely that the economic evidence suggesting greater cost efficiency for the prison-based units was a driver for the change in direction in 2011 with the coalition government's consultation document recommending the decommissioning of the high secure hospital DSPD units (Department of Health, 2011b, p. 6).

Psychiatric perspective

Traditionally, treatment of personality disorders had been in the domain of the psychiatric services, with the management of patients usually overseen by consultant psychiatrists. The government proposals (Department of Health, 1999) were closely scrutinised by doctors and misgivings about the role of psychiatry in the management of dangerous offenders were expressed (Morgan, 2004, p. 105). History has shown a cyclical pattern of looking to medicine and psychology to explain and 'solve' the perennial problem of recalcitrant criminals, and of such clinical interventions falling in and out of favour. It was perceived by some that the pattern was recurring (for example Morgan, 2004, p. 112). Furthermore, there may be issues about the implications of medicalising criminality and risk as it can imply reduced responsibility for one's actions (Morgan, 2004, p. 108; Gunn, 2000, p. 74; Morse, 2008, p. 205; see Tyson and Hall, this volume), which ironically is often the goal of interventions, and can distract from an understanding of the true causes of crime (Cox, 2002, p. 195). As it can be questioned whether psychiatrists are any more able to manage potential risk to others than the criminal justice system, some authors suggested that the medicalisation of dangerous offenders was a means to access powers over the individual that were not previously available to the judiciary (Morgan, 2004, p. 111).

A much documented challenge to the proposals was the assumption that they made that by involving prisoners with severe personality disorders in a therapeutic programme the risk that they posed of significant harm (as defined by the DSPD criteria) could be reduced. The challenge was mounted on two fronts. The first was based on the lack of evidence of the nature of the link between a diagnosis of personality disorder and violence. Research has demonstrated a link between a diagnosis of a personality disorder, most commonly antisocial personality disorder, and violence (Fountoulakis et al., 2008, p. 84; Vollm, 2009, p. 502) but the existence of a correlation between two factors does not imply a causative relationship (Howard, 2006, p. 21). It has been suggested that the link may be the effect of the research methodology used to explore the relationship, for example through factors such as social desirability, evaluation apprehension and rehearsal effects (Corbett and Westwood, 2005, p. 124). Alternatively other social and criminological factors may mediate the association (Duggan, 2011, p. 432). Substance misuse, particularly early onset alcohol use, has been implicated (Howard, 2006, p. 21; Pycroft and Green, this volume).

The second criticism related to the assumption that intervention would be effective in reducing risk (Duggan, 2007, p. 119). There had long been debate within the psychiatric community regarding the treatability of personality disorders in general, but the treatment of psychopathic offenders was particularly contentious. A 2004 literature review of the evidence for the treatment of individuals who scored highly on the PCL-R found that 'one cannot conclude that high-scoring psychopaths are untreatable or that treatment makes them worse', while acknowledging that the reviewed studies showed inconsistent findings (D'Silva, Duggan and McCarthy, 2004, p. 175). An alternative perspective that has some face validity is that the label of 'untreatable' may merely reflect a lack of available treatment (Meux, 2000, p. s3). In view of the lack of strong supportive evidence it could be surmised that the very characteristics of offenders that would make them suitable for a DSPD service would be associated with increased resistance to treatment (Maden et al., 2004, p. 379). One area that experts did appear to agree on was that even if interventions were effective in ameliorating some of the risks posed by these patients, the risks would remain 'well above the range of risk considered acceptable for discharge from a high secure hospital' (Maden et al., 2004, p. 380) and reoffending certainly could not be eliminated (Duggan, 2007, p. 119).

Therefore, psychiatrists who were to play a crucial role in the establishment, running and analysis of the DSPD programme expressed disquiet from the outset about the fundamental principles on which the proposals were based, namely that there was a causative association between personality disorder and violence, and that if the disorder was treated the risk would be reduced.

However, there were many professionals who attested that the DSPD programme was a positive step (Gordon, 2009, p. 164), and some of those who were vociferous in their criticism of the initiative at the beginning were later able to reflect on some of the benefits of the project (Mullen, 2007, p. s6).

The most lauded benefit was the recognition of the needs of a challenging group of individuals who, it was felt by many, had previously been ignored by both medicine and criminal justice (Mullen, 2007, p. s3; Duggan, 2011, p. 431). Not only were their needs being identified, a significant sum of money was being invested into addressing them. It was argued that the DSPD service provided an important function in offering previously unavailable specialised treatment while protecting the public (Beck, 2010, pp. 282–283). A further strength was the recognition of the shortage of evidence relating to the assessment and treatment of personality disorder (Gledhill, 2000, p. 445) and the investment in research, the outcomes of which have been published widely in mainstream and peer-reviewed journals (Duggan, 2011, p. 432).

Criminological perspective

Academics and criminological theory are also able to provide an insight into the timing and form of the government's proposals. Labelling Theory predicts that humans tend to pre-judge individuals and expect them to display particular characteristics based on the group they belong to (Rock, 2007, pp. 30–31). Furthermore, Goffman's Stigma Theory states that identifying people as abnormal or 'spoiled' can act to reinforce the 'normality' of everyone else, including oneself (Cordess, 2002, p. s15). Thus, we may tend to dismiss those who are frightening, and who commit horrendous crimes, to a category that epitomises their undesirability – for example DSPD. The negative stereotype allows for the justification of policies that further marginalise and punish them as a group (see also Göbbels, Thakker and Ward, this volume). This is an often recognised process with examples including apartheid, racism (see Tyson and Hall, this volume), and the treatment of asylum seekers. A further parallel with DSPD is the involvement of medicine and psychiatry in the definition and identification of the undesirable group (Cordess, 2002, p. s16). Stigma Theory provides an insight into the timing of the DSPD proposals; the stimulant to pursue such strategies can be when society feels vulnerable and isolated (Williams, 2001, p. 6; Cordess, 2002, p. s17).

DSPD provides a good example of the development of a 'maligned other' group. As Williams stated, 'it is always useful for both psychiatrists and sociologists to remember... the ways in which social problems are carefully framed by powerful institutions and definers for purposes of public regulation, consumption and debate' (Williams, 2001, p. 2; see also Arrigo and Bersot, this volume). There were clear motives for the government to be seen to exert some political power;

promoting public safety while vilifying the devalued group could gain public approval and ultimately votes (Corbett and Westwood, 2005, pp. 128, 131; Pilgrim, 2001, p. 263). The media played a significant role in projecting biased, but broadly accepted, views regarding the dangerousness of psychiatric patients and the number of DSPD offenders at large in the community (Corbett and Westwood, 2005, p. 128). This was set against a background of a popular perception that crime rates in general were high (Garland, 1996, p. 446) and that the criminal justice system was failing to contain this (Garland, 1996, p. 447). It has been postulated that this combination of social and political factors is associated with more punitive responses to crime and disorder as a figurative stance to demonstrate the government's authority (Garland, 1996, p. 460; De Koster et al., 2008, p. 730). Therefore the introduction of a programme with the stated purpose of managing dangerous offenders would be politically appealing in 1999 when the proposals were announced.

Ethical perspective

Perhaps some of the disquiet expressed by mental health professionals could be understood by a broader ethical critique of the DSPD programme (see also Canton, this volume). The first concern was the potential for a conflict of interests from the two 'masters' of the Department of Health and the Ministry of Justice and the different expectations of each of the role of mental health staff. Specifically, staff may feel tension between their role as a carer and the impetus to punish offenders and protect society (Haddock et al., 2001, p. 294; Lavender, 2002, p. s49; Szasz, 2003, p. 229). Doctors are guided by the ethical principles of beneficence and non-maleficence and there were some who felt simply that 'if we as clinicians refuse to treat people who are clearly unwell and distressed, we would be failing in our duty of care' (Mahapatra, 2001, p. 486; Tyrer, 2007, p. s1).

Psychiatrists have long contributed to public safety by detaining patients perceived to pose a risk to the public (Coid and Maden, 2003, p. 406). However, the legitimacy of this power is undermined if it is over-extended to apply to those who are not believed to fall within the accepted criteria for involuntary detention under the Mental Health Act (Appelbaum, 2003, p. 442). This argument is crystallised in the role of the psychiatrist in risk assessments for the purpose of assisting the judicial system, where the recommendations may not coincide with those that may be seen as in the patient's best interests (Nilsson et al., 2009, p. 405).

Legal perspective

Since 1991, three types of sentences had been introduced which had been particularly designed for public protection – the discretionary life sentence, the extended sentence for public protection and the automatic life sentence for a second serious violent or sexual offence. In addition, the Sex Offenders Act 1997 and the Crime and Disorder Act 1997 strengthened community conditions and required sex offenders to be registered (Forrester, 2002, pp. 330, 335–336). Some experts viewed the DSPD system as an extrapolation of these incapacitative measures (McAlinden, 2001, p. 108), seeing it as a form of preventive detention. This term was first coined at the beginning of the twentieth century, referring to legislation that provided for the incapacitation of habitual offenders by imposing additional sentences (Forrester, 2002, pp. 332–333). The trend throughout the 1990s was for the government to seek to use indeterminate detention to manage not only dangerous offenders, but also the public pressure to be seen to deal with them effectively (McAlinden, 2001, p. 113). In addition, the disposal of offenders by the extended sentences was based on an assessment of risk (albeit not necessarily carried out by a mental health professional), a parallel to the DSPD system (Maden, 2007, p. s10).

It would appear that the judiciary had a selection of sentences available for those perceived as being high risk, especially deriving from the premise of preventive detention. However they were reluctant to use them (Coid and Maden, 2003, p. 406). Only 2% of those eligible for a discretionary life sentence received one (Feeney, 2003, p. 351; Chiswick, 1999, p. 703). Examination of the characteristics of prisoners receiving an indeterminate sentence revealed a high proportion with mental health difficulties; 66% were assessed as requiring a clinical assessment for personality disorder, compared with 41% of life sentenced prisoners and 34% of the general prison population (Rutherford, 2009, p. s53). Such prisoners were more than twice as likely to fulfil criteria for transfer to the DSPD service (Rutherford, 2009, p. s53). This demonstrates that the dangerous offender that was to be the target of the DSPD programme was being, in many ways, identified and incarcerated by existing measures.

It has been postulated that there were a number of drivers for the increasingly cautious direction of sentencing. Hebenton and Seddon (2009) described the concept of 'precautionary logic', where the avoidance of risk is seen as imperative, even if the evidence for the existence of the risk or for the intervention is ambiguous (Hebenton and Seddon, 2009, p. 345). This drives decision-making that predicts the 'worst case scenario', rather than recognising the unlikelihood of this outcome. It is therefore underpinned by fear and anxiety, which can be amplified by the media (Hebenton and Seddon, 2009, p. 354). This can also be related to the second impetus, the concept of 'populist punitiveness' (McAlinden, 2001, p. 110). An alternative perspective is that the legislation of the 1990s reflected an 'exclusionist' philosophy that distinguished between deserving members of the public and an undeserving minority who should be excluded and incarcerated (Prins, 2001, p. 90).

The end of DSPD

In May 2010 the Labour government which had introduced the DSPD programme was replaced by a Conservative–Liberal Democrat coalition. A year later they produced a Consultation Paper on the Offender Personality Disorder Pathway Implementation Plan (Department of Health, 2011a). Again this was a joint publication between the Department of Health and the Ministry of Justice, and the Ministerial Foreword to the document referred to public protection as paramount and a 'key aim' (Department of Health, 2011a, p. 5). However, it set out the phased reduction of the DSPD pilots, concluding that treatments could be offered more effectively and at a lower cost in the prison service (Department of Health, 2011a, p. 7). It emphasised the need to develop opportunities for the rehabilitation of personality disordered offenders at lower levels of prison security and to develop pathways out of the higher secure units (Department of Health, 2011a, pp. 7–8). In effect, the focus shifted from the minority of extremely disordered offenders to the greater number of moderately mentally disordered offenders (Department of Health, 2011c, p. 1; see Rogers and Ormston, this volume). Furthermore, the onus was placed much more on the criminal justice system to manage such individuals within the prison service (Joseph and Benefield, 2010, p. 12). The response to the consultation phase was supportive (Department of Health, 2011b, p. 8) and the reconfiguration of services commenced. The DSPD programme, indeed the label DSPD, no longer existed.

Discussion and learning points

Throughout the chapter it has become clear that the impetus for the DSPD programme was not advances in medical expertise, but was predominantly potential political and cultural dynamics. Broadening the scope of the perspectives covered in this analysis demonstrated that the DSPD programme had not developed from a vacuum but was a continuation of previous government policy of increasingly punitive sentencing (McAlinden, 2001, p. 108), with indeterminate and discretionary life sentences. Exploring the theoretical underpinnings of preventive detention (Forrester, 2002, pp. 332–333) and Stigma Theory (Cordess, 2002, p. s15) reinforced that the proposals were a new incarnation of recognised responses to dangerous offenders. Indeed there is evidence that those who were serving indeterminate sentences were significantly more likely to meet the criteria for the DSPD service than other prisoners, which suggests that the target population was already being identified and subjected to special disposals (Rutherford, 2009, p. s53).

An improved understanding of the context to the DSPD proposals is crucial to appreciating how a scheme that was viewed with such scepticism by the key professionals was able to be implemented. The role that culture played in the development of DSPD can be summarised by the observation that 'provisions for the mentally ill have always reflected the dominant values and concerns of society at a particular time' (Morgan, 2004, p. 113; see Arrigo and Bersot, this volume). Many psychiatrists opined that DSPD was a misuse of psychiatry (Pilgrim, 2002, p. 7), citing the lack of clinical evidence in treating personality disorders. One of the conclusions for individual practitioners is that professionals should be more alert to the extraneous pressures that act upon them. This could develop from genuine multi-professional working, with all parties having an open attitude to the different theoretical and conceptual backgrounds of their colleagues. There should be debate about the fundamental issues and without presuming the superiority of one approach over another (see Rogers and Ormston, this volume; Hean, Walsh and Hammick, this volume). It is sobering that such an approach may protect practitioners against being led into potential violations of their profession's ethical codes.

While there was much to criticise about the DSPD programme, it can be concluded that it did make a significant positive contribution in changing professional attitudes to personality disordered offenders. It signalled a move away from the diagnosis being one of exclusion (Davies, 2007, p. 40) and prompted financial investment in the needs of a previously disparaged sector (Mullen, 2007, p. s3; Duggan, 2011, p. 431). Since the needs of personality disordered offenders were emphasised through the DSPD initiative they have remained on the political agenda, as demonstrated by the continued investment in the offender pathway currently being implemented. This is to be lauded and is a key area for future development.

A further positive aspect of the DSPD initiative was that it did acknowledge the paucity of research in the area and established programmes to develop this much-needed knowledge (see McGuire, this volume). However, the research that was an integral part of the programme identified that it was too soon to evaluate if the interventions started under the initiative were effective (Ramsay, 2011, p2). It is a concern that without the over-arching organisation of DSPD that the opportunities to formally assess the work that was begun, and expand the inadequate evidence base, will be lost. Of particular importance, the DSPD programme provided an opportunity to gain much-needed data about the treatment of personality disorders. Without this long-term vision, it is not implausible that future attempts to manage dangerous offenders will be criticised for the same fundamental flaw as the DSPD programme; a lack of an evidence base. Ensuring that research remains a central tenet of future initiatives will be crucial. As the lead provider of personality disorder services may have a health, prison, probation or social care background, a change of culture may be required to embed research as part of working with dangerous offenders. Professionals may need additional training, skills and support to maximise their ability to engage with this agenda (see Hean, Walsh and Hammick, this volume).

It has been suggested that policy-making requires knowledge, political will and social strategies (Coid, 2003, p. s7). This is a useful structure to summarise the impact of the DSPD programme. The literature is dominated by criticisms of the concept of personality disorders, the tools used to diagnose personality disorders and in particular psychopathy, risk assessment and the therapies offered. It can be concluded that the knowledge base to support the implementation was contentious. The political will for a programme to solve the problem of dangerous offenders was strong, related to a public perception of rising crime rates (Garland, 1996, p. 446) and media portrayals of the number of mentally disordered offenders on the streets (Corbett and Westwood, 2005, p.128). However, the strategies chosen to address it perhaps were less potent than they may have been. As the first reports from the studies that reported on the outcomes from the DSPD programmes coincided with the election of a new government it is difficult to establish the extent to which the replacement of the programme with a criminal justice-led service reflected a reasoned response to new evidence or a more partisan review of policy.

In conclusion, the rise and fall of DSPD is an example of a more positivist response to dangerous offenders and offending by seeking a psychological solution to a perennial problem. In this chapter the genesis of the DPSD programme has been placed within a wider context, providing an understanding of how such a controversial initiative could be implemented. While the DSPD programme may be regarded as dead and buried, the challenge of the management of dangerous offenders persists, and as so it is possible that in the future another variation of the DSPD programme will rise and fall again. The challenge will be to learn from the strengths and weaknesses of this incarnation to maximise the benefits to the offender and to the public.

References

American Psychiatric Association (1994). Diagnostic and Statistical Manual of Mental Disorders (4th edition) (DSM-IV). Washington DC: APA.

Appelbaum, P. (2003). Dangerous Persons, Moral Panic, and the Uses of Psychiatry. *Law and Psychiatry*, 54(4), 441–442.

Appelbaum, P. (2005). Dangerous People with Severe Personality Disorders. *Psychiatric Services*, 56(7), 874.

Beck, J.C. (2010). Dangerous Severe Personality Disorder: The Controversy Continues. *Behavioural Sciences and the Law*, 28, 277–288.

Bell, J., Campbell, S., Erikson, M., Hogue, T., McLean, Z., Rust, S. and Taylor, R. (2003). An Overview: DSPD Programme Concepts and Progress. *Issues in Forensic Psychology*, 4, 11–23.

Bennett, J. (2002). The Role of Prison Officers on the Dangerous and Severe Personality Disorder Unit at HMP Whitemoor. *Prison Service Journal*, 143, 9–14.

Chan, P. (2002). In Whose Best Interests? An Examination of the Ethics of the UK Government's White Paper 'Reforming the Mental Health Act'. *Journal of Psychiatric and Mental Health Nursing*, 9, 399–404.

Chiswick, D. (1999). Preventive Detention Exhumed and Enhanced. *Psychiatric Bulletin*, 23, 703–704.

Chiswick, D. (2001). Dangerous Severe Personality Disorder. From Notion to Law. *Psychiatric Bulletin*, 25, 282–283.

Coid, J. (2003). Epidemiology, Public Health and the Problem of Personality Disorder. *The British Journal of Psychiatry*, 182, s3–s10.

Coid, J. and Maden, T. (2003). Should Psychiatrists Protect the Public? *BMJ*, 326, 406.

Corbett, K. and Westwood, T. (2005). 'Dangerous and Severe Personality Disorder': A Psychiatric Manifestation of the Risk Society. *Critical Public Health*, 15(2), 121–133.

Cordess, C. (2002). Proposals for Managing Dangerous People with Severe Personality Disorder: New Legislation and New Follies in a Historical Context. *Criminal Behaviour and Mental Health*, 12, s12–s19.

Cox, J.L. (2002). Commentary Towards a More Integrated International System of Psychiatric Classification. *Psychopathology*, 35(2–3), 195–196.

Davies, J. (2007). Working with Personality Disordered Offenders: Where Are We At and Where Do We Need to Go? *Issues in Forensic Psychology*, 6, 40–46.

Davies, J. and Tennant, A. (2003). Dangerous and Severe Personality Disorder (DSPD). Integrating Education, Training, Teamwork and Supervision. *Issues in Forensic Psychology*, 4, 86–96.

De Koster, W., Van Der Waal, J., Achterberg, P. and Houtman, D. (2008). The Rise of the Penal State. Neo-Liberalization or New Political Culture? *British Journal of Criminology*, 48, 720–734.

Department of Health, The Home Office and HM Prison Service (n.d.). Managing Dangerous People With Severe Personality Disorder. Taking Forward The Government's Proposals. Retrieved on 31 May 2012 from http://www.dh.gov.uk/prod_consum_dh/groups/dh_digitalassets/documents/digitalasset/dh_120632.pdf

Department of Health and the Home Office (1999). Managing Dangerous People with Severe Personality Disorder. Proposals for Policy Development. Retrieved on 29 June 2012 from http://www.dh.gov.uk/prod_consum_dh/groups/dh_digitalassets/documents/digitalasset/dh_120634.pdf

Department of Health and The Ministry of Justice (2011a). Consultation on the Offender Personality Disorder Pathway Implementation Plan. Retrieved on 18 April 2011 from http://www.dh.gov.uk/prod_consum_dh/groups/dh_digitalassets/documents/digitalassets/dh_124489.pdf

Department of Health and the Ministry of Justice (2011b). Response to the Offender Personality Disorder Consultation. Retrieved on 31 May 2012 from http://www.dh.gov.uk/prod_consum_dh/groups/dh_digitalassets/documents/digitalasset/dh_130701.pdf

Department of Health (2011c). Impact Assessment of the Personality Disorder Implementation Plan. Retrieved on 31 May 2012 from http://www.dh.gov.uk/prod_consum_dh/groups/dh_digitalassets/documents/digitalasset/dh_132012.pdf

D'Silva, K., Duggan, C. and McCarthy, L. (2004). Does Treatment Really Make Psychopaths Worse? A Review of the Evidence. *Journal of Personality Disorders*, 18(2), 163–177.

Duggan, C. (2007). To Move or Not To Move – That is the Question! Some Reflections on the Transfer of DSPD Patients in the Face of Uncertainty. *Psychology, Crime and Law*, 13(1), 113–121.

Duggan, C. (2011). Dangerous and Severe Personality Disorder. *The British Journal of Psychiatry*, 198, 431–433.

Farr, C. and Draycott, S. (2007). 'Considering Change' – A Motivational Intervention with DSPD Offenders. *Issues in Forensic Psychology*, 7, 62–69.

Feeney, A. (2003). Dangerous Severe Personality Disorder. *Advances in Psychiatric Treatment*, 9, 349–358.

Forrester, A. (2002). Preventive Detention, Public Protection and Mental Health. *The Journal of Forensic Psychiatry*, 13(2), 329–344.

Forrester, A., Ozdural, S., Muthukumaraswamy, A. and Carroll, A. (2008). The Evolution of Mental Disorder as a Legal Category in England and Wales. *The Journal of Forensic Psychiatry and Psychology*, 19(4), 543–560.

Fortune, Z., Rose, D., Crawford, M., Slade, M., Spence, R., Mudd, D., Barrett, B., Coid, J., Tyrer, P. and Moran, P. (2010). An Evaluation of New Services for Personality Disordered Offenders: Staff and Service User Perspectives. *International Journal of Social Psychiatry*, 56(2), 186–195.

Fountoulakis, K.N., Leucht, S. and Kaprinis, G.S. (2008). Personality Disorders and Violence. *Current Opinion in Psychiatry*, 21, 84–92.

Fox, S., Jones, A., Meadows, L. and Savage, R. (2006). Prison Officers in a Multidisciplinary Team. The Role of Operational Staff in the DSPD Unit at HMP Whitemoor. *Prison Service Journal*, 168, 27–31.

Garland, D. (1996). The Limits of the Sovereign State. Strategies of Crime Control in Contemporary Society. *British Journal of Criminology*, 36(4), 445–471.

Gledhill, K. (2000). Managing Dangerous People with Severe Personality Disorder. *The Journal of Forensic Psychiatry*, 11(2), 439–447.

Gordon, H. (2009). Letter to the Editor. *The Journal of Forensic Psychiatry and Psychology*, 20 (1), 164–165.

Gunn, J. (2000). Editorial: A Millennium Monster is Born. *Criminal Behaviour and Mental Health*, 10, 73–76.

Haddock, A.W., Snowden, P.R., Dolan, M., Parker, J. and Rees, H. (2001). Managing Dangerous People with Severe Personality Disorder: A Survey of Forensic Psychiatrists' Opinions. *Psychiatric Bulletin*, 25, 293–296.

Hare, R.D. (2003). Hare Psychopathy Checklist – Revised (PCL-R), 2nd edition. Technical Manual. Toronto: MHS.

Hebenton, B. and Seddon, T. (2009). From Dangerousness to Precaution. Managing Sexual and Violent Offenders in an Insecure and Uncertain Age. *British Journal of Criminology*, 49, 343–362.

Hogue, T.E., Jones, L., Talkes, K. and Tennant, A. (2007). The Peaks: A Clinical Service for Those With Dangerous and Severe Personality Disorder. *Psychology, Crime & Law*, 13 (1), 57–68.

Howard, R. (2006). What is the Link Between Personality Disorder and Dangerousness? A Critique of 'Dangerous and Severe Personality Disorder'. *The British Journal of Forensic Practice*, 8 (4), 19–23.

Joseph, N. and Benefield, N. (2010). The Development of an Offender Personality Disorder Strategy. *Mental Health Review Journal*, 15(4), 10–15.

Kirkpatrick, T., Draycott, S., Freestone, M., Cooper, S., Twisleton, K., Watson, N., Evans, J., Hawes, V., Jones, L., Moore, C., Andrews, K. and Maden, T. (2010). A Descriptive Evaluation of Patients and Prisoners Assessed for Dangerous and Severe Personality Disorder. *The Journal of Forensic Psychiatry and Psychology*, 21 (2), 264–282.

Langton, C.M. (2007). Assessment Implications of 'What Works' Research for Dangerous and Severe Personality Disorder (DSPD) Service Evaluation. *Psychology, Crime and Law*, 13(1) 97–111.

Lavender, A. (2002). Developing Services for People with Dangerous and Severe Personality Disorders. *Criminal Behaviour and Mental Health*, 12, s46–s53.

Maden, A. (2007). Dangerous and Severe Personality Disorder: Antecedents and Origins. *The British Journal of Psychiatry*, 190, 8–11.

Maden, A., Williams, J., Wong, S.C.P. and Leis, T.A. (2004). Treating Dangerous and Severe Personality Disorder in High Security: Lessons from the Regional Psychiatric Centre, Saskatoon, Canada. *The Journal of Forensic Psychiatry and Psychology*, 15 (3), 375–390.

Mahapatra, P. (2001). Mental Health Act Reform. *Psychiatric Bulletin*, 25, 486.

McAlinden, A.-M. (2001). Indeterminate Sentences for the Severely Personality Disordered. *Criminal Law Review*, Feb, 108–123.

Meux, C. (2000). Editorial: Exploring the Assessment of Personality Disorder. *Criminal Behaviour and Mental Health*, 10, s1–s7.

Moore, C. and Freestone, M. (2006). Traumas of Forming: The Introduction of Community Meetings in the Dangerous and Severe Personality Disorder (DSPD) Environment. *Therapeutic Communities*, 27 (2), 193–209.

Morgan, D. (2004). Mad or Bad? A Critique of Proposals for Managing Dangerously Disordered People. *Journal of Community and Applied Social Psychology*, 14, 104–114.

Morse, S.J. (2008). Psychopathy and Criminal Responsibility. *Neuroethics*, 1, 205–212.

Mullen, P.E. (2007). Editorial. Dangerous and Severe Personality Disorder and In Need of Treatment. *The British Journal of Psychiatry*, 190, s3–s7.

Nilsson, T., Munthe, C., Gustavson, C., Forsman, A. and Anckarsater, H. (2009). The Precarious Practice of Forensic Psychiatric Risk Assessments. *International Journal of Law and Psychiatry*, 32, 400–407.

Pilgrim, D. (2001). Disordered Personalities and Disordered Concepts. *Journal of Mental Health*, 10 (3), 253–265.

Pilgrim, D. (2002). DSPD: From Futility to Utility. *Clinical Psychology*, 20, 5–7.

Pilgrim, D. (2007). New 'Mental Health' Legislation for England and Wales: Some Aspects of Consensus and Conflict. *Journal of Social Policy*, 1, 79–95.

Prins, H. (1995). Psychopathic Disorder: A Useful Label? In H. Prins, *Offenders, Deviants or Patients?* London: Routledge. 119–142.

Prins, H. (2001). W(h)ither Psychopathic Disorder? A view from the UK. *Psychology, Crime & Law*, 7, 89–103.

Ramsay, M. (2011). *Research Summary 4/11. The early Years of the DSPD (Dangerous and Severe Personality Disorder) Programme: Results of Two Process Studies*. Retrieved on 31 May 2012 from http://justice.gov.uk/downloads/publications/research-and-analysis/moj-research/early-years-dspd-programme-research-summary.pdf

Rock, P. (2007). Sociological Theories of Crime. In M. McGuire, R. Morgan and R.Reiner (eds). *The Oxford Handbook of Criminology*. Oxford: Oxford University Press. 3–42.

Rutherford, M. (2009). Imprisonment for Public Protection: An Example of 'Reverse Diversion'. *The Journal of Forensic Psychiatry and Psychology*, 20 (S1), s46–s55.

Sizmur, S. and Noutch, T. (2005). Dangerous and Severe Personality Disorder Services. *The British Journal of Forensic Practice*, 7 (4), 33–38.

Szasz, T. (2003). Psychiatry and the Control of Dangerousness: On the Apotropaic Function of the Term 'Mental Illness'. *Journal of Medical Ethics*, 29, 227–230.

Tyrer, P. (2007). Editorial. An Agitation of Contrary Opinions. *The British Journal of Psychiatry*, 190, s1–s2.

Tyrer, P., Duggan, C., Cooper, S., Crawford, M., Seivewright, H., Rutter, D., Maden, T., Byford, S. and Barrett, B. (2010). The Successes and Failures of the DSPD Experiment: The Assessment and Management of Severe Personality Disorder. *Medicine, Science and the Law*, 50, 95–99.

Vollm, B. (2009). Assessment and Management of Dangerous and Severe Personality Disorders. *Current Opinion in Psychiatry*, 22, 501–506.

Williams, J. (2001). The Costs of Safety in Risk Societies. *The Journal of Forensic Psychiatry*, 12 (1), 1–7.

World Health Organization (2007). ICD-10. Retrieved 23 April 2011, from http://apps.who.int/classifications/apps/icd/icd10online/

12
Prosecuting the Persecuted: Forgive Them, They Know Not What They Do
Taffy Gatawa

Introduction

NHS staff are among the most likely to face violence and abuse at work (Department of Health, 2011). Acts of violence committed against mental health professionals by psychiatric inpatients is a serious perennial workplace problem. It is acknowledged that crimes of violence are more prone to subjective judgement about whether to record a crime (ONS Crime Survey, 2015). A report published by Her Majesty's Inspectorate of Constabulary (HMIC) found that violence against the person offences had the highest under-recording rates across police forces in England and Wales. Indeed, nationally, an estimated one in three (33%) violent offences that should have been recorded as crimes were not. The link between mental disorder and offending behaviour has often been postulated in literature and in the media. In 1933 at an annual meeting for the South African Association of Probation in Johannesburg, his royal highness Prince George made the following observation:

> The problem of crime is a sad one when looked upon from the point of view of the offender and a troublesome one when looked at from that of the State. (HRH Prince George, 1933)

In this chapter, I explore one of the difficulties faced by mental health professionals working in high security hospitals; whether or not to prosecute inpatients who engage in violent / criminal behaviour within the hospital setting. The focus of this debate is one which has exercised professionals over a number of decades and one in which opinion is divided. This chapter is based on a service evaluation undertaken at Broadmoor Hospital, one of the three high security hospitals in England. It considers a framework for addressing this long-standing problem and explores the reluctance to prosecute this cohort of offenders.

Hospital or prison – patient or prisoner?

Despite their long-standing existence, the work of the high secure hospitals remains largely misunderstood by the public and is therefore subject to fantasy and conjecture. A common misconception is that these hospitals are, in fact, prisons in all but name. Having worked within a high secure hospital for nine years, I am very clear that this is not the case, as I have experienced that caring, therapeutic healing and rehabilitation are at the heart of the work of the hospitals. Arguably, although not impossible to find, these three characteristics are less prevalent within the prison estate. High secure psychiatric hospital services in England are provided across a small network of three hospitals, Ashworth, Broadmoor and Rampton. Each of the three hospitals is integrated within local National Health Service (NHS) mental health services that operate under license from the Secretary of State for Health to provide high security hospital services (Department of Health, 2008). Broadmoor Hospital is part of West London Mental Health NHS Trust and the other two high secure hospitals, Ashworth and Rampton, are part of Mersey Care NHS Trust and Nottinghamshire Healthcare NHS Trust respectively. The NHS Act 2006 places a specific duty on the Secretary of State for Health to provide hospital accommodation and services for persons who a) are liable to be detained under the Mental Health Act 1983 (as amended in 2007; 'the Act') and b) in the opinion of the Secretary of State require treatment in conditions of high security on account of their dangerous, violent and or criminal propensities. Patients detained within high secure hospitals are those defined as having a high risk of posing a grave and immediate danger to the public if at large (see Scally, this volume). The legal requirement for the Secretary of State to provide these services ensures a high level of political interest as well as a high level of public and media interest in the services provided by the high security hospitals and the patients they treat (Department of Health, 2008).

In the majority of cases, patients within high security hospitals will have had contact with the criminal justice system at some point in their psychiatric journey. This also means that most of the patients within high secure hospitals will not only be detained under the Mental Health Act but will also have a restriction order applied by the sentencing court. The Act is divided into nine parts. Part 2 of the Act sets out the civil procedures under which compulsory admission to hospital and guardianship may be instigated. Part 3 concerns patients involved in criminal proceedings or under sentence. It therefore provides powers for Crown or Magistrates' Courts to remand an accused person to hospital either for treatment or a report on their mental disorder (see de Lacy, this volume). Within Broadmoor hospital, most people are detained under this part of the Act.

An unrestricted hospital order indicates that the sentencing court found treatment more appropriate than punishment, and was persuaded that purely clinical risk management would suffice to protect the public. This means that decisions about the patient are not purely clinical and there has to be express agreement of the Secretary of State for Justice with regards to permission to leave the hospital, transfer to another hospital etc. The Ministry of Justice (2007) guidance for working with mentally disordered offenders points out that, in this case, the offender with a hospital order has no tariff to serve because he is not being punished (see Canton, this volume). Ideas about punishment relate to the concept that behaviour can be modified as a result of punishment as depicted in the old adage, 'spare the rod and spoil the child'. Where this conventional punishment is not deemed appropriate, a hospital order may be indicated.

The work of Monahan and Steadman (1983), cited in Gunn and Taylor (1993), reviewed the numerical relationship between violence, crime and mental disorder. They emphasised the distinction between 'true' rates of crime and mental disorder (that is the rate at which crime and mental disorder actually occur) and their 'treated' rates (that is the rate at which the criminal justice and the mental health systems respond to them). They found that most published research focused on true rates of disorder among 'treated' criminals or true rates of crime among 'treated' patients. Many studies referred to mental disorder or illness in broad terms and estimation of the contribution of psychosis was difficult.

Thirty years on, this difficulty remains. Although it is widely acknowledged that mental disorder may be a contributory factor to violent behaviour and much has been written about this (Chen et al., 2010; Vinkers et al., 2011), there has been relatively little written about prosecuting psychiatric inpatients. Cherrett (1996) points out that a great deal of the debate about how mentally disordered offenders are dealt with revolves around how they are defined. Bradley (2009) notes that some experts argue that to classify someone as a mentally disordered offender there has to be a demonstrable link showing that the disorder has contributed to the offending behaviour. The challenge of establishing this demonstrable link is central to this discussion and is a contributory factor to the reluctance to prosecute patients within high security hospitals. To that end, it is not uncommon for these mental health patients to have an extensive history of offending behaviour and not have any prosecutions and/or convictions for those offences (Norko et al., 1992; Rachlin, 1994; Brown, 2006).

The service evaluation at Broadmoor conducted in 2011 sought to investigate the experiences of staff working in Broadmoor high secure hospital in relation to this issue. It explored the complexity of the criminal justice system when applied in the context of attempting to prosecute patients detained in the hospital following criminal acts, and particularly incidents of assault on staff and other patients.

Above the law or just bending the rules?

As most healthcare professionals working within mental health are aware, it is increasingly difficult to prosecute mentally disordered offenders who are already detained within an inpatient mental health unit (Brown, 2006; Young et al., 2009). This has led to the despair sometimes expressed by mental health professionals, in particular nurses, that patients can assault [staff] with impunity. The question of impunity for the patients in Broadmoor is an interesting point. Tabloid headlines such as 'Comedy night for Broadmoor fiends' (The Sun, Oct 2008) can evoke public outrage and a sense that what is portrayed is inconsistent with the public perception of what constitutes punishment, and certainly does not reflect what the expected lifestyle ought to be for a mentally disordered offender detained at Broadmoor. There is therefore some disparity in the public expectation of such an institution and what the Government intends. Prosecuting inpatients in high security institutions is a multi-faceted problem. The first of these is that of the offender and determining their culpability in legal terms. The second is about the attitudes (conscious / unconscious) of the staff working in these institutions – often referred to as 'culture'. Finally, there is the pervasiveness of violence within the high secure estate which can sometimes leave others around desensitised to the violence or indeed lead to the resigned acceptance of violence as being a workplace hazard.

Brown (2006) asserts that the extent to which mentally ill individuals are prosecuted for violence varies. He adds that the recent history of psychiatry is littered with examples of those who are not (Norko et al.,1992; Rachlin, 1994), and that this is ultimately to their disadvantage. Brown's paper, which was written before the Act was amended in 2007, refers to mentally ill individuals, which is a classification no longer in use in the amended Act. However, the point he makes is relevant to all mental health patients alike, irrespective of the mental disorder classification. The idea of being disadvantaged by evading prosecution is often juxtaposed with the advantages of receiving treatment and therapy that may not otherwise be accessible. The Mental Health Act Commission's report, 'In Place of Fear' (2005), states that it may also be the case that excusing offending may not be in the patient's interests and that the legal process itself may be useful for a patient's reality testing, and a presumption that prosecution of violent behaviour is routine rather than exceptional may help patients take responsibility for their behaviour and instil a sense of justice amongst patients and staff. Needless to say, opinion on this is strongly divided between the mental health professionals and the so-called mentally disordered offenders. Whilst most patients acknowledge the need for treatment, few believe that this need follow prosecution. However, the professional viewpoint is that prosecution can lead to many more treatment options for patients particularly when the offending profile is multi-dimensional, i.e. a combination of different offences such as physical violence, sexual offences, and fire setting. Certainly initiatives like the court diversion scheme have been credited with helping in identifying individuals who may otherwise not have come to the attention of the mental health system, and enabling treatment of such individuals. In addition the Act does carry powers under Part 3 to direct an offender to a hopsital to receive treatment.

Throughout history there has long been recognition of the requirement for recompense for wrongdoing. This requirement is often associated with a consciousness of mind from the wrongdoer. The mode of recompense for certain crimes and acts of wrongdoing has evolved over time. However it appears that even in the past the requirement for recompense was not indiscriminately applied and so there was a need to consider the state of mind of the wrongdoer before deciding on the appropriate disposal. In legal terms this is known as 'mens rea' and is often at the centre of debates about the appropriate plea to submit. From Shakespeare to modern literature, we are reminded of many examples of the 'mad' being subject to a different yardstick and one of the early examples is the case of Daniel M'Naghten in 1843, who after being charged for the murder of Edward Drummond, whom he had mistaken for the British Prime Minister Robert Peel, was acquitted from a murder charge due to insanity. Equally there are many examples, both past and present, of madness feigned to escape harsh punishment for crimes committed.

With the passage of time, there has been more debate about the requirement to punish those who do wrong against an emerging idea that it is far better to attempt rehabilitation in the hope that this is more likely to affect lasting change in the behaviour and attitude of those perpetrating the crimes. Rehabilitation can take many forms. For example, restorative justice, which is based on the premise that bringing the victim and the perpetrator together to afford the opportunity for dialogue can be rehabilitative for the perpetrator whilst serving the needs of the victim, is one accepted concept along the rehabilitation spectrum. The tasks of restorative justice (such as apology, rehabilitation, reparation, healing, restoration and re-integration) as defined by Shapland et al. (2006) have informed recent criminal justice policy and programmes of prison reformation across England. These, along with the policy changes like those put forward in *Transforming the CJS: A strategy and action plan to reform the criminal justice system* (2013), have also had an impact on the treatment of those judged to be criminally insane and detained within psychiatric hospitals. This idea of supportive rehabilitation is in itself not a new concept in the world of psychiatry. Instead the ideas about the type of rehabilitation have evolved over time, often based on evaluation of their efficacy and the estimated recidivism rate for those undergoing the rehabilitation/ treatment.

To illustrate this, the model for caring for highly dangerous persons with a personality disorder known as the Dangerous and Severe Personality Disorder (DSPD) programme was largely based on a range of cognitive behavioural rehabilitation methods, with limited use of medication. The programme was disbanded in 2011 following evaluation of the efficacy of the model which arguably, according to Maden (2007), had very limited success. An evaluation of the DSPD programme by Professor Tyrer, referenced in a Channel 4 news programme, also came to a similar conclusion (Davies, 2010; see Scally, this volume). Indeed, many psychiatrists have noted how impossible it is to accurately predict risk and, because of high profile failures, such as those leading to the political construct of 'DSPD', psychiatrists have tended to over-predict as a safeguard (Smith, 2011).

Violence in psychiatric hospitals: the scale of the problem

In a survey of workplace violence, healthcare professionals were identified as among the most likely groups to experience violence (British Crime Survey, 2015). Behr et al. (2005, p. 7), cite the work of Wells and Bowers in 2002 which showed that nursing staff in the UK were four times more likely to experience work related violence than other workers. Behr et al. (2005, p. 7) also show, using the work of Hobbs and Keane, that violence towards doctors and other health professionals has also been identified. Violence against mental health service personnel is a serious workplace problem and one that appears to be increasing (Nolan et al., 1999; Kumar et al., 2006). Observation shows that assaulting a doctor is more likely to trigger a referral to a secure hospital (whatever the level of security) in comparison to assaulting a nurse or other junior member of staff (Gunn and Taylor, 2004). This sentiment was echoed by many nursing staff when asked to describe some of the frustrations in relation to the management of violence within the high secure estate.

In Broadmoor, between January and December 2010, there were 196 incidents of patient to staff assaults and 100 incidents of patient to patient assaults reported. This shows that staff were twice as likely to be assaulted compared to other patients. Between 2001 and 2005, there were 14 cases that were referred to the CPS for prosecution. Using the number of recorded incidents of assault for 2010 as a rough estimate of incidents each year, it is possible to conclude that the percentage of incidents that are taken forward to prosecution each year is extremely low. It is also significant to note that a small number of patients are responsible for the cases referenced above. This fits with observations from other researchers who note that in the most part, it is a small number of patients who repeatedly assault (Gunn, 2003). According to the National Reporting and

Learning Service report published in October 2014, there were 1078 patient safety incidents reported by WLMT between 1 October 2013 and 1 March 2014 (NRLS, 2014). Of these, 33.5% related to aggressive, disruptive behaviour. This figure is twice that reported for other mental health organisations.

The work of the high secure hospitals has been an area of fascination for a long time, with the media often providing sensational insights into the goings on within these premises. The hospitals have been described as closed institutions and efforts to shine a light on the true nature of the hospitals have been met with scepticism. Whilst there have been efforts to bring the high secure estate into the mainstream, which included making the three high secure hospitals in England part of the NHS, there remains a great degree of mystery and intrigue about the high secure hospitals and those detained within them. Another challenge can be the relationship and effectiveness of communication between the police, CPS and mental healthcare professionals. The quality of this is significant and is often critical to how strong, in legal terms, a case is when presented to the CPS. There are in place two memorandums of understanding (MoU) between the Association of Chief Police Officers (ACPO) and the CPS and NHS Protect which seek to outline best practice for joint working (CFSMS 2003a,b). On the occasions that this hurdle is overcome, there is for the staff the challenge of maintaining a therapeutic relationship with the patient and the impact that bringing criminal proceedings can have to the therapeutic alliance.

Prosecution?...not in the public interest

Modern sociology reminds us of the principles of citizenship and social responsibility and places great emphasis on public morality. One social ideal is that of reducing crime and violence and the high secure estate has a clear role in this. Exploring the value of prosecuting patients detained within high secure contributes to the debate of whether or not it is important for these social ideals to be upheld, as far as is practicable, within these institutions. In their review of security within the high secure estate, Tilt et al. (2000) offer a further reminder of the importance of appropriate responses to security matters within these institutions stating that '...the underlying dangerousness of the patient population and the potential threat which they present to members of the general public, and to staff and fellow patients within the hospitals should not be underestimated' (paragraph 3.2).

Eastman and Mullins (1999) state that prosecuting patients may help increase their capacity to accept responsibility for their crime and aid future clinical risk assessment. This view is generally accepted by most professionals (Brown, 2006; Young et al., 2009; Buchanan, 2008). Interestingly, this view was recently challenged in 2010 when a Crown Court judge queried whether it was in the public interest (i.e., whether this was an appropriate way to spend public money) for criminal prosecutions to be brought against persons who were already detained in hospital. These comments related to the case of a patient detained at Rampton (a high secure hospital) on a section 37/41 order (hospital order with restriction). The patient had been charged with five counts of common assault. The patient pleaded not guilty at a Magistrates' Court hearing. However when the case was tried, the patient was found guilty by the Magistrates' Court and ordered to pay compensation to each member of staff together with a fixed amount of legal costs.

The patient appealed against the conviction and a hearing took place at Nottingham Crown Court. It was at this appeal hearing that the comments about the appropriateness of prosecuting the patient were expressed by the judge. The hearing was subsequently adjourned in order to enable information to be gathered in relation to the rationale behind the patient's prosecution including a history of previous risk incidents. A further and final hearing took place and the Court came to the decision that there was no merit in the patient's appeal and it was dismissed (see briefing by Mills and Reeve, 2010, for a full explanation). A similar case is cited by Norko et al. (1992) who described a New Jersey Superior Court that also questioned the appropriateness of prosecuting patients for behaviours which precipitated their hospitalisation. The relevance of the comments from both these cases to this research is that the psychiatric high secure hospital is distinctly different from other psychiatric hospitals and its function is, as stated previously, often misunderstood. Even within the psychiatric community, some refer to the high secure hospitals as 'prisons' or 'prison hospitals'. This incorrect perception may also contribute to the reluctance to prosecute. However, it is important to note that, unlike the prison governor, the psychiatrist does not have the power to impose adjudications following assaults on others. It is therefore important that the law has equal application within the high secure estate and that, as argued by Murray (1989), the fact that an incident occurs in a hospital does not, in itself, determine what the judical response to that incident should be.

Another view is the idea that caring lies at the heart of mental health services so issues of social control, coercion and violence are rarely acknowledged or discussed (Nolan et al., 1999). This can often leave staff either feeling guilty about being assaulted or even considering prosecution (Phelan et al., 1984). Historically, the high secure hospitals have been accused of fostering a 'macho' culture in which being the victim of an assault was viewed negatively, therefore contributing to a reluctance to prosecute.

The road to prosecution

The CPS deal with prosecutions of offenders on behalf of the Crown. The code for Crown Prosecutors states that prosecutors must only start or continue a prosecution when the case has passed both stages of the Full Code test. The exception is when the threshold test may be applied where it is proposed to apply to the Court to keep the suspect in custody after charge, and the evidence required to supply the Full Code test is yet to be available.

The prosecution policy states that when violence occurs whilst staff are undertaking their duties, it should be considered an aggravating factor to the offence as laid down by the code for Crown Prosecutors (paragraph 5.9). This gives weight to the public interest criterion. The memorandum of understanding between ACPO, the CPS and the NHS asserts that criminal law has equal application both inside and outside mental health units, and that it should be assumed that all mental health service users have capacity in law for responsibility for their actions (CFSMS, 2007). It also recognises, however, that mental illness may be a negative factor in prosecution and that mental health professionals should be prepared to disclose confidential patient information to the police as requested. As mental illness is weighted against prosecution, this immediately presents the dichotomy of the problem: prosecuting assaults committed by the mentally disordered against those serving the public. It has been suggested that there are times when the public interest outweighs the mental illness, and in particular the severity of the offence will often have a bearing on this (Buchanan, 2006; Mills and Reeves, 2010; see also Canton, this volume).

However there are other factors that may influence the decision of the CPS to take no further action after an assault has been commited by a psychiatric inpatient, including the clinical presentation of the patient at the time of the offence. There are those who argue that, irrespective of this, there are times when it is clinically appropriate to pursue a prosecution (Buchanan, 2006), that 'allowing these people, most of whom are capacitous, to take responsibility for their action is an important therapeutic tool' (Behr at al., 2005, p. 8), and that shielding them from the consequences of their choices has the potential for undermining this and perpetuating that individual's psychological problems.

The dilemma in pursuing legal action is not only experienced by the clinicians, but indeed also by the police. Particular tensions for the police include the requirement to have an appropriate adult in interviews and police concerns about lack of understanding of mental disorder. A study by Mclean and Marshall (2010), where they interviewed front line police, is perhaps more successful in eliciting the views and perspectives of the police regarding their role in mental health services. Although the study focused on the increasing role of the police in the community management of people with mental health problems, some of the insights, particularly around issues of arrest, can be generalised to inpatient settings. One of the themes emerging from this study was the officers' recognition of the possible consequences of police intervention on mental health patients. 'At the end of the day how will that benefit the person, how will it benefit if they are going to end up with a criminal conviction and then it could...make it worse' (p. 65). This sits at odds with the clinical view that not being prosecuted can sometimes be ultimately detrimental to the individual (Brown, 2006). However this does present the tension that is at the heart of the reluctance to prosecute. In relation to the evaluation, it was evident that efforts had been made to establish good relationships with the local police and to improve their understanding of the high secure hospital.

Nevertheless, the notion of lack of responsibility on the part of the patient (mentally disordered offender) remains a particular concern for the police who are called upon to investigate cases occuring within Broadmoor. The Crown Prosecution Service (CPS) code guiding prosecution contains criteria similar to those followed by the police. The CPS use the term 'mentally disordered offender' to describe a person who has a disability or disorder of the mind who has or is suspected of committing a crime. From their perspective a mental disorder may be relevant to the decision to prosecute or divert; fitness to plead; and sentencing or disposal. In determining whether to prosecute a case the CPS may apply the Full Code test, which is made up of two stages: the evidential stage and the public interest stage. The public interest stage requires that the prosecutor considers a set of questions as outlined below:

a) How serious is the offence committed?
b) What is the level of culpability of the suspect?
c) What are the circumstances of and the harm caused to the victim?
d) Was the suspect under the age of 18 at the time of the offence?
e) What is the impact on the community?
f) Is prosecution a proportionate response?
g) Do sources of information require protecting?

All of these questions are then considered against the backdrop of a mental disorder. Indeed there may be public interest factors tending against prosecution that outweigh factors in favour of prosecution. In this instance the prosecutor may be satisfied that the public interest can be properly served by offering the offender the opportunity to have the matter dealt with by an out-of-court disposal rather than by bringing a prosecution.

The literature and my own research and experience highlights that where there is police involvement in dealing with these situations there are several benefits, and that the process of prosecution may have a positive effect on staff morale despite the effort involved (Bayney and Ikkos, 2003). Given the volume of assaults recorded in the hospital, maintaining staff morale is crucial. Other studies have also highlighted the possible deterrent effect of pursuing a prosecution (Behr et al., 2005; Gunn, 2003). This is important when considering that most incidents within Broadmoor are perpetrated by a small recidivist group. Some authors have argued that the tolerance of aggression leads to its encouragement and increasing frequency and that appropriate responses may decrease their frequency (Kumar et al., 2006).

Coyne (2002) explored how decisions to contact the police are made in mental health services. This study revealed that few incidents are reported to the police, who in turn take fewer matters beyond an initial discussion. Most staff were also found to be unclear about the benefits of prosecution, thus further perpetuating the failure to address the problem. For instance, staff believed that experiencing violence was an unfortunate part of their role which they were powerless to change. Staff also believed that the police were unlikely to pursue a case or that if they did this would not have an impact on the ongoing treatment of the patient and would therefore be pointless. Since then there has been significant investment in addressing the problem of violence in the health service with a memorandum of understanding first agreed between the CPS and the NHS in 2003 and also a further MoU agreed between the NHS and ACPO as discussed earlier. Whilst current practice at Broadmoor hospital stipulates that all incidents of assault are reported to the police the number of cases that proceed to prosecution continue to remain comparatively low for the reasons described above.

Benefits and disadvantages

Bayney and Ikkos (2003) discuss some of the contentious issues that arise when considering the referral of mentally disordered offenders to the criminal justice system, particularly where individuals are deemed to lack responsibility for their actions. Young et al. (2009) suggest that adopting the assumption that all psychiatric patients who commit offences lack responsibility and should therefore be exempt from prosecution lends itself to apparent justification of such behaviour in the eyes of the public. They suggest that this undermines staff and does little to facilitate prediction of further violent acts (Badgers and Mullan, 2004). Part of the assurance that the public expect from the high secure hospitals is the ability to predict future risk to ensure that the public protection element is satisfied. This is more easily facilitated if episodes of assaults are formally recorded via police investigation rather than merely recorded in the clinical notes. Ho et al. (2005) describe an ethical framework for clinicians to work from when considering prosecution of a detained patient. This framework describes five domains for ethical consideration in making a judgement about whether to seek prosecution of assaultive psychiatric patients. These domains encapsulate the factors that may be considered in the decision-making process including issues of responsibility and capacity. Taking these domains into consideration also helps to arrive at balanced decisions which are not too weighted on just one element, which may render the process flawed or not sufficiently thought through.

Treatment options and risk assessment

As discussed previously, an unrestricted hospital order indicates that the sentencing court found treatment more appropriate than punishment, and was persuaded that purely clinical risk management would suffice to protect the public. However the relevance for this dicussion is that most patients in Broadmoor have a restriction attached to their hospital order. This means that when considering decisions about discharge or transfer to conditions of lesser security, the hospital order must be reviewed by a first tier tribunal.

The role of the first tier tribunal is to decide whether at the time of the hearing a patient should remain subject to the relevant compulsory powers of the Act, and if appropriate to make statutory recommendations. It is however not its purpose to decide if the initial detention was lawful or justified. The first tier tribunal therefore has the right to discharge patients, including restricted patients, from detention. The burden of proof before the tribunal rests on those arguing for the continued use of the compulsory powers in relation to the patient. The standard of proof is the balance of probabilities. The implications for this is in relation to having a formal record of assaults which are admissible in a tribunal as these will be considered against decisions to discharge a patient. If assaults are formally recorded through police investigations, they help inform the tribunal's assessment of potential dangerousness. '[This] is therefore a crucial process, for the offender and the wider public because potentially huge harms or huge losses of rights rest upon it' (Nash, 2006, p. 83). Furthermore, Nash (2010) makes the observation that the approach by those working in these types of environment can at times be to minimise risk through lack of recording of incidents and dismissing these as insignificant, thus failing to see these in the context of future offending behaviour. Indeed, a prosecution that leads to conviction for a different offence to the one the patient is already detained for can sometimes open treatment options that may otherwise have been unavailable to the mentally disordered offender. For example, a patient with a known risk of arson who goes on to be convicted of a sexual offence. This also means that, for the treating clinicians, they have a more comprehensive risk profile of the patient.

Staff and patient perspectives (voices from inside the wall)

When I began my research, I started from the hypothesis that staff believed that patients can commit violent acts [in Broadmoor] with impunity. This was largely based on the frequent throwaway comments that I had heard made over the years when cases of violence occurred within the hospitals and seemingly nothing came of it by way of prosecution. The idea of impunity for patients in Broadmoor is in itself an interesting point. The literature is full of opinions from experts, politicians and scholars on this topical subject, including often sensational tabloid headlines about life within the high secure estate. However a voice that is less heard is that of the staff working within the high secure estate who manage this challenge on a daily basis. I was fortunate to have been able to interview staff at Broadmoor to elicit their views on this, including also interviewing a small purposive sample of patients. Below is my synthesis of some of those interviews.

In general most staff were in favour of prosecution following acts of violence although most agreed that this should be decided on a case-by-case basis. All staff were clear that the presence of a mental disorder should not in itself preclude a case from being referred for prosecution. Certainly staff felt that there were definite benefits to pursuing a prosecution, particularly for repeat offenders and more specifically for those patients with a diagnosis of personality disorder. However staff acknowledged that there were some patients whose mental illness was so debilitating that in these cases staff did not advocate prosecution. Interestingly, this was a view that was also echoed by the patients who were interviewed, who believed that there was a handful of patients within the hospital whose psychotic illness meant that they really could not be held accountable for their actions. However the patients who stated this were quick to warn me that this type of patient was in the minority and that most patients were often fully aware of the consequence of their actions. Whilst I too had believed this to be the case for some patients, it was nevertheless somewhat surprising to hear this articulated – with conviction – by these patients.

When staff described the benefits, these were often linked to treatment and risk assessment issues whilst some also spoke of the benefits from a sociological perspective, such as creating a safe culture and the impact upon staff morale and confidence in the judicial system. One doctor described the benefits of a prosecution when deciding future placements of the patients within a first tier tribunal, stating that if something is not documented and formalised then it is not admissible. In that context, prosecution therefore aids the recognition of that risk which otherwise cannot be discussed.

Staff talked about disadvantages as being the conflict that such a situation can bring to a therapeutic alliance with a patient. However some staff expressed a reluctance to prosecute on the basis that this presented an ethical dilemma for them and their professional role. One member of staff expressed the view that going through the prosecution process was likely to be stressful for the patient and therefore it would be unethical for a member of staff to be the cause of stress for the patient. They expressed that they held this view even when issues of responsibility and capacity were not a factor. This finding is consistent with findings from the literature (Murray, 1989; Norko et al., 1992; Rachlin, 1994; Bayney and Ikkos, 2003; Kumar et al., 2006). Ho et al. (2009) specifically discuss ethical tensions that may present to clinicians facing the decision to refer a case for prosecution. Others described their reluctance based on fear of reprisal from individual patients or fear of the impact of an unsuccessful attempt to prosecute. This was a real issue for most staff, particularly nurses, and one that requires very skilful management to overcome.

The often protracted nature of these undertakings was also perceived as a potential barrier if witness statements were not sought at the onset, as this could hamper the investigation if staff were unable to recall the events. Also, through continued contact with the patient during the proceedings, questions of suggestibility could be raised, thus weakening the case. Notwithstanding the above, staff felt that there were more benefits than disbenefits and these ranged from helping the development of risk profile and assessment to those staff who viewed this as part of the treatment continuum in which patients were appropriately held accountable for their actions in much the same way as the rest of society. Ambivalence was also evident amongst staff about the utility of prosecution, with some staff expressing the view that the courts may perceive detention in Broadmoor as equivalent to serving a sentence and therefore were less likely to encourage prosecution of these patients.

Conclusion

Over the last decade, there has been a noticeable shift in the mindset of mental health professionals about prosecuting patients following acts of violence. There are clearly some benefits to be realised by so doing. Although this chapter has focused on high security in the main, the benefits that I have discussed are equally relevant and applicable to patients in hospitals of lower security. Certainly it has been known that some patients have either consciously or unconsciously increased their level of offending in order to be detected with the aim of securing hospitalisation. However, decisions to prosecute must be carefully considered and, when made, require careful and skilful management, both in terms of the staff and the patient involved. In much the same way that we use a range of tools to assist the process of risk assessment, similarly, such decisions could be assisted by a decision tool. In Broadmoor hospital, staff have access to an incident decision management tool (known as the Criminal Justice Referral–Decision Hierarchy) which prompts them to consider a number of key facts when considering whether or not to pursue a prosecution. The benefits of such a framework mean that this can be a collaborative process amongst a group of multi-disciplinary staff, which is often helpful when trying to form a comprehensive view of the context in which the violence was committed, as different professionals will have different 'access' to the patient's persona. A decision framework such as this also enables staff to consider aspects such as how to preserve evidence to ensure a robust case for progressing to prosecution. Another key element is the development of a collaborative partnership with the police, and within Broadmoor the approach that the hospital has taken is to have a dedicated police officer who is available on site to give police advice in real time. This also means they are available to support the triage of incidents as they occur and staff can direct their efforts on those cases where a prosecution is likely, thus reducing wasting resources on cases that have no prospect of being taken forward by the CPS. The presence of the police officer on site arguably also helps to instil a sense of public order and I would argue that this conveys an important message about the hospital's attitude to safety and security of staff and patients alike. Even when conviction was not the outcome of a prosecution, other sanctions such a issuing of fines were also felt to be strong deterrents for future violence for capacitous patients. Therefore if the possibility of prosecution can act as a moderator of behaviour for some patients, then pursuing a prosecution where clinically appropriate, can be seen as one viable option along the treatment continuum.

References

Badgers, F. and Mullan, B. (2004). Agressive and Violent Incidents: Perceptions of Training and Support Among Staff Caring for Older People and People with Head Injury. *Journal of Clinical Nursing*, 13 (4), 526–533.

Bayney, R. and Ikkos, G. (2003). Managing Criminal Acts on the Psychiatric Ward: Understanding the Police View. *Advances in Psychiatric Treatment*, 9, 359–367.

Behr, G.M., Ruddock, J.P., Benn, P. and Crawford, M.J. (2005). Zero Tolerance of Violence by Users of Mental Health Services: The Need for an Ethical Framework. *The British Journal of Psychiatry*, 187, 7–8.

Bradley, (Lord) K. (2009). *The Bradley Report: Lord Bradley's Review of People with Mental Health Problems or Learning Disabilities in the Criminal Justice System*. London: Department of Health.

Brown, A.R (2006). Prosecuting Psychiatric Inpatients – Where is the Thin Blue Line? *Med. Sci. Law*, 46, 7–11.

Buchanan, A. (2006). Competency to Stand Trial and the Seriousness of the Charge. *The Journal of the American Academy of Psychiatry and the Law*, 34, 458–465.

Buchanan, A. (2008). Commentary: Facts and Values in Competency Assessment. *The Journal of the American Academy of Psychiatry and the Law*, 36, 352–353.

Cherrett, M. (1996). Mentally Disordered Offenders and the Police. *Mental Health Review Journal*, 2, 25–27.

Counter Fraud and Security Management Service (CFSMS) (2003a). Memorandum of Understanding between the Association of Chief Police Officers (ACPO) and the NHS Security Management Service. London: CFSMS.

Counter Fraud and Security Management Service (CFSMS) (2003b). Memorandum of Understanding between the Crown Prosecution Service and the NHS Security Management Service. London: CFSMS.

Counter Fraud and Security Management Service (CFSMS) (2007).Tackling Violence Against Staff. London: CFSMS.

Coyne, A. (2002). Should Patients Who Assault Staff Be Prosecuted? *Journal of Psychiatric and Mental Health Nursing*, 9 (2) 139–145.

Davies, A. (2010). www.channel4.com/news/dangerous-offenders-scheme-to-be-axed. 15 February 2010.

Department of Health (2008). *A Framework for the Performance Management of High Security Hospitals*. London: HMSO.

Department of Health (2011). *Guidance on the High Security Psychiatric Services (Arrangements for Safety and Security at Ashworth, Broadmoor and Rampton Hospitals)*. London: HMSO.

Eastman, N. and Mullins, M. (1999). Prosecuting the Mentally Disordered. *The Journal of Forensic Psychiatry*, 10 (3), 497–501.

Gunn, J. and Taylor, P.J. (1993). *Forensic Psychiatry. Clinical, Legal and Ethical Issues*. Oxford: Butterworth-Heinemann.

Ho, J., Ralston D.C., McCollough, L.B. and Coverdale, J.H. (2009). When Should Psychiatrists Seek Criminal Prosecution of Assaultive Psychiatric Inpatients? *Psychiatric Services*, 60, 1113–1117.

Kumar, S., Fischer, J., Ng, B., Clarke, S. and Robinson, E. (2006). Prosecuting Psychiatric Patients who Assault Staff: A New Zealand Perspective. *Australasian Psychiatry*, 14, 251–255.

Maden, A. (2007). Dangerous and Severe Personality Disorder: Antecedents and Origins. *British Journal of Psychiatry*, 190 (49), s8–s11.

McLean, N. and Marshall, L.A. (2010). A Front Line Police Perspective of Mental Health Issues and Services. *Criminal Behaviour and Mental Health*, 20, 62–71.

Mental Health Act Commission (2005). 'In Place of Fear'. London: Stationery Office.

Mills and Reeve. (2010). Briefing Paper- The Prosecution of Detained Patients. Prosecution of Violent offences Against Hospital Staff.

Ministry of Justice (2007). *Guidance for Working with MAPPA and Mentally Disordered Offenders*. London: Ministry of Justice.

Murray, K. (1989). *Calling the Police: Some Observations on a Professional Dilemma Following Assaults by Psychiatric Inpatients*. Unpublished.

Nash, M. (2006). *Public Protection and the Criminal Justice Process*. Oxford: Oxford University Press

Nash, M. (2010). The Art of the Possible – Public Protection in a Closed Establishment. *Prison Service Journal*, 198, 21–24.

National Reporting and Learning Service (2014). Organisational Reports. London: NRLS.

Nolan, P., Dallender, J., Soares, J., Thomsen, S. and Arnetz, B. (1999).Violence in Mental Health Care: The Experiences of Mental Health Nurses and Psychiatrists. *Journal of Advanced Nursing*, 30, 934–942.

Norko, M.A., Zonana, H.V. and Phillips, R.T (1992). Prosecuting Assaultive Psychiatric Patients. *Journal of Forensic Sciences*, 37 (3), 923–931.

Office of National Statistics (2015). Crime Survey. London: ONS.

Phelan, L.A., Mills, M.J., and Ryan, J.A. (1985). Prosecuting Psychiatric Patients for Assault. *Hospital and Community Psychiatry*, 36, 581–582.

Pyatt, J. (2008). Comedy Night for BroadmoorFiends. London: The Sun Newspaper.

Rachlin, S. (1994). The Prosecution of Violent Psychiatric Inpatients: One Respectable Intervention. Journal of the American Academy of Psychiatry. American Academy of Psychiatry and Law, 22 (2), 239–247.

Shapland, J., Atkinson, A., Atkinson, H., Colledge, E., Dignan, J., Howes, M., Johnstone, J., Robinson, G. and Sorsby, A. (2006). Situating Restorative Justice within Criminal Justice. *Theoretical Criminology*, 10 (4), 505–532.

Smith, L. (2011). Stuck in 'Dangerous and Severe Personality Disorder' Limbo. https://www.opendemocracy.net/.../stuck-in-"dangerous-and-severe-person. September 2014.

Taylor, P.J. (2004). Mental Disorder and Crime. *Criminal Behaviour and Mental Health*, 14, 31–36.

Tilt, R., Perry, B., Martin, C., Maguire, N. and Preston, M. (2000). *Report of the Review of Security at the High Secure Hospitals*. London: Department of Health.

Vinkers, D.J., De Beurs, E., Barendregt, M., Rinne, T. and Hoek, H.W. (2011). The Relationship Between Mental Disorders and Different Types of Crime. *Criminal Behaviour and Mental Health*, 21 (5), 307–320.

Young, C., Brady, J., Iqbal, N. and Brown, F. (2009). Prosecution of Physical Assaults by Psychiatric Inpatients in Northern Ireland. *The Psychiatrist* (formerly the *Psychiatric Bulletin*), 33, 416–419.

13
Successful Strategies for Working with Mentally Disordered Offenders within a Complex Multi-Agency Environment

Leighe Rogers and Gillian Ormston

Background

In 2009 Lord Bradley's review of people with mental health problems or learning disabilities in the criminal justice system was published (Bradley, 2009a). The government response, led by the Department of Health and Ministry of Justice, was to invest in Health and Criminal Justice Liaison and Diversion Schemes (CJLDs). Set against this, Stone (2003) stated that where multi-agency collaboration works well it is the most effective way of providing for the multiple and complex needs of offenders with mental health difficulties. However, he went on to add that such arrangements often collapse under the weight of festering personal differences rooted in the poor articulation of roles and responsibilities, restricted resources and professional and philosophical differences. How such issues were resolved will be addressed in this chapter.

With established mental health court assessment and diversion services in place since 1993 and a dedicated Mental Health Court in Brighton – the legacy of an earlier national 12 month pilot launched in 2009 (see Winstone and Pakes, 2010a; Pakes et al., 2010) – Sussex was well placed to deliver on this new initiative. The Sussex vision was initially borne out of the collaboration of leaders from Sussex Police and Surrey & Sussex Probation Trust. Each had experience of the earlier Sussex pilots and valued the outcomes achieved by criminal justice partners. The involvement of the local mental health provider Sussex Partnership Foundation Trust, local authority Community Safety partnerships in East Sussex, West Sussex and Brighton and Hove, and wider consultation with representatives from the voluntary and private sectors were all key to the early development of the scheme. A project manager was appointed who brought additional experience having project managed the Mental Health Court pilot, Brighton and Stratford (East London), on behalf of Her Majesty's Courts and Tribunals Service (HMCTS).

Sussex was successful in securing funding to deliver dedicated police custody and court assessment and diversion services across the area. This followed the submission of a detailed business case, the result of the best efforts of the partnership. Governance was through a newly created Sussex Health and Criminal Justice Board (SHCJB), which was jointly chaired by the CEO of Surrey & Sussex Probation Trust and an Assistant Chief Constable from Sussex Police. Almost all of the funding was invested in dedicated criminal justice mental health nurses (CJLNs) (see also de Lacy, this volume). The nurses were, and continue to be, responsible for assessment and diversion activity across all police custody and court sites in Sussex. The key strategic objectives of the scheme are development of:

- Processes to assess individuals arriving in the police custody suites for multiple vulnerabilities including mental health, substance misuse (see Pycroft, this volume) and learning disability.
- Opportunities to divert the assessed individuals away from the criminal justice process and into relevant support services, if appropriate.
- Credible options to provide sentencers with alternatives to a sentence of imprisonment, where individuals either plead guilty or are convicted of an offence.

The alignment of liaison and diversion services to existing criminal justice partnership activities was seen as critical to its success. This approach was designed to eliminate duplication of effort and avoid silo working which we recognised as a risk for all concerned, to the detriment of service users. An alignment with existing Integrated Offender Management (IOM) arrangements offered the best fit.

IOM is an approach to working with groups of offenders promoted by the Home Office and the Ministry of Justice (MOJ). It aims to reduce both crime and reoffending by targeting offenders who are responsible for causing the most disruption to their communities through their criminal behaviour. IOM enables police, probation, youth offending services, local authorities and other agencies to pool resources and tackle the root causes of offending in an effective and efficient way. Criminal justice partners work together to address the behaviour of those found suitable for the scheme (there are strict selection criteria based on the number and type of offences committed), by applying appropriate sanctions for failure to comply with court orders or prison licenses as well as tailored interventions to address their needs. Interventions are linked to key offending pathways, which include employment and education, accommodation, relationships, health and well-being, and attitudes and thinking skills (see McGuire, this volume; Göbbels, Thakker and Ward, this volume). The CJLD service objectives are similar to those of IOM, as are the available interventions. Governance of Sussex IOM schemes is through the Sussex Criminal Justice Board and local Reducing Reoffending Boards which are held in the counties of East and West Sussex and the Unitary Authority of Brighton and Hove. Membership of these Boards includes the key statutory criminal justice partners as well as representatives from Community Voluntary Organisations (CVOs). The Sussex Criminal Justice Liaison and Diversion (SCJLD) scheme was implemented in Brighton in April 2012 and went live in East and West Sussex on 2 July 2012.

The health and criminal justice partnership in Sussex were fortunate in being able to build on the foundations of previous approaches to the establishment of effective liaison and diversion arrangements. Although limited in scope, the existing service was well respected and had the confidence of sentencers and the broader criminal justice partnership. Our task was to put together a coherent framework that could inform national implementation whilst being sufficiently flexible to meet local need.

There were a number of considerations in the early stages of the project which are illustrated for ease of reference in the mind map below (Figure 13.1) and then in more detail under each section.

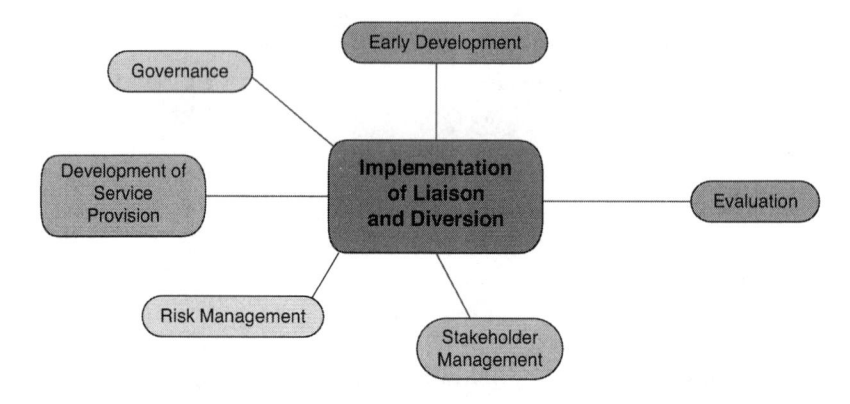

Figure 13.1 Mind map of early considerations

Governance of the service

Figure 13.2 shows the breadth of the task that we identified. One of the key challenges we encountered in working in a complex multi-agency environment

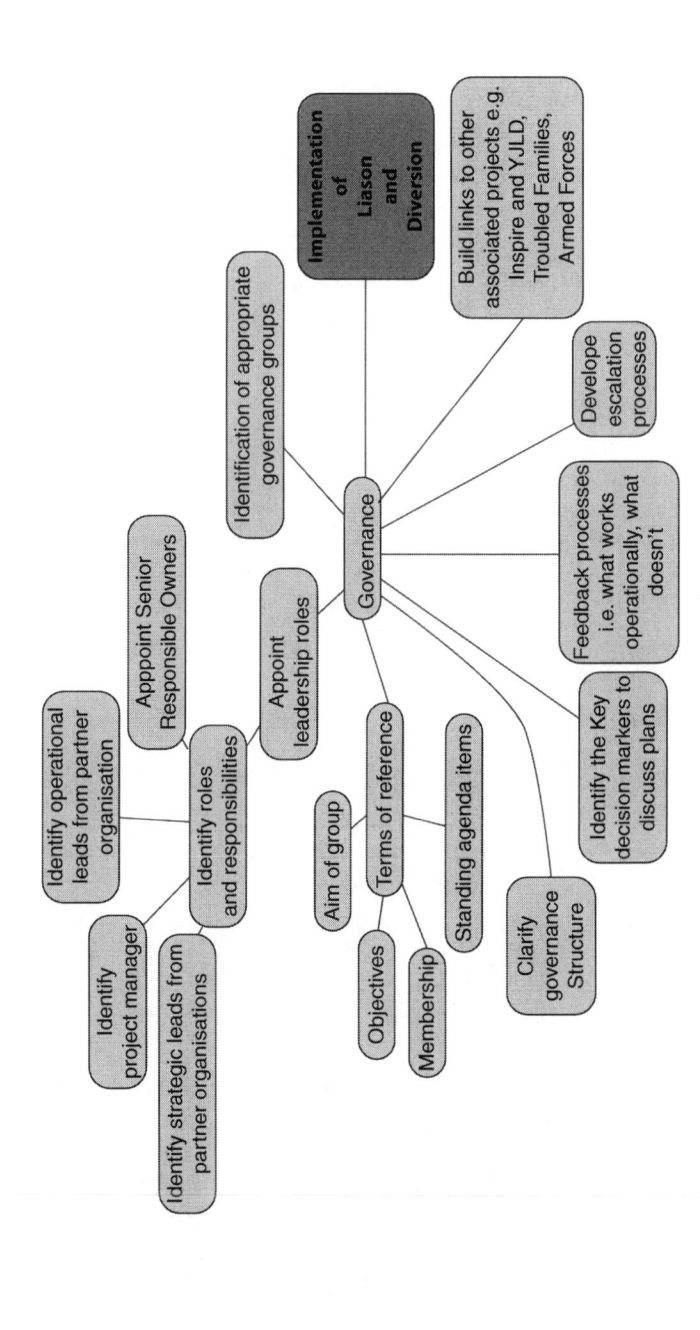

Figure 13.2 Breadth of identified task

was the need to establish clear and structured governance arrangements – see Figure 13.3 below. We recognised that clear lines of accountability, a shared ownership of service delivery, robust whilst measured monitoring arrangements, and a strong focus on shared outcomes were essential elements to success (Pakes and Winstone, 2009; Winstone and Pakes, 2010b).

```
                    Health and Criminal Hustice Organisation
                              Chief Excutives

     Local Strategic                        Sussex Criminal
     Partnership                            Justice Board

     Reducing                    ──────►    Sussex Health and Criminal Justice Liaison
     Reoffending Board  ◄ - - - - - - - -   Board Steering Group (Chair Nick Smart)

  ▲
  ¦  Reporting Process
  ¦
  ¦  Feedback Process                       Sussex Health and Criminal Justice Liaison Scheme
  ▼                                         Operational Groups East Sussex, West Sussex, Brighton
                                                                 & Hove
```

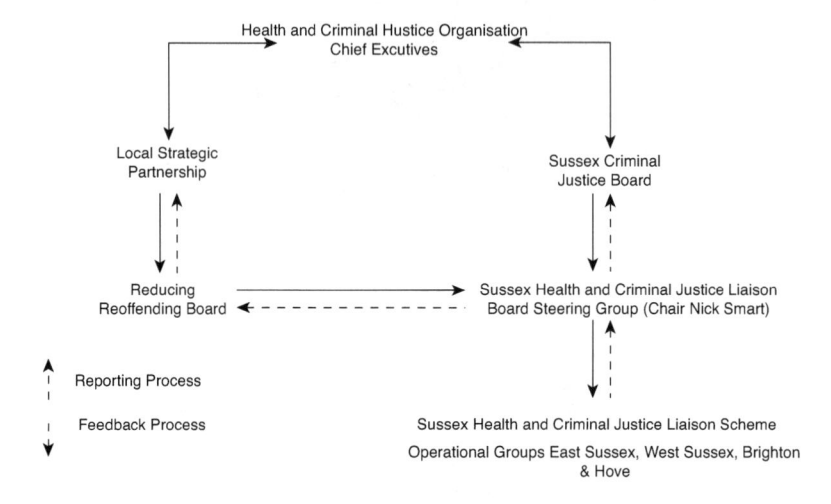

Figure 13.3 Complex multi-agency environment and emerging governance structures

Whilst governance arrangements were through a dedicated Steering Group, oversight of the scheme rested with the Sussex Criminal Justice Board (SCJB). This allowed any issues which were not capable of resolution by the Steering Group membership to be escalated to the SCJB. Initially there were two Senior Responsible Owners (SROs), from Sussex Police and Surrey & Sussex Probation Trust, who shared responsibility for the service, ensuring successful outcomes were achieved. This was supported by an experienced Project Manager, who had previously been responsible for the national Mental Health Court Pilot on behalf of HMCTS (see also Winstone and Pakes, 2010a). The professional relationships that developed alongside these formal structures were of equal importance in advancing the aims of the scheme, not least because when working well, these allowed for the informal resolution of issues without the need for escalation.

As time passed the governance arrangements transitioned into the existing criminal justice structures, utilising the SCJB to bring partners (across health and criminal justice including local authorities) together to share responsibility for the success of the service.

Whilst the current governance structure, in Figure 13.4 below, might look as if it has a solely criminal justice focus, the significant progress made in

Successful Strategies for Working 223

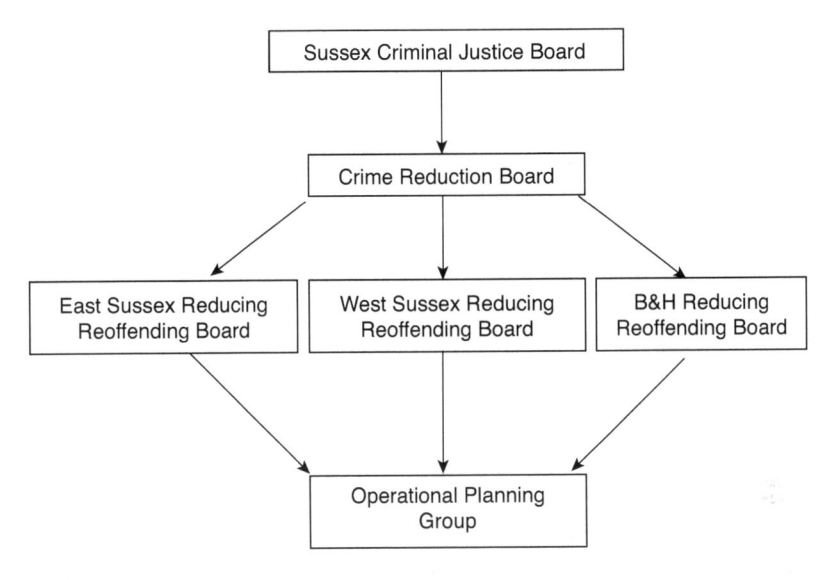

```
                  ┌─────────────────────────────┐
                  │ Sussex Criminal Justice Board│
                  └──────────────┬──────────────┘
                                 ▼
                  ┌─────────────────────────────┐
                  │    Crime Reduction Board    │
                  └──────────────┬──────────────┘
         ┌───────────────────────┼───────────────────────┐
         ▼                       ▼                       ▼
┌──────────────────┐   ┌──────────────────┐   ┌──────────────────┐
│ East Sussex      │   │ West Sussex      │   │ B&H Reducing     │
│ Reducing         │   │ Reducing         │   │ Reoffending Board│
│ Reoffending Board│   │ Reoffending Board│   │                  │
└────────┬─────────┘   └────────┬─────────┘   └────────┬─────────┘
         └───────────────────────┼───────────────────────┘
                                 ▼
                  ┌─────────────────────────────┐
                  │    Operational Planning     │
                  │           Group             │
                  └─────────────────────────────┘
```

Figure 13.4 Current governance structures

Sussex in developing multi-agency relationships has meant that Sussex NHS Partnership Trust colleagues attend the meetings at all levels of the governance structure.

Each of the groups involved in the governance structure, whether original or current structures, had 'Terms of reference'. The definition of 'Terms of Reference' is:

> Terms of reference describe the purpose and structure of a **project, committee, meeting, negotiation**, or any similar collection of people who have agreed to work together to accomplish a shared goal. (Wikipedia)

These terms of reference provided clarity around the objectives, roles and responsibilities of each of the groups including any potential overlaps that might need to be managed.

The terms of reference included:

1. **Aim of the group**, for example the Operational Groups in the original governance structure had the following aims: 'To take responsibility for operational delivery of the Sussex Liaison and Diversion Scheme on behalf of the Sussex Health and Criminal Justice Steering Group. To ensure the aims and objectives of the Liaison and Diversion scheme, as part of the wider Department of Health Liaison and Development network are achieved.'

2. **Core membership**, that is, the organisations and individuals involved in the group and the role that they play, for example, Chair. An example of the core membership of the original operational groups is set out below:
   - Sussex Partnership NHS Foundation Trust
   - CRI
   - Surrey & Sussex Probation Trust (Chair)
   - Addaction
   - Sussex Police
   - Youth Offending Service
   - Her Majesty's Courts and Tribunals Service (HMCTS)
   - Crown Prosecution Service
   - Local Authority
   - INSPIRE (Brighton)
3. **The core members** of the various governance groups changed as the project developed and were updated as and when new members were identified or the role of current members changed
4. **Objectives of the group** – in order that the group understood their shared purpose and the reason they had been asked to play a part in the governance of the liaison and diversion service.
5. **Standing agenda items** informed the purpose and function of the group and provided a framework for constructive discussion. Examples of standing agenda items included for example:
   - Updates from each hub
   - Case Studies
   - Review and update of Operational Policy
   - Lessons Learned
   - Data Review.

An early and arguably persistent challenge to the smooth running of the scheme was one of cultural difference. This was most evident between criminal justice and health colleagues (see Hean, Walsh and Hammick, this volume). In order to overcome this issue we had to make sure that there was a clarity about leadership roles across participating organisations and along with multi-agency 'buy-in' to the overall outcomes (see Winstone and Pakes, 2010b). Securing the attention and ownership of senior leaders from the key participating agencies was essential, as was an understanding of and respect for the differing cultures and values. There were times when we lost sight of shared goals and the resultant conflict and emergence of separate agendas had the potential to derail the project (Stone, 2003). Taking time to listen to and understand the differing perspectives of health and criminal justice organisations, whilst maintaining open and honest discussions, meant that potentially critical issues were resolved.

Organisational cultural issues aside, in delivering a project of this size and complexity there were inevitable tensions and areas of conflict within the partnership group. For example, it was necessary to incorporate national requirements into a locally developed service, which was designed to address local need. In this case there was a recognition that a compromise was required if the promised investment was to be secured. Senior leaders had to reconcile themselves to a shared vision and 'sell' this to other stakeholders. Throughout the life of the pilot, it was essential to maintain transparency and to manage expectations around deliverables. If these issues were to be resolved amicably time had to be dedicated to the development of trusting professional relationships, whilst consistent information had to be shared with all stakeholders in an accessible and timely way. By front-loading communications with the delivery of consistent messages and maintaining active participation with our stakeholder groups, we were able to drive key aspects of the project through ensuring major project milestones were fully met. Linking implementation into other key local priorities, for example IOM, further assisted in maintaining effective progress.

Critically, the context for delivery of the service was within a criminal justice environment. We faced the inevitable challenges of balancing the strong health values around choice and patient care with those of a criminal justice system which has a duty to hold individuals to account for their behaviour. The resultant and arguably healthy tensions surrounding this endured throughout the partnership.

Clarity about what success looked like for the scheme and for participating agencies was vital. For health there was an unequivocal focus on the needs of the individual and on improving their well-being whilst also (where consent was given), providing information to sentencers. This was shared by their criminal justice colleagues, who were equally clear that the information provided was helpful to managing the individuals' risk of harm and reoffending. Marrying the health goal with those of addressing criminal offending behaviour was required. Whilst it might seem obvious that in doing the former you will almost certainly achieve the latter, the reasons for commissioning the service do need to be recognised and understood by the offender themselves. Not least, because there is a financial cost to these interventions; a cost justified by the improvement in their well-being, a reduction in crime and that there are fewer victims, with the wider benefits of that to society as a whole.

All partners understood the need to support vulnerable offenders who struggle to access mainstream services in a different way to the 'norm'. Solutions to address this included the use of volunteers to support attendance and the broadest possible involvement of community and voluntary sector groups so that the diverse needs of offenders with complex needs could be met.

Escalation processes were developed to enable issues that could not be resolved at an operational level to be discussed by strategic leads. These processes were clearly defined and included within the Operational Policy described later in the chapter.

Communication presented a significant challenge in sectors with differing cultures and the lack of a shared 'language'. Governance arrangements were designed to ensure that clear and consistent messages were released in a timely way across the partnership. However, despite a belief from the SROs that consistent messages were being delivered, the European Foundation for Quality Management (EFQM) assessment that was undertaken identified there was a lack of clarity and leadership in relation to the local Operational Groups. This resulted in an absence of local ownership of the project's aims, as members said they were unclear about their responsibilities for local delivery. This, in turn, meant there was an inability to engage local partners who had the potential to bring their additional resources to the scheme. The key challenge was identifying a lead for the operational groups who took proactive ownership and had an ability to provide the effective local leadership necessary to embed the scheme into the existing local health and criminal justice landscapes.

Alongside robust governance arrangements we identified that an Information Sharing Agreement was essential to the effective running of the scheme. Consultations took place with the various stakeholder organisations to ensure their organisational values and outcomes were reflected within the agreement. There was a significant level of compromise required along with a need to understand each others' cultures. Multi-agency events, together with a series of individual meetings with key delivery partners, formed part of these consultation arrangements. Training sessions and shadowing opportunities for operational staff were set up so that the proposed content could be tested and further honed. The Information Sharing Agreement was based on an existing similar agreement to which all members of SCJB were signatories. The resulting document was formally signed off by Chief Officers from Sussex Police, Surrey & Sussex Probation Trust and Sussex NHS Partnership Trust.

Early development

Figure 13.5 shows the way in which the early development of the scheme was conceptualised. The ambition for the scheme, from the outset, was to forge a strong alliance of interested partners across the sector for the delivery of a flexible, ageless service that responded to individual service user needs. At the outset of the project potential partners were brought together to build the initial business case into a project plan and in doing so to build the good relationships, respect and understanding which we recognised as essential to success. By applying project management principles we were able to complete a stock take of the current service, undertake a gap analysis and develop our understanding of the requirements for the new service.

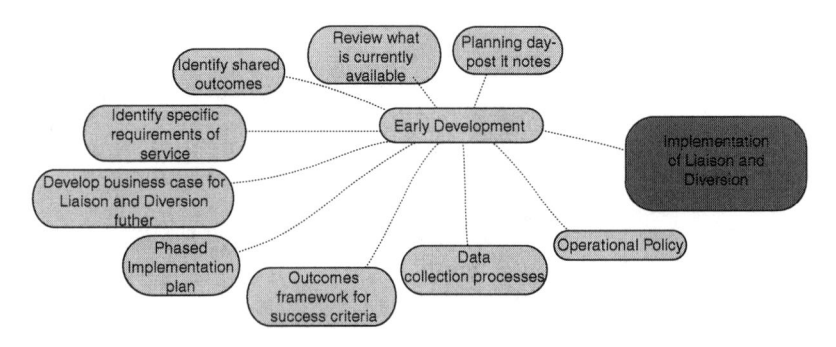

Figure 13.5 Early development of scheme

With a clear project plan in place we were able to monitor progress towards implementation. The main challenge was ensuring everyone owned their actions and made progress with them in between regular governance meetings. A common issue was that of reconciling the pull on senior resources to other projects and priorities. This was mitigated by constant contact, nudge / nagging and managing the tension between other priorities and in this way ensuring delivery was maintained in a timely way. Managing these different relationships required a variety of approaches. Sometimes it made sense to be direct; at other times a more circuitous route was needed and time had to be taken to acknowledge and empathise with the particular circumstances of the individual concerned. Knowing when and how to escalate was similarly key to the resolution of barriers to success.

By developing an understanding of the differing priorities, behaviours and personalities of key individuals, challenges were gradually overcome and the project plan kept on track without the need to escalate the majority of issues. Having the knowledge and confidence to flex individual ownership of actions as well as the actions themselves, whilst ensuring that the project remained on track for completion to the desired timescale was an important part of the project manager's role.

Development of service provision

Figure 13.6 illustrates the scoping of existing service provision to identify any gaps, and the likely fit with a new operating model was an early task for the project team. This led to discussions with the existing provider of services to all Sussex courts, Sussex Partnership Foundation Trust (SPFT). The Trust had a strong record of delivery of forensic health services locally and was keen to be involved with any extension of the service to include police custody suites. At the same time a judgement had to be made as to whether there were

228 *Leighe Rogers and Gillian Ormston*

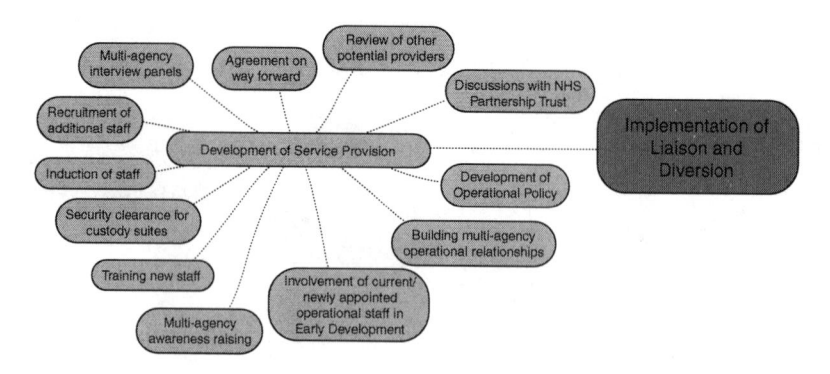

Figure 13.6 Scoping of existing service provision

other service providers who were in a position to deliver the service from what would effectively be a standing start. Partners agreed that it was important to maintain service delivery whilst testing out new procedures and processes. This led to the extension of the existing Liaison and Diversion service delivered by SPFT.

In order to ensure that there was a true multi-agency approach to the service, SPFT joined the governance meetings and played an active role in the further development of the service. Criminal justice partners also played an active role in recruitment of the additional practitioners required for the service.

An immediate challenge to the development of the existing service was how best to prepare the staff group for a change to the focus and the scope of their roles. The volume and type of client and working pattern were both subject to change. Whilst familiar with a court setting staff had to have access to and to understand the different working arrangements in police custody suites. Throughout the project there were several change management processes undertaken as the service developed. Full mobilisation took time to achieve as SPFT had to increase their staffing capacity. This involved a lengthy recruitment process.

The existing forensic health team was employed on a pay band a grade higher than that the project team deemed appropriate for the revised service. We addressed this by conducting a review of the nursing roles and responsibilities attached to the service. In this way we were, over time, able to clarify a distinct role for the more experienced nurses who were on the higher banding. Notably that their role was extended to include a supervisory element.

All health practitioners received a bespoke induction programme, which included input from criminal justice agencies. Opportunities shadowing colleagues working in criminal justice agencies such as the police and probation service were linked to the programme. By offering similar shadowing experiences to all key partners we were able to break down some of the myths surrounding different cultures and enable staff to build strong professional relationships and to see their own work in the context of outcomes for other agencies. Following successful negotiation with the police and HMCTS, arrangements for the co-location of health practitioners with police and probation colleagues was agreed. Health staff could access their own database from these sites whilst also being able to access information relevant to each assessment from their criminal justice colleagues. Whilst not every court or custody suite could easily provide office space for the practitioners, the project team recognised that provision of these facilities was essential to the success of the scheme. This was because staff were able to easily access the information they needed to do their job (Winstone and Pakes, 2010b) and because the close proximity of staff fostered good working relationships and information sharing.

Health practitioners required enhanced security clearance to be able to operate from police custody suites. While individual cases were being progressed (some took longer than others depending on their antecedent history) we decided to appoint a single point of contact whose role was to provide updates and challenge delays (see also de Lacy, this volume). In this way the team was able to fully function and a delay to implementing the service was avoided.

Prior to the formal launch of the new service we brought all the existing staff from health and criminal justice agencies together to 'walk through' plans for the new service. This was a Sussex-wide event held at a central training unit made available to us by Sussex Police. Over the course of a day staff worked through a mixed programme which included the exchange of information about different aspects of the service, group discussion and scenario planning. In this way the workforce were able to begin to develop working relationships and to gain a deeper understanding of the outcomes we were seeking to achieve.

The service specification clearly set out the problem we were seeking to address and what would be delivered. How this was to be delivered was incorporated into a new service role that was worked on by the group of agencies involved with the service, led by the Project Manager. The Operational Policy was key to ensuring that everyone involved understood their role and responsibilities and the inter-relationships between them. It was particularly important for the health practitioners to understand at what point referrals could be made to drug and alcohol workers. By working through interface issues with all participants we were able to ensure that the service users' experience of a potentially complicated and confusing system was as smooth as possible. We recognised that these interfaces were potential points of tension between agencies and that at each stage it was important to establish who was involved and why. It was equally important for us to develop a shared vision about what the service was there to do and what might be collectively achieved. The meetings in which the Operational Policy was drafted proved to be a good place for these issues to be aired and different perspectives taken into account resulting in a final document that was fit for purpose.

We recognised scaling up a service to cover all Sussex courts and custody suites presented its own challenges. Sussex extends over 1,461 square miles. It is bounded to the west by Hampshire, to the north by Surrey and to the north-east and east by Kent. To the south lies the English Channel with the distance by road from the west to the eastern edges of the scheme being 65 miles, a journey time of just under two hours outside of summer coastal traffic. We were for the first time seeking to place staff on a permanent (rather than a call-out) basis in custody suites in Crawley, Chichester, Worthing, Eastbourne, Hastings and Brighton. This is a large geographical area with poor transport links other than along the coastal strip and north to London. We wanted our staffing plan to work in a way that ensured an equality of access to the service was in place and sustained. If it were to work the staffing plan needed to be flexible. We learned to our cost very early on that our failure to fully incorporate sick leave and annual leave into our business case had the effect of compromising some service delivery due to the lack of available staff.

Managing risks and issues

Figure 13.7 demonstrates the way in which the key aspects of the risk management plan were identified. Our project plan included a comprehensive register of risks to the project with example headings set out in Table 13.1 below. This was subject to regular review at the Steering Group. A more detailed example of a completed risk log can be found in Table 13.2 further on in this section. Our aim was to ensure that we were able to identify risks and could be confident that these were being managed effectively without the process being overly bureaucratic. Ownership of individual risks were allocated to the relevant agency who were asked to update on a regular basis

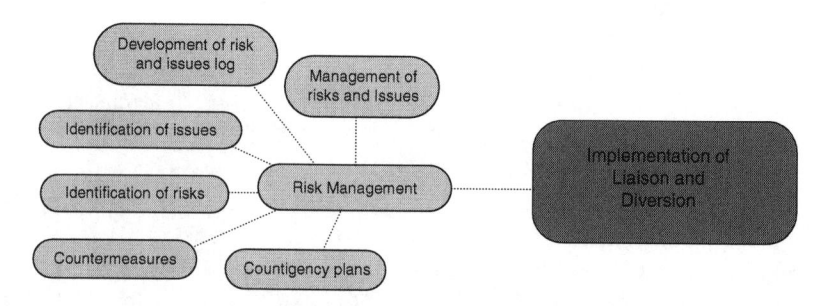

Figure 13.7 Key aspects of the risk management plan

Table 13.1 Comprehensive register of risks

Risk ID	Date Identified	Risk Description Specify Risk / Cause(s) / Effect(s)	Controls: In Place and Effective	Current I	Current L	Score (IXL)	Controls: Underway or Planned Include Date/ Action Officer	Next Review	Target I	Target L	Target Date

The risk ID number enabled effective tracking of each of the risks with everyone being able to identify the risk through shorthand without lengthy description. The date identified was also a key piece of information to assist in monitoring the age of the risk.

Risks were described in terms of 'cause and effect', a clarity that was designed to enable everyone to understand risk both in terms of what it was, and the effect it would have if the risk came to fruition. There was considerable negotiation with partners until all were satisfied of the nature of the risk and that there was a commitment to it being managed. By way of example, one of the key early risks for the project included recruitment of practitioners to the liaison and diversion team. Recruitment itself presented a risk, and there was an additional risk attached to the clearance procedures required before practitioners could be allowed to work in a police custody setting.

Further, there was a need to manage elements of risk which inadvertently placed a spotlight on any one of the partner organisations who were delivering a key element of the service for example, focus on Sussex NHS Partnership Foundation Trust in delivering against the key performance indicators (KPIs). This needed to be balanced with ensuring that wider partnership KPIs were also identified and managed in terms of delivery. Controls or counter-measures in place included specific actions identified by partners to ensure the risk did not turn into 'a live issue'. For example, in the risk identified report (see Table 13.2 below) there are clear actions to mitigate these, which were then transferred over to the project plan to be monitored. Should additional actions emerge these were added to the Controls Underway or Planned column.

Risks were scored so that appropriate focus was given to priority areas in need of discussion. A red, amber, green (RAG) rating system was a visual way of highlighting the most important for close oversight by the Steering Group and the lead operational group. Risks that were rated green were monitored by the Project Manager to ensure that there was no change in the impact or likelihood scores and that progress was being made with resolution. Later columns in the log identify the target impact and likelihood scores which we anticipated could be achieved if and when the control actions were completed.

Table 13.2 Risks identified and action taken

Risk ID	Date Identified	Risk Description Specify Risk / Cause(s) / Effect(s)	Controls: In Place and Effective.	Current Score (IxL) I L	Controls: Underway or Planned. Include Date/Action Officer	Next Review	Target I L	Date
1	14/02/12	**Risk** Unable to provide robust information for the purposes of DOH evaluation Causes Lack of consistent information from CVO and statutory service providers. Quality of data collection within each organisation leads to inaccurate data being reported to DOH. **Effect** Funding is withdrawn by DOH and the project cannot continue into the 2nd year.	A data sharing protocol has been agreed across both health and criminal justice agencies and further work is being undertaken to identify specific details to support the protocol. A data quality action plan has been developed and significant improvements achieved. Action plan attached. A database is currently under development to significantly improve data collection processes.	3 2 6	Additional Actions: Contingency Discussion with OHRN to identify solutions to the issues being faced, understand whether other areas nationally having issues, have found solutions and to share lessons learned regarding data collection.	01/06/13	2 1	18/03/13

Risk type headings were designed to simplify what was in truth a very complex set of partnership arrangements. By keeping these simple the task could be more easily defined and ownership assigned accordingly. The headings used were Responsible Clinicians, environmental, process and evaluation, and below are some examples of the potential risks under each of the headings identified.

Responsible Clinicians
- Vetting nurses in advance of starting work.
- Delays due to practitioners travelling significant distances between geographical sites.
Insufficient staff available to cover annual leave and sick leave.

Environmental
- Private interview space available at Courts and Probation to enable practitioners to have confidential conversations with offenders requiring assessment.
- Access to police custody suites in the early stages whilst practitioners were building relationships with their Police colleagues.
- Parking at police custody suites/courts for practitioners.

Process
- Information sharing agreements in place to enable confidential health information to be shared with criminal justice partners.
- Reporting of Serious Untoward Incidents.
- Clarity of assessment processes and how relevant information would be shared with partners.

Evaluation
- Quality of data collection.
- Data collection processes taking up significant practitioners meaning they have less time to assessment individuals.
- Lack of clarity of evaluation requirements.

Essential to the risk management process was ensuring that highlighted risks were discussed fully in multi-agency meetings to gain consensus on the way forward. The logging and monitoring of the risks significantly supported development of the service.

Stakeholder Management

At the start of the project we drew up a map (Figure 13.8) of our stakeholders. This was a collaborative exercise involving all key partners. Through the

234 *Leighe Rogers and Gillian Ormston*

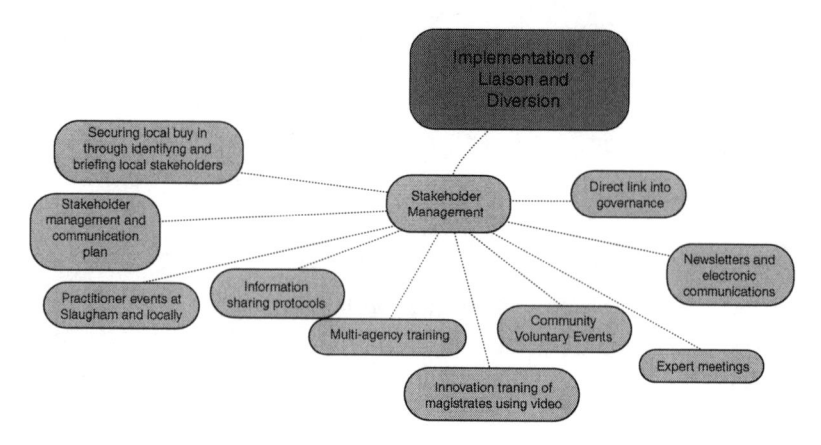

Figure 13.8 Map of stakeholders

stakeholder analysis we were able to identify local leaders who the service would be most likely to impact on. These included Directors of Public Health and Local Authority Chief Executive Officers for the three affected areas: East Sussex, West Sussex, and Brighton and Hove. Representatives from the project team held individual briefing sessions with these individuals who, seeing the benefits, were pleased to support the scheme. Similar discussions were held with police divisional commanders who were in a strong position to advise on the suitability or otherwise of our plans.

Key elements for consideration included:

- knowing who the stakeholders were
- identifying the appropriate stage to involve them
- assessing which stakeholders required active management, to be enlisted as necessary – those who needed to be kept satisfied and those who needed simply to be kept informed.

The easiest and most effective way to undertake the analysis was to plot stakeholders on the template shown below (Figure 13.9).

This created an instant visual map to enable both the steering group and the operational group leads to see immediately which stakeholders could influence the project along with those who had more of a stake in ensuring it was effectively managed and implemented.

In addition to the above map a stakeholder management plan was developed which included information as in Table 13.3.

The stakeholder management plan identified who would be communicated with, how and who was responsible for the communication.

Successful Strategies for Working 235

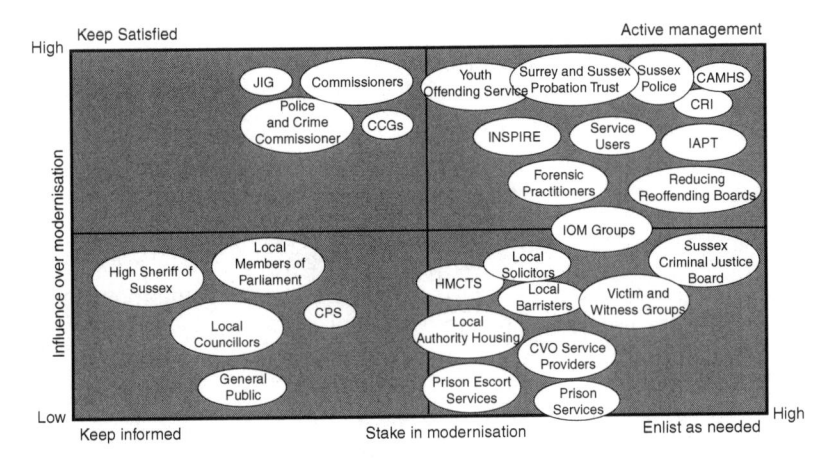

Figure 13.9 Map of stakeholders and proximal relationships

Table 13.3 Management stakeholder plan

Ref	Circulation	Information description	Information provider	Frequency	Method & media	Feedback method and media
	Local judiciary and magistracy Justices issues group Local probation Local criminal justice boards Regional and area directors Presiding judges Defence solicitor Local court staff	Progress newsletter	Local co-coordinators	Monthly or as and when important information needs communicating	Email	Email

The earlier Mental Health Court evaluation conducted by Dr Jane Winstone and Dr Francis Pakes (2010a) identified that the following are core requirements of any future Mental Health Court:

- training and awareness events for practitioners and stakeholders
- identification of, and engagement with, local resources for signposting and referral of defendants.

These were included in the development of new Sussex Liaison and Diversion Service. The stakeholder management plan enabled events to be planned effectively and for us to engage with appropriate stakeholders. Our aim being to empower them to move forward and involve themselves with the service in whatever capacity seemed right.

A number of events were held ranging from provision of information to stakeholders, development workshops and training sessions for key operational staff to enable both the steering group and the operational development of the service. A good example of this is that a consultant psychiatrist from SPFT agreed to be videoed talking about forensic aspects of mental health with particular reference to severe and enduring mental health issues. We used this material in briefings with staff and a range of stakeholders including local magistrates.

Bespoke events were held with Community Voluntary Sector (CVS) colleagues to inform them of the services that were being developed and to invite them to consider how the services they offered might align with or contribute to the project. In this way we were able to identify and engage with those CV organisations that were willing and able to provide onward referral services for individuals assessed as having a specific need by the Liaison and Diversion practitioners.

Evaluation

In order to evaluate the effectiveness of any service or project, data collection is a core requirement, which in the case of this Liaison and Diversion service was complex due to the multi-agency nature (see Figure 13.10). Significant work needed to be undertaken initially in collaboration with the Department of Health to identify the core data requirements.

As a result of the Sussex history within the Mental Health Court pilot in 2009 significant elements of the data were already being collected by the service. However, there was a need to review information sharing policies that were in place to ensure they were fit for purpose.

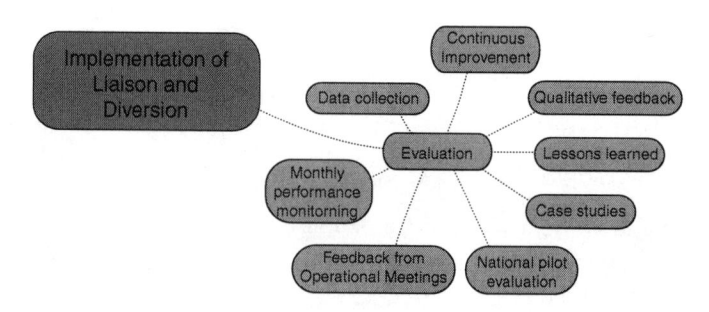

Figure 13.10 Data collection for evaluation

Additionally a review of the existing consent forms used by the service identified a need to ensure that the service user from whom data is being collected is aware that they were consenting to the sharing of data throughout their involvement with the service not just on the one occasion that they were asked to sign the consent form.

There were many challenges to overcome in securing the provision of robust and accurate data to evaluate the service which included:

- the format for data collection
- who would input the data being collected
- how could the accuracy of the data be monitored
- what mechanism needed to be in place to collect data automatically where possible
- who were the key people in each organisation to support the process
- what data was essential to monitor performance
- misrecording of information leading to significant amounts of data cleansing.

Key lessons learned included:

- The data needed to be input by someone other than the practitioners where possible to avoid unnecessary time being spent away from the key roles that the practitioners undertook within the service.
- Identifying ways of collecting the data from existing systems through the use of Information Technology (IT) could reduce the time involved within data collection.
- Ensuring the data is not being handled by several different organisations reduces the potential for inaccuracies/misrecording of data, for example in early development the data would be entered into a spreadsheet by the practitioners and then would need to be transferred over to another format for the purposes of the national evaluation. This led to inaccuracies which in turn took up extra resources in undertaking data cleansing. The more automated the data collection can be made the more accurate the data becomes.
- Having a multi-agency information sharing agreement was essential in supporting the evaluation process. This was also a joint Health and Criminal Justice information sharing policy which in itself supported the development of cross-cultural relationships between organisations.

A data report was produced in advance of each of the Steering Group and local Operational meetings to enable a review of performance and identification of potential issues to be addressed.

Another challenge, in terms of evaluation, is achieving robust and valuable service user feedback (see Pycroft and Green, this volume [PPI involvement]). There were many facets to be considered when we investigated securing feedback directly from the service users. For example, the timing of asking them for their feedback was crucial, as asking for it too soon might have unwittingly given the impression that the outcome of their pending case could be different if they gave positive feedback – an important ethical compliance issue. Leaving the request for feedback until after the case also presented a challenge as individuals simply wanted to move on. Various methods of collecting service user feedback were utilised, for instance, comment cards, invitations to organisations supporting service users to attend events, feedback from practitioners, and the later introduction of inviting service users to attend Operational Planning Group meetings.

An equally essential form of evaluating the service being provided is the completion of an Equality Impact Assessment (EIA) at regular intervals. Having the EIA completed and an action plan in place as a result supported the need to hard-wire equality into the service provision.

The ongoing evaluation supported continuous improvement and development of the service provision over a sustained period of time. This included regular identification of lessons learned through a number of forums including operational meetings and the regular steering group meeting which took place as part of the overall governance of the service. A lessons learned log was developed in a fairly simple format to make it easy for everyone to contribute to. The example format used is in Table 13.4 below.

Table 13.4 Lessons learned log

Issue	Lesson	Solution	Where identified
Lack of information about the local Community Voluntary Organisations available to support Diversion or Alternatives to Custody.	Need to find a centralised source of information that nurses can access to get a picture of the services available locally.	Find out if there is a CVO Forum Directory and/or web information available in each locality that nurses can access quickly and easily.	Slaugham Manor away day

Case studies were particularly valuable in being able assess the Liaison and Diversion service and the potential benefits that could be achieved as well as the lessons that could be learned. The practitioners developed case studies on a regular basis to enable discussions at the operational planning and steering group meetings. Case studies were always anonymised and included information about the individual brought into the police custody suite, the alleged offence, the needs identified during the assessment and the outcome of the case including details of the sentence received where appropriate. Sufficient detail was included in each of the case studies to provide a clear picture of the process and context around the individual progressing through the criminal justice process.

In April 2014 the SCJLD scheme was renamed as the Police and Courts Liaison and Diversion Service (PCLDS) and became part of the national pathfinder programme (see NHS England, n.d.). As a result, the Sussex PCLDS will be subject to independent evaluation and will work with partners to provide data to the evaluators to enable national best practice to be further developed.

Conclusion

Government's acceptance of the recommendations contained in the Bradley Report and its willingness to invest in a number of national pilot schemes offered the established criminal justice partnership in Sussex a timely and valuable opportunity to expand the scope of the existing (rather limited) liaison and diversion services. For the first time an assessment and diversion service was available to all detained persons entering police custody, or transferring through for prosecution into their local court. Central to the success of the scheme was a shared vision which envisioned a seamless service across health and criminal justice organisations along with better health outcomes for people taken into police custody. Partners also saw wider benefits for society including confidence that individual needs were being met, offering the prospect that fewer might be sentenced to imprisonment with all the attendant costs and future risks to their health.

To secure the overall vision we needed to engage with key stakeholders on a regular basis. This meant sharing and defining how we would make it happen with a wider audience, which included community voluntary organisations. In this way we were able to sustain the necessary energy and momentum to deliver a project of this scale to a nationally determined timeframe and budget. Ours was a committed partnership of people from a number of local agencies, each of whom brought their different skills, experience and organisational cultures to the task at hand. An independent Project Manager was a further strength; ours came with previous experience of implementing a similar, though smaller-scale, scheme. Proven project management tools were utilised and combined with the necessary commitment, drive and use of interpersonal skills, notably: persuasion, influence, negotiation and judgment when necessary, to ensure commitment was maintained to the direction of travel.

Robust governance arrangements were secured by the early 'buy in' of senior leaders from our main delivery partners; police, probation, health (in its various forms) and HMCTS. These endured through the start-up and implementation phases before being successfully passed to the Sussex Criminal Justice Board and local Reducing Offending Boards where they remain to this day. Partnership decisions were informed by the collection and analysis of relevant data, which contributed to the overall national evaluation of the scheme.

Liaison and Diversion is now established in all Sussex Custody Suites and Courts. In addition to a health professional undertaking assessments, health outreach workers have been assigned to support individuals in accessing recommended treatment options. Health outreach workers or their equivalent are an essential component of any service for this vulnerable group (who typically struggle to access mainstream services). Liaison and Diversion remains aligned to partnership Integrated Offender Management arrangements. Sharing governance at a local (West Sussex, Brighton, East Sussex) level, and a pan-Sussex basis, ensures the energies and interest of both are maintained. Future joint commissioning of supportive interventions is also facilitated.

The Sussex journey to a seamless meaningful and effective Liaison and Diversion service continues. We will strive to improve on what we have developed to date. At a time when partners and structures will change (witness changes to probation services throughout 2013–2014), the lessons learned remain valid and are a solid foundation on which we will continue to build for the future.

References and resources

Adebowale, V. (2013). Independent Commission on Mental Health and Policing Report. http://news.bbc.co.uk/1/shared/bsp/hi/pdfs/10_05_13_report.pdf

Bather, P., Fitzpatrick, R., and Rutherford, M. (2008). Briefing 36: Police and Mental Health. *Sainsbury Centre for Mental Health*. www.centreformentalhealth.org.uk/publications/references.aspx

Bradley, K. (2009). *The Bradley Report: review of people with mental health problems or learning disabilities in the criminal justice system*. London: Department of Health.

Brooker, C., Sirdfield, C., Blizard, R., Denney, D. and Pluck, G. (2012). Probation and Mental Illness. *The Journal of Forensic Psychiatry and Psychology*, 23 (4), 522–537.

Brooker, C., and Glyn, J. (2012). Probation Service and Mental Health. *Centre for Mental Health*. www.centreformentalhealth.org.uk

Durcan, G. (2014). Keys to Diversion: Best practice for offenders with multiple needs. *Centre for Mental Health*. www.centreformentalhealth.org.uk

Durcan, G., Saunders, A., Gadsby, B. and Hazard, A. (2014). The Bradley Report five years on: An independent review of progress to date and priorities for further development. *Centre for Mental Health*. www.centreformentalhealth.org.uk/

England, E. and Lester, H. (2005). Integrated mental health services in England: a policy paradox. www.ncbi.nlm.nih.gov/pmc/articles/PMC1475728/

Goodwin, N. and Lawton-Smith, S. (2010). Integrating care for people with mental illness: the Care Programme Approach in England and its implications for long-term conditions management. *Journal of Integrated Care*, Mar 2010. ISSN 1568–4156. Available at: http://www.ijic.org/index.php/ijic/article/view/516

NHS England (n.d.). Liaison and Diversion Initiative. http://www.england.nhs.uk/2011/11/

Pakes, F. and Winstone, J. (2009) Effective Practice in Mental Health Liaison and Diversion. *Howard Journal of Criminal Justice*, 48 (2), 158–171.

Pakes, F., Winstone, J., Haskins, J. and Guest, J. (2010) Mental Health Court Feasibility Study. www.justice.gov.uk/publications/research-and-analysis/moj/2010/mhc-process-feasibility-evaluation

Parsonage, M. (2009). Diversion: A Better Way for Criminal Justice and Mental Health. *Sainsbury Centre for Mental Health*. www.centreformentalhealth.org.uk/

Revolving Door Agency in association with Clinks and Making Every Day Matter (MEAM) (2013). Supporting Vulnerable People in Custody at Court. www.revolving-doors.org.uk/

Scott, G. and Moffatt, S. (2012). The Mental Health. Treatment Requirement: Realising a better future. *Centre for Mental Health*. www.centreformentalhealth.org.uk

Stone, N. (2003). *A Companion Guide to Mentally Disordered Offenders*. Crayford: Shaw and Sons.

Winstone, J. and Pakes, F. (2010a). Mental Health Court Process Evaluation. www.justice.gov.uk/publications/research-and-analysis/moj/2010/mhc-process-feasibility-evaluation

Winstone, J. and Pakes, F. (2010b). Offenders with mental health problems in the criminal justice system: the multi-agency challenge. In: A. Pycroft and D. Gough (eds). *Multi-agency working in criminal justice: control and care in contemporary correctional practice*. Bristol: Policy Press. 169–178.

14
Training to Improve Collaborative Practice: A Key Component of Strategy to Reduce Mental Ill Health in the Offender Population

Sarah Hean, Elizabeth Walsh and Marilyn Hammick

Introduction

Internationally there are unacceptably high numbers of people in contact with the criminal justice system (e.g. in police custody, in court, or in prison) who have mental health issues (Fazel and Danesh, 2002). Addressing mental health in the offender population is essential to maintain public safety, improve the well-being of the offender and their family, and reduce reoffending and the impact of this on the public purse. Poor interagency and interprofessional working have been highlighted as key factors that have severely compromised patient and public safety in the past: working at the interface of the mental health services and criminal justice systems has been shown to be particularly challenging, with complex communication and information-sharing strategies being required. A key aspect of improving joint working is the delivery of a continuous or integrated rehabilitation pathway characterised by early diagnosis, treatment, appropriate sentencing or diversion of people away from the criminal justice system and into mental health services (see Rogers and Ormston, this volume). Integrated, effective partnership working is required between these two systems. Training and development to assist and support staff involved in this team working endeavour is essential. Within the mental health/criminal justice arena the Bradley Report (Bradley, 2009) in the UK calls for joint training between agencies. To date there is little that suggests the content or format this training should take.

This chapter responds to this shortfall by exploring how the enhancement of collaborative practice between mental health services (MHS) and the Criminal Justice System (CJS) can be seen as one element of the armoury necessary to combat the issues posed by mental illness in the offender population (Durcan et al., 2014). We explore why collaborative practice between different professionals and agencies is high on the agenda globally (World Health Organization [WHO], 2010) and why professionals within the MHS and CJS need to be trained to be able to work collaboratively in the interest of reducing mental ill health in the offender population. Although training of this type is largely absent in this area, we explore potential approaches to training, focussing on both a systems and an interpersonal level of analysis, giving some examples of interprofessional training used in the MHS and CJS context to illustrate these approaches. A triple-phase model of collaborative practice training for professionals within the MHS and CJS is proposed.

Offender mental ill health is a major societal challenge. Globally, there are unacceptably high numbers of people in contact with CJS who have mental health issues with 7–9 out of 10 prisoners demonstrating signs of at least one mental disorder (Fazel and Baillargeon, 2011). This is far higher than the average population level of mental illness and as such represents an area of severe health inequality. A meta-analysis of 62 surveys of 23 000 prisoners in 12 Western countries, for example, showed the prevalence of psychosis to be around 4%, compared to 1% in the general population, major depression 10–12% compared to 2–7% in the general population, and personality disorder 42–65% compared to 5–10% in the general population (Fazel and Baillargeon, 2011; Fazel and Danesh, 2002). When offender mental health is not addressed, this leads to a deterioration of the mental disorder (Nurse et al., 2003; see Göbbels, Thakker and Ward, this volume). In turn, this impacts on offender well-being as well as their failure to adjust to community life on release, resulting in their social exclusion and increasing the likelihood of reoffending (World Health Organization, 2005). Offender mental ill health also affects the well-being of the offender's family, fellow prisoners, frontline police/court/prison staff and public safety. Further, the CJS, if uninformed, can impose inappropriate sentences on offenders and as mentally ill offenders are likely to reoffend, this places an economic strain on the public purse and prison and mental health hospital places (World Health Organization, 2005).

Multi-agency training has been tried before, but often in a piecemeal fashion and usually as part of a local initiative to respond to identified cross-agency needs in mental health support (see Pakes and Winstone, 2009; Bradley, 2009; Durcan et al., 2014). This chapter focusses on the importance of collaborative practice between the MHS and CJS as a key factor in work to address the issues posed by mental illness in the offender population. We then explore the vital role of inter- (rather than multi-)agency training for MHS and CJS practitioners to enable them to work collaboratively in the interest of reducing mental ill health in the offender population. We explore potential approaches to this training with a focus on systems and the interpersonal, drawing on joint training used in the MHS and CJS context to illustrate these approaches and to identify successful strategies which could be pursued over the long term.

Addressing mental health in through enhanced collaborative practice

Enhancing collaborative practice between professionals, and between agencies, from a wide range of services and disciplines, is high on current political agendas. National inquiries into critical incidents breaching patient safety (e.g., Laming, 2003; Kennedy, 2001) highlight consistently poor collaborative practice between a wide range of professionals including those in the police and health services. A global ageing population (reflected in the prison population – Fazel and Baillargeon, 2011) is associated with greater incidence of longer-term conditions that require the input of several professionals and agencies in their resolution. In addition, we live in a rapidly changing and complex world of service provision, with high levels of specialisation of services and professionals. Professionals are increasingly required to provide integrated care across professional and disciplinary boundaries. Key policy drivers *IOM Health Professions Education: A Bridge to Quality* (2003), Lancet Commission (Frenk et al., 2010), *Framework for Action on Interprofessional Education and Collaborative Practice* (World Health Organization, 2010) and professional consortia such as the UK (National Collaboration for Integrated Care and Support, 2013) reflect this need.

Collaboration and collaborative competencies are also essential for social innovation. Defined as 'the development and implementation of new ideas (products, services and models) to meet social needs' (European Commission, 2013, p. 6), social innovation occurs through the creation of new social relationships or collaborations across disciplinary or professional boundaries. In this way disciplinary knowledge is shared and new innovative solutions created by a synthesis and co-production of these diverse knowledge resources (Hean et al., 2012a; Hammick, 1998). Social innovation and collaborative practice between MHS and CJS professionals is required if the issues that arise when mentally ill individuals come in contact with the criminal justice system (e.g. in the police station, court or prison) are to be addressed (World Health Organization, 2005; Bradley, 2009; Durcan et al., 2014). Effective partnership working between these systems means early diagnosis of the offender, treatment, appropriate sentencing or diversion into the MHS. However, collaborative practice at the interface of the MHS and CJS can be challenging, (Hean et al., 2009a and b), lacking shared protocols and agreed timeframes, poor information sharing and lack of clarity on lines of responsibility.

There is a range of practice models aimed at reducing mental illness in offenders. These include diversion and liaison schemes (see Rogers and

Ormston, this volume), specialist mental health courts, care coordination and service level agreements (Bradley, 2009). For success in these innovative service re-organisations, zones of collaborative practice between professionals from the culturally distinct mental health and criminal justice systems need to be established and to function effectively. Similar innovation is required to fill the grey spaces that lie between services (Department of Health and Welfare, 2013) into which complex offenders fall when no agency takes responsibility for the offender or their mental health needs (see Pycroft and Green, this volume).

We argue that whatever the service model or innovation used, professionals within the MHS and CJS systems need preparation and training for collaborative practice. In this way current models of interagency working will be sustained and the socially innovative models of interagency working required in the future will be developed.

The case for training for collaborative practice

To improve offender mental health, the UK Bradley report (Bradley, 2009) called for joint training between MHS and CJS organisations. It failed to suggest the content or format this should take as does the subsequent *Report on Bradley five years on* (Durcan et al., 2014). Staff training has subsequently focussed on training frontline staff in the CJS on how to recognise mental illness (Ministry of Justice and Department of Health, 2011) with only passing reference to referring clients to the appropriate mental health specialists. Hean et al. (2011) proposed that this joint training should not only be about mental health awareness in the CJS but also include training that crosses organisational and professional boundaries and prepares professionals from both systems to collaborate; to learn with, from and about each other to achieve better offender mental health outcomes (see Canton, this volume; Rogers and Ormston, this volume).

A distinction should be drawn at this juncture between uniprofessional, multiprofessional and interprofessional training and interagency training. Professionals can learn about the role of other professionals in a uniprofessional environment in which no contact or interaction with other professional groups or professionals takes place. They may also learn multiprofessionally, where multiprofessional education is defined as: 'Occasions when two or more professions learn side by side for whatever reason' (Barr et al., 2002, p. 6). Multiprofessional learning often involves large numbers of students being taught together at the same time, in the same space and about the same topic. Whilst there may be efficiency savings, Carpenter and Hewstone have indicated that 'simply putting students together in mixed classes...(may be)...unproductive and breed poor intergroup attitudes' (Carpenter and Hewstone, 1996,

p. 241). On the other hand, interprofessional education is defined as occurring 'when two or more professions learn about, from and with each other to enable effective collaboration and improve health outcomes' (WHO, 2010, p. 13). In operational terms, this leads logically to a model of small group learning rather than large group didactic teaching. It is in this latter environment that students develop the internal resources they require to be effective collaborators and/ or team members. A focus on the professional mix of the student group takes a micro level of analysis. However, in a patient's care pathway, interactions between professionals often occur at a more macro level of work organisation. Multiple agencies can be involved. It is in this context that interagency training approaches are to be considered. Although there will be overlap between the interprofessional and the interagency, the distinction between these two levels of analysis is not entirely clear. Although interagency training will have a component of the interprofessional, interagency training must also take into account greater levels of complexity as students learn to cross both professional and organisational boundaries.

The development and evaluation of interagency training has received less attention than interprofessional training. Where it is developed, in the context of safeguarding children, it is shown to impact positively on collaborative practice (Patsios and Carpenter, 2010). Interprofessional education is more widely reported in the literature, but where this occurs it is largely described at the interface of health and social care professional training (Department of Health, 2001). There is no equivalent that includes professionals from the CJS. Despite limited interagency or interprofessional training, MHS and CJS professionals strongly endorse the need for this type of training and its contribution to enhanced collaborative competence across the workforce and, in the long term, improved offender mental health (Hean et al., 2012b). Higher educational institutions and educational commissioners from Ministries of Health and Justice are amongst the key players that must address this deficit.

Interdependence between education and practice systems

The Lancet Commission Report (Frenk et al., 2010), when addressing future directions in medical education, emphasises the importance of interdependence between education and health systems: practice, social and policy drivers demand a workforce able to work collaboratively. Educators need to provide collaborative training that responds to this demand in both quality (the right type of collaborative skill) and quantity (sufficient number of workers with these skills). The same interdependence exists between the criminal justice systems and the systems of education training new legal and security professionals. Health and/or criminal justice systems respond to population needs (in this case offender mental health) by harnessing the range of professionals/

agencies required to deliver integrated services that are best placed to address the rapidly changing and complex needs of mentally ill offenders. We suggest that only with close interaction between the education systems and health/criminal justice systems will there be a workforce of sufficient quality and quantity to meet this service demand.

In other words, education systems must supply qualified professionals that are collaborative-practice ready (WHO, 2010) and able to cross professional and disciplinary boundaries in such a way that best serves current and future practice needs. The education systems need to keep abreast of rapidly changing practice needs through continuous dialogue between themselves and health/criminal justice systems. An example is described by Hean et al. (2012b), reporting on a series of focus groups that explored the opinions of mental health and criminal justice professionals' attitudes towards interagency training. Focus group participants from both the MHS and CJS called for training that would enable them to understand the other agency from both a systems level and at a more micro level in which positive relationships between individual professionals could be built. Following on from this, a UK higher education institution engaged with professionals from both the MHS and CJS systems to explore the current requirements of collaborative interagency training that MHS and CJS professionals believed would improve professionals' ability to collaborate and innovate with the common goal of enhancing the mental health of the offender population (Hean et al., 2012b) (see Box 14.1).

Box 14.1 Example of the outcomes of engagement between the MHS/CJS systems and a higher education institution regarding training needs for professionals related to collaborative practice skills

At a systems level, MHS and CJS professionals say that they would value training that gave them a greater knowledge of the components of other agencies, especially to understand the roles and responsibilities of professionals in other agencies and gain an overall understanding of systems and how they fit together (Hean et al., 2012b). They wanted to understand the legal and political environment of other professionals/agencies. This is important as they currently find it difficult getting hold of the right person/service they require in other agencies. This sentiment is not unique to the CJS and MHS. The need for an increasing knowledge of other agencies and interagency training has been at the forefront of many other service interfaces including those linked to the child safeguarding agendas for several decades, although the impact of interagency training on practice change and patient/client well-being is notoriously difficult to establish (Charles and Horwath, 2009).

At a micro level of interpersonal relationships, MHS and CJS professionals saw interagency training as a means by which to network and build those relationships necessary to enhance interagency working, and improve and share good practice. They wanted to learn to work together to enhance their professional practice and ultimately the well-being of the offender with mental issues. They recognised that

> other agencies have different priorities and values and that understanding their alternative perspectives, targets and priorities will facilitate the building of more effective interagency relationships. They wanted to build empathic relationships with other agencies. Without this interagency empathy, they believed prejudice builds, communication channels and information sharing are blocked, and misunderstanding of where lines of accountability lie occurs. These empathic relationships are important at all levels of the professional hierarchy but were seen as particularly important horizontally between senior managers across agency boundaries (Hean et al., 2012b).

We now turn to specific approaches to collaborative practice training within the MHS and CJS context. The first takes a systems approach to training and the second focusses on enhancing collaborative practice professional relationships at a micro level of analysis.

A systems approach to collaborative practice training between MHS and CJS professionals

Social innovations are defined as:

> complex process(es) of introducing new products, processes or programs that profoundly change the basic routines, resource and authority flows or beliefs of the social system in which the innovation occurs. Such successful innovations have durability and broad impact… social innovation strives to change the way a system operates. (Westley, 2010, pp. 2–3)

Social innovation, viewed at this systems level, requires the variety of actors working together to take an organisational or macro level view to the process of knowledge exchange and co-production between different professional groups and organisations. At this macro level of analysis, training aimed at enhancing collaborative practice must focus on preparing individuals or teams of individuals to be able to improve the management structures that promote interagency collaboration and through which contemporary policy drivers and guidance on mental health issues may be implemented (see Rogers and Ormston, this volume). Collaborative practice between the MHS and CJS at this level is described as a process of inter-organisational integration, one which describes the quality of joint effort put in by two or more organisations and their constituent professionals to collaborate with one another (e.g. between the police force and a community mental health team).

Levels of inter-organisational integration exist on a continuum from full segregation, with no contact between service providers, to full organisational integration where newly established organisations are created to promote collaborative behaviours. Linking, cooperation and coordination are levels of integration that lie between these two extremes. There is no one model that is generically better than another; the optimum level of inter-organisational integration depends on context and service user need (Ahgren and Axelsson, 2005). Service managers from the MHS and CJS respectively must develop the skills and knowledge to be able to judge the right level of integration between their constituent organisations to achieve the best outcome for offenders' mental health within their own context. These skills can be developed, for example, through application of an assessment tool such as the Scale of Organisational Integration, which quantifies levels of inter-organisational integration required for optimal interagency collaboration (Ahgren and Axelsson, 2005). This tool has made a unique contribution in other clinical areas (namely child health and rehabilitation) and has potential for both service development and collaborative practice training within the MHS/CJS context.

Another systems level approach that has relevance to collaborative practice training and integrated working across the MHS and CJS at a macro level is that of the Activity System (Engeström, 2001). The activity system framework is an evolution of socio-cultural learning theory (Vygotsky, 1978). The basic tenet of this theory is that the meaning we make of an activity, or the learning that takes place during this activity (see de Lacy, this volume), is a function not only of the individual's own cognition, ability or dedication; it is also mediated and influenced by factors external to the individual within the social world (Engeström, 2001). Professionals in the CJS (e.g. lawyers, judges and probation officers) (Figure 14.1) and professionals in the mental health and related services (e.g. psychiatrists, community psychiatric nurses, psychologists) (Figure 14.2), represent two separate activity systems.

In each single activity system (see Figures 14.1 and 14.2), the **subject** is the person within an agency undertaking a particular activity. The **object** is the purpose of this activity. In the legal system (see Figure 14.1), the subject is illustrated by a magistrate dealing with a defendant, who has been identified as having potential mental health issues. In the interest of the defendant, and to inform sentencing (the object), the magistrate requests an assessment and a report on the mental health of the defendant (the activity). In order to achieve this, the magistrate may complete a written assessment request or negotiate with legal advisors or liaison workers in court to make these requests. The latter are tools that mediate the activity (see de Lacy, this volume).

Surrounding this mediated activity is a range of other variables that may have influence on the actions of the key players. These include the unwritten social norms and formal rules that govern the way in which the legal system functions (see Arrigo and Bersot, this volume), for example, government imposed targets that specify the times in which court cases need to be completed. Also surrounding the activity are members of the wider legal community who

Figure 14.1

Mediating tools
Liaison workers, assessment requests

Object/Activity
Request for info on mental illness of defendant & relationship with crime for disposal and support of defendant

Subject
Magistrate

Rules
Cost effectiveness; disposal time targets

Community
Legal advisors, liaison workers, lawyers, probation, judges, magistrates, Reliance (police)

Division of labour
Probation, lawyers, liaison

Legal advisors, magistrate

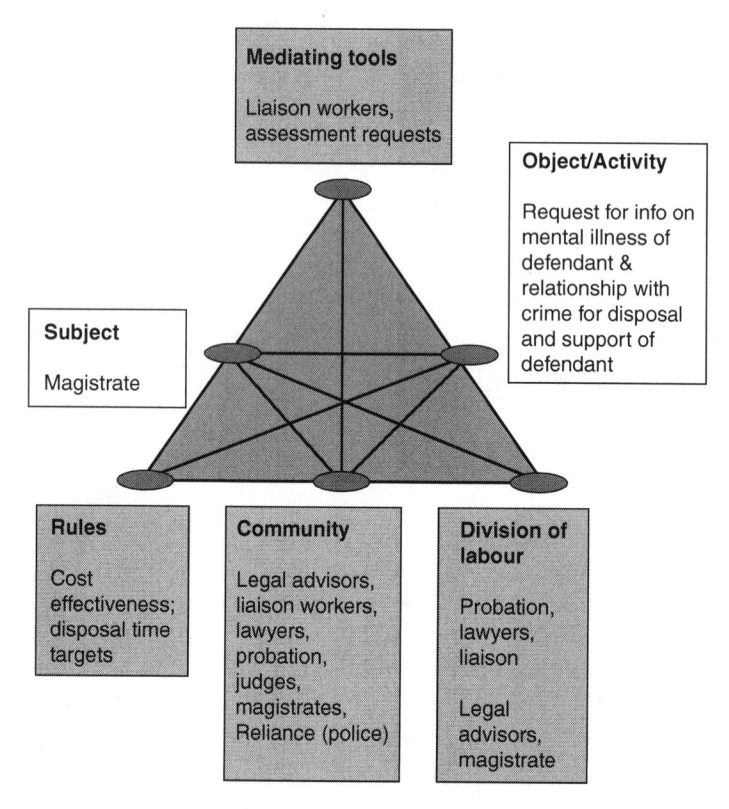

Figure 14.1 An activity system surrounding the requests for psychiatric reports made by the criminal justice system

include defence lawyers, probation officers, court ushers, other magistrates and security personnel. Each of these members may fulfil a particular role within the criminal justice system that will dictate how the activity under focus can be achieved (division of labour). There may be a range of contradictions within the activity system. For example, there is a contradiction in the activity system (see Figure 14.2) when this system interacts with that of the mental health services. There is a mismatch between the need to request a report (object) and governing rules that stipulate that court cases need to be completed in a set time frame (see de Lacy, this volume). These time targets, and conflict with the time it takes for a report to be produced by the mental health services, mean that the magistrate may decide it is not worth asking for a report as it delays proceedings.

In Figure 14.2 the subject is illustrated by a psychiatrist undertaking an assessment and making a report on a service user in contact with the CJS. The psychiatrist does this using the assessment tools available to her/him as part of

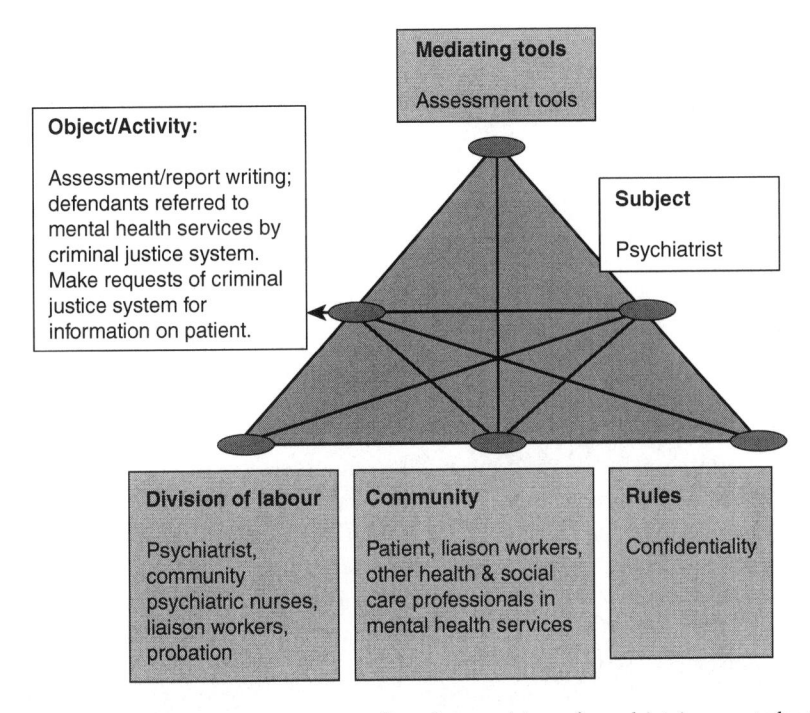

Training to Improve Collaborative Practice 251

Figure 14.2 An activity system surrounding the provision of psychiatric reports by the Mental Health Services

their normal practice. The way in which the report is written is underpinned by norms and rules, e.g.:

- the psychiatrist's view that their first responsibility is to the defendant and his/her treatment (and not punishment);
- patient confidentiality;
- in most places psychiatrists choose to complete reports for the court on a private consultancy basis over and above their current workload.

A community of other professionals surrounds the psychiatrist and their report-writing activity. This community includes other psychiatrists, community psychiatric nurses and social workers. A clear-cut division of labour between these professionals occurs during report writing with psychiatrists being responsible for the full assessment and psychiatric reports required on the more seriously mentally ill or more serious offenders. Although, abbreviated health and social circumstances or screening reports are conducted by other health professionals in some areas. The outcomes of this activity can be challenging because of the mismatch in expectations between the content the MHS (the psychiatrist in this case) believes should be in the report and what, on the other hand, the CJS (the magistrate in this case) requires of the report. The magistrate hopes for guidance on the relationship between the offence and the offender's mental health as well as advice on appropriate sentencing that protects both the interests of public safety and the health of the offender. However, the psychiatrist is bounded by norms of patient confidentiality: they may be ill-informed on sentencing options etc., or may argue that offering advice on appropriate sentencing is not within their professional remit. The end result of the interaction between the two systems is that expectations of report content and time frames are not clearly communicated (Hean et al., 2009a and b).

In considering interagency working, service leaders within the MHS and CJS need to look beyond the two separate activity systems in isolation and review them in parallel, identifying how the objects of each activity may be synchronised, where contradictions in the systems lie (as illustrated above) and how joint solutions can be created in partnership and tested out in practice (see Figure 14.3). Collaborative practice training can facilitate this process by bringing MHS and CJS professionals to perform this task, enabling them to share their disciplinary knowledge of their own activity system and co-construct new ways of working collaboratively. The innovative solutions they develop are contextually specific to the agencies involved in these crossing boundary activities (Engeström, 2001; Hean et al., 2012b).

A micro level approach to collaborative practice training between professionals within the mental health and criminal Justice systems

Building empathic relationships

MHS and CJS joint working can also be visualised at a micro level. Here collaborative practice training focusses more on the individual behaviour of different professionals and the relationships between them rather than the whole system in which they operate.

Building empathic relationships between MHS and CJS professionals is essential for effective interprofessional collaborative working (Adamson, 2011) and can, in turn, enhance professionals' ability to empathise with the patient/client (Reynolds and Austin, 2000). Such relationships originate from:

- an understanding of roles; appreciating differences;
- exploring the perspective of the other professionals;
- recognising professionals from other agencies are 'people first and co-workers second';

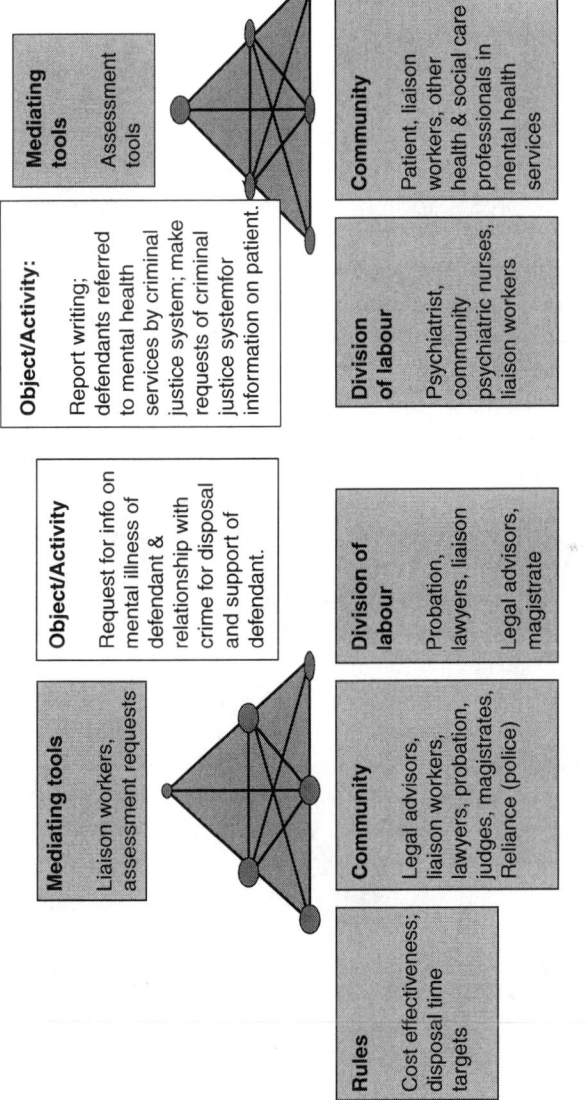

Figure 14.3 The two activity systems of mental health and court services interacting as defendants with mental issues overlap between the two

- developing an intentionality around interagency engagements and how these are managed;
- creating dialogic (rather than monologic) verbal communication channels;
- the development of collective spirit (e.g. through shared workload, being inclusive, accepting the expression of another's vulnerability) .

Adamson (2011) suggests that an understanding of the roles and responsibilities of another professional, and their scope of practice, is not sufficient to build interprofessional relationships. Professionals must also develop an understanding of the working context of the other agency professionals and how they perform the roles they are tasked with. This suggests that a divide between systems level and micro level approaches to collaborative training is not always feasible. Indeed, we would argue that an approach that balances systems level approaches with those that take into account the professional as a person are ideal.

In the current financial climate and with restrictions placed on training and the release of staff to participate in this, there is a temptation to rely on online e-provision or self-directed study. Collaborative training may be limited to access to an online directory of the roles of other agency professionals, and training may be restricted to uniprofessional or uniagency events. These forms of *arms length* training do not encourage an understanding of the context in which the roles of other agencies are performed and hence are not conducive to building interagency empathy. Actual contact between agencies is essential to build the necessary interagency relationships, interprofessional empathy, and the verbal dialogic communication recommended by Adamson (2011).

Contact between professionals from MHS and CJS agencies can be provided in several ways including interagency placements, visits and shadowing opportunities (see Rogers and Ormston, this volume). Whatever approach is taken, it is essential that a valid interagency learning experience is provided. Interagency placements, shadowing opportunities or formal visits between agencies all provide this validity through inspection of real-life, practice-based learning opportunities in future interagency training packages. A need for valid training steeped in practice experience also underpins MHS and CJS professionals' preference for training being delivered by fellow professionals rather than outsiders who may be unaware of the localised and practice issues at hand (Hean et al., 2012b).

Although establishing contact between agencies is a recognised tool in building relationships and minimising intergroup stereotypes and prejudice between the criminal justice system and mental health services, contact alone is insufficient (Dickinson and Carpenter, 2009). Whilst interagency placements, visits and shadowing opportunities provide contact, a range of contact conditions must be present for these positive effects to occur. These conditions include that:

- agencies should be working on common goals;
- there should be institutional buy-in from those in authority;
- intergroup contact should be such that participants are on a level and equal footing;
- similarities and differences between professions to be acknowledged (Dickinson and Carpenter, 2009).

If these contact opportunities are left unmanaged, however, and left open to serendipitous interagency learning, then the impact of contact may have quite the opposite effect, stereotypes being reinforced and interagency relationships harmed. Facilitation is key in these events.

Training focussing on the individual or micro level of analysis should not only consider the conditions required for training, as above. It should consider also the specific collaborative practice competencies that professionals need to achieve.

Collaborative competencies

The Lancet Commission on Education of Health Professionals (Frenk et al., 2010) recommend the generation of core collaborative competencies drawn from global knowledge but adapted to local contexts. These competencies include:

- interprofessional team working;
- interprofessional communication;
- role clarification;
- conflict resolution;
- second order reflection; and
- collaborative leadership.

Collaborative leadership is stressed as particularly important for 21st century public service professionals who, as service leaders, must operate in multiprofessional, multiagency environments to achieve change within and around their own services. They are responsible for establishing structures to ensure communication, information flow and that collaboration takes place. Part of this competence is awareness of the impact of management on staff collaboration and service user outcomes.

A range of competency frameworks are available for trainers to draw upon that spell out the domains and detail of collaborative competencies that MHS and CJS professionals should be able to demonstrate (see Table 14.1).

Table 14.1 Exemplars of collaborative competency frameworks and competencies to be attained by MHS and CJS professionals

Model	Country	Domains	Exemplar competence
Metacognitive Interprofessional competencies model (Wilhelmson et al., 2012)	Sweden	• Teamwork/group processes • Reflection and documentation • Communication • Shared knowledge • Ethics	Shared knowledge: Awareness of general laws/rules for all health/social professions.
Core competencies for collaborative practice framework (IECEP, 2011)	US	• Teams and Teamwork • Roles/Responsibilities • Communication • Values/Ethics	Roles and responsibilities: Communicate one's roles and responsibilities clearly to patients, families, other professionals.
National interprofessional competency framework (Orchard and Bainbridge, 2010)	Canada	• Team functioning • Communication • Patient-centred care • Role clarification • Conflict resolution • Collaborative leadership	Collaborative leadership: co-creation of a climate for shared leadership and collaborative practice.
Interprofessional capabilities framework (Walsh et al., 2005)	UK	• Interprofessional working • Knowledge in practice • Reflection • Ethical practice	Interprofessional working: ability to lead/participate in interprofessional team and wider interagency work, to ensure responsive, integrated approach to care/service management focussed on the needs of the patient/client.

Although the Lancet Commission (Frenk et al., 2010) recommends a move towards competency-based training for collaborative practice, training for MHS and CJS professionals that adopts a purely competency-based focus may be accused of taking an overly behaviourist focus on the outcomes or required skills and knowledge of training in isolation. A constructivist approach offers insight into *how* training is delivered, provides some balance and is exemplified by adult learning methods. We offer here action learning as one example of an adult learning approach, one that focusses on the process of learning in addition to its outcomes.

Action learning

McGill and Brockbank (2004) define action learning as 'a continuous process of learning and reflection that happens with the support of a group or "set" of colleagues, working on real issues, with the intention of getting things done' (p.11). This approach has been used successfully in the prison setting to enable particular developments in practice, such as:

- implementing clinical supervision in prison healthcare (Walsh et al., 2007);
- promoting partnership working amongst prison officers and nurses (Walsh, 2009);
- developing a learning environment in the prison health care setting (Walsh and Bee, 2012); and in
- developing a multiprofessional assessment tool to identify the health and social care needs of older prisoners (Walsh et al., 2014).

The use of action learning in the prison setting has two functions. Firstly, specific issues for practice (both security and health care) can be identified and addressed. However, as a result of using action learning as the approach to supporting developments in practice, professionals from a range of services engage in experiential learning, both from and with one another, that brings significant improvements in cross-disciplinary understanding and appreciation, leading to more effective interprofessional working.

Using two examples from practice, we demonstrate how action learning that includes both health care and prison staff not only develops practice and impacts on prisoner patient care, but can promote learning and strengthen professional relationships through mutual understanding and respect.

Example One: developing clinical supervision in prison health care settings

In the first of our examples, action learning was used to develop clinical supervision in prison health care settings, and included both health care staff and prison officers. Specific details of the methodological aspects of this project can be found in Walsh et al., 2007.

Bishop (2007, p. 1) defines clinical supervision as:

> a designated interaction between two or more professionals within a safe and supportive environment, that enables a continuum of reflective critical analysis of care, to ensure quality patients services, and the well being of the practitioner.

In general, clinical supervision has a number of functions including emotional support, opportunity for reflection and constructive critique, enabling the maintenance of practice standards, and the acquisition of new knowledge. Whilst the terminology may reflect a 'clinical' perspective, it is suggested that clinical supervision is important and valuable for non-clinicians who have responsibility for the care of others, including prison officers.

The initial phase of this three-phase project was centred on the provision and development of a training programme that prepared 35 staff from five prisons in England to facilitate clinical supervision back in their own prisons. The subsequent evaluation of this programme led to its refinement and further adaptation to enable the second phase of the study where 71 nurses and prison officers were trained as clinical supervisors across England and Wales. It is phase three of this study which is of interest to us here, as it is in this phase where the 71 nurses and prison officers were configured into seven regional action learning groups in England and Wales in order to support them to develop clinical supervision back in their own prisons. Thirty-one prisons were represented across the seven action learning groups, with the composition in five of them consisting solely of nurses. However, there were two action learning groups in which prison officers were members alongside nursing staff. One comprised of two prison officers working as suicide prevention officers, and the second consisted of one mental health nurse and four prison officers working together on a specialist unit for prisoners with dangerous and severe personality disorder (DSPD) (see Scally, this volume).

The evaluation of the work and experiences of these action learning groups led to debate about the importance of terminology when engaging professionals from any background to undertake clinical supervision. Therefore, what would be known as clinical supervision was termed practice facilitation by one group, who felt this better reflected their aims and purpose. Underpinning effective clinical supervision is the ability to reflect on practice, the ability to think explicitly, review and plan change in one's own professional behaviour and its outcomes (Schon, 1987). This was viewed as quite a challenge to some group members, particularly prison officers, who work in what we term a 'closed culture' where prising open practice for exploration is not commonplace (Freshwater et al., 2012). By remaining closed to reflection, prison staff protect themselves from the emotional challenges and potential impact on their own mental health. This reluctance to engage is what Menzies Lyth (1998) refers to as a defence against anxiety, The value of a psychologically safe space for prison staff to reflect on their practice and engage in both clinical supervision and action learning cannot be underestimated. Through this project, it became clear that the venue for the meetings, which was always away from the prison, was valued by participants as distractions from practice were avoided. In addition to the venue, all action learning groups worked to a contract, which outlined expectations and highlighted particular issues around confidentiality. This assisted in ensuring a safe space for open and honest discussion of issues and enabled effective reflection. In those action learning groups where officers and healthcare staff worked alongside one another, it was noted that there was an increased appreciation of professional roles and perspectives, leading to new understandings and shared knowledge. Members of both interprofessional action learning groups reported benefits that included a better understanding of each other's roles but also improved opportunities for networking amongst others in their prisons.

In the second of our examples, we report the experience of a project where action learning was used to promote shared reflection on practice between nurses and prison officers working in prison segregation units.

Example Two: promoting shared reflection on practice between nurses and prison officers working in segregation units

Following work to develop reflective practice in prison health care settings (see Walsh et al., 2007) the importance of reflection and its significance for interprofessional working led us to consider the value promoting shared reflection between prison officers working in segregation units and mental health nurses working with them in caring for segregated prisoners.

A study was designed to support prison officers and nurses to learn and work together to promote and improve partnership working through reflection on practice (Walsh, 2009). There are significant challenges for prison officers working in segregation units, where violent and difficult to manage prisoners are often located. The high incidence of mental ill health amongst the prison population has led to a greater awareness of prisoners in segregation units whose violent and aggressive behaviour can be linked to mental health issues. Consequently, there is usually a close relationship between healthcare staff and segregation unit staff, where a joint approach to care can be adopted (see Gatawa, this volume). Indeed, some segregation units have been renamed 'care and separation units' as their focus shifts to incorporate a rehabilitative, treatment-focussed approach. However, some prison staff find the rehabilitative focus challenging where segregated settings have predominantly been modelled on philosophies that are rooted in punishment and control (see Canton, this volume; Arrigo and Bersot, this volume). Similarly, mental health nurses can struggle with practising in an extreme secure setting where care and discipline are competing priorities (see Coyle, 2005; see Gatawa, this volume).

In order to promote effective interprofessional working between health care and segregation settings, action learning was employed as the means of delivering training that promoted collaboration between MHS and CJS professionals. Two action learning groups, with representation from four prisons in each, met monthly over a six-month period. From each prison, one segregation unit officer and one nurse attended. The groups were held away from the prison, where distraction would be minimal. From the evaluation of this work two key gains were identified, which were prisoner care and staff support. The shared reflection on practice enabled a better understanding of roles and culture, which fed through into changes to the way staff interacted and supported one another. Interestingly, whilst nurses and prison officers are deemed to be from different professional groups, staff in this project identified very little difference in their overall aim for attending the group. The improvement of prisoner well-being was noted by both professional groups as their primary and common goal.

Following the completion of this study, the project team received reports that some action learning group members found the experience of action learning and reflection so valuable that they continued to meet back in their prisons to ensure developments and support could continue to progress. It was felt that the action learning groups provided members with the opportunity to take control of their practice and try new ideas with the support of their colleagues. We are certain that prisoner patient care was positively affected by this work as strategies to manage difficult prisoners and situations were discussed in the action learning group, enacted back at the workplace, then reflected on at the next action learning group meeting. Further details of this study can be found in Walsh (2009).

Our reflection on these two examples from practice clearly demonstrate the value of interprofessional action learning and reflection on practice where professionals that come from a different philosophical base, i.e. caring and discipline, can come together to improve prisoner patient care, whilst developing a supportive environment for themselves, in what is a particularly challenging place to practise.

Towards a model of collaborative practice training for the MHS and CJS

A three-phase model of training for collaborative practice (Table 14.2) is proposed based on the above discussion. Participants should be drawn from regional services in the MHS/CJS deemed by service leaders to be at the MHS/CHS interface. A mapping exercise may need to be performed to identify the services and individual professionals that work at this interface, and who should therefore be best placed to benefit from such interagency training.

It is essential at the end of this model of training that an evaluation phase is included, with participants reconvened for this activity. The acquisition of the range of collaborative competencies by participants should be assessed and their perception of the interagency networks and relationships they have developed evaluated. In addition, the success of the strategic plans implemented by

Table 14.2 A triple-phase model of training for enhanced collaborative practice (TCP) at the interface of the MHS and CJS

Phase of training model	Content/mode of delivery
Intra-agency Phase 1 General awareness training	This phase may be delivered separately within each agency. For criminal justice staff training on mental health awareness could be included (Ministry of Justice and Department Health, 2011) These might vary in content but could include awareness about: neurosis; psychosis; personality disorders; learning disability; the difference between primary and secondary care; country-specific mental health legislation; and mental health treatment pathways. This training could be delivered by local mental health services and local criminal justice agencies, or be provided by local training agencies or universities. On the other hand, mental health staff working in local community mental health teams could receive training around how the criminal justice system works – what happens at the police station, courts, probation and prison, and basic information on policy driving these services (in the UK for example, the Police And Criminal Evidence (PACE) Act 1984 and sec. 136 of the Mental Health Act 1983 (as amended 2007) (Hean et al., 2012b). All agencies should receive some basic input on contemporary social innovations at the interface of the MHS/CJS (e.g. in the UK, the Mental Health and Learning Disability Liaison and Diversion agenda including the purpose of the agenda, what the benefits will be and how agencies might work together to achieve them). (Hean et al., 2012b).
Intensive phase 2 An induction to interprofessional and interagency training	An intensive face-to-face workshop for all MHS/CJS participants (e.g. one or two full days). This serves as a preliminary introduction to collaborative practice. Participants are introduced to definitions of collaborative practice and its importance relative to offender mental health and social innovation within services. Key concepts around collaborative practice at both systems and inter-relational levels of analysis are introduced. Conditions required for effective contact between professional groups (Carpenter and Hewstone, 1996), the processes behind building empathic relationships across professional and agency boundaries (Adamson, 2011), key collaborative competencies and how these are developed are discussed to promote awareness of relational factors in cross-agency working as well as to build empathic relationships and networks between workshop participants. Activity systems models (Engeström, 2001) are used to articulate interaction between MHS and CJS at a systems level. The workshop should heavily focus on interactive elements, using a cross-boundary workshop method (Engeström, 2002) with an offender case study to mirror the work at the MHS/CJS interface. Here participants form interagency teams to explore where contradictions in the overlap between the MHS and CJS systems occur. The Scale of Organisational Integration (SOI) assessment tool (Ahgren and Axelsson, 2005) is also employed within these groups to articulate current levels of integration between services and the desired level of integration required to promote offender mental health. Participants then work in their interagency teams to co-produce a strategy and implementation plan to take back into practice to address these contradictions and move towards an optimum level of integration.

Continued

Table 14.2 Continued

Phase of training model	Content/mode of delivery
Graduated phase 3 Implementation of co-production of interagency strategic and implementation plans and continuous, facilitated learning opportunities to reflect, with support of peers from all agencies, on these plans as well as individual collaborative practices and partnerships.	Action learning sets are set up between the teams formed in the Intensive phase 2 of the training. Action learning sets are scheduled for short periods (e.g. a couple of hours) across an extended period (e.g. a year). Here participants discuss personal development of collaborative competencies as individuals. They also explore the progress of any strategies designed and implemented as part of the Intensive phase 2 of the training that aimed to resolve contradictions with the overlapping system or achieve optimum integration between services. Authentic learning opportunities are also introduced during this phase that may include a portfolio of shadowing, placements, visits and case conferences.

each team should be explored in terms of the effectiveness of these plans in reducing contradictions between services and achieving optimal levels of integration between them. Last but certainly not least, the impact on offender mental health in the longer term should be assessed.

Conclusion

Collaborative practice is an essential skill required of professionals in both the MHS and CJS if they are to work together in such a way that offenders who cross MHS /CJS boundaries do not fall into the grey gaps between services that leads to poor mental health outcomes and reoffending. It is also essential to realising policy and practice developments which have followed from the Bradley Report (see Durcan et al., 2014). Although training in collaborative practice is currently undersupplied, despite the demand for these skills, there is a wide range of approaches to training in collaborative practice available. These warrant further support and development. Training of this type must take into account a systems-level approach where the position of the individual professional within the wider organisational systems can be viewed, and viewed as a function of the interaction between the individual and the components of these systems. Training must also look at a micro level of analysis, building good interpersonal relationships between professionals within the MHS and CJS. It is important at this level that that the outcomes of collaborative practice training for each professional are clearly articulated and there is opportunity now to transfer and adapt the well-developed competency frameworks developed elsewhere to the MHS and CJS training setting. A balance must be achieved, however, between the outcomes of training and how to achieve this: processes framed by various adult learning approaches including action learning must be kept in mind in achieving these goals. If this is achieved, and training of this form is commissioned by local and national bodies, the MHS and CJS workforce will be better able to work collaboratively in the interest of reducing mental ill health in the offender population. The proposed triple-phase model of collaborative training is a step in this direction.

References

Adamson, K. (2011). *Interprofessional Empathy in an Acute Healthcare Setting*. Wilfrid Laurier University, unpublished thesis.

Ahgren, B., and Axelsson, R. (2005). Evaluating integrated health care: a model for measurement. *International Journal of Integrated Care*, 5, e03–e09.

Barr, H. (2002). *Interprofessional Education: Today, Yesterday and Tomorrow*. London: LTSN – Centre for Health Sciences and Practice.

Bishop, V. (2007). *Clinical Supervision in Practice*, 2nd edition. Basingstoke: Palgrave McMillan.

Bradley, Lord (2009). *The Bradley Report*. London: Department of Health.

Carpenter, J., and Hewstone, M. (1996). Shared learning for doctors and social workers: Evaluation of a programme. *British Journal of Social Work*, 26, 239–257.

Charles, M., and Horwath, J. (2009). Investing in Interagency Training to Safeguard Children: An Act of Faith or an Act of Reason? *Children and Society*, 23 (5), 364–376.

Coyle, A. (2005). *Understand Prisons: Key Issues in Policy and Practice*. New York: Open University Press.

Interprofessional Education Collaborative Expert Panel (IECEP) (2011). *Core Competencies for Interprofessional Collaborative Practice*. Washington, D.C.: Interprofessional Education Collaborative.

Department of Health and Welfare (2013). *Morgendagens omsorg: Norwegian Government White Paper no. 29*. Norway: Helse og Omsorg Departement.

Department of Health (2001). *Working together – learning together: A framework for lifelong learning for the NHS*. London: Department of Health.

Dickinson, C. and Carpenter, J. (2009). 'Contact is not enough': an intergroup perspective on stereotypes and stereotype change. In I. Colyer, H. Helme, and M. Jones (ed.). *The Theory-Practice Relationship in Interprofessional Education*. London: Higher Education Academy.

Durcan, G., Saunders, A., Gadsby, B., and Hazard, A. (2014). *The Bradley Report five years on*. London: Centre for Mental Health.

Engestrom, Y. (2001). Expansive learning at work: towards an activity theoretical reconceptualisation. *Journal of Education and Work*, 14, 133–156.

European Commission (2013). *Guide to social innovation*. Brussels: European Commission.

Fazel, S., and Baillargeon, J. (2011). The health of prisoners. *Lancet*, 377 (9769), 956–965.

Fazel, S. and Danesh, J. (2002). Serious mental disorder in 23000 prisoners: a systematic review of 62 surveys. *Lancet*, 359 (9306), 545–550.

Frenk, J., Chen, L., Bhutta, Z., Cohen, J., Crisp, N., Evans, T.,...Zurayk, H. (2010). Health professionals for a new century: transforming education to strengthen health systems in an interdependent world. *Lancet*, 376 (9756), 1923–1958.

Freshwater, D, Cahill, J, Walsh, E, et al. (2012). Art and science in health care: Pushing at open doors or locked in institutions? *Qualitative Health Research*, 22 (9), 1176–1183.

Greiner, A.C. and Knebel, E (2003). *Health Professions Education: A Bridge to Quality*. Institute of Medicine. Washington DC.

Hammick, M. (1998). Interprofessional education: Concept, theory and application. *Journal of Interprofessional Care*, 12, 323–332.

Hean, S., Craddock, D. and Hammick, M. (2012a). Theoretical insights into interprofessional education. *Medical Teacher*, 34 (2), 158–160.

Hean, S., Heaslip, V., Warr, J. and Staddon, S. (2011). Exploring the potential for joint training between legal professionals in the criminal justice system and health and social care professionals in the mental-health services. *Journal of Interprofessional Care*, 25 (3), 196–202.

Hean, S., Staddon, S., Clapper, A., Fenge, L.-A., Jack, E. and Heaslip, V. (2012b). *Interagency training to support the liaison and diversion agenda*. Bournemouth, UK: Bournemouth University and SW Offender Health.

Hean, S., Warr, J. and Staddon, S. (2009a). Challenges at the interface of working between mental health services and criminal justice system. *Medicine, Science and the Law*, 49 (3), 170–178.

Hean, S., Warr, J., Heaslip, V. and Staddon, S. (2009b). *Final report: Evaluation of the South West Mental Health Assessment and Advice Pilot.* Bournemouth: Bournemouth University and SW Offender Health.

Kennedy, I. (2001). *Learning from Bristol: the report of the public inquiry into children's heart surgery at the Bristol Royal Infirmary 1984–1995.* London: Department of Health.

Laming, L. (2003). *The Victoria Climbie Report.* London: Department of Health.

McGill, I., and Brockbank, A. (2004). *The Action Learning Handbook.* Abingdon: RoutledgeFalmer.

Menzies-Lyth, I. (1988). *Containing Anxiety in Institutions: Selected Essays (Vol. 1).* London, UK: Free Association Books.

Ministry of Justice and Department of Health (2011). *Working with personality disordered offenders: A practitioners guide.* London: Ministry of Justice and Department of Health.

National Collaboration for Integrated Care and Support (2013). *Integrated Care and Support: Our Shared Commitment.* London: National Collaboration for Integrated Care and Support.

Nurse, J., Woodcock, P. and Ormsby, J. (2003). Primary care within prisons : focus group study. *BMJ,* 327 (August), 1–5.

Orchard, C. A. and Bainbridge, L. A. (2010). *A National Interprofessional Competency Framework.* Vancouver: Canadian Interprofessional Health Collaborative.

Pakes, F. and Winstone, J. (2009). Effective Practice in Mental Health Diversion and Liaison. *Howard Journal of Criminal Justice,* 48 (2), 158–171.

Patsios, D. and Carpenter, J. (2010). The organisation of interagency training to safeguard children in England: a case study using realistic evaluation. *International Journal of Integrated Care,* 10. http://www.ijic.org/index.php/ijic/article/view/548

Reynolds, Scott and Austin, W. (2000). Nursing, empathy and perception of the moral. *Journal of Advanced Nursing,* 32, 235–242.

Schon, D. A. (1987). *Educating the Reflective Practitioner.* San Francisco: Jossey-Bass.

Vygotsky, L. (1978). *Mind in Society.* Cambridge, MA: Harvard University Press.

Walsh, E. (2009). Partnership work with health professionals in segregation units, *Prison Service Journal,* January, No 181, 34–36.

Walsh, E. and Bee, A. (2012). Developing a Learning Environment in Prison Health Care. *International Practice Development Journal,* 2 (1) [6], 1–15.

Walsh, E., Dilworth, S. and Freshwater, D. (2007). *Establishing Clinical Supervision in Prison Health Care Settings: Phase Three, A report for Offender Health, Department of Health.* Bournemouth: Bournemouth University.

Walsh, E., Forsyth, K., Senior, J., O'Hara, K. and Shaw, J. (2014). Undertaking action research in prison: Developing the Older Prisoner Health and Social Care Assessment and Plan. *Action Research,* 12 (2), 136–150.

Walsh, C. L., Gordon, M. F., Marshall, M., Wilson, F. and Hunt, T. (2005). Interprofessional capability: a developing framework for interprofessional education. *Nurse Education in Practice,* 5 (4), 230–237.

Westley, F. (2010). Making a Difference Strategies for Scaling Social Innovation for Greater Impact. PhD Candidate. *Planning,* 15 (2), 1–19.

Wilhelmsson, M., Pelling, S., Uhlin, L., Dahlgren,O., Faresjö,T. and Forslund, K. (2012). How to think about interprofessional competence: A metacognitive model. *Journal of Interprofessional Care,* 26 (2), 85–91.

World Health Organization (2005). *Mental health and prisons: Information Sheet.* 1–6. Retrieved from http://www.who.int/mental_health/policy/mh_in_prison.pdf

World Health Organization (2010). *Framework for Action on Interprofessional Education and Collaborative Practice.* Geneva: WHO.

15
Psychological Jurisprudence: Problems with and Prospects for Mental Health and Justice System Reform

Bruce A. Arrigo and Heather Y. Bersot

Introduction

Critical scholars working at the intersection of mental health and criminal justice continue to raise concerns about the embedded socio-cultural dynamics that underlie, inform and shape institutional (and community) levels of service delivery (e.g., Allan et al., 2009; Dobransky, 2014; Fox et al., 2009). These dynamics typically construct and limit the identities of various offender groups or other stakeholders (Arrigo et al., 2011), specify and restrict the form and function of legitimate treatments (Polizzi et al., 2014a; see Mathews, this volume), and regulate and enforce programmatic compliance through methods of bureaucratic efficiency and/or measures of disciplinary control (Crewe, 2009; Rhodes, 2004). We submit that responding to crime and reforming through treatments that further these dynamics are clinically problematic. Indeed, as we have demonstrated elsewhere, maintaining these *relations of humanness* is habitually totalising because they engender the power to harm (e.g., Arrigo, in press; Bersot and Arrigo, 2010; Sellers and Arrigo, 2009). This is the power to reduce and repress the humanity of everyone involved given that the institutional realities outlined above are based on and sustained by processes of intensifying dehumanisation and depersonalisation (see Mathews, this volume). Those impacted by these processes include the kept (the imprisoned) and those on whom confinement depends (the collective keepers of the kept). Currently, the condition of this relationship (and the struggle to be human within and throughout it) signals that we are living in and among a 'society of captives' (Arrigo, 2013, p. 672; see also Sykes, 1958).

Captivity extends to and governs over many. Examples include those who criminally offend and those who are civilly confined (see Mathews, this volume); those who administer clinical treatments and those who provide other corrective services; those who legislate, lobby for and regulate punishments and those who discuss, monitor and absorb information about the same. Sustaining this condition of shared captivity or *totalising confinement* increasingly makes inconceivable, unknowable and immaterial alternative relations of humanness (Arrigo, in press). These are forms of human relating that communicate a different humanity; a humanity that could be more restorative and could become more transformative for the kept and for their collective keepers (Arrigo and Milovanovic, 2009).

Accordingly, in this chapter, we examine the above outlined concerns by presenting and discussing a number of concepts central to the critical philosophy of psychological jurisprudence (PJ) (for an overview, see Arrigo, 2004; Arrigo et al., 2011). As we argue, PJ helps to account for the response (to crime) and reform (through treatment) problem operating at the intersection of criminal justice policy and mental health service delivery. Thus, this chapter explains why institutional change is all too frequently unimaginable, and it describes how such conceptualised progress could be made more realisable for a 'people to come' (Deleuze and Guattari, 1994, p.108). The selected concepts under review include: (1) the relations of humanness; (2) the management of risk; (3) the jurisprudence of the mind; (4) the politics of subjectivity; (5) the microphysics of power; (6) the society of captives; and (7) the technologies of human excellence. These notions are examined within PJ's framework of socio-cultural diagnostics, and the framework consists of several core assumptions, operating principles and practice components.

PJ and its core assumptions

PJ is a philosophy about the ongoing project or risk of being human in contemporary society. This is the risk of living one's humanity as much or as fully as possible (i.e., ever more virtuously, excellently, productively) in all of one's relationships (Aristotle, 1976; Levinas, 2004), and the struggle to dwell habitually within this potentially restorative and transformative reality (Deleuze, 1983). As clinical diagnosis, PJ probes the conditions that deny and limit (or affirm and free) this humanness. Stated differently, PJ evaluates the relations of humanness that members of a society or group inhabit. By 'inhabiting' we mean the space of exchange, protocols and presence in which each of us pre-reflexively resides as we fulfil the duties or pursue the interests of our routine roles and/or statuses (e.g., as psychiatrist, incarcerated offender, correctional administrator; as parent, teacher, student). This is the micro-sociological space of communicative intra (within) and inter (between) action (Garfinkel, 1967; see also Laing, 1983), and it consists of signs and symbols (Lacan, 1977, 1981), codes and texts (Derrida, 1973, 1977, 1978), and customs and practices (Foucault, 1965, 1973, 1977). These influences on the relations of humanness often go unnoticed but, nonetheless, they do impact the ritualised construction and normalised version of relating that governs our social affairs and the project (and progress) of being ever more fully human. To be clear, the history of correctional psychiatry does not indicate much success with growing palliative interventions. Curatives and correctives advanced by the logics of moral treatment, public hygiene, deinstitutionalisation and managed care have not been persuasive, especially with respect to humanising the offender beyond psychological assessment schemas and diagnostic classification systems (Arrigo and Trull, in press).

As a philosophical critique and as a socio-cultural diagnosis, PJ is composed of several core assumptions. Chief among these are the following three: (1) *how* we are human is a choice; (2) our choice-making is influenced by dynamic and mostly pre-conscious cultural forces, and (3) foreclosing or growing the relations of humanness depends on how we choose to manage human risk (i.e., living ever more fully, or as virtuously, productively, authentically as possible). These assumptions are reviewed in brief below.

To suggest that our humanity is a choice is to argue that existence precedes essence (Sartre, 1956). In other words, the choices that we make in our interactions with others – whether as mental health clinicians, correctional administrators, offenders in custody, community service providers, etc. – tell us a great deal about who we are or who we could become (see Mathews, this volume). This view does not dismiss biologically derived or trait-based theories of psychological or moral development (Nietzsche, 1966, 1968). Instead, the notion that our existence precedes our essence indicates that, mindful of how such variables as genetic history or personality predisposition establish important human parameters for each of us, our relations of humanness emerge from how any one of us chooses to be and chooses to interact with others in various situations and/or settings. Our humanity is never reducible to the categories and taxonomies into which we are inserted and out of which we perceive, choose and act (see Mathews, this volume). If our 'awaiting' humanity is to be seized upon, mobilised and unleashed, then the relations of humanness that grow restoration and deepen transformation can only originate outside of such static cognitive maps and summary representations. Thus, status-limiting identifiers such as 'patient', 'criminal', 'mentally disordered offender' and 'desistor' are problematic in that they populate the current humanising space of recognition, insight and change. This is the harm-intensifying space into and out of which the choices of treatment and recovery are reasoned and reached (Arrigo, 2013). When the nature of our relational humanness is understood to be a choice, then every micro-sociological aspect of intra/inter-relating (e.g., exchanging, protocoling, presenting) can be the subject of examination. Indeed, choice-making blankets, and is inexorably linked to, all of our communicative intra/ interactions. What is studied and diagnosed are the choices made in instances of ritualised communication with another person or group (Goffman, 1961, 1963). These moments occur in many contexts: in therapy between the forensic psychologist and the criminal offender, in critical incident debriefings between prison administrators and the press as an extension of the public, in release (or discharge) planning between treatment advocates and community service providers. This is the critique and diagnosis of human subjectivity or the social person as a communicative intra/inter-actor or relator.

How can we diagnose the condition or status of human subjectivity as manifested through our choice-making? For PJ, the answer is sourced in an assessment of how the relations of humanness are culturally and constitutively formed. The structuring or formation of human relatedness consists of very active, porous and pre-conscious forces that populate a society, collective or group's communicative affairs. These micro-forces include the influence that consumerism, politics and technology exercise in normalising some and marginalising (even ceremonially degrading) other forms of human relating (Garfinkel, 1956). These micro-forces are found in and among civil commitment hearings, pre-trial competency evaluations, custody classification reviews, parole board hearings and post-sentencing planning panels. These settings and contexts exemplify how human relatedness is ritualised, normalised, marginalised and, in some instances, even degraded through scripted and choreographed institutional logics. The force of these logics extends to the kept as well as to their collective keepers. To put this notion in the form of an illustrative question: how, and to what extent, does the psychologist exchange signs and symbols (i.e., cognitive representations) that reflect the mentally disordered offender's (and the therapist's) humanity and dignity when engaged in forensic treatment? The consumption of and interaction through (the offender's) humanity and dignity is a choice that clinicians can (and should) make.

Politics refers to how the choice-maker thinks about and speaks of/to the interlocutor. To put this point in the form of an illustrative question: how, and to what extent, does the psychologist dialogue and reason through protocols (i.e., narratives) that honour the mentally disordered offender's humanity and dignity when completing a forensic assessment or other psycho-legal report? The protocols of treatment, recovery and re-entry are a choice that clinicians can (and should) make.

Technology refers to how the choice-maker acts to restore and/or to transform the interlocutor. To put this idea in the form of an illustrative question: how, and to what extent, does the psychologist utilise best practices and therapeutics that build upon and endorse the science of human dignity, compassion and respect (i.e., methods and measures of co-habitable change) when treating mentally disordered offenders? The tools of therapy, insight, recovery, etc., are a choice that clinicians can (and should) make.

Consumerism (how the choice-maker perceives the interlocutor in consciousness), politics and technology structure all relations of humanness, and their influencing force and micro-sociological forms further a cultural diagnosis about the condition of human subjectivity as found within a given group, collective and/or society.

For PJ, the project of being human and of dwelling ever more routinely within the space of human excellence and virtue is a function of *risk management*. What is managed is the risk of relating another way; a way that is different (e.g., more authentic, more transparent, more 'in the moment') from how we typically undertake our communicative rituals. Relating through risk constitutes a process of awareness or mindfulness in which the communicative intra/interaction (i.e., sign and symbols, dialogue and reasoning, customs and practices; see Canton, this volume) when assembled as such constitutes a different response to crime, a different pathway to reform and, consequently, a different humanity. Inhabiting this difference (i.e., in conscious perception, routine protocols, and best practices and therapeutics) is risky because it depends on the choice (we make or not) to honour and affirm the interlocutor's humanity and dignity unconditionally, even in the absence of unconditional reciprocity and regardless of the existence fashioned by the other's choice-making (Rogers, 1976). In this regard, one's being (and becoming) is never finalised (Bakhtin, 1982).When this difference fills the space of our ritualised communicative intra/interactions, then the risk of being human (e.g., as a correctional officer, forensic clinician, service provider, governmental official, peer-group member, parent or teacher) is for the sake of unleashing relational human capital or untapped shared potential. This is the potential to be otherwise; that is, to make different choices about how we will exchange, dialogue and reason, and be present in various contexts. When we relate through this risk as a habit of character or as a more fully lived expression of our otherwise unharnessed dynamism, then the communicative rituals that follow offer us the nearest promise for overcoming the growing problem of being's captivity in contemporary society; the mounting captivity of co-habited (i.e., collective and interdependent) human existence. Prospects for overcoming this increasingly dehumanising and depersonalising existence extend to the kept and to their collective keepers. The manifestation of these relations of humanness and the cultural forces necessary to sustain them constitute a system of service delivery in offender therapy and a system of justice policy in correctional treatment that awaits conceptualisation and composition (see Canton, this volume).

PJ's operating principles

PJ examines the project of being human. This includes choice-making, the forces that influence this humanity, and the risk on which the relations of humanness depend for any given collective or social group. PJ does this by diagnosing the condition of three cultural forces that influence the microstructure and quality of human relating. These forces include the trade in signs and symbols (i.e., the realm of cognitive representation, consumption and exchange), the performativity of texts and codes (i.e., the realm of certified narratives, dialogue and reasoning), and the making of customs and practices (i.e., the realm of presentation, relational restoration and transformation). When the forms that these culturalising micro-forces take are communicatively ritualised (e.g., reproduced and reenacted), then they (these ritualised forms) fill the space of ongoing human relating or communicative intra/interaction. Three operating principles from PJ (described below) help to diagnose the status of being ever more human, the struggle to grow this humanity, and the conditions (that is, the status of being human given how the space of communicative intra/interaction currently is populated and configured) within and through which the risk of being human takes place. These operating principles include: (1) the jurisprudence of the mind; (2) the politics of subjectivity; and (3) the microphysics of power.

The jurisprudence of the mind

The manifestation of our humanity depends on the choices that we make. This includes the cognitive representations that we choose to govern our own perceptions, the protocols and narratives that we select to define the parameters of our contextualised human relationships, and the methods and measures of co-habitable change that we construct and/or utilise to live best with others inter-relationally, institutionally and communally. In the lexicon of PJ, the above-mentioned 'governance' is a reference to the *jurisprudence of the mind* and the influence that it (this mindfulness) wields in communicative intra/interaction. This influence and governance emerge from the dominant or preferred forms that one's cognitive representations and exchanges assume in consciousness. The mind's jurisprudence, or the signs and symbols that saturate conscious perception, is derived from the laws of the unconscious. The mapping of the unconscious is limitless; however, the signs and symbols that we choose to consume, exchange and ritualise (i.e., to trade in) tell us a great deal about the topography that governs our unconscious (see Lacan, 1977, 1981).

For example, when one considers criminogenic terms such as 'drug user', 'sexually violent predator', or 'mentally ill offender', a picture is registered in one's mind consisting of certain aesthetic qualities ascribed to that particular offender type (see Canton, this volume). In these instances, the images that are formed stem solely from or otherwise depend on the knowledge of a person's addiction(s), transgression(s) and/or disorder(s). Relational exchanges communicated through these cognitive representations perceive (i.e., sign and symbolise) the dignity and the humanity of the 'criminogenic' other (Crewe, 2013).

As such, the mind's jurisprudence is incomplete. When 'cognitive distortions' such as these are reproduced and re-enacted in consciousness, then harmful (i.e., reductive and repressive) perceptions of, for and about human relating prevail (see McGuire, this volume). This harm extends throughout the project of being human, and it (this harm) thwarts untapped opportunities for what could be more genuine connectivity, restorative healing and mutual flourishing in ritualised moments of exchange.

The politics of subjectivity

According to PJ, our communicative rituals also depend, in part, on the narratives (i.e., the dialogue and reasoning) that define the contours of our contextualised human relationships. In the lexicon of PJ, these narratives are a reference to the *politics of subjectivity*, and the influence that preferred systems of narration (e.g., the language of law, prison argot, codes of professional conduct) exert in communicative intra/interaction (Sykes, 1958). This influence follows from the cognitive representations that govern the mind's jurisprudence. When this jurisprudence is spoken or written, then the trade in signs and symbols become performative. The performances that follow are the certified texts or codes of human relating (e.g., in therapy between forensic psychologists and criminal offenders), the authorised account of human affairs (e.g., in critical incident debriefings between prison administrators and the general public), and the official history of ritualised discourse and reasoning (in responding to crime and in reforming punishments for the kept and by their collective keepers).

PJ considers how these constructed narratives are (or might be) flawed (e.g., fragmented, incomplete or otherwise unfinished), and it examines how these performances limit the dignity and/or deny the humanity of all parties in ritualised exchanges, protocols and presentations within the relations of humanness (see Mathews, this volume). Thus, the performances that we select tell us a great deal about the potentially therapeutic (i.e., reformative and transformative) landscape of our speech, our writing and our self-and-other textmaking (Derrida, 1973, 1978). Summarising how this intra/inter-relational state of affairs disturbingly populates the prison milieu, Polizzi et al. (2014a, p. 4) noted,

> Current attitudes in corrections and offender treatment, and the policy initiatives these evoke, reveal an underlying set of negatively defined socially constructed meanings about offenders that effectively contradict and undercut any superficial [let alone detailed] discussion about the benefits of rehabilitation, re-entry, or restorative justice practices. It is very difficult to envision what successful work in corrections, offender psychotherapy, or rehabilitation would actually look like in such an environment. Successful

work with offender populations will be difficult to achieve without first thoroughly addressing the way in which these socially-generated definitions, concerning who and what the offender is, both restrict and actually prevent the type of success the criminal justice [and mental health] system[s] appear willing to pursue.

The microphysics of power

Following PJ, our communicative rituals also depend, in part, on the methods for and measures of co-habitable change that we construct and/or utilise in order to further our inter-relational, institutional and communal human affairs. These methods and measures consist of the protocols of discourse and reasoning that each of us develops, lives, shares and routinises. They (these protocols) represent a body of knowledge, and when this knowledge is acted on, disseminated and reproduced it makes evident our intra/inter-relational histories. These are the histories of discourse and reasoning presented and taken up as a code of (ethical) comportment, of 'how to be', in ritualised relations of humanness (see Canton, this volume). This discourse and reasoning exhibit the power to inscribe our humanity through the establishment of customs and practices. In the lexicon of PJ, the influencing force of these customs and practices is a reference to the *microphysics of power* (Foucault, 1973, 1977). This is the power to make, act on or alter the relations of humanness through forms of inhabitable (i.e., exchangeable, dialogical, presentable) communicative intra/interaction. However, when the dialogue and reasoning, and the signs and symbols, of this power are foreclosed, forestalled or fragmented, then the project of being human will always be less than what it could be or could become. In the extreme, this is the presentation of the social person as a 'docile' body, a body of 'abject utility', a 'mere functionary of the state' (Foucault, 1977, p. 210). Under these conditions, the possibilities of co-habiting the space of growing change (i.e., emergent relational restoration and transformation) is reduced to fixed exchanges (methods) and finite declarations (measures) of customised and formulaic relations of humanness.

This problem of docility is particularly prescient in offender therapy. The locus of change is often externalised and dependent on the use of a range of industry apparatuses. These include devices, instruments and mechanisms that represent the standard for promoting best treatment practices and therapeutics. These assembled technologies (and the discourse and reasoning that breathe meaning and vitality into them), then, constitute a schema of knowledge; a regime of truth. As methods for and measures of co-habitable change, these industry apparatuses fill the space in which the social person (e.g., the mental health therapist, the correctional officer and the criminal offender) dwells, makes meaning, chooses to act and exists. As a practical matter, however, these technologies and their bio-power can only further status quo dynamics (customs) or equilibrium conditions (practices) such that the norms of utility, efficiency and obedience prevail (Arrigo, 2013). This ordering of human existence follows as such because the methods for and measures of change ceremonially empiricise the prediction of dangerousness, the management of disease and the treatment of disorder. Thus, making and then developing technologies of the self (i.e., the industries of human capital) remain inactive and undone while technologies of the marketplace (i.e., the rehabilitative machine) prevail uninterrupted. When the imperatives of evidence-based corrections and solution-focussed change increasingly depend on apparatuses that manufacture engineered selves derived largely from habitualised inventories and checklists to further, at best, fabricated relations of humanness, then prospects for ritualising ever more authentic recovery and for co-habiting ever more mutual transformation are regrettably thwarted (Polizzi et al., 2014b). Indeed, excessive reliance on these marketplace technologies can only ritualise customs and practices that undo personal, institutional and even structural change for the kept and their collective keepers. This, then, is the ruin of human potential; the foreclosing of being more vital in ritualised moments of our intra/inter-existences. To be clear, this absent or deferred body of knowledge is the awaiting (co-habitable) space of creativity, innovation, experimentation and risk.

The jurisprudence of the mind, the politics of subjectivity and the microphysics of power are three PJ operating principles that help to explain the condition or status of our relations of humanness in contemporary society. With respect to criminal justice policy and mental health treatment, we submit that the trade in signs and symbols are incomplete, that the therapeutic protocols in dialoguing and reasoning are fragmented, and that the making of restorative and transformative customs and practices (i.e., a science that grows and affirms human dignity) remains mostly and lamentably unmade (e.g., Arrigo, 2013; Bersot and Arrigo, 2010; Sellers and Arrigo, 2009; Trull and Arrigo, in press; see Canton, this volume). These harmful conditions populate the relations of humanness for the kept and for their collective keepers. The ritualised communicative exchanges, protocols and presentations that ensue both reproduce and re-enact power-to-harm cultural conditions. When the influencing force of these limit-setting and denial-imposing conditions gradually structure human relating, then *a society of captives* is made more immanent (Arrigo et al., 2011; Arrigo and Milovanovic, 2009).

In the philosophy of PJ, this socio-cultural diagnosis of captivity extends to those who criminally offend and to those who are civilly confined; to those who administer clinical treatments and to those who provide other corrective services; to those who legislate, lobby for and regulate punishments, and to those who discuss, monitor and absorb information about the same. This diagnosis is reached based on a micro-sociological assessment of the relations of humanness that increasingly structure our interpersonal, institutional and communal affairs. Under the debilitating conditions of this ritualised captivity, the forms that our communicative intra/interaction assume can only produce and re-enact responses to crime and reforms through treatment that (unwittingly) invalidate the project of being ever more fully human. The normalisation of this condition, then, is the manifestation of totalising confinement in which the subject of crime (the response/reform agenda) morphs into the crime of subjectivity, the harm of being less than who we could be or could become uniquely, collectively and ever more interdependently (Arrigo, in press).

According to PJ, overcoming the crime of subjectivity and a society of captives depends on whether we still choose to invest in human capital rather than the *summary* representations into which our human existences are reductively categorised and out of which we repressively exchange, dialogue and reason, and are present in ritualised human affairs. If so, we must choose to revolutionise the project of being human, choose to reconfigure the influences that micro-sociologically condition our communicative intra/interaction, and choose to revisit the restorative and transformative power of risk-taking in being human within ritualised moments of intra/inter-relating. Three PJ practices help to usher in this different humanity. These component practices include common-sense justice, therapeutic jurisprudence and restorative justice.

PJ and its component practices

In order to appropriately explain how PJ's three component practices help to advance the project of being human, it will be useful to diagram how PJ's operating principles function to establish a socio-cultural diagnosis about contemporary society's response-to-crime and reform-through-treatment agenda. Figure 15.1 depicts the processes of assessment on which PJ relies to reach a diagnosis about the relations of humanness given the current micro-structuring of ritualised communicative intra/interaction.

Figure 15.1 depicts three streams of clinical inquiry. These include the processes of: (1) consumption and exchange, (2) certification, and (3) inscription and presentation. The processual dynamics that are relevant to each stream should be evaluated independent of the other two but they (these processes) should also be understood to function in concert with one another. This view of inter-relational forces at work is consistent with PJ's underlying constitutive philosophy.

The process of consumption and exchange refers to the unconscious and conscious dynamics that prefigure perception. In order to access these dynamics, PJ considers how the mind's jurisprudence operates in ritualised encounters (e.g.,

The process of consumption and exchange

- Cognitive Representations
- Jurisprudence of the Mind
- Perception
- The Tradein Signs and Symbols
- Laws of the Unconscious

The processes of certification

- Protocols as Narratives
- Politics of Subjectivity
- Dialogue and Reasoning
- The Performativity of Texts & Codes
- Histories

The processes of inscription and presentation

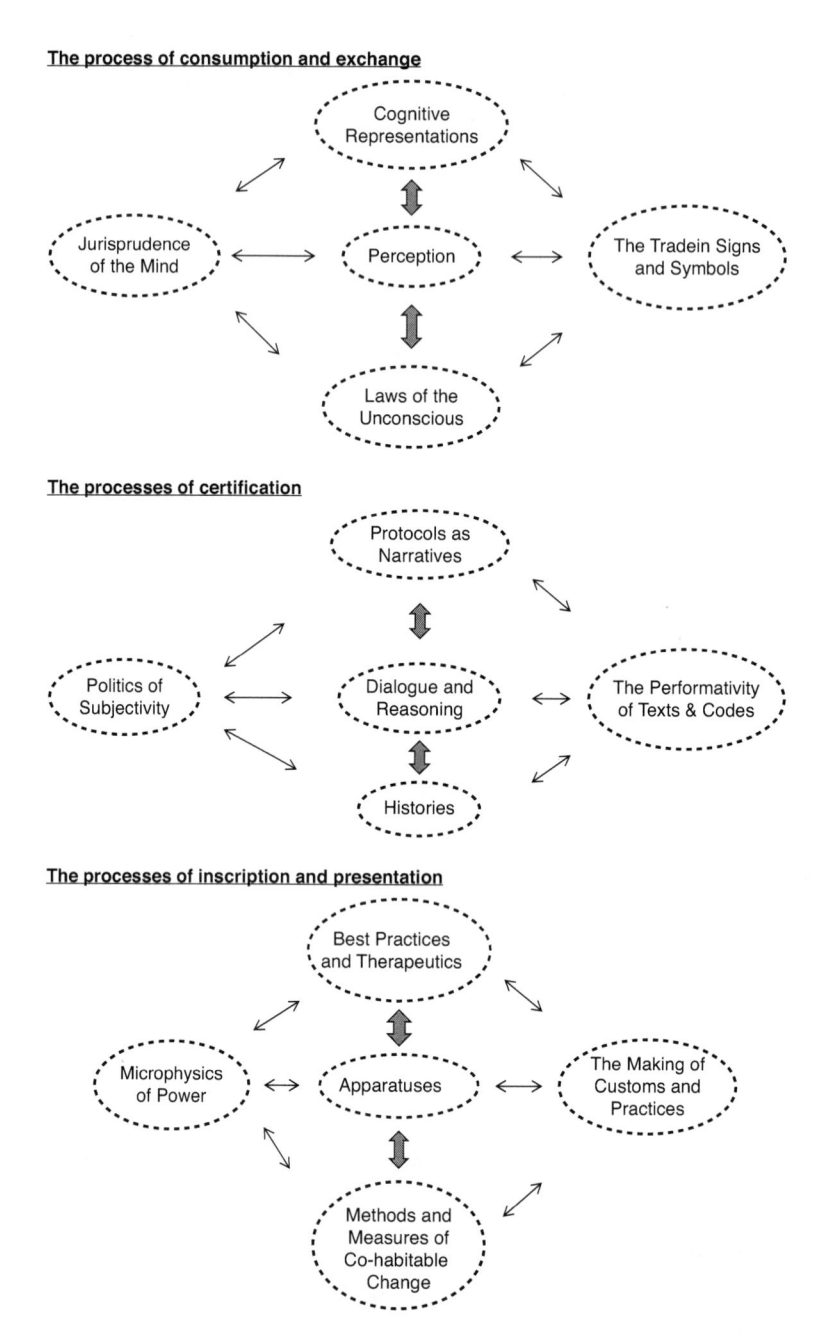

- Best Practices and Therapeutics
- Microphysics of Power
- Apparatuses
- The Making of Customs and Practices
- Methods and Measures of Co-habitable Change

Figure 15.1 Diagnosing the relations of humanness in ritualised communicative intra/interaction

in offender therapy as a forensic clinician). This governance is made evident by reviewing the images that dominate one's cognitive representations. Psychically trading in signs and symbols that form and re-form the criminogenic other does not advance the imaginative project of being more fully human for the kept or for their collective keepers. The process of certification refers to the unconscious and conscious dynamics that preconfigure dialogue and reasoning, making them into scripted protocols (i.e., performances). These protocols are the habit-forming codes and texts that narratively contextualise our ritualised human relationships. In order to evaluate these dynamics, PJ considers how the politics of subjectivity operates in ritualised moments of human relatedness. This politics is made apparent by examining the dialogue and reasoning that codify (i.e., legitimise) and historicise (i.e., routinise) one's protocols. Linguistically performing through texts and codes that frame and reframe the criminogenic other as diseased and disordered, or as deviant and dangerous, does not further the narrative project of being more fully human for the kept or for their collective keepers. The process of inscription and presentation refers to the unconscious and conscious dynamics that preconfigure our methods for and measures of co-habitable change. In order to review these dynamics, PJ considers how the microphysics of power operates to manufacture lived and shared customs and practices. This power is made obvious by surveying the apparatuses on which current practices (i.e., criminal justice policy) and therapeutics (i.e., mental health service delivery) are based. Physically relying on formulaic customs and simulated practices to ritualise human relatedness does not further the embodied project of being more fully human for the kept or for their collective keepers.

We contend that the influencing force of extant socio-cultural conditions establishes micro-forms of ritualised exchanges, protocols and presentations that grow a society of captives, and that replicate and re-enact the crime of subjectivity. How do we overcome these harmful intra/inter-relational processes of intensifying dehumanisation and depersonalisation? For PJ, the answer is simple. A series of choices need to be made. Overcoming requires novel image-crafting in correctional treatment and offender therapy, new vocabularies for and about responding to crime and reforming through treatment, and a nascent industry of restoration and transformation designed to more completely surmount the pains of imprisonment and to more fully realise virtuous, authentic and productive relations of humanness for a people yet to be.

In the philosophy of PJ, overcoming is understood to require unleashed will (i.e., the human potential of being) and harnessed way (i.e., the human possibility of becoming). When we exchange in, dialogue and reason through, and are present to these untapped dimensions of our dynamic humanity, then we have the nearest promise of revitalising (growing) the relations of humanness for any given group or collective – including the kept and their keepers. How can we increasingly inhabit this dynamic and yet-to-be-realised humanity, and how could these dynamics revitalise communicative intra/interaction for a society of captives?

In the lexicon of PJ, the will of being and the way of becoming constitute *technologies of human excellence*. The will of being is the dynamic power that follows when choosing to live differently (i.e., to be more authentic, more transparent) in all the moments of our existences within and throughout our (ritualised) relations of humanness. The potential of this unleashed power is intra/inter-relational restoration (i.e., the recovery of being, the rebuilding of our interpersonal, communal and even interdependent humanities). The way of becoming is the dynamic power that follows when choosing to channel our experience of restoration another way (i.e., more as a habit of character, more fully and productively in our lives). The possibility of this channelled power is intra/inter-relational transformation (i.e., overcoming how we ritually choose to be, and being 'otherwise' or ever more human in these intra/inter-relational moments). Unleashing and harnessing technologies of human excellence represent a socio-cultural revolution in the making. They (both unleashed will and harnessed way) constitute the project (and the promise) of unrealised human capital. They are risky precisely because of what they require from us – the release of our latent humanity (or more of it) in ritualised exchanges, protocols and presentations. Deploying the technologies of human excellence, then, is virtue's revolution actualised socio-culturally.

Commonsense justice, therapeutic jurisprudence and restorative justice (see Gatawa, this volume; Roger and Ormston, this volume) are three PJ practices that habitualise the technologies of human excellence. Our view of commonsense justice is derived from the work of Finkel (e.g., 1995). The average citizen's sense of fairness and decency, reasonableness and equality, etc., emerges from a common conscience, a shared story about right and wrong, and settled ways (measures and methods) by which to judge (e.g., to reach a verdict, to administer punishment and/or treatment). For Finkel, all of this is the administration of justice in action. We agree. However, for PJ the questions to be asked are as follows: which common conscience does each of us choose and what does it (this choice) reveal about our individual humanities as we visualise (i.e., sign and symbolise, cognitively re-present) the offender? Regrettably, in far too many instances and for far too many people, these visualisations convey less about who any of us is or could become. The current status of criminal justice policy and mental health service delivery makes this point both clear and compelling. Commenting on this status, Arrigo (2013, p. 687) noted the following:

> [W]hen psychiatrically disordered convicts are placed in long-term disciplinary isolation, how and for whom does this practice exhibit courage, compassion, and generosity? When criminally adjudicated sex offenders are

subsequently subjected to protracted civil commitment followed by multiple forms of communal inspection and monitoring, how and for whom is dignity affirmed, stigma averted, and healing advanced? When cognitively impaired juveniles are waived to the adult system, found competent to stand trial, and sentenced and punished accordingly, what version of nobility is celebrated and on whom is this goodness bestowed?

According to PJ, we need to restore and then to transform the common conscience as a pre-condition to this community administering its vision and version of visceral justice. This revolutionary work is the project of being ever more fully human in shared and communal intra/interaction as conceived in consciousness. The restoration and transformation that PJ has in mind, then, begins with choosing the project of reconceiving, rewriting and re-inscribing the relations of humanness, in order to be more fully human and to become otherwise than being in ritualised self-in-society affairs.

Our view of therapeutic jurisprudence is derived from the work of Winick and Wexler (e.g., 2003). They contend that the law can be an effective agent that heals and changes when the choices and actions of judges, attorneys and other legal professionals are guided by the human welfare of the parties in dispute. This is the administration of justice in action in which the salubrious and salutary effects of such decision-making ostensibly are limitless. Indeed, when the insights of therapeutic jurisprudence are in operation, then 'the law's potential for increasing [the] emotional well-being of the individual and society as a whole will [similarly] increas[e]' (Winick, 1997, p. 1). We agree. However, for PJ the questions to ponder are as follows: which therapeutic narratives are selected to advance the emotional well-being of participants in dispute; which version of healing, recovery, and/or change do these narratives endorse; and how does this rendering of justice certify (dignify and affirm) ever more so the humanity of all involved?

To be sure, the narrative performances that currently populate 'living with mental illness', or 'making good on one's desistance', or 'adopting the good lives model of recovery', offer well-intentioned responses to crime and reforms through treatment (see Göbbels, Thakker and Ward, this volume). However, this dialogue and reasoning often pre-reflectively codifies and historicises the status quo, including the political-economics (the industries and apparatuses) that empiricistically normalise, sanitise or correct the offender. Legitimising and routinising only these performances heals and helps based on fragmented depictions and finite declarations of being human. Much of our unrealised (i.e., unspoken, unwritten) humanness extends beyond the current parameters of dialogue and reasoning. Developing more authentic and productive protocols for and about mental illness, desistance, recovery, etc., awaits narration. Charting the therapeutics of this landscape requires a different jurisprudence.

Our view of restorative justice is derived from the work of Braithwaite (e.g., 1989, 2006). Ritualising a justice that is restorative (even transformative) in correctional treatment and rehabilitative therapy brings together the offender, victim and community in order to establish conditions for healing-focussed exchanges, dialogue and reasoning, and presentations. The intention of this communalising is reparative. The aim is to promote understanding, responsibility and forgiveness. The ritualised practice of restorative justice recognises that crime engenders harm (i.e., to self and others) and, as such, reparative interventions must be utilised in order to return participants to a state of moral equilibrium. We agree. However, for PJ the questions to consider are as follows: which tools of recompense are deployed to grow the space of change (i.e., restoration and change), and how do the communalising participants dwell (ever more humanly) within it? Regrettably, even the term 'restorative justice' has been manipulated to suit the ideological aims of managing offenders. As such, the promise of remediation and reconciliation strategies (e.g., victim–offender rehabilitative programming) increasingly is removed from its original intention (Polizzi et al., 2014b).

The technologies of human excellence are PJ's tools of reparative engagement. We maintain that ritualising a restorative (even transformative) justice built on being more virtuous, authentic, transparent and in the moment has the nearest power to grow mutual understanding, shared responsibility and genuine forgiveness. The human social injury that stems from drug abuse, sexual violence, untreated or undertreated mental illness, etc., warrants greater recognition and fuller expression within the mediation process. More completely owning our humanity (our choices) is pivotal to the success of this reintegrative enterprise. This includes the choice of how we respond to the pain of crime. We can suffer through it or we can soldier through it. The former does not grow anyone's humanity – least of all our own. The latter has the power to restore and to transform everyone. This is the power that follows, in the moment, when inhabiting the will of being and the way of becoming. These technologies affirm and dignify the healing human potential and possibility of each of us so that every one of us can overcome the injury of crime. When we dwell within this space, habit-transforming change more completely fills our relations of humanness.

Conclusions and summary

In this final, very brief portion of this volume, we wish to make clear that PJ's purpose is not to dismiss or to condemn the good work and steady progress made by well-meaning and evidence-based professionals who toil tirelessly on behalf of their clients' treatment needs and the public's general welfare. We refer to researchers who continue to do their very best to reach reasoned conclusions from work in their research settings; clinicians who characteristically exercise sound judgements in their institutional and community-based forensic assessment and treatment practices; or educators who thoughtfully instruct, train or otherwise mentor students in the complexities of criminal justice policy and mental health service delivery. Their efforts and accomplishments are worthy of respect.

That said, far too many of us are 'caught up' in our increasingly dehumanising and depersonalising relations of humanness. Our communicative intra/interaction rituals are less than what they could be and less than what they could become in our everyday relations of humanness. Indeed, captivity extends to the many that are both in and out of prison – the kept and their collective keepers. The harm of this captivity is socio-cultural. It includes the trade in sign and symbols (aesthetic harm, perceiving the other as criminogenic other, reduction and repression), the protocols of dialogue and reasoning (epistemological harm, the codifying and historicising of subjectivity's fragmentation), and the making of best practices (ethical harm, the formulas for and customising of bodies made docile). The ritualised reproduction and re-enactment of these micro-cultural forms signal the undoing of humanity, the forestalling and foreclosing of human relationships in terms of their awaiting progress and unrealised promise. Thus, something of a shift, a change, is in order.

In this volume, we have argued that the revolution begins at the micro-sociological level of analysis. In order to make this restorative and transformative metamorphosis more attainable, we need to take more risks and choose to be more human in our ritualised communicative intra/interactions. To put it plainly, then, we need to choose different images for and about mentally disordered offenders and those who police or manage them; we need to choose a different vocabulary for and about crime and punishment, law and disorder, desistance and recovery, and those who endeavour to treat, educate or correct; and we need to choose a different set of change-oriented and solution-focussed technologies that make being more fully human in our customs and practices how we prefer to be in moments of ritualised human relatedness. Seizing upon this difference begins with a philosophy that critiques the project of being human and a clinical diagnosis that explains the social-cultural conditions that limit and deny (or affirm and free) this humanness. We submit that the insights of PJ provide a platform for unleashing this difference and for harnessing this change. This difference is human capital for the kept, for their keepers, for a people yet to be.

References

Allan, J., Briskman, L. and Pease, B. (2009). *Critical social work: Theories and practices for a social justice world*. Sydney, Australia: Allen & Unwin.

Aristotle (1976). *Ethics*. Trans. J. A. K. Thomson. New York: Penguin.

Arrigo, B. A. (ed.) (2004). *Psychological jurisprudence: Critical explorations in law, crime, and society.* Albany, NY: SUNY Press.
Arrigo, B.A. (2013). Managing risk and marginalizing identities: On the society of captives thesis and the harm of social disease. *International Journal of Offender Therapy and Comparative Criminology,* 57, 6, 672–693.
Arrigo, B. A. (in press). Responding to crime: Psychological jurisprudence, normative philosophy, and trans-desistance theory. *Criminal Justice and Behavior,* 42, 1.
Arrigo, B. A., Bersot, H. Y. and Sellers, B. G. (2011). *The ethics of total confinement: A critique of madness, citizenship, and social justice.* New York: Oxford University Press.
Arrigo, B. A. and Milovanovic, D. (2009). *Revolution in penology: Rethinking the society of captives.* New York: Rowman and Littlefield.
Arrigo, B. A. and Trull, S. L. (in press). The history of imprisonment. In K. L. Appelbaum, J. L. Metzner and R. L. Trestman (eds.). *The Oxford textbook of correctional psychiatry.* New York: Oxford University Press.
Bakhtin, M. (1982). *The dialogic imagination: Four essays.* Austin: University of Texas Press.
Bersot, H. Y. and Arrigo, B. A. (2010). Inmate mental health, solitary confinement, and cruel and unusual punishment: An ethical and justice policy perspective. *Journal of Theoretical and Philosophical Criminology,* 2, 3, 1–82.
Braithwaite, J. (1989). *Crime, shame, and reintegration.* Cambridge, UK: Cambridge University Press.
Braithwaite, J. (2006). Doing justice intelligently in civil society. *Journal of Social Issues,* 62, 2, 393–409.
Crewe, B. (2009). *The prisoner society: Power, adaptation, and social life in an English prison.* Oxford: Oxford University Press.
Crewe, D. (2013). *Becoming criminal: The socio-cultural origins of law, transgression, and deviance.* Basingstoke: Palgrave Macmillan.
Deleuze, G. (1983). *Nietzsche and philosophy.* New York: Columbia University Press.
Deleuze, G. and Guattari, F. (1994). *What is Philosophy?* New York: Columbia University Press.
Derrida, J. (1973). *Speech and other phenomena.* Evanston, IL: Northwestern University Press.
Derrida, J. (1977). *Of grammatology.* Baltimore, MD: Johns Hopkins University Press.
Derrida, J. (1978). *Writing and difference.* Chicago, IL: University of Chicago Press.
Dobransky, K. M. (2014). *Managing madness in the community: The challenge of contemporary mental health care.* New Brunswick, NJ: Rutgers University Press.
Finkel, N. (1995). *Commonsense justice: Jurors' notions of the law.* Cambridge, MA: Harvard University Press.
Foucault, M. (1965). *Madness and civilization: A history of insanity in the age of reason.* New York: Vintage.
Foucault, M. (1973). *The order of things.* New York: Vintage.
Foucault, M. (1977). *Discipline and punish: The birth of a prison.* New York Pantheon.
Fox, D., Prilleltensky, I. and Austin, S. (eds.) (2009). *Critical psychology: An introduction,* 2nd edition. London: Sage.
Garfinkel, H. (1956). Conditions of successful degradation ceremonies. *American Journal of Sociology,* 61 (5), 420–424.
Garfinkel, H. (1967). *Studies in ethnomethodology.* Englewood Cliffs, NJ: Prentice-Hall.
Goffman, E. (1961). *Asylums: Essays on the social situation of mental patients and other Inmates.* Garden City, NY: Anchor Books.

Goffman, E. (1963). *Stigma: Notes on the management of spoiled identity*. New York, NY: Simon & Schuster.

Lacan, J. (1977). *Ecrits: A selection*. New York: W. W. Norton.

Lacan, J. (1981). *The four fundamental concepts of psychoanalysis*. New York, NY: W. W. Norton.

Laing, R. D. (1983). *The politics of experience*. New York, NY: Pantheon.

Levinas, E. (2004). *Otherwise than being*. Pittsburgh: Duquesne University Press.

Nietzsche, F. W. (1966). *Beyond good and evil: Prelude to a philosophy of the future* (new edition) (W. Kaufmann, ed.). New York: Vintage.

Nietzsche, F. W. (1968). *The will to power* (new edition) (W. Kaufmann, ed.). New York: Vintage Books.

Polizzi, D., Braswell, M., and Draper, M. (eds.) (2014a). *Transforming corrections: Humanistic approaches to corrections and offender treatment*. Durham, NC: Carolina Academic Press.

Polizzi, D., Draper, M. and Andersen, M. (2014b). Fabricated selves and the rehabilitative machine: Toward a phenomenology of the social construction of offender treatment. In B. A. Arrigo and H. Y Bersot (eds.). *The Routledge handbook of international crime and justice studies*. London: Routledge. 233–255.

Rhodes, L. (2004). *Total confinement: Madness and reason in a maximum security prison*. Berkeley: University of California Press.

Rogers, C. (1976). *On becoming a person*. New York: Houghton Mifflin.

Sartre, J. P. (1956). *Being and nothingness: A phenomenological essay on ontology*. New York: The Philosophical Library.

Sellers, B. G. and Arrigo, B. A. (2009). Adolescent transfer, developmental maturity, and adjudicative competence: An ethical and justice policy inquiry. *Journal of Criminal Law and Criminology*, 99, 2, 435–488.

Sykes, G. (1958). *Society of captives: A study of a maximum security prison*. Princeton, NJ: Princeton University Press.

Trull, L. S. and Arrigo, B. A. (in press). U.S. immigration policy and the 21st century conundrum of 'child-saving': A human rights, law and social science, political economic and philosophical inquiry. *Studies in Law, Politics, and Society*.

Winick, B. J. (1997). *Therapeutic jurisprudence applied: Essays on mental health law*. Durham, NC: Carolina Academic Press.

Winick, B. J. and Wexler, D. B. (eds.) (2003). *Judging in a therapeutic key: Therapeutic jurisprudence and the courts*. Durham, NC: Carolina Academic Press.

Index

Note: 'f' indicates figure, 't' indicates table.

21st century
  services, 24, 255
  thinking, 11–12

absolute rights, 31
abuse, 29, 34, 68, 119, 124, 132, 136, 137, 139
  childhood, 133, 140, 147
  domestic, 133, 135
  drug, 68, 124, 280
  physical, 135, 142
  sexual, 133, 134–135, 140, 142
  substance, *see* substance abuse
  at work, 201
action learning, 256, 257, 260
  definition, 257
  in prison health care settings, 257–259
  reflection between nurses and prison officers, 259–260
activity system framework, 249–252, 250f, 251f, 253f, 261t
addiction theory, 140
ADHD, *see* attention deficit hyperactivity disorder (ADHD)
Aggressive Behavioural Control (ABC), 61
alcohol, 151, 162
  abuse, 68, 133
  as coping means, 135
  dependency, 148, 153, 168
  misuse, 147, 156–157
  policy, 152
  services, 154
  use, 35, 148, 152, 157, 158, 190
  workers, 229
Alcohol Strategy, 152
alcoholism, 133, 137
All Party Parliamentary Group (APPG), 163
Allport, G., 99, 100
Alred, D., 74–77

American Psychiatric Association, 7, 68, 102, 105, 107, 115, 149, 184
Andrews, D. A., 53, 68, 76
Anthony Rice case, 7–8
anti-depressants, 21, 22, 23, 40
anti-psychotics, 21, 25
antisocial behaviour, 4, 56, 59, 60, 76, 80, 113–114, 116–117, 119, 120–121, 124, 126, 187
antisocial/dissocial personality diagnoses, 57, 58–59
antisocial pathological bias, 104
antisocial personality disorder (ASPD), 54–59, 103, 104, 107, 184, 188, 190
anxiety, 39, 51, 55, 101, 102, 103, 110t, 111–112, 117, 119, 132, 133, 134, 143, 193, 258
Appleby, J., 5, 17
Appropriate Medical Treatment Test, 10
Ashworth Hospital, 202
ASPD, *see* antisocial personality disorder (ASPD)
Asperger's syndrome, 91, 117
assessment
  actuarial, 9, 188
  clinical, 9, 193
  forensic, 9, 269, 281
  psychiatric, 22, 37, 39
  of risk, *see* risk assessment
Association of Chief Police Officers (ACPO), 93, 172, 207, 209, 211
attention deficit hyperactivity disorder (ADHD), 68, 112, 113, 116–117, 118, 119
attitudes, 21, 22, 96, 185, 195, 204, 215, 220, 245, 247, 272
  criminal, 76, 205
  to mental illness, 26, 28
  objective, 34, 35
  reactive, 34

autism, 68, 117
  see also Autistic Spectrum Disorder (ASD)
Autistic Spectrum Disorder (ASD), 21, 24, 68, 110t, 117
automatic life sentence, 171, 193
avoidant pathological bias, 103

Baird, G., 117
behaviour, 14–16, 33, 49–50, 73, 76, 97–98, 100, 103, 104, 114–117, 122, 123
  abnormal, 93, 102, 106
  antisocial, see antisocial behaviour
  attitudes to, 34
  bad/troublesome, 42, 57
  coping, 133
  criminal, 52, 58, 76, 78, 80, 81, 92, 94, 95, 107, 118, 136
  disruptive, 207
  maladaptive, 112, 133
  normal, 93, 102, 105, 106
  offending, see offending behaviour
  self-harming, 133, 137
  suicidal, 113
  violent, 55, 133, 203–205, 259
  of women, 138–139
behavioural control, 77, 114
behavioural difficulties, 114, 117, 123, 124
behavioural problems, 118, 152
Bell, C. C., 100, 102–104
Bennett, C., 34
Bentham, J., 154–155
Berkman, L. F., 81
bigotry, 93, 100, 101
bipolar disorder, 21, 23, 24, 54, 68, 103, 133–135
Blackburn, R., 77
Bloom, B., 136, 137, 139, 140
Bonta, J., 42, 53, 68, 76, 81, 82
borderline personality disorder (BPD), 56–58, 103
Bowling, B., 97, 98
Bradley, K. (Lord), 3–5, 7, 9, 11, 15, 156–157, 180, 203, 218
  see also Bradley Report (2009)
Bradley Commission, 157
Bradley Report (2009), 1–2, 3, 4, 123, 125, 148, 157, 167, 239, 242, 245, 263

Broadmoor Hospital, 15, 187, 201, 202, 203–204, 206, 210–215
Brown, A. R., 203, 204, 207, 210
Budge, S. L., 58

CARAT service (Counselling, Assessment, Referral, Advice and Through care), 152
CARE accredited programme, 138
Care Act (2014), 3
Care cluster, 16, 154
Care Programme Approach (CPA), 153
CBT, see cognitive-behavioural therapy (CBT)
Central and North West London NHS Foundation Trust, 169
Central Criminal Court, 10, 14, 167, 169, 178, 180–181
Central Criminal Court Mental Health Liaison Scheme, see Mental Health Liaison Scheme (MHLS)
Centre for Mental Health, 147, 153, 154
charity User Voice, 159
  see also service user(s), voice of
childhood
  abuse, 133, 140, 147
  ADHD, 116–117
  communication disorders, 116, 122
  neurodisability, 114, 124
  trauma, 104
  victimisation, 134
Choinski, M., 7
Christopher Clunis case, 10
CJLDs, see Criminal Justice Liaison and Diversion Schemes (CJLDs)
CJLNS, see criminal justice mental health nurses (CJLNs)
CJS, see criminal justice system (CJS)
claim rights, 28, 30
  good lives and, 42–43
Clarke, A. Y., 76
Clearwater programme, 61–62
Clinical Nurse Specialist, 167, 169
  assistance when defendant is fit to plead, 171–172
  communication with the Court, 173, 174–175, 177, 180–181
  as a facilitator, 170–177, 180–181
  liaison with defence, 172, 175, 177

Responsible Clinician and, 173, 175–177
   responsibilities when defendant is unfit to plead, 172–177
   role during post sentence of defendant, 180
   support to intermediaries, 178
   and transfer of defendant to hospital from prison, 178–180
   see also Crown Court
clinical recovery, 74–75
clinical supervision, 163
   definition, 257
   in prison health care settings, 257–259
Clunis, C., 10
CMHT, see Community Mental Health Team (CMHT)
cognitive-behavioural approach/strategies, 38, 76, 123, 188, 206
   see also cognitive-behavioural therapy (CBT)
cognitive-behavioural therapy (CBT), 51–52, 53, 57, 59, 76, 83, 138, 141f
collaborative competencies, 255–257, 256t
collaborative practice, 242–244
   enhanced, 244–245
   interdependence between education and, 246–248
   micro level approach to
     action learning, 257
     collaborative competencies, 255–257, 256t
     empathic relationships, 252–255
     examples of, 257–259
   outcomes of engagement between MHS/CJS systems, 247–248
   systems approach to
   activity system framework, 249–252, 250f, 251f, 253f, 261t
   social innovations, 248–249
   training for, 245–246
   see also training
Committee for the Prevention of Torture, 37
commonsense justice, 275, 278–279
communication disorders, 110t, 116, 122
Community Act (1990), 153
Community Mental Health Team (CMHT), 22–26
Community Rehabilitation Companies (CRC), 5
community voluntary organisations (CVOs), 220
community voluntary sector (CVS), 236
comorbidity, 14, 57, 68, 80, 118, 157
Comprehensive Health Assessment Tool (CHAT), 14, 122, 125
Comprehensive Screening and Assessment Tool, 14
conflict(s), 31, 99, 100, 101, 131, 135, 213, 224, 225, 250
convention rights, 31–32
Cornford, C., 156
courts, 2, 4, 6, 7, 9, 10–11, 14, 31, 32, 35–38, 40, 70, 74, 122, 125, 143, 157, 167
   see also Crown Court
Covington, S., 136, 137, 139, 140
CPS, see Crown Prosecution Service (CPS)
Crime and Disorder Act
   1997, 193
   1998, 93
   1999, 171
crime control models, 8–9
criminal behaviour, 52, 58, 76, 78, 80, 81, 92, 94, 95, 107, 118, 136, 201, 219
   hate as motivation for, 97–98
Criminal Justice Act (CJA) (2003), 3, 5, 7, 35, 42, 168
Criminal Justice Liaison and Diversion Schemes (CJLDs), 218, 220
   see also Sussex Criminal Justice Liaison and Diversion (SCJLD)
criminal justice mental health nurses (CJLNs), 219
Criminal Justice Referral–Decision Hierarchy, 214–215
criminal justice system (CJS), 3, 29, 82, 131, 158
   black and minority ethnic groups in, 9–10
   collaborative practice between MHS and, see collaborative practice; training
   co-production within, 158–160
   and the DSPD programme, see Dangerous and Severe Personality Disorder (DSPD) programme

criminal justice system (CJS) – *continued*
  dual diagnosis in, *see* dual diagnosis
  guidance and legislation for, 3–4
  and hate crime, 92, 98, 107
  health care in, 155
  health inequality in, 151
  interventions in, 52–53
  and mental health needs, 2–11, 38, 48–50, 77, 156–157, *see also* interventions
  prosecution of offenders in the, *see* prosecution
  rehabilitation in, 76–77
  rights of prisoners, 31–32
  RNR model in, 53–54
  and women, *see* women and mental health needs
  and young people, 111, 117, 119, 123, 125, *see also* young offenders
  see also Crown Court
Criminal Procedures and Insanity Act (1964), 175
criminal recidivism, 49, 52–53, 55, 56, 60, 76
Crown Court, 167, 168–169
  Central Criminal Court Mental Health Liaison Scheme, 169–170
  Experts, role in, 174–175, 178
  intermediaries for defendants, 177–178
  legal realities of, 170–171
  Nottingham, 208
  post sentence of defendant, 180
  responsibility of, 170
  transfer of defendant to hospital from prison, 178–180
  trial process
    fitness to plead, 171–172
    unfit to plead, 172–177
  see also Clinical Nurse Specialist
Crown Prosecution Service (CPS), 11, 93, 94, 171, 177, 206–211, 215, 235f
Crown Prosecution Service and Her Majesty's Court and Tribunal Service, 176
Cullen, A. E., 76, 77
custody time limits (CTL), 171
CVOs, *see* community voluntary organisations (CVOs)

CVS, *see* community voluntary sector (CVS)

Dangerous and Severe Personality Disorder (DSPD) programme, 1, 15, 41, 42, 206, 258
  criminological perspective of, 191–192
  criticisms of, 195
  developmental background of, 185–186, 194–195
  end of, 194
  ethical perspective of, 192
  implementation of, 188–189
  legal perspective of, 192–193
  legislative changes in, 186
  management of people with PD, 186–188
  'populist punitiveness' concept, 193
  positive aspects of, 195–196
  'precautionary logic' concept, 193
  prison sites in, 185, 187–189
  psychiatric perspective of, 189–191
  role of culture in, 195
Daniel M'Naghten case, 205
Dano Sonnex report, 8
data collection, 227f, 232t, 233, 236–238
Davis, M., 67–68
De Silva, M. J., 81
decisive momentum
  in MDOs, 72–75
  in ITDSO, 70–71
delusion, 36, 101, 102, 106, 111
democratic therapeutic community (DTC), 138–139
Department of Health, 3, 9, 15, 137, 148, 150, 153, 156, 157, 184, 186–188, 189, 192, 194, 201, 202, 218, 223, 236, 245, 246
depression, 22, 39, 40, 51, 52, 55, 57, 68, 78, 112–113, 119, 132–136, 142–143, 243
desistance, 13, 29, 42–43, 44, 67, 83
  ITDSO, 69, 70–72, 78, 79, 83
  in MDOs, 67–68, 79
    barriers to, 79–81
    decisive momentum, 72–75
    maintenance of, 81–82
    normalcy, 82–83
    recidivism in, 69–70

re-entry, 79–82
rehabilitation, 75–79
types of, 68–69
in youth crime research, 67
see also recovery
Diagnostic and Statistical Manual of Mental Disorders (DSM), 7, 54, 55, 102, 105, 106, 121
III, 149–150
IV, 57, 58, 117, 184, 188
V, 56, 58, 115, 158
discretionary life sentence, 192–193, 194
dissocial personality disorder, *see* antisocial personality disorder (ASPD)
diversion, 15, 29, 37, 38, 40
see also liaison and diversion initiatives
Doren, D. M., 60
Drake R., 150
Drennan, G., 74–77
driving while intoxicated (DWI), 59
drug(s)
abuse, 68, 124, 180, 280
addiction, 140, 148
'British System' of control, 152
courts, 157
dependency, 148, 153, 156, 168
illegal/illicit, 35, 74, 80, 117, 147, 151, 152
-induced disorders, 149–150
legislations, *see* Mental Health Act, 1983; Misuse of Drugs Act (1971)
psychotropic, 49
services, 154
strategies, 152, 157
therapies/intervention, 22, 23, 25, 30, 39, 142
users, 152, 156, 157, 158, 271
-using offenders, 67, 75, 132, 133, 135
workers, 148, 229
see also substance abuse; substance misuse
DrugScope, 154
Drug Strategy of 2010, The, 157
Drug Treatment Outcome Research Study (DTORS.org), 152
Drummond, E., 205
DSM, *see Diagnostic and Statistical Manual of Mental Disorders* (DSM)

DSPD, *see* dangerous and severe personality disorder (DSPD) programme
DTC, *see* democratic therapeutic community (DTC)
dual diagnosis, 147–149
case studies
ethical considerations, 161–162
PPI consultation, 160–161
co-production, 158–160
empowerment of service users, 158
legislations, 149, 151–154
less eligibility principle, 154–156
policy guides, 150
problems, 148, 156–157
sociopolitical determinants of, 151
strategies, policies and guidance, 149–151
training and education in, 162–163
see also Bradley Report (2009)
Duggan, C., 57
Dunbar, E., 100, 102–104
Duncan, E. A. S., 76
Duncan, J. C., 82
dyscalculia, 115
dyslexia, 115
dyspraxia, 115

EBTs, *see* evidence-based treatments (EBTs)
Edgington, N., 10–11
EFQM, *see* European Foundation for Quality Management (EFQM)
empathic relationships, 252–255
'empirically supported treatments' (ESTs), 52
engagement therapy, 73–74
Equality Impact Assessment (EIA), 238
escalation processes, 221f, 225–226
ESTs, *see* 'empirically supported treatments' (ESTs)
European Convention on Human Rights, 31, 41
European Court of Human Rights, 32, 36
European Foundation for Quality Management (EFQM), 226
evidence-based treatments (EBTs), 58
Expert Reports, 7, 173, 181

Expert Witnesses, 11
extended sentences, 193

Fazel, S., 55, 111, 113, 116, 119, 242, 243, 244
female offender, *see* offender(s), female
Ferguson, A., 69
Ferguson, G., 78
Filer, N., 34
Fisher, W. H., 68, 75, 80, 84
fitness to plead, 171–172
  see also Clinical Nurse Specialist, assistance when defendant is fit to plead
forensic assessment, 9, 269, 281
forensic mental health services, 54, 58
forensic psychiatry, 33–34
Framework for Action on Interprofessional Education and Collaborative Practice, 244
Full Code test, 209, 210
functional recovery, 75
Fundamental Freedoms, 31

Gannon, T. A., 71, 72, 78, 79
Garland, D., 29, 41
Gaylin, W., 95, 96, 98, 100, 101, 102
gender bias
  in gender-neutral service provision, 131–132
  and mental health and substance misuse, 132–134
gender-responsive interventions
  addiction theory, 140
  evaluations of, 142–143
  pathways theory, 139
  principles of, 136–140, 141f
  relational theory, 140
  trauma theory, 140
gender-responsive treatment (GRT), 131, 139, 140, 142
Gibbon, S., 59
Göbbels, S., 79
Goffman, E., 191, 269
Golzari, M., 110, 118
good life plan (GLP), 71, 72, 78–79
good lives, claim rights and, 42–43
Good Lives Model (GLM), 13, 28–29, 71, 75, 77–79, 83, 279

Good Lives Model–Forensic Mental Health (GLM-FMH), 77–78
Greenley, D., 75
Gudjonsson, G. H., 74
Guest, C., 148, 163

Haines, D., 104, 106
Hale, B., 38–39
hallucination, *see* delusion
Hare, R. D., 60
hate
  definition of, 93–94
  and hate crime, 92–97
  as motivation for criminal behaviour, 97–98, 105
  as pathological bias, 102–105
  see also hate crime; hatred
hate crime
  conceptualisation of, 94–96
  core elements of, 94
  definition of, 94–95
  examples of, 91, 104–106
  and hate, 92–97
  and mental disorder, 13, 39–40
  and prejudice, 94–96, 99
  and racism, 100–101, 102, 106–107
  as social construct, 94–96
  see also bigotry; hate; hatred
hatred, 13, 91–92, 94–98, 105
  components of, 101
  and the hater, 97, 98, 100–102
  and the individual
    psychiatry, 100–104
    psychology, 98–100
  mental ill-health and, 91, 105, 107
  prejudice versus, 100
  as socio-legal problem, 105
  see also hate; hate crime
Hawker, R., 164
Health and Justice, 2, 16, 246
health care, 5, 123, 155–156, 257–259
  see also mental health
Healthcare Standards for Children and Young People in Secure Settings, 122
Hebenton, B., 193
Helping Women Recover: A programme for treating substance abuse and Beyond Trauma: A healing journey for women, 142

Her Majesty's Courts and Tribunals Service (HMCTS), 219, 222, 224, 229, 235f, 240
Her Majesty's Inspectorate of Constabulary (HMIC), 201
Hiday, V. A., 68, 81, 84
Higgins, J., 33, 40
HMCTS, see Her Majesty's Courts and Tribunals Service (HMCTS)
HMIC, see Her Majesty's Inspectorate of Constabulary (HMIC)
HMP Send, 138
Hockenhull, J. C., 55
Hodge, J. E., 73, 74
Holland, M., 148, 163
'Home Crisis Team', 23
hospital(s)
 forensic, 69, 83
 high secure, 185, 187, 189, 190, 201, 202–204, 207–208, 210, 211
 mental, 137
 order, 175, 176, 203, 208, 212
 psychiatric, 15, 202, 205–207
 secure, 10, 15, 69, 76, 181, 187
 transfer from prison to, 169, 173–174, 176, 177, 178–180, 181, 203, 212
 violence in, 206–207
 see also Ashworth Hospital, Broadmoor Hospital; Rampton Hospital
hostility, 32, 93–94, 104
Howard League, 32
human rights, 13, 28, 30–32, 44
 claims, 28, 30, 32
 conventions, 43
 discourse of, 30–32
 implications for, 41
 legal standing of, 32
 liberties, 28, 30, 32
 mentally disordered offenders and, 30–31, 41
 principles, 75
 see also Human Rights Act (1998); Human Rights Watch
Human Rights Act (1998), 8, 31–32
Human Rights Watch, 136–137
humanness, relations of, 266–280, 276f

incarceration, 3, 7, 10, 15, 37, 59, 72, 80, 118, 135, 136, 142, 193, 267
 see also prison(s); prisoners
identity, 70, 72, 74, 78
 and hate, 99
 non-offending, 69, 75, 79
 offending, 83
 social, 99
Indeterminate Sentences for Public Protection (IPP), 42, 194
induction, 228, 261t
 bespoke programme, 228–229, 236
Information Sharing Agreement, 226, 233, 237
Integrated Offender Management (IOM), 219–220, 225, 235f, 244
Integrated Theory of Desistance from Sex Offending (ITDSO), 69, 70–72, 78, 79, 83
 decisive momentum, 70–71
 normalcy/reintegration, 72
 re-entry, 71–72
 rehabilitation, 71
Intensive Supervision and Surveillance Programme (ISSP), 116
interagency training, see training, interagency
intermediaries, 177–178, 181
International Classification of Diseases, 184
inter-organisational integration, 248–249
interprofessional education, see training, interprofessional
interventions, 48–50
 for antisocial/dissocial personality diagnoses, 58–59
 in criminal justice, 52–53
 effectiveness of, 76–77
 for offenders with major mental illness, 53–55
 for personality disorders, 55–58
 psychological therapies, 50–52
 for psychopathic disorders, 59–62
IOM, see Integrated Offender Management (IOM)
IOM Health Professions Education: A Bridge to Quality, 244
IPP, see Indeterminate Sentences for Public Protection (IPP)
irrationality, 33–34
ISSP, see Intensive Supervision and Surveillance Programme (ISSP)

ITDSO, *see* Integrated Theory of Desistance from Sex Offending (ITDSO)

Jacobs, J., 94–97, 105
Jacobson, N., 75
Johansen, M., 56
jurisprudence of the mind, 267, 271–272, 274, 276f

Kawachi, I., 81
Kings Fund and Centre for Mental Health, 147
Kroll, L., 111–114, 116

Labelling Theory, 101
Lambert, M. J., 51
Lancet Commission on Education of Health Professionals, 255–256
Lancet Commission Report, 246–247
League, H., 32
Leahy, N., 164
learning disability, 35, 114–115, 122, 123, 132, 156, 218, 219, 261t
Learning Service report, 207
Leff, J., 39, 45
Legal Aid Agency, 169
legislations, 32, 193
  criminal justice system and, 3–4
  DSPD programme, 186
  in dual diagnosis, 149, 151–154
  see also Care Act (2014); Community Act (1990); Crime and Disorder Act; Criminal Justice Act (CJA) (2003); Criminal Procedures and Insanity Act (1964); Human Rights Act (1998); Mental Health Act, 1983; Misuse of Drugs Act (1971); Offender Rehabilitation Act (2014); Sex Offenders Act (1997)
Leibing, E., 57
Leichsenring, F., 57
liaison, 167, 169–170, 175, 178, 179, 180, 181, 222f, 249, 250f, 251f, 253f, 261t
  see also liaison and diversion initiatives
liaison and diversion initiatives, 2, 5, 15, 16, 125, 157, 170, 180, 218–220, 220f, 223–224, 227f, 228f, 230f, 231, 234f, 236, 238–240, 244
Liaison and Operating Model, 157
liberty rights, 28, 30, 43
life plan, 71, 72, 79
  see also good life plan (GLP)
limited rights, 31
Lindqvist, P., 79
Lipsey, M. W., 50, 53
Lund, C., 70

MacArthur Violence Risk Assessment Study, 61
madness, 10, 34, 205
'Managing Dangerous People with Severe Personality Disorder', 184, 186–188
MAPPA, *see* Multi Agency Public Protection arrangements (MAPPA)
Martin, M. S., 54, 76, 81
Maruna, S., 42, 67, 71, 72, 74, 76, 78, 82, 83
Mathews, L. J., 21–27
McDevitt, J., 95, 96
MDFT, *see* multi-dimensional family therapy (MDFT)
MDOs, *see* mentally disordered offenders (MDOs)
Mendota Youth Treatment Center, 62
'mens rea', 36, 205
mental distress, 26, 28, 30, 37, 39, 42, 43
Mental Health Act, 6, 153, 175, 180, 186, 192, 201, 204
  1983, 3, 10, 14, 23, 149, 151, 152, 158, 169, 185, 202, 261t
  2007, 1, 3, 7, 10, 14, 151, 152, 158, 169
Mental Health Casework Section, 176, 178–179
Mental Health Court Pilot, 219, 222, 236
mental health courts, 74, 218, 219, 235–236, 245
Mental Health Liaison Scheme (MHLS), 169–170, 175, 178, 180
mental health needs
  and criminal justice system, 2–11, 38, 48–50, 77, 156–157, *see also* interventions
  gender and ethnicity, 119–120
  media reporting of people with, 6–7, 10
  of women, 131–143
  of young people, *see* young offenders

mental health problems, 9, 36, 48, 49–54, 57, 62, 132–135, 137, 139, 143, 147, 148, 149, 151, 153, 156–157, 209, 218
mental health professionals, 25, 39, 178, 189, 192, 201, 204–205, 209, 214
mental health services (MHS), 76, 121, 125, 142, 185, 208
  access to, 148, 152, 153, 155–157
  collaborative practice between CJS and, *see* collaborative practice; training
  in England, 38
  forensic, 54, 58
  prison, 172, 176, 178, 179
  role of police in, 209, 211
  secondary, 153
  within NHS, 21, 22, 24, 26, 202
Mental Health Strategy, 14, 157
Mental Health Treatment Requirements (MHTR), 3–4
mental health trusts, 4, 150, 153–154
mental ill health, 12, 35, 36, 39, 50, 91, 105, 151, 156, 243, 259, 263
mentally disordered offenders (MDOs), 6–7, 12, 13, 33, 210
  assault of mental health staff, 201, 204, 206–207
  clinical improvement in, 77
  definition of, 32–33, 68
  desistance in, 67–68
    barriers to, 79–81
    decisive momentum, 72–75
    normalcy, 82–83
    rehabilitation, 75–79
    re-entry, 79–82
  effectiveness of interventions in, 76–77
  and engagement therapy, 73–74
  and hate crime, 13, 39–40
  with hospital order, 203–204
  human rights and, 30–31, 41
  indeterminacy and public protection, 41–42
  maintenance of desistance in, 81–82
    employment, 82
    pro-social capital, 81–82
  management of, 29–30
  motivation for change, 73–74
  prosecution of, 204–205, *see also* prosecution
  Reasoning and Rehabilitation programme (R&R) for, 76–77
  reasons for offence, 34–36
  recidivism in, 69–70
  rehabilitation of, 75–76, 77
  rights of, 28, 32–40, *see also* right(s)
  social dysfunction of, 74
  strength-based approaches for, 77–78
  and substance misuse, 35
  treatment for, 39–40
  types of, 68–69
  well-being of, 78
Metropolitan Police Murder Investigation Team, 172
MHLS, *see* Mental Health Liaison Scheme (MHLS)
MHS, *see* mental health services (MHS)
MHTR, *see* mental health treatment requirements (MHTR)
Michael Stone case, 6–7, 185
microphysics of power, 267, 271, 273–275, 276f, 277
Ministry of Justice (MOJ), 178, 219
Misuse of Drugs Act (1971), 14, 149, 151–152
M'Naghten, D., 205
Moffitt, T., 116, 119, 120, 121
Monahan, J., 61, 203
Moore, B., 34
Morgan, R. D., 54
Moulin, L., 1
MST, *see* multi-systemic therapy (MST)
multi-agency collaborations, 2, 4, 218
  deficiencies in, 6–11
  early development, 226–227, 227f
  evaluation
    case studies, 238–239
    data collection for, 236–237, 236f
    lessons learned log, 238t
    service user feedback, 238
  governance structures, 220–226, 222f, 239
    current, 222–223, 223f
    deliveries, 225
    escalation processes, 225–226
    terms of reference, 223–224
  risk management

multi-agency collaborations – *continued*
  key aspects of plan, 230f
  potential risk types, 233
  red, amber, green (RAG) rating system, 231
  register of risks, 231t
  risk identification and action, 232t
  service provision development, 227–230
    bespoke induction programme, 228–229, 236
    key performance indicators, 231
    Operational Policy, 229–230
    scoping of existing service provision, 227–228, 228f
  stakeholder management
    key partners in, 233–235, 234f, 235f
    plan, 234–236, 235t
  in Sussex, 218–220, 239–240
  tasks, 220, 221f
Multi Agency Public Protection arrangements (MAPPA), 8
multi-dimensional family therapy (MDFT), 124
multiprofessional learning, *see* training, multiprofessional
multi-systemic therapy (MST), 124
My Twisted World, 91

NACRO, 5, 9, 119
narcissist/labile pathological bias, 103–104
Narcotics Anonymous, 137
Nash, M., 6, 8
National Autistic Society, 117
National Confidential Inquiry into Suicide and Homicide (NCISH), 169
National Health Service (NHS), 5, 10, 15, 138, 153–155, 169, 180, 201, 202, 207, 209, 211, 223, 226, 228f, 231
  England, 1–3, 15, 157, 239
  Five Year Plan, 1, 2, 4
  'Home Crisis Team', 23
  Liaison and Operating Model, 157
  mental health services in, 21, 22, 24, 26, 202
National Health Service and the Prison Service, 138

National Institute for Health and Clinical Excellence (NICE), 111, 116, 117, 124, 158
National Offender Management Service (NOMS), 5, 176, 178
National Reporting, 206–207
National Service Framework for Mental Health: Modern Standards and Service Models, 150
The Nature of Prejudice (Allport), 100
NCISH, *see* National Confidential Inquiry into Suicide and Homicide (NCISH)
Neal, S., 10
NEF, *see* New Economics Foundation (NEF)
neurodevelopmental disorders
  anxiety disorders, 111–112
  attention deficit hyperactivity disorder (ADHD), 116–117
  autism, 117
  in children, 111, 112, 113, 114, 116, 122, 124
  communication disorders, 116
  comorbidity, 118
  depression, 112–113
  gender and ethnicity, 119–120
  learning disability, 114–115
  neurodisability and, 114
  policy and practice implications, 120–125
    developmental pathways, 120–121
    interventions, 123–125
    recent developments in, 125
    screening, 121–123
  posttraumatic stress disorder (PTSD), 112
  prevalence rates, 109–110, 110t
  psychiatric disorders, 110–111
  psychotic disorders, 111
  self-harm and suicidal behaviour, 113
  substance misuse disorders, 112
  traumatic brain injury (TBI), 117–118
  see also *individual disorders*
neurodisability, 14, 109, 114, 119–124, 126
New Economics Foundation (NEF), 159
New Jersey Superior Court, 208
New Liaison and Diversion Arrangements and Operating Model, 157

NHS, *see* National Health Service (NHS)
NICE, *see* National Institute for Health and Clinical Excellence (NICE)
Nicola Edgington case, 10–11
Nilsson, N., 8, 9
Nilsson, T., 70, 192
nonvictimization adversity, 135
normalcy
  in MDOs, 82–83
  in ITDSO, 72
North West Juvenile Project (NWJP), 110–111, 112, 116, 118, 119, 120
Nozick, R., 31
NWJP, *see* North West Juvenile Project (NWJP)

offence, 10, 35, 36, 39, 41, 53, 62, 68, 80, 94–96, 105, 132, 136, 139, 172, 179, 185, 187, 203, 209–211, 219, 239, 252
  criminal, 38, 48–49, 69, 93, 168, 176
  drug-related, 133
  -free life, 78, 83
  indictable, 171
  hate, 93
  sexual, 7, 70, 137, 193, 205, 212
  violent, 61, 70, 72, 137, 193, 201, 205
  see also offending behaviour
Offender Personality Disorder Strategy for Women (OPDSW), 137–138
Offender Rehabilitation Act (2014), 3, 5
offender(s)
  adult, 53, 67, 82
  dangerous, 185, 189, 192–196
  dual-diagnosed, 80–81
  ex-, 71–72, 79, 82
  female, 80, 115, 119, 133, 189
  habitual, 193
  high risk, 184, 189
  interventions for, *see* interventions
  male, 80
  management of, 4, 5, 29–30
  mentally disordered, *see* mentally disordered offenders (MDOs)
  'mission', 95
  personality disordered, 185, 187, 188, 194, 195
  readiness of, 71–74, 83
  sexual, 54, 61, 67, 69, 70, 78, 193, *see also* Integrated Theory of Desistance from Sex Offending (ITDSO)
  young, *see* young offenders
offenders with mental illness (OMI), 54–55, 67
offending behaviour, 3, 4, 7, 15, 16, 43, 49, 53, 68, 95, 114, 120–121, 125, 131, 133, 136–137, 158, 185, 201, 203, 212, 225
Office of the Children's Commissioner for England, 109
OMI, *see* offenders with mental illness (OMI)
Operational Groups, 223, 226
Operational Policy, 229–230
Oxleas NHS Foundation Trust, 169

paranoia, 101–102
paranoid pathological bias, 103
pathological bias, 102, 105
  antisocial, 104
  avoidant, 103
  narcissist/labile, 103–104
  paranoid, 103
  trauma-induced, 103
pathways theory, 139
Payment by Results approach (PbR), 5, 154
PCLDS, *see* Police and Courts Liaison and Diversion Service (PCLDS)
PD, *see* personality disorders (PD)
Peay, J, 29, 33, 34, 38, 41, 42
Peel, R., 205
perpetrators, 81, 94, 97, 99, 147, 181, 205
Perry, B., 92–93, 97, 98, 99
personal recovery, 75
personality disorders (PD), 6, 10, 24, 37, 41, 55–58, 102, 106, 168, 261t
  antisocial, 54, 57
  assessment for, 193
  borderline (BPD), 56–58
  case studies of, 132–134
  clusters (A, B or C), 57
  and crime, 56
  definition of, 188
  diagnoses of, 56, 213
  model of, 56

personality disorders (PD) – *continued*
  narcissistic, 103
  obsessive-compulsive, 103
  and offending behaviour, 68, 185
  prevalence of, 243
  psychopathic, 60
  therapies/interventions for, 57–58
  treatment of, 49, 58, 189, 191, 195
  types of, 58–59, 184
  violence and, 190–191
  women with, 137–139, 187
  see also antisocial personality disorder (ASPD); borderline personality disorder (BPD); Dangerous and Severe Personality Disorder (DSPD) programme; Offender Personality Disorder Strategy for Women (OPDSW)
pharmacotherapy, 51
PJ, *see* psychological jurisprudence (PJ)
police, 15, 40, 125, 169, 170, 172, 181, 201, 207, 209–212, 215, 235f, 240, 242–244, 248, 250f, 253f, 261t, 281
  see also Association of Chief Police Officers (ACPO); police custody
police custody, 157, 219, 227–229, 231, 233–234, 239, 242
Police and Courts Liaison and Diversion Service (PCLDS), 239
politics of subjectivity, 267, 271, 272–273, 274, 276f, 277
posttraumatic stress disorder (PTSD), 103, 112, 119, 134, 135, 136, 142
Potter, K., 94–97, 105
PPI, *see* Public and Patient Involvement (PPI)
precautionary logic, 193
prejudice, 7, 13, 93, 99, 105–106, 162, 248, 254
  hate crime and, 94–96, 99
  and hatred, 100
  psychology and, 99
preventive detention, 193, 194
primary goods, 71, 78, 79
principle of less eligibility, 151, 154–156
prison(s), 3, 5, 15, 30, 62, 69, 136–137
  action learning in, 257
  clinical supervision in, 257–259
  health care in, 155–156, 257–259

  hospitals as, 202–204, 208
  interventions in, 52–53
  mental health services in, 172, 176, 178, 179
  officers, challenges for, 259–260
  reflective practice in, 259–260
  release from, 71
  sites in the DSPD programme, 185, 187–189
  'Supermax', 37
  transfer of prisoners to hospital from, 178–180
  see also incarceration; prisoners
prisoners, 5, 23, 52, 81, 83, 178–180, 202
  access to services, 148, 152, 153, 155–157
  and the Clinical Nurse Specialist, *see* Clinical Nurse Specialist
  conditions of, 30
  and Crown Court settings, *see* Crown Court
  drug-addicted, 148
  and dual diagnosis, *see* dual diagnosis
  female/women, 3, 9, 37, 132–133, 136, 138–139, 142–143, 155, 156
  fitness to plead, 171–172
  male, 3, 37, 132–133, 156
  morbidity in, 168
  older, 257
  with personality disorders, 190, 193, 194, 195
  prevalence of mental disorders, 243
  released, 80
  remand, 9, 168
  rights of, 31–32
  transfer of, *see* transfer of prisoners
  unwell, 169, 172–177, 180
  young, 118
  see also incarceration; prison(s)
Pritchard Criteria, 171–172
'Proposals for Policy Development', 186–187
prosecution
  benefits and disadvantages of, 211
  Full Code test, 209, 210
  of offenders, 201, 203–206
  role of the police in, 201, 207, 209–212, 215
  policy, 209

and public interest, 207–208
road to, 208–211
staff and patient perspectives, 212–214
treatment options and risk assessment, 212
see also Crown Prosecution Service (CPS)
psychiatric disorders, 102, 110–111, 113, 115, 118
psychiatric hospitals, *see* hospitals, psychiatric
psychodynamic therapy, 51, 57
psychological jurisprudence (PJ)
  captivity and, 266–267, *see also* society of captives
  commonsense justice, 275, 278–279
  component practices of, 275–280
    certification, 277
    consumption and exchange, 275–277, 276f
    inscription and presentation, 277, 276f
  core assumptions of, 267
    choice-making, 269–270
    humanity as choice, 268–269
    risk management, 270
  operating principles, 270
    jurisprudence of mind, 271–272
    microphysics of power, 273–275
    politics of subjectivity, 272–273
  restorative justice, 272, 275, 278, 280
  technologies of human excellence, 278, 280
  therapeutic jurisprudence, 275, 278, 279
  and will of being, 278, 280
psychological therapies
  cognitive-behavioural therapy (CBT), 51–52
  pharmacotherapy versus, 51
  positive effects of, 50–51
Psychologically Informed Planned Environments (PIPEs), 3, 138
psychopathy, 8, 41, 54, 59–62, 184, 196
  sexual offence and, 60–61
  violence and, 60
Psychopathy Checklist (Revised) (PCL-R), 60, 61, 184
Psychopathy Checklist, Youth Version (PCL:YV), 62
psychosis, 11, 74, 78, 111, 132, 133, 158, 168, 172, 175, 203, 243, 261t

psychotherapy, 51, 52, 54, 58, 59, 272
see also psychological therapies
psychotic disorders, 68, 110t, 111, 119, 133
PTSD, *see* posttraumatic stress disorder (PTSD)
Public and Patient Involvement (PPI), 160, 238
  consultation, 160–161
  ethical considerations, 161–162
public fear, 7, 10, 15
Public Health England (PHE), 154
public health strategy, 157
public protection, 2, 7, 8, 10, 35, 43, 186, 194, 211
  risk and, 41–42, 186, 202–203, 211
  sentences for, 192–193
'Public Protection Agenda', 2, 186
punishment, 29, 30, 34–37, 39, 41, 50, 151, 152, 154, 159, 203–205, 212, 251, 259, 267, 272, 274, 278, 281

qualified rights, 31

racism, 100–101, 102, 106–107, 191
Rampton Hospital, 187, 202, 208
randomised controlled trials (RCTs), 51, 55, 57, 59
Rapid Cycling Bipolar Disorder, 21, 23, 24
Reasoning and Rehabilitation programme (R&R), 76–77
recidivism, 5, 56, 76, 83
  criminal, 49, 52–53, 55, 56, 60, 76
  in Germany, 70
  in Japan, 70
  in MDOs, 42, 69–70, 81, 83, 84, 206
  outcomes of, 80
  reduction of, 49, 52–53, 76, 77, 83, 136
  violent, 61, 69–70, 77
  see also reoffending/reoffence
recovery, 22, 24, 39, 71–76, 79, 83, 268, 269, 274, 278, 279, 281
  clinical, 74–75
  economic, 98
  functional, 75
  personal, 75
  secure, 71, 75
  social, 75
  see also rehabilitation

red, amber, green (RAG) rating system, 231
Reed, J., 1, 2, 167
Reed Report, 2, 167
re-entry
  in MDOs, 79–82
  in ITDSO, 71–72
rehabilitation, 35, 42, 124, 194, 242, 249, 272
  in ITDSO, 70, 71
  in MDOs, 75–79, 202, 205–206
  meaning of, 76
  vocational, 82
Reidy, D. E., 60
relational theory, 139, 140
Renwick, S. J., 73, 74
reoffending/reoffence, 5, 12, 28, 42, 43, 53, 55, 62, 70–71, 81, 82, 84, 124, 143, 159, 188, 190, 219, 220, 222f, 223f, 225, 235f, 242, 243, 263
  see also recidivism
Responsible Clinician, 173–174, 175–176, 177, 233
  see also Clinical Nurse Specialist, Responsible Clinician and
restorative justice, 205, 272, 275, 278, 280
Rice, A., 7–8
right(s)
  absolute, 31
  claim, 28, 30, 42–43
  human. *see* human rights
  liberty, 28, 30, 43
  limited, 31
  of MDOs, 28, 32–40
  not to be punished, 35–37
  not to be treated, 38–40
  of prisoners, 31–32
  to be punished, 34–35
  qualified, 31
  to be treated, 37–38
  of victims versus offenders, 31
risk, 29, 38, 55, 56, 68, 83–84, 122, 137, 138, 176, 193
  assessment of, *see* risk assessment
  aversion, 151
  avoidance, 193
  environmental, 233
  evaluation, 233
  of reoffending, 187, 188
  of harm, 4, 6, 9, 14, 136, 190, 225
  identified and action taken, 232
  managing, *see* risk management
  of mental health, 135
  prediction, 9, 206
  of neurodevelopmental disorders, 111, 113, 114, 118, 120–126
  public protection and, 41–42, 186, 202–203, 211
  of recidivism, 60, 70, 71–72, 84
  reduction, 61, 71, 76, 78, 79, 83, 138, 190
  register of, 231
  scores, 60, 61, 62
  of suicide, 113, 147, 156
  in transfer of prisoners, 179
  violence, 61, 73, 77, 81
risk assessment, 6, 8–10, 41–42, 60, 61, 78–79, 192, 193, 196, 207, 212, 213, 214
risk management, 5–11, 41–42, 75, 76, 83, 179, 203, 212, 230–233, 267, 270, 274
risk-needs-responsivity (RNR) model, 53, 71, 75–78
Robertson, P., 75
Rodger, E., 91
Rowe, M., 74, 82
Ruchkin, V., 112, 113, 118

Sainsbury Centre for Mental Health, 153
Saskatoon Regional Psychiatric Centre, 61
Scale of Organisational Integration, 249, 261t
schizophrenia, 10, 11, 39, 54, 69, 76, 80, 132, 135, 172
SCJB, *see* Sussex Criminal Justice Board (SCJB)
SCJLD, *see* Sussex Criminal Justice Liaison and Diversion (SCJLD) scheme
screening, 10, 11, 14, 55, 60, 109, 111, 120, 121–123, 125, 126, 141f, 251
Scull, A., 29, 30
secure recovery, 73, 75
Seddon, T., 193
self-harm, 76, 113, 119, 131–132, 133, 136, 137, 156
  see also suicide/suicidal ideation

sentences, 11, 37, 41–42, 219
  in Crown Court, 168
  post, 180
  for public protection, 192–193
service user(s), 9, 12, 14, 16, 21–27, 49, 147, 148–149, 219, 226, 229, 235f, 237, 249, 255
  dually diagnosed, 153–154, 162–163
  empowerment of, 158
  engagement and co-production, 159–160
  feedback, 238
  mental health, 148, 209
  report on, 250–251
  voice of, 21–27, 159–162
Sex Offenders Act (1997), 193
sexual offenders/offences, 54, 60–61, 67, 69, 70, 78, 193
  see also Integrated Theory of Desistance from Sex Offending (ITDSO)
Shapland, J., 205
SHCJB, see Sussex Health and Criminal Justice Board (SHCJB)
Singleton, N., 3, 168
Skeem, J. L., 61, 76
Skipworth, J., 79
Smith, M. L., 50
social capital, 13, 43, 44, 68, 75, 78, 84
  pro-, 80, 81, 83
social care 4, 5, 123–125, 148, 195, 246, 251f, 253f, 257
social exclusion, 4, 5, 7, 9–10, 13, 28, 39, 78, 147, 148, 151, 243
Social Exclusion Unit (SEU), 148
social innovation, 244, 248, 261t
social psychology, 98, 99
social recovery, 75
society of captives, 266, 267, 274, 275, 277, 278
Sonnex, D., 8
Soppitt, S., 74, 82
South African Association of Probation, 201
SPFT, see Sussex Partnership Foundation Trust (SPFT)
stakeholder management, 233–236
  key elements, 234
  map of, 234, 235
Stangor, C., 98, 99
Steadman, H. J., 61, 203

Steering Group, 230, 231, 238
stereotyping, 6, 9, 10, 28, 162
Stern, K., 98, 99
Steury, E., 7
Stevens, S., 1, 2
stigma, 6, 7, 21, 39, 48, 68, 75, 78, 80, 121, 122, 137, 159, 162, 279
Stigma Theory, 191, 194
Stone, M., 6–7, 8, 185
Strawson, P., 34, 35
strength-based approaches, 84
  GLM-based interventions, 79
  on well-being of MDOs, 78
substance abuse, 54, 59, 61, 68, 73, 80, 142
substance misuse, 4, 6, 35, 53, 57, 154, 156–157, 190, 219
  disorders, 110, 112, 113, 118, 119, 122, 123, 124, 150
  policy, 150
  practitioners, 162
  problems, 136–137, 143, 158
  services, 160
  in women, 132–134
suicide/suicidal ideation, 27, 91, 113, 132, 133, 135, 147, 156, 258
Sullivan, A., 93, 94, 96, 97, 105
Surrey & Sussex Probation Trust, 218, 219, 222, 224, 226
Sussex, 218–220, 222, 223, 229, 230, 231, 234, 239, 240
Sussex Criminal Justice Board (SCJB), 222, 226
Sussex Criminal Justice Liaison and Diversion (SCJLD), 220, 239
Sussex Health and Criminal Justice Board (SHCJB), 219
Sussex Partnership Foundation Trust (SPFT), 218, 227, 228, 236
Sussex Police, 218, 219, 222, 224, 226, 229, 235f

TAU, see treatment as usual (TAU)
TBI, see traumatic brain injury (TBI)
technologies of human excellence, 267, 274, 278, 280
Teplin, L. A., 109–112, 116, 119
terms of reference, 221f, 223–224
therapeutic jurisprudence, 275, 278, 279
Thornicroft, G., 4, 6, 7, 39

Tomblin, J. B., 116
training
　interagency, 242, 245, 246, 247–249, 252, 254, 255, 256t, 260, 261t
　interprofessional, 242, 243, 245, 246, 252, 254, 255, 256t, 257, 259, 260, 261t
　multiprofessional, 245, 255, 257
　systems approach to, 248–252
　three-phase model of, 260–263, 261t
　uniprofessional, 245, 254
　see also collaborative practice
transfer of prisoners
　to the DSPD service, 193
　to hospital from prison, 169, 173–174, 176, 177, 178–180, 181, 203, 212
Transforming the CJS: A strategy and action plan to reform the criminal justice system, 205
trauma, 114, 118, 119, 133
　birth, 120
　childhood, 104
　definition, 134–135
　rates, 112, 113
　symptoms, 134, 143
　theory, 140
　see also trauma-informed approaches; traumatic brain injury (TBI)
trauma-induced pathological bias, 103
trauma-informed approaches, 14
　as gender-responsive approach, 136, 142–143
　gender-responsive interventions
　　evaluations of, 142–143
　　principles of, 136–140, 141f
　　theories of, 139–141
traumatic brain injury (TBI), 117–118
treatment as usual (TAU), 50, 57, 58, 59

Uggen, C., 82
UK Drug Policy Commission, 154
UK Government's Social Exclusion Unit, 148
unfit to plead, 172–177
　see also Clinical Nurse Specialist, assistance when defendant is fit to plead
United Kingdom, 48, 52, 62, 150
United States, 52, 61, 110
unrestricted hospital order, 203, 212
　see also mentally disordered offenders (MDOs), with hospital order
Uzieblo, K., 9

Valley State Prison for Women, 142
victims, 7, 8, 11, 12, 16, 31, 40, 81, 84, 92–95, 97–98, 101, 103, 104, 132, 134–137, 139, 142, 143, 175, 177, 181, 187, 205, 208, 210, 225, 235f, 280
violence, 41, 53, 58, 91, 99, 112, 138
　domestic, 40, 147, 174
　in hospitals, 201, 203–209, 211–215
　interpersonal, 56, 135
　personal disorder and, 190
　psychopathy and, 60
　risk, 61, 73, 77, 81
　sexual, 147, 280
Violence Risk Scale (VRS), 61–62
violent recidivism, 69–70
vocational rehabilitation, 82
VRS, see Violence Risk Scale (VRS)

Ward, T., 67, 71–74, 76, 78, 82
WASI, see Wechsler Abbreviated Scale of Intelligence (WASI)
Wechsler Abbreviated Scale of Intelligence (WASI), 114–115
Wexler, D. B., 279
Williams, A., 6, 8
Wilson, D. B., 50
Wilson, H. A., 59
Wilson, N. J., 59, 62
Winick, B. J., 279
women and mental health needs
　gender bias in gender-neutral service provision, 131–132
　gender-responsive interventions in, 136–142, see also gender-responsive interventions
　substance misuse in, 132–134, 136
　and trauma, 134–136
　trauma-informed approaches, 136–141
　see also Women Offender Case Management Model (WOCMM)
Women Offender Case Management Model (WOCMM), 137
Wong, S. C. P., 61
wrongdoing, 36, 205

Yates, P. M., 60
Yoshikawa, K., 70
young offenders, 53, 62, 67–68, 109
　anxiety disorders in, 111–112
　attention deficit hyperactivity disorder (ADHD) in, 116–117
　autism in, 117
　communication disorders in, 116
　comorbidity in, 118
　depression in, 112–113
　female/girls, 110, 111, 113, 115, 116, 117, 118, 119, 121
　gender and ethnicity of, 119–120
　learning disability in, 114–115
　male/boys, 110, 111–112, 113, 115, 116, 117, 118, 119, 121, 122
　neurodisability and neurodevelopmental disorders in, 114
　policy and practice implications, 120
　　developmental pathways, 120–121
　　interventions, 123–125
　　recent developments in, 125
　　screening, 121–123
　posttraumatic stress disorder (PTSD) in, 112
　prevalence of, 109–110
　psychiatric and neurodevelopmental disorders in, 110–111, 110t
　psychotic disorders in, 111
　rights of, 32
　self-harm and suicidal behaviour in, 113
　substance misuse disorders in, 112
　traumatic brain injury (TBI) in, 117–118
youth justice system, 14, 109–110, 115, 117, 120–122, 125, 126
Yu, R., 56